THE ROAD FROM
SARAJEVO

Praise for *A Cold War:*

'An important reflection of commanding on operations. It recounts a very significant period in history, but does so in a very personal manner'

The Bugle, journal of the Rifles

'Barry describes with admirable calm the obstacles and frustrations he faced. Where Barry's book stands out is in the intermingling of personal experiences and anxieties (both his and his men's) with clear expositions of the complexities of the chain of command'

Journal of the Royal United Services Institute

'Unrivalled view of the Bosnia quagmire as viewed from the perspective of a British battalion on the ground. Excellent on the process of command.'

Professor Gary Sheffield, Chair of War Studies, University of Wolverhampton

'Really explained what life was like in a battalion and the pressures that officers and soldiers are under.'

General Lord Guthrie of Craigbank, Former UK Chief of Defence Staff

'An invaluable resource and a key insight at the tactical level.'

General Lord Richard Dannatt, Former Chief of the General Staff, 2006–2009

'Ben Barry has written the definitive account of how the hard-won peace was achieved. This book tells it all, from the political to the personal, with numerous comments and observations from the men under his command ... *A Cold War* is much more than a personal account of an operational tour; it is a testament to the courage and ingenuity of the British soldier, who under the most demanding and difficult circumstances made the difference.'

Les Howard, former British soldier and author of *Winter Warriors*

'All I wanted to know about why I froze my arse off for 6 months! Actually a very good read and explains a lot about command and the reasons why we hurry up and wait.'

Anonymous blogger on the Army Rumour Service website

THE ROAD FROM SARAJEVO

British Army Operations in Bosnia, 1995–1996

Brigadier Ben Barry

Front cover image: British troops near Sanski Most, Bosnia, January 1996. (Author's collection)

Map artwork on page 255 by the Map Studio, from ESS 63, *The Collapse of Yugoslavia 1991–99* by Alastair Finlan, © Osprey Publishing Ltd, www.ospreypublishing.com

First published 2008 as *A Cold War* by Spellmount
This new edition published 2016

The History Press
The Mill, Brimscombe Port
Stroud, Gloucestershire, GL5 2QG
www.thehistorypress.co.uk

British Library Cataloguing in Publication Data.
A catalogue record for this book is available from the British Library.

ISBN 978 0 7509 6199 8

Typesetting and origination by The History Press
Printed and bound in Malta by Melita Press

Contents

Foreword by Martin Bell,
UNICEF Ambassador

Warfare fascinates. There are people who write about it, people who read about it, and people who risk their lives to get close to it. I confess that in my former life I belonged to all three categories. But the battalions of books about soldiering, which jostle for attention on the shelves, are generally the work of academics, military theorists and even journalists. Too few of them are written by soldiers. Yet it is the soldiers who live through these experiences, who put their lives of the line in the course of them, and who understand better than any commentator the rapidly changing nature of the profession of arms – the emphasis on peace-making as well as war-fighting, the devolution of responsibility down through the ranks, and the complex problems of command and discipline in a multinational force.

Two groups of people with a unique insight into all this were the soldiers of the Light Infantry and the Royal Regiment of Fusiliers who served in Bosnia during the winter of 1995 to 1996. They began their tours of duty as the UN's soldiers and ended them as NATO's – for which they were properly rewarded with two medals. Those medals were earned the hard way in hard weather. The troops enforced the military provisions of the Dayton Agreement, risked their lives to save the lives of others, swept away the road blocks and restored a minimal peace in Bosnia after three and a half years of war. It was NATO's first ever ground operation, and it was substantially led by the British. At the time of the transfer of authority, on 21 December 1995, the Americans, for all their logistical power, had actually failed to arrive.

I observed these operations close up and personally, since I was still in the service of my own civilian regiment, the BBC. My subsequent career as a citizen politician was at the time not even dreamed of, and there was more than enough politics going on around us, in the manoeuvres and manipulations of the Bosnian warlords with whom our soldiers dealt. I remember reflecting, not for the first time, on the extraordinary quality of the British troops participating, on the dangers they faced across a mine-strewn landscape, and on the unique and unprecedented nature of the task before them. I wished that one of them would write an account of it, not just in an an Army journal but for an audience wider than the regimental family, and provide a soldier's eye view of these events. They owed that to the history they were making.

Fortunately Colonel Ben Barry, the Commanding Officer of the Second Battalion the Light Infantry (2LI) had the same idea. This book is the result. It stands as a companion volume to Colonel Bob Stewart's *Broken Lives*, which chronicled the Cheshires' tour of duty in 1992–93. Both men, like most who served in Bosnia, were deeply affected by what they saw there – one at the start of the UN's involvement and the other at the very end. They are two very different characters. But they both interpreted their mandates bravely. They saved lives. They made a difference. They served with distinction in the world's best army, which happens to be British. And, best of all, they had the sense to write about it.

Martin Bell

Glossary

A Vehicle A tracked or wheeled armoured fighting vehicle.

A 10 A US Air Force strike aircraft used over Bosnia.

ABiH Abbreviation for the Army of Bosnia-Herzegovina, the Army of the Bosnian Government. Largely made up of Bosnian Muslims.

ACFL Agreed Cease-Fire Line as shown on the maps agreed at Dayton, showing the front line between Federation and Republika Srpska forces at the cessation of hostilities in autumn 1995.

Adjutant A captain serving in the headquarters of a British battalion or regiment, responsible for personnel matters, including discipline, routine administration and career management.

AGC Adjutant General's Corps. The battalion had a small detachment of AGC officers and soldiers providing clerical support, personnel administration and pay experts.

Airmobile An Army sub-unit, unit, or formation trained and equipped to move around the battlefield in helicopters. As a response to the hostage crisis of summer 1995, the British Government deployed the 24th Airmobile Brigade to the Croatian port of Ploce, close to Bosnia's southern border.

AK47 Term for a common type of Warsaw Pact assault rifle.

AMX A type of French Army wheeled armoured car. Foreign legion cavalry with AMX 10 RC vehicles sporting 105mm guns were attached to Task Force Alpha.

'Anvil' The largest area of transfer in Bosnia, centered on the town of Mrkonjić Grad. It was territory from which the Bosnian Croats had driven the Bosnian Serbs in autumn 1995. It was transferred back to Bosnian Serb control in February 1996.

APC Armoured Personnel Carrier. An armoured vehicle, with the primary function of transporting people and equipment under armour, not primarily designed to fight. We used the FV432 and Spartan APCs. The Mechanised Battalions (1 RRF and 1 QLR) used the Saxon APC.

Area of Responsibility (AOR) An unofficial term, widely in use at the time. It denoted the area of ground allocated to a subordinate to define the geographic limits in which they may conduct operations.

'Area Of Transfer' An area of land being transferred from one Bosnian faction to another.

Armed Islamic Extremists See Mujahideen.

Armija Bosnian term for army – often used to describe the predominantly Muslim Bosnian Government army, the ABiH.

ARRC The Allied Command Europe Rapid Reaction Corps. NATO's high-readiness rapidly deployable land component headquarters, the ARRC commanded all land forces involved in the NATO IFOR from December 95 to November 96. The framework of the ARRC headquarters and its communications, including the commander, chief of staff, 60% of the staff officers and a Signal Brigade were all provided by the British Army.

Artificer A highly trained senior rank of the REME, leading a team of soldiers involved in the repair of equipment. Often known as 'Tiffy'.

Assault Pioneers Infantry soldiers trained in various combat engineer skills.

AVRE Armoured Vehicle Royal Engineers. A Chieftain tank modified for use by Royal Engineers, in order to provide mobility support to battle-groups. Some AVREs carried rapidly laid bridges, whilst others were configured for breaching minefields using rocket-fired explosive hoses and mine ploughs.

B Vehicle A wheeled unarmoured vehicle, not employed primarily in a combat role, including Land Rovers, trucks and logistic vehicles.

Battalion A major unit, invariably commanded by a lieutenant colonel and comprising between 400 and 1000 people.

BATCO Literally Battle Code. A paper-based code to provide security on insecure tactical radio nets.

BATES Battlefield Artillery Target Engagement System. An artillery computer system used to assist in the control and planning of artillery fire.

BATUS British Army Training Unit Suffield conducts the training of battle-groups in war fighting. The exercises take place in a large Canadian Forces training area – the size of the county of Hampshire. Training involves live firing exercises against target arrays and two-sided exercises using tactical engagement simulators.

Battery An artillery regiment contains three or four batteries, each of 6 or 8 guns. A battery equipped with 105mm howitzers or AS 90 self-propelled guns would usually provided a tactical group of its commander and forward observers to a battlegroup.

Battle Procedure The procedures and techniques of preparing for operations, including reconnaissance, planning and the production and issue of orders. The aim is to ensure, by concurrent activity, that the time available to prepare for battle is used efficiently, so that troops are properly prepared and briefed.

Battlegroup (BG) A British Army term describing a tactical grouping of combat arms, usually with armour and infantry under command, based on the HQ of an armoured regiment, armoured infantry battalion, mechanised infantry battalion, aviation regiment or armoured reconnaissance regiment.

BBGT Brigade and Battle Group Trainer. A facility using simple simulation to train brigade and battlegroup commanders and their headquarters staff in planning, command, control and tactical decision-making. In 1995, both

10

2 LI and HQ 4th Armoured Brigade conducted pre-Bosnia command and staff training at the BBGT at Sennelager.

BCV Battery Command Vehicle. The Warrior variant issued to an artillery battery commander.

Bergen A slang term for any military pattern rucksack.

BGEEO Battle Group Engineer Operations Officer. An captain from an engineer regiment who joins a battlegroup HQ to plan and co-ordinate engineer work in support of the battlegroup. He also advises the battlegroup commander and battlegroup HQ on all engineer matters and terrain analysis.

B-H Bosnia-Herzegovina.

'Bird Bath' Washing from a bowl of water when no baths or showers are available.

'Bluey' Slang term for Forces Free Aerogrammes, blue air mail letters that could be sent free between the UK and Germany and British forces on operations.

BMP An armoured infantry fighting vehicle widely used by countries of the former Warsaw Pact. Equipped with a 30mm cannon and machine gun, it was used by the Czech Mechanised Battalion in IFOR.

BONDI BEACH An IFOR-controlled crossing point at Sassina between the Bosnian Muslim-controlled territory and Bosnian Serb-controlled territory. Throughout 2 LI's tour a platoon or troop controlled it.

Bosniac A term used to describe a person, organisation or force aligned with the Bosnian Government in Sarajevo.

Brigade (Bde) In the British Army and many NATO armies, the term is used to describe a grouping of battalions and regiments, the lowest level of 'formation'. 2 LI served in the Anglo-French-Dutch, Multinational Brigade in November and December 1995, transferring back to British command, becoming a unit of the 4th Armoured Brigade. The faction armies used the term much less precisely, in part because of casualties. Few faction 'brigades' approached the size of British formations, most being much smaller.

Brigadier (Brig) A senior officer commanding a brigade. In many armies, but not the British, the rank is called 'brigadier-general'.

BTR A wheeled armoured personnel carrier widely used by countries of the former Warsaw Pact. Equipped with a heavy machine gun, it was used by the Czech Mechanised Battalion in IFOR.

BV 206 An unarmoured tracked oversnow vehicle, with exceptional cross-country mobility and ability to traverse snow and ice conditions impossible to any other vehicles.

Cadre Term used in British infantry to describe certain training courses. For example the NCO cadre trained soldiers to become lance-corporals.

Call sign An alpha-numeric designation used to identify a vehicle, an individual or a unit or sub-unit when speaking on a radio net. Examples from the 2 LI Battlegroup Net:

> Battlegroup Commander – Zero Alpha
> Battlegroup Main Headquarters – Zero
> A Company – One Zero
> B Company – Two Zero … and so on.

Campaign A sequence of military operations designed to achieve a strategic objective within a given theatre of operations. Campaign planning is the responsibility of the operational commander

Cantonment Term used by IFOR to refer to the place where the Bosnian faction armed forces would be authorised to store weapons and military equipment to meet the requirements of the Dayton Peace Agreement.

Capt. Captain.

'Celebratory' Fire UN and NATO term describing Bosnian troops and civilians firing weapons in celebration – for example festivals, coming off the front line and drunken parties.

Challenger The Challenger tank was the single British tank deployed to Bosnia.

Cheshires First Battalion the Cheshire Regiment, the first British battalion to conduct UN operations in Bosnia.

Chinook A large transport helicopter used by the RAF to support IFOR.

Chobham Armour A specific type of armour fitted to certain British armoured vehicles. Challenger tanks had Chobham armour fitted as standard, whilst Warrior's had large plates of Chobham armour added to the front and sides as a part of preparation for service in Bosnia.

Chief of Staff (COS) The principal staff officer in a British formation headquarters, responsible for the overall co-ordination of all staff work and planning, especially operational and intelligence matters. In a brigade HQ, the COS would be a major, in a divisional HQ, the COS would be a colonel and the Chief of Staff of the NATO Rapid Reaction Corps would be a major-general.

CO Commanding Officer. A lieutenant colonel commanding a major unit of the British Army.

Command The exercise of legal authority by a military commander for the planning direction, control and co-ordination of a military force.

Comd. Commander.

Company Armoured infantry companies usually had about 150 people, with 19 Warriors (of various types) and a few other vehicles. Support and HQ Companies had different organisations.

Company Fleet Manager A serjeant responsible for co-ordination of armoured vehicle supply and maintenance within the company.

Company Group A company with attachments from other arms and services.

Compo Nickname for Composite Rations. Vehicles were supplied with two types of Compo; boxes of tinned food and one-man packs.

Corimec The UN logistics organisation had procured a large number of temporary buildings for use in UN bases. Most of these were small, collapsible, white painted buildings. Most bore the name the Italian manufacturer, 'Co. Ri. Mec.' They were therefore known as Corimecs.

Corps In NATO armies, a formation of several divisions. The NATO Allied Command Europe Rapid Reaction Corps in Bosnia comprised three multinational divisions. The Bosnian Serbs attempted to maintain divisions and subordinate formations, although casualties made this only partially possible. The ABiH corps usually commanded a number of brigades directly, although some divisional HQs were used.

Counter Battery Fire Fire from artillery or mortars designed to neutralise enemy artillery or mortars.

CQMS Company Quartermaster Serjeant, responsible for bringing logistic support forward to his company.

Crew Shelter A small tent made of green canvas, carried by some armoured vehicles. Crew shelters were designed to be quickly fixed to the side of a vehicle.

CVR(T) General term for members of the Combat Vehicle Reconnaissance (Tracked) family of light armoured vehicle. The battalion was equipped with Spartan APCs, Sultan command vehicles and Samson recovery vehicles, with the Recce Platoon having Scimitars. The battlegroup's armoured recce squadron was predominantly issued with Scimtar but employed Spartan and Samson as well.

D Day The day on which an operation is due to commence. For the takeover from the UN by NATO, D Day was 20 December 1995.

1 D&D First battalion the Devon and Dorset Regiment. They were the other armoured infantry battalion in Paderborn and preceded 2 LI as the British Armoured Infantry Battalion in Bosnia.

Dayton Agreement See GFAP.

Deputy Chief of Staff (DCOS) After the Chief of Staff, the next most important staff officer an a British formation HQ – responsible for the planning and co-ordination of all logistic and personnel support to the formation. Rank the same as Chief of Staff.

Division (Div) A formation of two or more brigades. In NATO armies usually commanded by a major-general.

DROPS Literally Demountable Rack Offloading and Pick-up System. A medium-mobility lorry, able to carry palletised ammunition and other supplies, as well as ISO containers. Issued to logistic units and artillery regiments, but not to armoured infantry battalions.

EOD Literally explosives ordnance disposal. The detection and neutralisation of unexploded ordnance. In Bosnia Royal Engineer EOD teams took the lead in British mine-clearing operations and in monitoring and supervising faction mine-lifting operations that were executed under British control.

Ethnic Cleansing A process carried out by all 3 Bosnian factions of forcibly evicting people of the other faction from an area.

Electronic Warfare (EW) Military operations involving the use of electromagnetic radiation; either to gather information, or to deny information to the enemy.

Entity The Dayton Agreement formalised the division of Bosnia into two 'entities', the Republika Srpska and the Federation of Bosnia-Herzegovina.

Estimate The process of making a decision and/or a plan for an operation or battle. It begins by analysing the requirements of the mission, followed by anlaysis of the key factors involved. From this possible courses of action are developed, before the analysis of the factors is used to select the best option as a basis for planning. The process can be very short, for example a quick combat estimate in the heat of battle may take a few seconds. Or it can take much longer, for example 2 LI's estimate process for NATO operations began a month earlier as soon as the Dayton treaty was signed.

Factions Common term for the three parties to the Bosnia war.

Federation Literally Federation of Bosnia-Herzegovina, the uneasy combination of Bosnian Muslim- and Croat-controlled mini-states that opposed the Bosnian Serbs.

Field Firing A form of training exercise in which troops employ live ammunition against targets that simulate enemy forces.

Fighting Power That which defines an Army's capability to fight. The British Army recognises three components to fighting power; the conceptual (the thought process), the physical (the aility to get people to fight) and the physical (the means of fighting).

Friction The force that, in military operations or combat, can make simple operations difficult, and difficult operations virtually impossible.

Fusileers A term describing members of British Army Fusilier battalions.

FV 432 A British-designed and -manufactured armoured personnel carrier, known universally as '432'. It was used by the Mortar Platoon to carry the mortars, ammunition and crews and by the Signals Platoon to carry radios and as a command post. The battlegroup also used ambulance variants.

FWF Commonly used abbreviation for 'Formerly Warring Factions'.

Geneva Convention An expression relating to a series of international treaties specifying agreed limitations on the conduct of war and armed conflict.

GFAP General Framework Agreement for Peace in Bosnia-Herzegovina, the 'Dayton Peace Agreement'.

GREY CAT Nickname for the IFOR-controlled crossing point between Bosnian Muslim and Bosnian Serb territory opened in January 1996. A Company were based in an abandoned village in the middle of no-man's-land between the two faction front lines.

Grizzly A Canadian wheeled light armoured vehicle.

'Groundhog Day' A day or series just like those before them – in other words a very monotonous period of time. A nickname taken from the film 'Groundhog Day' where the protagonist becomes trapped in a repeating time loop, resulting in an endlessly repeating cycle of events.

Gucci Slang term taken from the name of an Italian fashion house, used to praise clothing or personal equipment. For example the special hats, gloves and boots issued for the Bosnian winter were universally perceived by the battalion as being 'Gucci'.

H Hour (H Hr) The specific time at which an operation is due to commence.

Hats Deputy Dawg Slang term universally used by the battalion to describe camouflage, fur-lined Arctic hats issued for the Bosnian winter.

HQ Company (HQ Coy) Headquarter Company contains all the battalion's logistic and personnel assets. This includes the quartermasters and their staffs, the MT Platoon, a platoon of cooks from the Royal Logistic Corps and a team of clerks and pay specialists from the Adjutant General's Corps. The battalion has its own doctor and small medical section, maintaining health in peace and dealing with casualties in war.

Hummvee Slang term for an American light all-terrain vehicle, officially designated High Mobility Multipurpose Wheeled Vehicle (HMMWV).

HV The Croatian army.

HVO The Army of the Bosnia Croats in Bosnia. There was much evidence of HV soldiers, officers, units and formations fighting for the HVO, albeit disguised as HV troops.

IEBL Inter Entity Boundary Line. The final boundary between the Federation and Republika Srpska, after transfer of territory had taken place between the two entities.

IFOR The NATO Implementation Force, responsible for monitoring, supervising and enforcing the Dayton Peace Agreement.

INMARASAT International Maritime Satellite. The battalion was equipped with a few terminals that could access this civilian satellite telephone system.

IPTF International Police Task Force. An unarmed UN-sponsored police operation with contingents from a wide variety of nations. The Dayton Agreement required it to monitor, observe and inspect Bosnian civil police forces, as well as assisting with training.

ITN Independent Television News – British TV news company.

JCOs Joint Commission Observers. The 1994 US-brokered Washington Treaty engineered a cease-fire between the warring Bosnian Muslims and Croats. UNPROFOR established Joint Commissions, chaired by UN Sector commanders to help co-ordinate the military and civil implementation of this peace. The UNPROFOR commander, Lieutenant General Sir Michael Rose also needed his own independent observers who could operate throughout Bosnia, in order to provide him with accurate information, unfiltered by the UN chain of command. The JCOs comprised specially selected and trained volunteers from all regiments and corps of the British Army. Operating with little more than small arms for personal protection, Land Rovers and portable satellite radios, they had a key role in the remainder of UNPROFOR operations. On transition to IFOR they were to become Corps troops, carrying out a similar role, reporting to both Divisional Commanders and COMARRC.

JHQ Joint Headquarters. The tri-Service headquarters exercising operational command over all British forces in the Balkans.

JMC Joint Military Commission. A formal meeting between an IFOR commander and faction commanders. A practice begun by UNPROFOR in 1994 and continued by NATO as a way of formally informing faction military commanders of NATOs requirements for military compliance. Commissions were conducted at all NATO levels of command from battle-group to corps.

Kalashnikov A slang term covering most faction rifles and light machine guns. Taken from the name of the Russian designer of the AK 47 assault rifle, copies of which were made in Yugoslavia.

Kit Term commonly used for any piece of clothing or personal equipment.

2 LI Second Battalion the Light Infantry.

LAD REME Light Aid Detachment. A large platoon of approximately 50 REME soldiers charged with carrying out a wide range of repairs to the battalion's weapons, vehicles and equipment.

Law of Armed Conflict A term that covers the application of the Geneva Conventions and other laws of war, not only in wars, but also in situations where wars have not been formally declared.

LD Light Dragoons. A reconnaissance regiment that provided an armoured reconnaissance squadron to 2 LI throughout the tour.

LO Liaison Officer. An officer trained and equipped to conduct liaison with the factions, other UN or NATO forces, or with non-governmental organisations. 2 LI had trained three captains to act as company LOs, whilst three more captains were used as battlegroup LOs, the overall liaison effort being directed by the Support Company commander. An LO travelled in a single Land Rover accompanied by a driver and interpreter, the requirement for security dictating the strength of any escort.

Logistics Defined as 'the science of the movement and maintenance of forces'. Logistics at battlegroup level included provision of combat supplies (fuel, food, water, ammunition) and spare parts – as well as maintenance and repair of battlegroup equipment, weapons and vehicles. It also included negotiation and monitoring of contracts for supply of fresh food, clean water and waste disposal, as well as the handling of incoming and outgoing mail. This activity required the full time attention of over a hundred soldiers and four officers.

2 Lt Second Lieutenant, a rank junior to lieutenant and the junior officer rank in the Army.

Lynx A British Army light helicopter, capable of reconnaissance, transport of up to 6 people, or armed action with anti-tank missiles.

MALIBU CORNER A patrol base opened by B Company between Muslim and Serb territory.

Manoeuvre The British Army has formally adopted the manoeuvreist approach to operations and the philosophy of manoeuvre warfare. This seeks to defeat the enemy by shattering his moral and physical cohesion – his ability to fight as an effective, co-ordinated whole – rather than by destroying him physically through incremental attrition.

Married Quarter Houses and flats for married army personnel.

Matterhorn An insulated, waterproof boot supplied to 2 LI specifically for use in the Bosnian winter.

MENTOR A secure satellite telephone installed in British UN bases.

MFCs Mortar Fire Controller parties. 2 LI's mortar platoon had four of these parties, each comprising a pair of NCOs, trained and equipped to control mortar and artillery fire, travelling in a Spartan APC.

MILAN Anti-tank missiles fired from a manportable launcher, with a range of 1,950 metres. The Anti-tank Platoon's Warriors each carried two launchers and crews.

Minefield An area of ground in which land mines have been placed. They may be fenced and marked on the ground. In Bosnia, most minefields were not marked.

Mission Analysis Mission Analysis is a logical process for extracting and deducing from a superior's orders the tasks necessary to fulfil a mission. A commander establishes what constraints apply, and determines, as the campaign, major operation, battle or engagement progresses, whether further decisions are required. As such it is a dynamic process that 'triggers', and then regulates, the remainder of the estimate. It is continued thereafter as the situation and the mission are reviewed.

Mission Command A central pillar of the Army's doctrine and training. Mission Command is designed to promote a robust system of command and to achieve unity of effort at all levels; it is dependent on decentralisation. It requires the development of trust and mutual understanding between commanders and subordinates throughout the chain of command, and timely and effective decision-making, with initiative (a quality of a commander) at all levels: the keys to 'getting inside' the enemy's decision–action cycle. The successful employment of Mission Command on operations rests on its principles being fully understood, fostered and frequently practised in training. Its application, however, cannot be stereotyped. A commander's style of command must also reflect the situation, including the capability and understanding of his subordinate commanders. It has the following key elements:

a. A commander gives his orders in a manner that ensures that his subordinates understand his intentions, their own missions and the context of those missions.

b. Subordinates are told what effect they are to achieve and the reason why it needs to be achieved.

c. Subordinates are allocated the appropriate resources to carry out their missions.

d. A commander uses a minimum of control measures so as not to limit unnecessarily the freedom of action of his subordinates.

e. Subordinates then decide within their delegated freedom of action how best to achieve their missions.

2 LI sought to apply mission command as much as possible, in barracks, during training and on operations.

MNB Multi National Brigade. An ad hoc formation assembled out of British, French and Dutch troops, it operated in Bosnia from August to December 1995. The brigade had no dedicated logistic assets and its HQ and staff were ad hoc. 2 LI was part of the brigade from 1 November to 20 December 1995.

MND (SW) Multinational Division Southwest. The Divisional HQ responsible for southern and western Bosnia from December 1995. The British 3rd Division provided the commander and majority of the staff.

MT Platoon Mechanical Transport Platoon. Holds all of a battalion's logistic vehicles. Commanded by the MT Officer (MTO).

Mud Factory Nickname for an extremely muddy and uncomfortable IFOR base outside Sanski Most occupied December 1995 – January 1996.

Mujahideen Sometimes known to US and NATO forces as 'Armed Islamic Extremists'. Forces made up of a mixture of foreign Muslim volunteers and fanatical Muslims, making up special units of the Bosnian Muslim Army. Known for a highly truculent and aggressive attitude to the Western contingents of UNPROFOR. Once IFOR arrived, the Americans considered the Mujahideen a great threat to their security and were determined that they should leave the country.

NAAFI Literally Navy Army and Air Forces Institute. A semi-official company supplying goods and services to the British armed forces.

NCO Non Commissioned Officer.

NGO Non-governmental Organisations. A term used to describe the multitude of national and international charities and aid organisations working in Bosnia, such as the UN High Commission for Refugees, Save the Children and Médecins Sans Frontières, but excluding government organisations, such as the UK Government's Overseas Development Administration.

Obstina Bosnian term for county.

OC Officer Commanding. A general term for an officer commanding a sub-unit ranging from platoon/troop to company/battery/squadron.

ODA Overseas Development Administration. A British Government department responsible for overseas development and humanitarian aid. Now succeeded by the Department for International Development (DfiD).

Orders Group (O Group) A group of subordinates assembled to receive a commander's orders. Its composition is usually specified in standing orders, but may be adjusted as required.

Op. Operation.

Operational Level Campaigns and major operations are planned and directed at the operational level.

Operations Officer (Ops Officer) A captain in Battlegroup HQ responsible for both operational planning and the routine conduct of operations.

OPFOR Opposing Force, the troops acting as enemy during a training exercise.

OPV Warrior Observation Post Variant. Used for artillery forward observation officers, equipped with powerful surveillance and target acquisition equipment, including laser range-finder, thermal imager and radar.

Padre Term for battalion chaplain.

Peace Enforcement Operations of a coercive nature, to maintain or re-establish peace or enforce terms specified in a mandate. British operations during the NATO IFOR 1995–96 are considered to be peace enforcement.

Peacekeeping Operations conducted with the consent of the belligerents in support of efforts to achieve or maintain peace, in order to promote security and save life in areas of potential or actual conflict. See also Wider Peacekeeping.

Peace Support Operations A term describing the wide range of operations to settle armed conflicts. They include peacekeeping, peace enforcement and peace-building operations.

Platoon (Pl) A sub-unit of approximately 30 infantry soldiers. In 2 LI officers command all platoons. Armoured infantry platoons were equipped with 4 Warriors.

Platoon House A small base for a platoon, using a house or similar-sized building for shelter.

Poncho Not a cape, but a shelter of thin waterproof green or camouflaged nylon fabric. Light enough to be carried by the soldier, it is used as an improvised one- or two-man tent.

Pooh Sticks A children's' game, immortalised in the book *Winnie The Pooh*, in which sticks are dropped from a bridge over a river or stream. The winner is the person whose stick emerges first from under the bridge.

'Portishead Radio' A method of linking high-frequency radios to a civilian station at Portishead in the UK, allowing the radio to link into the civilian telephone network. Used by 2 LI to allow soldiers to talk to their families when this could not be achieved in any other way.

Procovnik Serbo-Croat term for the military rank of colonel.

Psychological Operations (Psyops) Defined as operations directed to enemy, friendly and neutral audiences in order to influence attitudes and behaviour affecting the achievement of military and political objectives. In the US forces in Bosnia these were executed by Psyops specialists, in 2 LI Psyops were conducted by all.

Ptarmigan The British trunk communications system that provided secure voice and data channels to users. For most of the tour, 2 LI's access to Ptarmigan was limited to the Single Channel Radio Access (SCRA) a type of secure military mobile telephone.

QM Quartermaster. An officer responsible for logistic support within a unit. 2 LI had two QMs, one responsible for barracks and infrastructure support, the other for equipment and combat supplies. Both deployed to Bosnia.

RAChD Royal Army Chaplains Department, the British Army branch that chaplains belong to.

'Radio Big' A privately owned independent music station in Banja Luka.

Raki A local home-brewed liquor.

RARDEN The 30mm cannon fitted to Warrior and Scimitar.

Rebro Rebroadcast Station. Two radios connected together to allow a signal received by the first to be re-transmitted on a different frequency by the second. All 2 LI rebroadcast stations consisted of one or two vehicles, with crew.

Relief in Place An operation for the relief of troops in combat, in which an outgoing force is replaced in sector by an incoming force.

REME Royal Electrical and Mechanical Engineers. The corps responsible for equipment support, repair and recovery.

Republika Srpska The Bosnian Serb entity within Bosnia.

RMP Royal Military Police.

ROE Rules of Engagement. A way of constraining the operations and use of lethal force by troops, to conform to legal and political constraints.

Rover Group (R Gp) The vehicles, crew and staff that support a commander moving around the battlefield.

RQMS Regimental Quartermaster Serjeant. A warrant officer responsible for assisting a quartermaster with their logistic responsibilities.

R&R Rest and Recuperation. All British personnel on 6-month tours were entitled to a two-week period of R&R in England or Germany.

RRF (1) Royal Regiment of Fusiliers. First Battalion the Royal Regiment of Fusileers (1 RRF) were the UK mechanised battalion in Bosnia September 95 – March 96.

RRF (2) Rapid Reaction Force. The UNPROFOR Rapid Reaction Force was set up in mid 95 as a response to the hostage crisis. It included the Franco-British-Dutch Multinational Brigade, the British 24 Airmobile Brigade and a French brigade held at high readiness to reinforce Bosnia from France.

RRFOS The Rapid Reaction Force Operational Staff, established at the same time as the Rapid Reaction Force to give Commander UNPROFOR a planning staff. Their framework was provided by the British Headquarters Royal Marines, augmented by French and Dutch personnel.

RSM Regimental Serjeant Major. A Warrant Officer Class 1, the senior warrant officer in a battalion or regiment.

Samson A light armoured recovery vehicle.

Sandhurst The Royal Military Academy Sandhurst trains officer cadets of the British Army to be officers.

Saxon A light wheeled armoured personnel carrier (APC) used by British mechanised infantry. A larger vehicle than Warrior, it was faster on roads, but had less cross-country mobility, protection and only a single machine gun for armament.

Scimitar A light armoured reconnaissance vehicle. Thinly armoured, equipped with a machine gun and 30mm cannon. Crewed by 3 men and issued both the battalion reconnaissance platoon and armoured reconnaissance squadrons. Part of the CVR (T) series.

SCRA See Ptarmigan.

Sea King A Royal Navy battlefield support helicopter used to carry troops and cargo.

Sector Southwest (SSW) The UNPROFOR HQ commanding south-west Bosnia. Brigadier Richard Dannatt was the last commander of the sector, which disbanded when NATO took over from the UN.

Secure A term used to describe encryption of radio signals, so as to prevent others from gaining intelligence that could be revealed from 'clear' unencrypted radio traffic. 2 LI had three secure speech radios, for use on the brigade secure command net, as well as three Ptarmigan SCRA terminals with the ability to conduct secure speech or data transfer. The KL 43 data entry device provided a limited secure data transmission capability to the battlegroup insecure VHF radio net. All other security came from the use of the complex paper-based code BATCO.

'Send for Agent Scully' A humorous slang expression used when someone or something was lost and needed finding. Refers to female lead in the X Files TV series.

Separation of Forces The withdrawal of the opposing faction forces 2km back from the cease-fire line.

Shamargh A large Arab headscarf dyed dark green that can be wrapped thickly around the face, leaving only the eyes uncovered.

The *Silver Bugle* Regimental magazine of the Light Infantry.

Slivovitz A Bosnian plum brandy. Often locally distilled and very strong.

SNCO Senior Non-Commissioned Officer. A serjeant, colour-serjeant or staff serjeant.

Spartan A light tracked APC used by infantry signals and mortar platoons and armoured reconnaissance.

Spyglass A handheld thermal imager used by infantry mortar fire controllers and reconnaissance platoons.

Squadron (Sqn) A company sized sub unit of engineers (three troops), tanks (12), army helicopters (8–10) or armoured reconnaissance (up to 20 light armoured vehicles). British Army squadrons are normally commanded by majors.

Stag Slang expression for a period of time spent on sentry duty or radio watch. 'Stagging On' was a loose expression with various positive and negative meanings.

Standard Operating Procedure (SOP) Standard procedure laid down for the conduct of operations at battlegroup, company/squadron and platoon/troop level.

Strategy The application of national resources to achieve policy objectives. Military strategy is subordinate to wider grand strategy. Strategy can be conducted in both a national or coalition context.

Sub-Unit A component part of a British Army unit. Battalions broke down into companies, which are divided in turn into platoons, sections and fire teams. Armoured and reconnaissance regiments break into squadrons and troops, whilst artillery regiments break into batteries with component troops.

Support Company (Sp Coy) The company contained 2 LI's combat support; the mortar, anti-tank, reconnaissance and signal platoons.

Surveillance The continuous watch over the battlefield and detection, recognition and identification of targets.

TA Territorial Army, the Army's reserve force made up of volunteers conducting military training in their spare time. Forty TA soldiers and two TA officers volunteered to accompany 2 LI to Bosnia.

Tactical Group (Tac Gp) At battlegroup level, the artillery tactical group consists of a battery commander, his fire planning cell and observers. They are responsible for planning, co-ordinating and integrating all battlegroup fire support operations.

Tactics The tactical level sits below the operational level. Tactics is the art of conducting battles, engagements and lower level operations, in order to achieve operational objectives.

Task Force Alpha (TF-A) A British battlegroup based initially on the Devon and Dorsets and then on 2 LI that made up one of the two manoeuvre units of the Anglo-French-Dutch Multinational Brigade in 1995. The battlegroup included a large armoured engineer troop.

Team Medic A soldier given a short course in advanced battlefield first aid.

Theatre of Operations A theatre of operations is the whole geographical area assigned by a strategic commander to an operational commander. For both UNPROFOR and IFOR we regarded the 'theatre' as being Bosnia and Croatia.

Thermal Imager (TI) A surveillance or target acquisition device producing an image of an object's thermal signature. The thermal image can be detected through some kinds of obstruction, including smoke, which would defeat optical sights and image intensifiers.

Tiffy See artificer.

Troop A British military term for a platoon-sized sub-unit of artillery, engineers, tanks or armoured reconnaissance.

Underslung Load. Cargo, vehicles or weapons carried beneath a hook on the underside of a helicopter.

UNHCR United Nations High Commission for Refugees.

Unit In the British Army, a unit is a battalion or regiment.

UNMOs United Nations Military Observers. A force of unarmed officers from a wide range of UN member states, deployed to observe and monitor the conflict in Bosnia. They use in Bosnia preceded the UNPROFOR operation and they worked to a UN HQ in Zagreb, rather than the UNPROFR HQ In Sarajevo. Their quality and value were both highly variable. When NATO took over from the UN the UNMOs withdrew.

UNPROFOR The United Nations Protection Force, the UN force in Bosnia 1992–95.

VBL A French APC. Small, light and wheeled, it was the size of large car. The Multinational Brigade allocated a VBL to 2 LI, crewed by French-speaking British officers and two French signallers. It carried radios on the French radio nets.

VRS Vojna Republika Srpska. Literally the Army of Republika Srpska, the Bosnian Serb entity. Previously known by the UN and NATO as the Bosnian Serb Army (BSA).

Warrior A 32-ton armoured infantry fighting vehicle, two-thirds the size of a tank, mounting a machine gun and a 30mm 'Rarden' cannon. The basic vehicle carries a section of infantry and is crewed by a driver, gunner, commander and seven infantrymen in the rear crew compartment. Variants of the vehicle are used as command vehicles (equipped with extra radios and masts and issued to company HQs and Battalion HQs), anti tank vehicles (with Milan firing posts and crews carried in the back) and REME repair and recovery vehicles (fitted with cranes and winches).

Warrior Serjeant Each armoured infantry platoon had a warrior serjeant, responsible for supervising the maintenance of the vehicles and commanding them when the platoon commander dismounts.

Watchkeeper A person controlling the radio net and routine passage of information.

Webbing A term describing British Army personal load carrying equipment.

Welfare Telephone An official telephone available to British personnel to call their friends and family in Germany or UK.

WHITE FANG The IFOR-controlled crossing point between the Bosnian Muslim-controlled territory of Sanski Most and the Bosnian Serb controlled town of Prijedor. Throughout 2 LI's tour a platoon or troop controlled it.

Wider Peacekeeping Peacekeeping operations carried out with the consent of the belligerents, but in an environment that is highly volatile. British operations in Bosnia between 1992 and May 1995 could be considered to fall into this category.

Zeroing The process of aligning the sights of weapons to ensure they are as accurate as possible. Usually applied to small arms.

ZOS Zone of Separation. The area for 2km on either side of the ACFL and IEBL, in which neither faction was allowed to deploy any weapons, forces or military equipment.

The Agreed Cease-fire Line. Map courtesy the Silver Bugle.

Introduction

People sleep peacefully in their beds only because rough men stand ready to do violence on their behalf.

George Orwell

In 1992 Bosnia descended into a savage and bitter war, which by 1995 had claimed over a quarter of a million lives. The United Nations Protection Force (UNPROFOR) was deployed to protect the delivery of humanitarian aid. It succeeded in bringing this aid to the suffering civilian population which was being ravaged by the fighting, and lives were saved as a result. But its efforts to promote a cessation of hostilities between the Bosnian factions met with only occasional and partial success.

The first British troops in Bosnia were First Battalion the Cheshire Regiment, who joined UNPROFOR in November 1992. Further armoured infantry battalions continued to form the core of the ever-growing British UN forces in central Bosnia. In 1994, the British General Sir Michael Rose took command of UNPROFOR.

As the fighting between the Bosnian Serbs and the uneasy alliance of Bosnian Muslims and Croats intensified, the risk to the UN troops increased and their influence on the warring factions decreased. By May 1995 the UNPROFOR operation was in a state of perpetual crisis, with British, European, United States and UN policies on the Bosnian war under great pressure. Three years of international efforts to end the war had come to nothing. The UN mission appeared close to failure and, it seemed, would have to withdraw. Extracting the UN troops from a civil war would have been very difficult – NATO had contingency plans to do this by intervening in Bosnia in force – but no one doubted that this would be a hazardous undertaking.

Throughout that long bloody summer, the state of affairs in Bosnia continued to deteriorate, but the strategic situation was altered by a series of successful offensives by Bosnian Croat forces in western Bosnia. At the end of August NATO responded to Serb shelling of Sarajevo market by unleashing a massive air attack on Bosnian Serb forces. The effects of these actions reinforced each other, the Serb military position in western Bosnia collapsed and a truce was negotiated. A dynamic US negotiator, Richard Holbrooke, exploited this politically, persuading the three Bosnian factions to sign a peace agreement at Dayton. Many politicians, diplomats and senior UN officials considered this to be the very last chance for peace.

On 20 December NATO began its first land operation when the Implementation Force (IFOR) took over from the UN Protection Force. The alliance was to ensure the factions complied with the military provisions of the peace agreement, and had the mandate and rules of engagement to use force to achieve this. That same day a British battlegroup moved from Sarajevo to north-west Bosnia. Two thirds of the forces allocated to the battlegroup for this mission had not yet been released from other tasks in central Bosnia. The battlegroup had a single armoured infantry company, a reconnaissance platoon and six mortars – a total of two hundred men with thirty armoured vehicles. They had no tanks or artillery. Three liaison teams, a dozen more men, completed the force: the only British troops in this part of Bosnia.

It had an area of responsibility a hundred kilometres wide by seventy deep. Winding through it was a front line a hundred and twenty kilometres long, separating territory held by the Bosnian Muslims from that held by Bosnian Serb forces. Every single road or track through the no-man's-land between the two forces was sown with land mines. During the previous three and a half years of war, the factions had denied the UN access to almost all of this area. The commanders of the two Bosnian Government corps manning the front line were renowned for their obduracy, intransigence and desire to constrain the freedom of action of UN forces. The Bosnian Serb forces had allowed the UN even less access across the front line.

As soon as it arrived, the battlegroup opened a crossing point between the two armies and began patrolling its vast territory. Little was known about the faction armies' strength and locations, and intelligence was almost non-existent. The battlegroup set out to find the factions for itself. Liaison officers were despatched to the few known faction headquarters and patrols of Warrior and Scimitar armoured vehicles began working from the base at Sanski Most, forward towards the front line. All this movement was conducted with the support of the battlegroup's mortars, ready to bring down fire on any potential opposition.

Communications with the British headquarters sixty kilometres to the south-east were tenuous and intermittent. Snow and ice covered the narrow, winding mountain roads, making vehicle movement dangerous and slow. Logistic support was severely overstretched – food and mail got through, but it was proving very difficult to provide the battlegroup with sufficient fuel and spare parts for its vehicles. The battlegroup commander was worried that these accumulating difficulties might make evacuation of casualties too slow.

The troops saw much evidence of recent fighting: minefields, damaged and burned out vehicles, shell cases, empty ammunition containers, enormous piles of rubbish and all the discarded paraphernalia of war. Patrols frequently came across corpses and body parts. Some were from livestock, killed in the fighting but most seemed to be the pathetically sad remains of soldiers from both sides.

Close to the front line, buildings and villages were occupied by faction soldiers: tired, dirty, hungry-looking men in assorted shabby uniforms and civilian clothes. Although a few were friendly, many seemed ill-disciplined, sullen characters who scowled truculently at passing British vehicles. Some villages were empty, their occupants having fled. Bosnian soldiers and civilians were systematically looting these settlements. Other villages were destroyed and abandoned. Most of these appeared to have been wrecked not by fighting, but by 'ethnic cleansing' – where one of the factions had expelled people from other ethnic groups. Violence had been threatened or applied to civilians to achieve this.

Each of the factions had approximately seventy thousand men under arms in the battlegroup's area of responsibility. Both sides had more armoured fighting vehicles than the British force. The Bosnian Muslim forces included a battalion of thirty tanks and the Bosnian Serbs had over a hundred pieces of heavy artillery and an armoured brigade with a hundred tanks. A mere six weeks ago these soldiers had been fighting each other in a war of savagery and atrocity that was medieval in its excess. Both sides were very suspicious of each other. Their attitude to NATO was unknown, but so far the faction forces seemed to be conforming to most of the military requirements of the peace agreement. British NATO troops had been granted 'freedom of movement', something that was always denied to UN troops, although Warriors had forced open a Bosnian Muslim checkpoint that had attempted to stop a NATO vehicle.

A cease-fire was supposed to be in force. During the day it seemed to hold, but at night there was a constant sound of firing. There were exchanges of fire between the two front lines, and armed civilians fired at shadows, at suspicious movement and into the air to reassure themselves and deter looters.

In three weeks' time, the formerly warring armies would be required to withdraw from their front lines to create between them a zone of separation four kilometres wide. During the previous three years' fighting all three factions had continually undermined the UN mission in Bosnia. Attacks on UN troops, obstruction at every level, duplicity, endless wrangling and repeated refusals to implement cease-fires had made it impossible for the international community to broker a lasting peace. No one knew if the factions would attempt to frustrate the NATO mission in the same way. If they failed to comply, NATO could use military force to compel them to do so. This would mean NATO ground troops attacking non-compliant faction forces. If so, would NATO take casualties? Would the Dayton Peace Agreement survive? For the soldiers and officers of the battlegroup, this was the source of no small anxiety and tension, alleviated only by their confidence in their training and each other.

On 23 December a British engineer party travelling in two Land Rovers set out to conduct a route reconnaissance. Without notifying the battlegroup, they drove through the Bosnian Muslim front line at the village of Sassina, five kilometres north-east of the town of Sanski Most. Passing through the front line held by Bosnian Muslim troops, they carried on into no-man's-land, where the leading Land Rover drove over an anti-tank mine. The front of the vehicle was totally destroyed. Both of the crew were injured, one seriously. The battlegroup sent an armoured infantry platoon of four Warriors to the scene. They evacuated the casualties from the minefield and brought in a helicopter to fly them to the field hospital. The platoon provided protection for an engineer mine clearance party, who lifted six anti-tank mines from the frozen track, allowing the recovery of the wrecked vehicle.

The next day was Christmas Eve. The Bosnian Corps Headquarters delivered a protest note complaining that Serb troops at Sassina had directed machine-gun fire towards the Muslim lines. Unless the factions conformed to the peace agreement, and military tension and suspicion were reduced, the NATO mission would not succeed. The armoured infantry company was ordered to investigate the allegations. They decided to get the two opposing commanders together in neutral territory to sort out the problem.

26 December 1995

The armoured infantry platoon that responded to the mine strike is now halted on the same snow-covered track a hundred metres short of the shallow crater left by the explosion. They wait level with a line of trenches, bunkers and fortified buildings: the front line of the Bosnian Muslim troops.

They represent almost a quarter of the combat power available to the battlegroup. The sheer size of the four Warrior armoured vehicles with their huge slabs of armour, powerful diesel engines and turret-mounted cannon and machine guns impresses the Bosnian Muslim troops. These citizen soldiers have never before encountered either such large fighting vehicles or professional NATO troops.

It is intensely cold in this narrow snow-covered valley with rolling hills rising on either side. As the twenty-four soldiers wait, all thickly bundled in winter uniforms, some in the back of the vehicles smoke and drink tea to keep warm. Others doze, or read letters and Christmas cards. But the vehicle turrets are on full alert. Cannons, machine guns and rifles are loaded and commanders and gunners are using their high-powered sights to watch activity in the trenches and bunkers that mark the two opposing front lines. They are ready to open fire. The whole valley is also covered by the battlegroup's mortar platoon, ready to bring down high-explosive or smoke bombs on any positions that fire on the British troops.

The platoon commander and a liaison officer are meeting the Muslim brigade commander. Four hundred metres further up the valley is the Bosnian Serb Army's front line. Behind it, a liaison team of Joint Commission Observers, all highly trained specialists, is negotiating with the headquarters of the Serb brigade controlling the area. Both British parties are proposing a meeting between the Serb and Muslim commanders in no-man's-land, under NATO protection and mediation. After some difficult negotiations this is agreed.

The Warriors deploy into firing positions to provide cover and respond to any firing by Muslims or Serbs. The patrol of Joint Commission Observers arrives with the Serb brigade commander, stopping on the Serb front line. Four hundred metres of snow-covered track separate the two forces. No one knows for sure whether or not the track is free from land mines.

There are protracted discussions between the British troops and the faction officers. The Muslim commander firmly states that all Muslim-laid mines were recovered during the clearance operation after the Land Rover was destroyed. The Serb commander is adamant that his side has not laid any mines at all. It is impossible to know if they are telling the truth. Either side could have laid mines without records being kept. The British forces confer by radio. There are two options: either they do nothing or they start taking risks.

Slowly and cautiously the vehicle advances. After a short distance, the platoon commander sees a lump in the snow. Trying to see if it is an anti-tank mine, he hauls himself out of the turret and carefully climbs down from the front of the vehicle to look more closely ...

This book is a personal account of operations conducted by Second Battalion the Light Infantry (2 LI) in Bosnia between November 1995 and May 1996. As commanding officer I was responsible for making sure that the battalion carried out all the missions assigned to it.

The Bosnian war had created great tension inside both the UN and NATO and between the two alliances. Before the transfer of authority from UNPROFOR to IFOR, there was understandable Western apprehension about the outcome of NATO's first ever land operation. Would the formerly warring factions comply with the General Framework Agreement for Peace, so hastily negotiated at Dayton just a month earlier? Would NATO troops suffer the same harassment, obfuscation, non-cooperation and attacks as had UNPROFOR? Would NATO have to use force? In the event, the military implementation of the Dayton Agreement was a great success, especially in areas where British IFOR troops operated.

This account demonstrates how the powers granted to NATO in the Dayton Agreement were used to conduct peace enforcement operations to compel the factions to comply with the treaty's military requirements. There was no existing theory or doctrine for this. Tactics were developed on the job by the forces conducting these operations, while they also overcame the inherent frictions of operating in a multinational force, and coped with the harsh and unforgiving environment of a Balkan winter.

Key to this was our ability to change our approach quickly from UN peacekeeping operations that relied on the consent of warring factions, to peace enforcement operations under a NATO mandate that allowed the use of force to make the factions cooperate with us. Peace enforcement explicitly relied on our demonstrated combat capability. We used force to defend ourselves and we twice mounted operations to attack the faction troops.

The achievements of NATO forces operating under a robust and assertive *modus operandi* would influence future political and military planning for peace support operations. The success of British NATO troops in rapidly bringing stability to war-torn Kosovo in 1999 owed much to lessons learned in Bosnia in 1995 and 1996. Indeed, General Jackson, who had so dynamically commanded the first six months of British operations in Bosnia, led the NATO ground force entering Kosovo three and half years later.

The battalion that I had the privilege to command, Second Battalion the Light Infantry, was the seventh British armoured infantry battalion to serve in Bosnia. It was the last to be part of the UNPROFOR and the first to form part of the NATO Implementation Force responsible for making the military aspects of the Dayton Agreement work.

These six months in Bosnia were unlike anything any of us had ever experienced before. They featured danger, uncertainty, rapid movement over long distances at short notice, unforeseen problems, logistic and communications challenges and a unique multinational military environment. Operations were very different from those conducted by any of the other British battalions and regiments that served in Bosnia.

I found the tour sometimes frustrating, often taxing, but ultimately immensely rewarding. The combination of comradeship, success on operations and the unpredictable and bizarre incidents that were so much a feature of our activities made the tour fun – something that was not necessarily the case for our wives, families and friends in Germany and England.

After the tour, as the battalion most recently returned from Bosnia, we ran the preparatory training for troops deploying to the Balkans from Germany at the end of 1996. Subsequently I was invited to brief military training establishments about our operations. As I did so, I began to feel that there was a tale to tell concerning our operations in the last months of the UN mandate and in the first four ground-breaking months of the NATO mission.

I have read many first-hand accounts of British military operations. Apart from books on Special Forces, it is disappointing that so few have dealt with operations since 1945. Even fewer deal with operations other than war, and the number of books covering the British peacekeeping operations in Bosnia can be counted on one hand – with some fingers to spare. I do not know of any books analysing the highly successful NATO peace enforcement operations that ended the Bosnian civil war.

This book shows how the British Army operated in the Balkans, adapting its tactics, techniques, procedures and conceptual approach to this constantly changing and unpredictable environment. I want to take the reader into the platoons, troops, companies, squadrons and Battlegroup HQ that used both modern technology and the timeless principles of military leadership to achieve their mission. The young people of the battlegroup achieved some quite remarkable things. Because all their work was part of a collective team effort, it is easy to overlook the individual courage, endeavour and determination that contributed to the battlegroup's success. Deliberately I have not censored myself. I want the reader to understand the reasoning behind key decisions and to get a feel for the highs and lows of the roller-coaster ride that is command on operations.

The battalion was engaged in a large number of different operations simultaneously, often having to work 'in parallel' rather than 'in series'. But the printed word conveys information only in a linear fashion. I have sometimes described events sequentially which in fact occurred simultaneously.

I want to give the reader an impression of the actions of the whole battlegroup. Many incidents, operations and events are described in the words of those who took part. These accounts were written for various Army publications, including newsletters, the Light Infantry's regimental magazine the *Silver Bugle*, and the *Infantryman*, the house journal of the British infantry. Many were written when time was short. They have an immediacy that a retrospective, deliberate account lacks.

Most of this account is written in the past tense. I occasionally use the present tense for immediacy. The terminology, jargon, slang and abbreviations of the British Army can be impenetrable to the uninitiated. A glossary is provided on pages 9–23.

Acknowledgements

Over a thousand people served with the 2 LI Battlegroup in 1995–96. Many others directly and indirectly helped us achieve our mission. Inevitably, it is impossible to acknowledge the contribution made by all of them. I thank them all, and apologise in advance to anyone whose contribution to our operations is not described.

I would also like to thank the people who have helped me write the book. These include Colonel Ben Bathurst, Mr Martin Bell, Tom Boswell, Lorraine Brooks, Mrs Sappho Clissit, General Sir Richard Dannatt, Major General Simon Mayall, Rob Lynam, Major Steve Noble, Serjeant Dryhurst-Smyth, Corporal Palframan, John Harding, Kate Paice, Andrew Lownie, Colonel Chris Vernon, Adrian Weale, my agent Robert Dudley and Shaun Barrington at The History Press. Colonels Jan de Vos, Paul Kellett, Rex Sartain and Brigadier Richard Smith have been particularly helpful with advice concerning the activities of the companies they commanded. Especial thanks are due to my parents and my wife Liz and children Jamie and Charlotte.

CHAPTER ONE

'Naming of Parts'

The British Army is organised into units called *battalions* or *regiments*. All are commanded by lieutenant colonels, aged between thirty-seven and forty-two, and have between four hundred and a thousand men and women. Some recruit their soldiers and officers from all over the UK, others from particular regions. Although many armies have specifically organised and equipped light infantry battalions, in the British Army the name 'Light Infantry' was applied to a particular infantry regiment.

Our origins were in the special purpose light infantry units first raised by the British Army to fight the French, Native Americans and rebellious colonists in North America, and subsequently for Wellington's army in the Peninsular War. Not only were these regiments lightly equipped to move faster and clothed in green uniforms for camouflage, both innovations of their times, but they also developed a new concept of operations, with more speed of movement, decentralised command, and freedom of action at low levels.

The First Battalion was an airmobile infantry battalion based in England and we, the Second Battalion the Light Infantry (abbreviated to 2 LI), were an armoured infantry battalion based in Paderborn, Germany.

We are equipped to take part in high-intensity warfare as part of an armoured brigade. The most important component of the battalion is the infantryman. Equipped with an SA 80 assault rifle, he is grouped into a fire team of three or four men led by a lance corporal or a corporal (the next step up the promotion ladder). All of the fire team will be capable of engaging targets out to a range of three hundred metres with their rifles. One of the soldiers will have a Light Support Weapon (LSW), a heavier version of the SA 80 rifle with a range of six hundred metres. The fire team will normally carry one or two Light Anti-Tank Weapons (LAW), large, heavy rockets with powerful anti-tank warheads. The weapon is heavy, bulky, and difficult to carry for any distance, but could destroy any of the tanks or armoured vehicles we might encounter in Bosnia.

The corporal is the section commander, responsible for both fire teams. The whole section lives and travels in the thirty-two-tonne Warrior armoured infantry fighting vehicle, with a crew of three more soldiers, a driver, a gunner and the deputy vehicle commander.

Warrior is over six metres long, three high and three wide, some two-thirds the size of a tank. In the centre of the vehicle is a squat turret, mounting a machine gun and a 30mm 'Rarden' cannon. The machine gun can engage infantry and soft targets, as well as suppress bunkers and fortifications out to eleven hundred metres. Similar targets can be engaged at longer ranges by high-explosive shells from the cannon, which also fires armour-piercing rounds to destroy light armoured vehicles. In the turret, the commander and gunner have excellent optical sights. At night image intensification sights amplify moonlight and starlight several thousandfold.

Despite having armour sufficiently thick to defeat small arms fire, the vehicle is fast and more reliable than any other armoured vehicle then in service with the British Army. But it still requires the crew to maintain it regularly. Replacing old, worn track with a new one is a tedious and back-breaking task for the whole section.

The back of the vehicle contains a rectangular crew compartment for the passengers. There is space for storing equipment, weapons, food and ammunition. Even so a Warrior carrying ten soldiers and a full load of combat supplies is extremely crowded. The infantry whose job is to fight on the ground (who we call the 'dismounts') and their vehicle should be considered as a single fighting system. Much of our training is devoted to integrating both of these components.

A platoon comprises three such sections, each in a Warrior. The platoon commander is a young officer, a second lieutenant or lieutenant. He and his platoon HQ, who travel in their own Warrior, comprise two serjeants, one his deputy for dismounted operations and one 'Warrior serjeant' who co-ordinates the maintenance of the vehicles. (The Light Infantry traditionally use the antique spelling of serjeant, with a 'j'.)

Three platoons comprise an armoured infantry company. All of 2 LI's company commanders are in their early thirties. A Company commander, Major Jan de Vos, B Company commander, Major Stuart Mills, and C Company commander, Major Rex Sartain, are all experienced and respected officers. Jan de Vos is the only Light Infantryman in the battalion to have war experience, having served as a staff officer in the 1991 Gulf War.

Armoured infantry companies have two captains. One is the company second-in-command, the commander's deputy and responsible both for co-ordinating the company's logistics and for running the company headquarters. The other officer is the company 'second captain'. Often known as the 'Warrior captain', he manages the company's armoured vehicles. If the company commander dismounts to lead the battle on foot, the Warrior captain commands and fights the Warriors.

All companies have a warrant officer as company serjeant major, supporting the commander in many functions, including discipline and administration. The company headquarters has two Warrior Command Vehicles with additional radios, tables and map boards. The vehicles are crewed by the small company signals detachment commanded by a corporal.

The company also has a small logistic team commanded by the company quartermaster serjeant (CQMS). He and his small team have a Land Rover and truck which they use to supply us with the essential commodities required by sustained operations.

All the battalion's weapons, vehicles and equipment need both maintenance and repair. Although simple routine tasks are the responsibilities of the soldier, weapon crew or vehicle crew, more demanding work is carried out by the Royal Electrical and Mechanical Engineers (REME). Each company is invariably accompanied by its affiliated 'fitter section' of two Warrior repair and recovery vehicles crewed by expert REME tradesmen. Commanded by a staff serjeant artificer or 'tiffy', they repair the company's vehicles and equipment, and can use power winches to recover vehicles bogged in soft ground or stuck in ditches or culverts.

The battalion's REME Light Aid Detachment (LAD) carries out more complex repair tasks. This seventy-strong group of electrical and mechanical engineers is fully committed to keeping the maximum amount of equipment 'on the road'. Our forward repair and recovery capability is invaluable in minimising the amount of time that the company's vehicles spend 'off the road'.

The battalion has its own combat support grouped in Support Company, commanded by Major Ian Baker. The reconnaissance platoon has eight Scimitar reconnaissance vehicles. Although these look like small tanks, armed with a 30mm cannon and machine gun, they are lighter than Warrior, with thinner armour. The platoon's role is to gain information and it fights only as a last resort.

The anti-tank platoon has twenty MILAN anti-tank missile launchers. They can knock out any armoured vehicles to be found in Bosnia, including tanks, which cannot be destroyed by the cannon of our Warriors. Like LAW 80, it also has a useful capability against bunkers and fortifications. An anti-tank detachment consists of six men in a Warrior with two MILAN systems. Three detachments make up a section, the platoon having three sections. We affiliate each anti-tank section to an armoured infantry company, thus guaranteeing each company an anti-tank capability with longer ranges than LAW 80 and greater punch than the 30mm cannons. The bulky firing posts and missiles are just about man portable and can be carried in helicopters or smaller vehicles such as Land Rovers, allowing us to deploy the missile and its thermal imaging night sight to places that could not be reached by Warriors.

The mortar platoon gives the battalion its own indirect fire support. It has nine 81mm mortars, each firing an extremely effective anti-personnel bomb with a range of over five kilometres. They can also fire smoke and illuminating bombs. The mortars travel in FV 432 armoured personnel carriers, known universally as '432s', which are little more than steel boxes on tracks. The mortars deploy in sections of three weapons in mortar 'lines', out of sight of their target. Their fire is directed by mortar fire controllers (MFCs) equipped with laser range-finders and hand-held thermal sights, who travel in Spartan, an armoured personnel carrier based on the same chassis as Scimitar. Each MFC party and mortar section is affiliated to an armoured infantry company, although the mortar lines are usually controlled at Battalion HQ.

The signal platoon mans all the vehicles of Battalion HQ. These consist of a 'command' variant of the FV 432, equipped with more radios and configured inside as a cramped armoured office. The platoon also has a few Spartan APCs and the commanding officer's Warrior.

All these men, weapons and armoured vehicles have to be capable of continuous operations for however long it takes the battalion to accomplish its mission. It is essential that ammunition, food, water, spare parts and other supplies reach the companies and platoons as and when they are needed. Obtaining these from logistic units and arranging distribution within the battalion is the role of our in-house logisticians in Headquarters Company, overseen by the battalion's two quartermasters. Fetching, carrying and delivering these supplies requires a fleet of trucks and fuel dispensers manned by the mechanical transport (MT) platoon.

Headquarter Company is commanded by Major Dave Wroe, the longest-serving member of the battalion. An immensely experienced officer, he and I had served together some years earlier in Northern Ireland, where I had acquired great respect for his logistic expertise and good-humoured common sense. The company also contains a small platoon of cooks from the Royal Logistic Corps and a team of clerks and pay specialists from the Adjutant General's Corps. At this time, women are not permitted to serve in roles involving direct combat, and the only women in the battalion are five clerical staff. The battalion has its own doctor and small medical section, maintaining health in peace and dealing with casualties in war.

There is much more to the British Army than armoured infantry. The battalion is part of 1 Armoured Division. This contains a reconnaissance regiment, tank regiments, engineers, artillery and armed helicopters, as well as a complex network of communications and logistics. We train to fight the 'All-Arms' battle, using the strengths and capabilities of each arm to achieve an effect greater than the sum of our parts. This requires us to train with armoured squadrons of tanks and an affiliated battery of artillery and combat engineers. We have to be able to combine our tactics with those of reconnaissance and armed helicopters and close support aircraft. This process of grouping forces for battle is called 'task organisation'. A battalion task organised in this way is called a battlegroup.

I had taken command of 2 LI at the beginning of June 1994, nineteen years after I had joined the Army. In 1976 I spent five months as a private soldier before officer training at the Royal Military Academy Sandhurst. Joining the First Battalion as a lieutenant, I commanded a platoon in Hong Kong, and on operations in Northern Ireland. As a captain I had been an intelligence officer on the Cold War's front line in West Germany and again on operations in Belfast. After staff training, I spent two years working in the Ministry of Defence, and commanded an infantry company in Berlin as the Wall was opened and the Cold War ended. A year as a battalion second-in-command, mostly spent in the hostile environment of South Armagh, was followed by promotion to lieutenant colonel. Eighteen months as an instructor at the Royal

Military College of Science had been a frustrating time, as I watched television reports of the war in Bosnia with interest, especially the work of the British troops pitchforked into this three-way civil war.

As a student officer at Sandhurst I had studied Yugoslavia. The Cold War was at its height and the country was seen as a potential flashpoint. Yugoslavia was a young state, its provinces coming from the disintegration of the Austro-Hungarian and Ottoman empires. The Second World War had seen the military defeat of the Yugoslav state by Germany, its occupation and the subsequent partisan campaign led by Tito. It had also seen nationalist tension between Croats, Muslims and Serbs flaming into bloody inter-ethnic conflicts. These were suppressed by Tito, who sustained himself in power with techniques of repression and manipulation similar to those employed by the communist regimes throughout Eastern Europe. For the next three decades the potential centrifugal forces of ethnic nationalism, were held in check stabilised by Tito's authority striking a delicate balance between the various Yugoslav republics and autonomous regions. But our instructors forecast that when Tito died, tensions between the different ethnic groups that made up the state would erupt, and the resulting sparks would have the potential to ignite a superpower confrontation.

Tito died in 1980. The predicted explosion did not happen, but throughout that decade the Yugoslav economy declined, and inter-ethnic tension rose, especially after Slobodan Milošević became Serbian Prime Minister in 1989. In 1991 Croatia and Slovenia seceded from Yugoslavia; the fighting that resulted was especially intense in the Serb minority areas of Croatia. The next year British troops deployed as part of the UN peacekeeping force in Croatia. But no sooner had they arrived than Bosnia imploded into civil war between the Bosnian Government and the Bosnian Serbs. A British armoured infantry battalion became part of the UN Protection Force (UNPROFOR), conducting both humanitarian operations and peacekeeping.

In 1993 the battalion had set aside its newly learned skills in armoured warfare in order to conduct six months' operational duty in Northern Ireland. It returned to Paderborn at the end of the year with some relief, knowing that it would spend 1994 training in its primary 'war fighting' role.

I took over 2 LI in mid-June 1994. I was looking forward to getting to grips with command. With me in Paderborn I had my wife Liz and our young son, James. I had seven weeks to find my feet and to prepare for a period of war-fighting training in Canada. Exercise MEDICINE MAN, run by the British Army Training Unit Suffield (BATUS), required the battalion to train on the Canadian prairie as the framework of an all-arms battlegroup of more than two hundred vehicles and twelve hundred men. Formed around Battalion HQ, two armoured infantry companies and our recce platoon, the battlegroup included two squadrons of tanks from the Queens Dragoon Guards, our affiliated artillery battery, engineers, logistic troop and two reconnaissance helicopters. All training was conducted with live ammunition (of which a prodigious amount was expended) against a sophisticated target array.

The aftermath of the Gulf War, the reduction of the Army after the Cold War and the battalion's Northern Ireland tours meant that this was the first time the battalion had achieved a concentrated period of all-arms war fighting training since 1990. The battlegroup spent a month on the vast and desolate prairie, mastering individual and collective skills and living in the harsh arid environment, little dissimilar to a desert. The single component of the battalion least prepared or 'worked up' before the exercise had been Battalion HQ. To put this right required the replacement of one officer who was not meeting the demands of his appointment.

I spent a lot of time during the first two weeks on the prairie training the headquarters and myself in the critical functions of command and control, without which the battlegroup could not function. We achieved a great deal and battalion HQ improved beyond all recognition. It had to climb a steeper learning curve than the other components of the battlegroup, but on the final part of the training, Exercise GAZALA, everything suddenly seemed to gel. This exercise was a continuous five-day operation in which the battlegroup fought eight separate battles, including all the phases and operations of war that might be required of it.

We all learned a great deal about war-fighting tactics, our machines and ourselves. I had taken command only two months before, but was delighted with the way everyone thrived on the challenge, working extremely hard through the sweltering heat and choking dust. The exercise had thoroughly tested all parts of the battalion and all had passed with flying colours.

As we returned from Canada, the battalion was formally warned that it would spend six months in Bosnia, beginning in November 1995. The armoured infantry companies were to return to BATUS the next year, this time under command of the two tank regiments in 20 Armoured Brigade, the Queen's Dragoon Guards and the Royal Dragoon Guards. There had been many personnel changes in Battalion HQ and I decided to send all the officers who had not been to BATUS out to Canada.

Human Factors

The battalion's rank structure was a pyramid of more than seven hundred people. At the top were forty officers, with more than double that number of warrant officers, colour serjeants and serjeants. Below that were the corporals and lance corporals and the private soldiers, most of whom had only three years' service or less.

The function of an army is the controlled use of force to further the interests of the nation. The infantry's role is defined as 'close combat'. All the training of infantrymen is directed to this end, making infantry soldiers robust characters, physically and mentally tough men who are capable of fighting and killing the enemy without being killed.

The majority of infantry soldiers join the Army with few educational qualifications. We liked to consider ourselves a tough and uncompromising battalion who trained hard and played hard. There was no room for oversensitive characters or introverted loners in the battalion. You cannot train soldiers in the controlled use of aggression and not expect some of that aggression to carry over into some soldiers' off-duty time. It was little surprise that this led to problems when soldiers let off steam in the bars and clubs of Paderborn.

Half the battalion was married and almost all had their families with them living in married quarters all over Paderborn. Most had children, the majority of whom attended the excellent Service Children's Education Authority Schools in the same area.

The senior soldier in the battalion was the Regimental Serjeant Major WO1 Matthews. The head of the Serjeants Mess, he oversaw the maintenance of standards in the battalion, particularly discipline. He was also my advisor on all matters to do with the life, routine and culture of the battalion. I was lucky to have Captain Mark Goldsack as adjutant, my staff officer for personnel issues, including career management, overseeing all our routine personnel administration and running my office. This thin and wiry individual had established an unquestioned authority over the battalion and had also acted as battlegroup operations officer during our month's training in Canada. An immensely able young staff officer, with a wry sense of humour, he had been of enormous assistance in my first months in command.

We recruited soldiers from the counties of our former regiments: Cornwall, Somerset, Herefordshire, Shropshire, Yorkshire and Durham. In 1993 the Light Infantry had reduced from three battalions to two. Our battalion had received more than a hundred and fifty men from the two UK-based battalions as they merged into a single battalion. Despite this, by mid-1994, the battalion was significantly under strength. Too many soldiers were leaving and the number of recruits forecast to pass out of training was insufficient to return the battalion to full manning.

Goldsack, Matthews and I analysed who was leaving and why. Corporals and above were not leaving, but we were suffering a haemorrhage of private soldiers. We constructed a 'league table' showing the total number of soldiers leaving each of the battalion's companies and specialist platoons and made no secret of its existence. It showed graphically that some companies were much better at retaining their soldiers than others. One specialist platoon was losing its private soldiers at a rate three times higher than the battalion average.

This needed remedial action. A key part of this would be improving the standard of man-management in the battalion. We concentrated on officers, warrant officers and serjeants, running study periods in which they were taught the knowledge they needed concerning soldier's engagements, terms and conditions of service and how to handle family and welfare problems.

I left the officers, serjeants and corporals under no illusions regarding the improvements in retention I wanted. We improved our procedures for handling soldiers expressing a desire to leave, including a series of formal interviews; I was at the end of this chain and would expect the company to have done everything possible to persuade the soldier to stay.

We did a lot to plan private soldiers' careers – and to explain that we could offer them a career – in order to encourage them to stay in the battalion. This was particularly important for newly trained soldiers joining the battalion. The recruit training regime had allowed them plenty of leave and they had seen a lot of their friends and families. They seemed psychologically unprepared for extended separation from their loved ones and the other difficulties that overseas service would bring. They could easily be led astray. Although most were well trained in basic infantry skills, they had no training in the special skills required of armoured infantry.

To give them the best possible introduction into the battalion we ran a five-day introductory cadre. This included training in living and fighting from a Warrior, as well as instruction in administration, welfare, discipline, money and a host of other issues. I personally briefed them on how they could get themselves promoted, on their career prospects, what I expected of them and what they could expect to be doing over the next year. Their company commanders wrote to their parents or guardians to let them know how we would be looking after their sons.

Other measures were taken, to improve battalion morale. I had identified that some of the Serjeants' Mess and Corporals' Mess, although up to the minimum standard required for their rank, were potential sources of weakness in our overall effort. It was important to create a climate in the battalion in which the prevailing attitudes and morale were so positive that the weaker commanders were dragged up by the stronger influence of their better and stronger colleagues.

We needed to increase everyone's sense of self-worth, particularly among private soldiers and JNCOs. They had to feel that they were no longer at the bottom of the battalion's food chain. I began formally interviewing all those who had achieved something, even private soldiers who had just achieved a pass on a comparatively minor course or cadre. At the same time, we had to improve the passage of information to junior ranks. I adopted an uncompromising attitude with commanders who did not brief the junior ranks on what was going on.

As we implemented these measures, retention got better – and kept on getting better. The retention measures improved morale and the measures to improve morale and discipline improved retention.

The converse of improving retention of good soldiers was that no attempt would be made to retain people whom we did not wish to keep. Indeed, with a Bosnia tour looming, measures were taken to identify weak individuals and either improve their performance or, if this could not be achieved, remove them from the battalion. A number of weaker commanders were posted out of the battalion. A concerted effort was also made to improve the minority of soldiers with serious disciplinary problems, known malingerers, troublemakers and bullies. All of these could have a negative influence on morale during the tour. Where these efforts failed, the individuals concerned were discharged. At the same time the regimental police and guardroom were strengthened and a battalion regime of zero tolerance of misconduct was instituted. These measures had a good effect on the morale of the battalion as a whole.

Unfortunately, this was not going to be enough to bring the battalion up to the to seven hundred people we needed in time for the start of pre-tour training. To bridge the gap, I decided to recruit part-time soldiers from the Territorial Army (TA). These members of the reserve forces gave up a significant proportion of their weekday evenings and weekends as well as attending a two-week annual camp to conduct military training. The TA could help bring us up to strength for our tour, so I wrote to all TA infantry commanding officers seeking volunteers. This was successful, with an excellent response from the six TA battalions of the Light Infantry and Royal Green Jackets and the two TA battalions of the Parachute Regiment.

Planning and Reconnaissance

In early summer 1995 while the companies were training for war on the vast, empty prairies of Alberta, Battalion HQ and I began closely monitoring events in Bosnia. I read Colonel Bob Stewart's book describing the operations of the Cheshire Regiment in 1992 and 1993 and the post-operation reports of all the battalions that subsequently served in the country.

When the country broke down in the fighting of 1992, the war that resulted was a three-sided conflict between the Bosnian Serbs, the Bosnian Croats and the Bosnian Government. Although the government and their army, known as the *Armija* or ABiH, professed multi-ethnicity and included a small number of Serbs and Croats, the vast majority of them and their supporters were Bosnian Muslims.

Our administrative officer from the Adjutant General's Corps, Captain Jason Medley, had commanded an armoured infantry platoon in the Prince of Wales' Own Regiment of Yorkshire during this period. They had succeeded the Cheshires in Bosnia while the Muslim–Croat war was at its height. Jason had had many adventures, including evacuating civilians from a village in the middle of fighting between Bosnian Muslims and Croats. Awarded the Queen's Commendation for Brave Conduct, he had thought-provoking tales to tell and sound advice to offer.

The three warring armies contained a large number of citizens under arms with little or no understanding of the Geneva Convention and laws of armed conflict. Ancient ethnic hatreds had reasserted themselves, with vengeance and spiralled into a vicious cycle of atrocities. Some UN contingents took a pretty minimalist attitude to this. But the British battalions originally sent to escort humanitarian aid extended their mission to include the 'implied tasks' of creating an environment stable enough to allow the aid convoys to move. Bob Stewart had articulated this as 'creating the conditions by which humanitarian aid can pass freely', by attempting to stabilise the conflict and reduce fighting.

A particular problem in the mountainous terrain was the proliferation of checkpoints, which the warring parties (known universally to the British Army as the 'factions') used to block movement on roads and tracks. Manned by highly suspicious local soldiers, usually ill-disciplined, untrained and often frightened, drunk, or both, they were an expression of the communist mentality of many military and political leaders. They also became a way by which the factions attempted to restrict UNPROFOR's freedom of movement. They wanted to ensure that the UN did nothing that would directly or individually aid their opponents. They needed to protect their operational security and suspected the UN would pass information to their enemies. And many faction commanders simply wanted the UN out of their way as they got on with the fighting. Getting through checkpoints without having to fight required negotiating skills of the highest order.

This triangular war continued until February 1994 when the US brokered a peace deal between two of the factions, establishing the Federation between Muslims and Croats. The fighting between the two sides finished with the ABiH and HVO strongly entrenched behind minefields, and with no movement between the factions other than UNPROFOR and aid vehicles.

By the end of the year, remarkable progress had been made in central Bosnia in reducing tension and restoring some degree of 'normality'. British troops and the British commander in Bosnia, Lieutenant General Rose, played a major role in this. Rose's more robust approach to the factions achieved unexpected success in promoting peace, but this success could not be developed into a final settlement between the Federation and the Bosnian Serbs.

All three sides continuously attempted to manipulate UNPROFOR to serve their own ends. It appeared that the strategy of the Bosnian Government was to attempt to draw the international community NATO and the US into the conflict on the Bosnian side. They would often attack the Bosnian Serbs, suffer heavy military and civilian casualties from Serb artillery and counterattacks, then exploit the international media reporting of the resulting suffering to launch a propaganda effort to generate international sympathy for themselves.

The Bosnian Serbs compensated for inferior numbers of infantry by superior numbers of tanks and artillery, occasionally mounting well-coordinated offensives which resulted in an increasingly shrill political response by the Bosnian Government. The Muslims had considerable success both in portraying themselves as the victims of Serb aggression, and in achieving a high degree of public and political support in the West, particularly in the US.

There was much tension in the NATO alliance, which was providing air support to UNPROFOR. NATO jets were operating in the Bosnian skies to support the UN, and many in NATO seemed to find UNPROFOR's reluctance to request massive air strikes frustrating. There were shrill cries that this reduced NATO's 'credibility'. There was little apparent political co-ordination between NATO, the UN and the Contact Group of nations attempting to negotiate a peace deal. Unsurprisingly, there was little success in brokering any sort of lasting peace with the Serbs, but at the end of 1994 a winter truce between the loose and uneasy Muslim/Croat Federation and the Bosnian Serbs had been brokered.

The battalion had an officer with experience of serving in Bosnia during that time, Captain Paul Sulyok. A tall, imposing man, he had spent the winter in Bosnia, supporting the small British garrison of the isolated Muslim enclave of Goražde. Their line of communication ran through territory controlled by the Bosnian Serbs, who applied severe restrictions on all UN traffic. That and the parlous state of the civil infrastructure meant that the small garrison – from the newly formed Royal Gloucestershire, Berkshire and Wiltshire Regiment – had to make maximum use of improvisation to survive and operate in an extremely austere environment. For example, Goražde Force never received enough radio batteries to fulfil its requirements and the soldiers responded by having their REME craftsman build a water wheel to power a battery charger.

Trained to speak Serbo-Croat, Paul was responsible for leading convoys through Bosnian Serb territory to Goražde. At one stage, the Bosnian Serbs detained him and his soldiers for ten days. Effectively hostages, his small force had acted quickly to retain the initiative over their captors. This included a regime of parades, regular fitness training and constructing a make-believe television from a wooden box. Paul explained the difficulties of operations and the harshness of the climate in a way that bald statistics could not, showing that for us to be effective in a winter tour, we would need to be mentally and physically robust and as self-reliant as possible.

During the spring and summer of 1995, the situation in Bosnia deteriorated. The winter cease-fire between Bosnian Serbs and the Muslim-Croat Federation collapsed and there was no peace of any meaningful sort to keep. UNPROFOR's roles of protecting humanitarian relief and peacekeeping became increasingly difficult to execute. The Muslims and Croats were quite content for UNPROFOR to help provide security for their rear areas while they fought the Bosnian Serbs, and only paid lip service to such tattered fragments of peace process as staggered on. It was also clear that the UN 'safe areas' were more than pockets of beleaguered and helpless non-combatant civilians – indeed, Bosnian Government forces were extremely active in these places. In the words of the UN Secretary General, the safe areas had 'been incorporated into the broader military campaign of the Government's side'.

There also appeared to be a strategic disconnect between Britain and France, who had troops at risk on the ground in Bosnia, and the US, who had no troops on the ground but had no shortage of politicians volubly advocating the use of US air power against the Bosnian Serbs. To better understand the situation, I attempted a formal analysis of the political and military situation at the strategic level. My efforts foundered on the difficulty of identifying where UNPROFOR was going, what it was trying to do and what it could achieve. If I had not been careful I could have allowed myself to become profoundly depressed at the incoherence of the Western position and the increasingly contradictory position in which UNPROFOR was finding itself. But the distractions of the battalion and family life allowed no time for this.

In May, the Bosnian Serbs repossessed some of their tanks and artillery which were held at UN-controlled 'weapons collection points'. The new UNPROFOR commander, General Rupert Smith, issued an ultimatum, demanding the return of the weapons and that the Serbs cease shelling the so-called 'safe areas'. When they refused, General Smith authorised NATO air strikes against the Bosnian Serbs. The Bosnian Serbs seized UN personnel as hostages, including Royal Welch Fusileers from the British battalion in Goražde. The Bosnian Serbs closed Sarajevo airport and obstructed humanitarian relief, and their tanks and artillery engaged UN convoys and positions.

France and Britain both announced that they were sending reinforcements, including 24 Airmobile Brigade. At the same time the UN conducted intense negotiations with Bosnian Serbs. These two initiatives proved successful. Within a month, the UN hostages had all been released.

A Closer Focus

On paper, 2LI was under command of 20 Armoured Brigade. In fact Brigadier Andrew Pringle, the brigade's commander, and its HQ were already in Bosnia, providing the framework for the UNs Headquarters Sector Southwest commanding all UNPROFOR units in central Bosnia, and also the British national logistic headquarters in Split. Twenty Brigade's tour in Bosnia would end as we deployed, under command of 4 Armoured Brigade. Although this HQ was two hours' drive away in Osnabruck, I decided that we should get to know the Brigadier and his staff, who we would regard as our Brigade HQ for everything to do with our forthcoming tour.

The commander was Brigadier Richard Dannatt. An officer of the Green Howards, he was an impressive man, with a natural air of relaxed authority. He not only took immense pains to analyse and plan our training and operations, but, a firm believer in delegation, he kept his guidance and direction to the absolute minimum necessary for us to accomplish our missions. The brigade chief of staff Major James Everard and the deputy chief of staff Major Paul Baker were most helpful. We could not have worked under a better team.

At the end of June I led our initial reconnaissance of Bosnia. With the second-in-command, operations officer, intelligence officer and quartermaster, I found myself in a Royal Navy Sea King helicopter descending to a bleak limestone plateau near Tomislavgrad. Below was the battalion we were to relieve, First Battalion the Devonshire and Dorset Regiment (1 D&D, or the 'Devon and Dorsets'), lined up in row upon row of white-painted armoured vehicles. Apart from the white paint I could have been flying over training in Germany or Canada. I felt the familiar surge of confidence I had last felt in Canada. It was good to be with an armoured infantry battalion at a high peak of operational readiness.

While the Devon and Dorsets returned to their base at Vitez, we visited UN Sector HQ at Gornji Vakuf and other British and French units. The situation was military stalemate between the Federation and the Bosnian Serbs. UNPROFOR was obstructed by the Bosnian Serbs and both detested and despised by the Federation for its unwillingness to join their battles. There were plenty of Bosnian politicians, warlords and black marketeers, with an interest in keeping the war going. The international community wanted UNPROFOR to keep the peace between the Federation and the Bosnian Serbs, but there was no peace to keep.

With the cessation of hostilities between Muslims and Croats and the exclusion of the UN from the front line, much of UNPROFOR in central Bosnia was making only a very limited contribution. This included some UN contingents that appeared to have come to Bosnia structured, equipped, trained and conditioned for peacekeeping in a benign environment. These contingents were being marginalised, with their national governments unwilling to allow them to be put in harm's way. UN commanders had little or no authority to direct the operations of these forces, particularly to work in new areas or in any operations that increased risk.

The Bosnian Serbs had closed the main road into Sarajevo, and the French and other UNPROFOR contingents in the city now depended on the exposed and difficult route down the north face of Mount Igman, under the eyes of Bosnian Serb tanks and guns.

The Devon and Dorsets had begun their tour in May conducting 'framework' peacekeeping operations in central Bosnia. As soon as the hostage crisis erupted, they became the core of a British theatre reserve under 20 Armoured Brigade's command, together with a light artillery regiment and armoured engineers, the British national 'Task Force Alpha'. They spent five weeks training and preparing contingency operations, including reopening routes into the beleaguered city of Sarajevo. These involved some danger and, while 20 Brigade and the Devon and Dorsets clearly had the high morale necessary to fight their way into the city, it was equally clear that the UK was not prepared to take the risk.

The UN Rapid Reaction Force was being assembled from French, British and Dutch troops, with the role of 'protecting' UNPROFOR. British engineers were building a base for 24 Airmobile Brigade at Ploce and a battlegroup of the French Foreign Legion had landed from French ships and encamped in the Croat-held area of Herceg-Bosna. The ABiH and HVO were intensely suspicious of all these developments. If the forces were to support UNPROFOR, as the West had declared, why, they asked, were they not being used to force open routes to Sarajevo and Goražde? Was the Rapid Reaction Force to be used, not to fight the Bosnian Serbs, but to support withdrawal by UNPROFOR?

The ABiH and HVO accordingly placed severe restrictions on the movements of UN troops in Sector Southwest, leaving relations between them and UNPROFOR at a low ebb. My recce party and I were able to travel by helicopter, but we could see UN columns being subjected to considerable delay and harassment at Federation checkpoints. Of course these reinforcements for UNPROFOR did nothing to improve the already strained relations with the Bosnian Serbs, who saw them as a threat.

Impressions there were aplenty, including stories from hardened British veterans of the Gulf War and Northern Ireland who had appalling tales to tell of atrocities by all three parties to the conflict. They also told of being harassed by Bosnian soldiers at the many faction checkpoints. Most of the population was living under siege conditions, as shown by their sallow, unhealthy skin and tired, lined faces. There were few men aged between sixteen and fifty around: most of them were at the front, apart from invalids and a few who appeared to be running the highly lucrative black market.

We came back with plenty of food for thought. I resumed training Battalion HQ so as to avoid the problems of the previous summer. Key to this was 'battle procedure', the art of preparing for operations and the production and issue of orders. I had the company commanders run a series of exercises which would require Battalion HQ to plan operations while moving between locations and organising itself and its communications in the field. After giving the company commander some initial direction I left him to write the exercise, which began with me receiving orders from a superior headquarters. Battalion HQ and I practised our role in mission planning and controlling operations. We learned a multitude of lessons.

Our training in Canada and in Germany taught me that I was merely a component of the battalion's brain, eyes and nervous system. My role was not to duplicate the functions of my subordinate commanders or staff officers. When planning was the main effort I had to receive orders from Brigade HQ, carry out reconnaissance and, by leading the mission analysis and estimate process, formulate the battlegroup mission, articulate the concept of operations and allocate missions and key tasks to the components of the battlegroup. If I did this clearly enough, Battlegroup HQ would have no difficulty in co-ordinating the details. Once battle was joined, my place was to be forward, seeing what was going on, reading the battle, anticipating the enemy's next move, encouraging, directing and leading.

I could also help the battalion prepare for the tour by making sure that our training was as effective as possible. I wanted to draw out everyone's talents, promoting initiative, original thought and 'situational awareness', particularly amongst commanders. Where I assessed that people were going wrong, I had to tell them and encourage them to do better.

The battalion second-in-command, Chris Booth, managed the training. New to the role, Chris was a perpetually cheerful and extremely experienced major. He had just come from commanding an airmobile infantry company in 1 LI. Often jokingly commented on as the only officer in the battalion as bald as me, he had a vital role, both as my deputy and in overseeing the work of Battalion HQ.

Young captains held key appointments in headquarters. As well as Jason Medley and Captain Kevin Stainburn, an immensely experienced AGC officer newly commissioned from the ranks, I had Captain Tony Allport as intelligence officer. I had once fulfilled this role myself and knew how important it was to have someone in Battlegroup HQ who could see events from our adversaries' perspective, as well as an intelligence section to support him. I was delighted when Colour Serjeant Lawrence, an intelligence expert, volunteered to leave 1 LI to come to Bosnia with us. In the Balkans an equally important role would be to liaise with and handle the media, and I selected Captain Steve Noble for this role. Both these officers would be key members of my command team and I lost no time in making sure that we all understood how each of us thought.

Men joined us from other regiments, including the Highlanders, the Cheshires and even a regular colour serjeant from the Parachute Regiment – attached to us to gain Bosnia experience. Officers also volunteered to accompany us for the tour, and were affectionately labelled 'medal hunters' by some. From the Royal Marines came Lieutenant Steve Liddle to command a Warrior platoon; from the Royal Air Force Regiment (normally responsible for defence of airfields) came Flight Lieutenant Mark Jacklin, who qualified as a platoon commander at BATUS before moving up to A Company's Warrior captain slot. The Royal Dragoon Guards provided two captains, Peter MacFarlane who joined B Company as second-in-command, and Ed Cresswell who was leaving the Army, but who wanted to go out on a high – as did Captain Toby Ellwood who joined us from the Royal Green Jackets. Finally, from the Royal Irish Regiment came a new operations officer, Captain Ross Gillanders, a volunteer for the tour, his dry humour concealing an enormous appetite for hard work.

These reinforcements meant that the Officers' Mess was bursting at the seams. The volunteers from outside the Light Infantry created a very cosmopolitan atmosphere, with a considerable amount of light-hearted leg-pulling and inter-regimental banter. By the end of the summer there was a palpable 'edge' to the Mess, with tangible anticipation and a sense of adventure.

In the meantime, events in Bosnia deteriorated further. The Muslim-held enclaves of Srebrenica and Žepa fell to the Bosnian Serb commander General Mladić and the media reported massacres of the Muslim defenders. The British troops in Goražde were more isolated than ever. General Smith reduced the number of UN troops in isolated positions that were exposed to further Bosnian Serb hostage-taking attempts. Privately I wondered how 2 LI would have performed we had been in Srebrenica or Goražde. I resolved to make sure that we would not be found wanting.

The British Task Force Alpha was re-subordinated from Sector Southwest into the Multinational Brigade, part of the UNPROFOR Rapid Reaction Force, where it joined French and Dutch reinforcements. It immediately painted its vehicles green to show combat capability. This occurred just as we had started to paint our Warriors UN white! As we were about to go on summer leave, the Devon and Dorsets escorted artillery onto Mount Igman overlooking Sarajevo.

The British, French and US governments agreed with the UN that the previous tight controls on the use of NATO air power would be relaxed. At the beginning of August NATO warned that the existing threat to use air power to deter attacks on the 'safe area' of Goražde now applied to the other 'safe areas', including Sarajevo, and that any future air strikes would be on a much larger scale than before.

I paraded the whole battalion just before they went on summer leave and gave them my assessment of the rapidly developing situation and what it meant for us:

Extract From Notebook – Talk to Battalion Before Summer Leave

Everybody did really well in Canada

Current Situation. Devon & Dorsets on Mount Igman with British and French artillery.

Recce showed that anything could happen – same applies to us.

Training begins 29 August with lecture package that all will attend.

Cadre to brief and train commanders then main recce.

Summer Leave. Aim is that everyone sees friends and families.

Recharge batteries BUT let's all keep fit.

FINALLY – Really congratulate everyone on hard work this summer.

I spent summer leave with my family in a cottage in Brittany. As we drove through France the BBC World Service reported the Croatian offensive against the Krajinas – parts of Croatia that had been forcibly occupied by nationalist Serbs during the break-up of Yugoslavia. The military capability of the Croat Army had been improved by training from US military contractors and the Serb defences collapsed. I heard reporters describing clashes between attacking Croat forces and UN troops. There were heart-rending reports of the huge columns of Serb refugees either fleeing from the Croat attacks or evicted during ethnic cleansing. I wondered how we would measure up in such a situation. I was sure that, now the Krajinas had been liberated, some of the victorious forces would be re-deployed to the Bosnian Croat Army inside Bosnia.

CHAPTER TWO

'Actors Waiting in the Wings of Europe'

Returning from leave, at the end of August, I and all the battalion's commanders down to serjeant spent two days being trained on a 'commander's cadre'. This mixture of lectures and practical demonstrations by a specialist training team was designed to give us the knowledge and understanding so that we could train our subordinates in the different tactics and approaches required for Bosnia.

New skills were taught and practised. A particular problem would be posed by land mines. These had been laid in large numbers in and around the front lines. Some were properly marked and recorded, but many more, laid by untrained, undisciplined or drunk faction soldiers, were neither. We learned to read the current and historic front lines so as to predict where the mine threat would be highest. This skill was called 'Mine Awareness'.

As the training began a shell hit a Sarajevo market, killing thirty-seven civilians. The evidence was that the Bosnian Serbs had fired it. General Janvier was on leave, with his authority delegated to General Smith, who requested NATO air strikes. We watched these on our television screens and saw the British and French guns of the Multinational Brigade shelling Serb positions around Sarajevo.

The command team was to return to Bosnia for a second 'confirmatory' reconnaisance. The night before we were due to leave, Colonel Simon Young, the deputy commander of the British forces in Bosnia, rang me at home. Our recce could go ahead but I would only be able to bring half the people I had intended. Overnight we reconfigured our recce party in time to catch an RAF plane the next day. Accompanied by key Battalion HQ officers and the company commanders and Steve Noble, I landed in Split just as NATO and the UN announced a temporary suspension of hostilities. This was to give the Serbs a chance to show their compliance with the NATO/UN ultimatum that they withdraw their artillery and heavy weapons from around Sarajevo. There was some banter that we had 'just missed being in a war zone'. I wrote in my notebook:

DAY 1. Comprehensive briefing on situation by D&D [Devon and Dorset] officers at Vitez. Meet Jeff Cook CO 1 D&D at Kiseljak conducting orders group. Battalion assembling for operation to reopen main route into Sarajevo, as soon as Serbs agree to NATO demands. Fly to Mount Igman in French helicopter. They get lost! Visit HQ Multinational Brigade. Meet chief of staff – Colonel Hamish Fletcher – old chum from Germany ten years earlier.

Tour of mountain positions. Overlook Sarajevo glinting in late afternoon sun. So near and yet so far and not a single sign of any fighting visible to naked eye. Invited for supper with CO Foreign Legion battalion. Bizarre experience of meal in his tent, bedecked with regiment's standards and memorabilia. Charming, fluent English speaker and clearly a dynamic leader.

DAY 2. Trip to Headquarters Sector Southwest. Meet old friends Brigadier Pringle and his chief of staff. Listen to secure telephone conversation between Pringle and General Smith. If no compliance from Serbs, air strikes to resume. If air and artillery campaign unsuccessful, UNPROFOR will be untenable and would need to withdraw, which will require NATO assistance. Helicopter flight to visit Foreign Legion battalion in south Bosnia. Not expecting us, no one speaks English, my schoolboy French exhausted too soon. Back to Vitez where Brig. Pringle comes to supper with 2 LI officers. Gives us a comprehensive and frank brief and answers probing questions.

DAY 3. Return to Igman with D&D padre. Conducted tour by company commander. South flank of UN position spread across huge mountain complex similar to Brecon Beacons. Currently screened by Warrior platoon and Milan section! What will it be like in winter? Visit small village, appears war-damaged but closer inspection shows this to be extreme disrepair – caused by rural depopulation? Occupied by single large family. Father treats us like honoured guests with Balkan coffee thick as glue, huge chunks of warm bread and wonderfully piquant goat's cheese. Wife totally subservient and silent. Two charming shy children watch wide-eyed from a tent. Return to 1 D&D HQ listening to BBC World Service reporting UN/NATO announcement that air attacks are resuming. Troops to 'alert rouge', donning helmets and body armour. Suddenly familiar chainsaw buzz of a heavy cannon – American A10 jets attacking Bosnian Serb positions. Warrior exchanges fire with Serb heavy weapons crew, BBC filming engagement. Multinational Brigade HQ under pressure planning for opening of routes to Sarajevo. Meet commander 24 Airmobile Brigade (former CO 2 LI) arriving on Igman as I leave. Meet him again in midst of huge traffic snarl up at ABiH checkpoint on road to Kiseljak. At Kiseljak the D&D battlegroup is assembled in disused brick factory. Return to Vitez for discussion over a few beers with rest of recce party. Watch CNN news on satellite TV and see BBC report of Warrior firing on Serb position as we had heard in real time five hours earlier.

DAY 4. End of recce. Helicopter flight to Split and then by RAF transport back to Germany. Several officers travelling on leave from UN theatre HQ in Zagreb. Most openly cynical about overall ineffectiveness of UN forces in Krajinas and evidence of US assistance to Croatian Army. General agreement that if NATO attacks fail, UNPROFOR will have to withdraw, likely hostility of factions, especially Muslims expected. Many consider we will have to fight our way out. Arrive less than twenty-four hours after leaving Mount Igman. Extreme contrast of stable dull German countryside.

While we were away, our wives and families watched news broadcasts of the NATO preparation and the Warriors firing on Serb positions below Igman. This gave me food for thought about our arrangements for briefing our families – how could our passage of information to Paderborn match the speed with which the media worked?

The next night, US cruise missiles struck targets near the Bosnian Serb city of Banja Luka. Concurrent with the NATO and UNPROFOR air and artillery strikes, the HVO and to a lesser extent the ABiH achieved startling success in their offensives against the Bosnian Serb army, who were rapidly evicted from a huge swathe of territory in the west of Bosnia. Shortly afterwards, the US brokered a cease-fire and Richard Holbrooke, their chief negotiator, began attempting to set up peace talks.

All previous peace plans had foundered – with the Bosnian Serbs controlling much of the country neither their opponents nor the international community had much leverage over them. Now the Bosnian Serbs' share of Bosnia had been reduced to half. Would the US be able to exploit this to clinch a peace deal? Only time would tell, but if the peace negotiations succeeded quickly, we could be going to Bosnia early to help implement the peace. If the negotiations failed, we would become part of the NATO force sent to extract UNPROFOR, again earlier than we expected. In this case, it appeared likely that fighting would flare up with increased intensity, probably including attempts by the Federation to frustrate the withdrawal of UNPROFOR or to involve us in their war. We would need to be prepared to fight our way in and fight our way out.

The battalion now began the 'in barracks phase' of its preparation. Chris Booth had organised training into a number of self-contained packages, and commanders and Battalion HQ trained and prepared themselves and those under their command. The soldiers laboured long and hard to ready their weapons, equipment and the vehicles on which their effectiveness, even their survival, could depend. This included painting names on all our armoured vehicles. All vehicles already bore a 'call sign', the short combination of numbers and letters that gave them an identity on their company radio net. In addition, each Warrior and Scimitar would carry the name of one of the Light Infantry's battle honours. Our Warriors' protection was improved by fitting huge slabs of special armour originally developed for the Gulf War. Later our regimental magazine, the *Silver Bugle*, described this period:

The Warriors had to be up-armoured. Great white slabs of 'Chobham' armour were bolted to the sides and front of each wagon, making us as close to invincible as science allows. More importantly each plate needed several men to lift it, and toes to be kept well away. As Chobham (or at least what's inside it) is secret, a whole new guard commitment appeared. For two months the garages were wired off and patrolled. As it turned out practice at 'stagging on' was excellent pre-Bosnia training!

Every battalion that has served in Bosnia has found its tour totally different from the last. However they have all needed the same skills. Each company, therefore, ran a range of cadres. In particular, emphasis was put on assault pioneers, team medics and gunnery. In anticipating the worst, the battalion set about preparing for six months of Arctic war. Temperatures of minus 57° had been clocked up on Mount Igman the previous winter. Not to be caught out, lecture after lecture was given on cold weather injuries, medicine and equipment. The quartermaster produced an excellent stock of Arctic clothing.

For subalterns there was a platoon commanders' cadre, which ranged from basic Serbo-Croat coaching, through watch-keeping, to watching some singularly ghastly BBC footage of atrocities they felt too disturbing to broadcast. The presence of Captain Sulyok, a real live ex-hostage, convinced us that Serbs were odd – they released him.

It had been Chris Booth's initiative that all platoon commanders should spend a week considering how they would command in this new environment. He came up with an excellent programme, which made maximum use of our in-house expertise in the forms of Captains Jason Medley and Paul Sulyok. The cadre included Serbo-Croat language training and significant instruction in logistics and the human factor. We knew that battalions preceding us had been exposed to much raw human suffering and soldiers had witnessed many deeply disturbing sights. The best way to counter this potential source of stress would be to have the highest possible standards of morale and leadership. I led a discussion about these issues – a vehicle to put over my own views on the standards I expected of commanders.

We continued to train Battalion HQ in its role. This included map exercises and training in logistic and personnel issues. We made sure that everyone had sound pay and banking arrangements, an up-to-date will and life insurance. I always found this aspect of preparing for operations a profoundly depressing reminder of my own mortality, and this occasion was no exception. At the same time, each of the five companies briefed the wives of its married personnel. I attended all of these meetings and would begin the meeting with a short talk.

Extract From Notebook – Talk to Wives Briefing Evenings

Roles of UN. Help with displaced persons, relief supplies.
Makes a difference to ordinary people, especially women and children.
I am personally responsible for the battalion carrying out the mission as effectively as possible. Have to make sure that operations are properly planned and that any threats are minimised.
Training and Preparation. A lot of people are very busy. Your husbands are really earning their pay. You should both prepare yourselves as well – wills, insurance.
Bosnia is operational theatre. Not as stable as Northern Ireland, more or less at war.

Leave – do all we can but can't guarantee arrival until he arrives.

Telephones in bases, but not in field locations.

Real privilege to command battalion. 2LI is best-prepared armoured infantry battalion in Army. Doing all I can to prepare us all for what we have to do, to do it as well as we can and as safely as possible, to get your husbands back to you in one piece, both for R&R and at the end of tour.

It was particularly difficult to explain to wives that on deployment to Bosnia their husbands would receive a cut in income. In Paderborn all members of the battalion received a local overseas allowance to make up the extra costs of living in Germany, a country more expensive than the UK. Since there were no extra costs of living in Bosnia, single soldiers had their allowance removed and married soldiers had theirs reduced. Although the logic of this was clear, equally clear was the great difficulty of convincing a soldier's wife that the family income should be reduced by four hundred German marks a month while her husband was away.

We made time for the companies, the Serjeants' Mess and the Officers' Mess to fit in a series of lively parties. Everyone also took seven days' leave. Like many others I returned to England for a final chance to see friends and family before Christmas.

In this period Lance Corporal Dawson, a promising and extremely popular member of C Company was killed in a traffic accident. His friends and C Company were devastated. We had a moving memorial service and as the gut-wrenching mournful notes of the Last Post rang out, I again resolved to do everything I could to bring as many people back from Bosnia as I took out.

Field and Command Training

The next two phases of training were described in the *Silver Bugle*:

The range package took us from zeroing personal weapons to live firing patrol incidents and defence shoots. Everyone was introduced to the mine threat and taught what to do if involved in a mine incident.

The final phase was the Field Training Exercise. Sennelager training area was cast as a divided segment of Bosnia with three warring factions vying for it. The Stapel area to the north was portrayed as a Srebrenica-type enclave. Later we had to break the siege of Stapel. The exercise was highly successful and culminated in a company Warrior live firing circuit around the training area perimeter. The Warriors were then prepared for shipping, not to be seen again until Split.

This three-day exercise required the battlegroup (the battalion plus its armoured engineers, artillery and a forward air controller) to move to a new area, and attempt to re-establish peace between the factions. A company of Royal Highland Fusiliers, who had spent the previous winter in Bosnia, portrayed the irreconcilable factions of Serbs, Muslims and Croats. Battlegroup HQ and I were under considerable pressure as we moved into bases, attempted to establish contact with local leaders, arranged the exchange of prisoners between the factions, withstood mortar and artillery attacks and dealt with attempts to take our soldiers hostage, mine strikes and the aftermath of atrocities.

At the same time, the UN was demanding access to an enclave of 'Muslims' surrounded by 'Serbs' to our north. After the breakdown of negotiations a Security Council resolution authorised use of all necessary means to restore access to the enclave. This allowed us to conduct a full rehearsal of the type of operation that might be needed to force open routes to real enclaves such as Sarajevo or Goražde. In the event of a UN withdrawal, we might well have to use this sort of operation both to go forward to relieve encircled groups of UN troops, and even to withdraw ourselves. I chose not to explain this to anyone.

As I had intended, the battlegroup achieved its mission, but not without difficulties, including huge obstacles that had been constructed to deny entry to the enclave. Great earth mounds and burned-out buses fixed together with huge chains were augmented by simulated anti-tank mines, which released huge clouds of yellow smoke when detonated. By the time the exercise ended, our three engineer tanks had either worn out their gearboxes or been 'destroyed' by mines. I drove back through Sennelager training area, the trees glowing with the bright chemical colours of a rich, voluptuous autumn, reflecting that the battlegroup was capable of functioning for long periods under great pressure. It had a large number of experienced officers whom I could trust to think for themselves and get the job done.

The final phase of training was five days spent at the Brigade and Battlegroup Trainer (BBGT). This allowed unit and formation commanders to practise their command skills in a simulated Bosnian environment. The permanent staff of the BBGT ran the exercise for 4 Armoured Brigade, 2 LI, the engineer regiment and various support units. Company commanders and their headquarters acted as the 'lower control', sending and receiving information and messages, as if we were on operations in Bosnia.

Great realism was created by the lower controls and BBGT staff playing their roles with considerable imagination and enthusiasm, aided and abetted by officers flown back from appointments in Bosnia who acted as up-to-date expert advisors. Astonishingly realistic local colour was injected into the exercise by the presence of Bosnian interpreters employed by the British contingent of UNPROFOR. This was particularly important for our liaison officers, or LOs. Several young officers, all captains, were nominated to conduct the important task of liaising between the battalion and the factions. Each of the three company second captains was similarly trained. I appointed the support company commander, Major Ian Baker, as chief liaison officer to co-ordinate all the battlegroup's liaison efforts.

BBGT included an excellent package of training in their duties. After a short period of theoretical instruction this 'virtual Bosnia' environment allowed the LOs to practise their skills of liaison and negotiation on interpreters pretending to be faction commanders. Captain Sean Harris described this training:

Experienced LOs had been flown from the theatre; the stories they told seemed too far-fetched to be true. During the training, potential LOs were exposed to the warring factions' least publicised but most potent weapon, slivovitz, more commonly known as 'slip in a ditch'. We were also introduced to some of the interpreters, the first Bosnians we had met. These scruffy, mischievous individuals tried their best to cause us as many problems as possible during scenario training, often succeeding in making us lose our tempers, something I was to learn a LO should never do.

The period climaxed with two days of simulated operations, a useful final focus to our training. I described the lessons learned in my notebook:

PHASE 1: Sarajevo Route Opening Problem. Mission to forcibly reopen main route into Sarajevo, a maverick Bosnian Serb commander having closed it. Difficulty of negotiations with HVO and ABiH. How do you retain impartiality when you actually need their help? Considerable discussions with 4 Armd Bde over use of force. Significant issue. Need to give factions maximum excuse to back down, but if negotiation fails, will have to be prepared to open route using whatever force is necessary. Operation was easier than negotiations!

Followed by simulated press conference. Included real journalists and very hostile. I started badly and got steadily worse. Must do better! Stage management and my briefing to be improved.

PHASE 2: Preparation for implementation of a peace plan. Mission: to implement peace in western Bosnia under UN auspices until NATO reinforcements arrive. Considerable tension between ourselves (who wanted to focus on future ops) and Multinational Brigade (who wanted to keep us for their ops until last moment).

Decide priority is to implement the Buffer Zone (four kilometres wide and demilitarised) between Federation and VRS. Intelligence a total vacuum apart from what factions choose to tell us or we find out for ourselves. An extremely long move and significant logistic problems. Difficulty of getting there in time leads us to deduce that priority is to establish some sort of presence in zone and open British-controlled crossing points between factions. Other potential problems included armed civilian police in buffer zone, verification that factions have actually withdrawn, handling of civilians and soldiers who live in zone and faction minefields.

OVERALL LESSONS
Value of negotiation and liaison.
Proper use of media: internal to Bosnia and international.
Seize opportunities as they are offered.
Use of Force.
If attacked by factions respond decisively. Rules of engagement allow us to use sufficient force to respond.

May be necessary to use force to compel factions to do what we want: for example to force our way through a route they are attempting to block. If so, we must succeed. Therefore maximum force should be concentrated, so as to neutralise faction obstruction as quickly as possible and minimise risk of our own casualties. Old German army expression 'clout doesn't dribble' applies, as does modern British expression 'the more you use, the fewer you lose'.

Tension on transfer from Multinational Brigade back to British control.

Deterrence to overawe potential opposition – particularly air.

Limitations of ad hoc arrangements for artillery, engineers, medical support and logistics. Need to be properly 'joined up'.

I reflected on military training: the way in which disparate groups of individuals are transformed into military organisations capable of fighting against an opponent who has both modern weapons and the ability to employ them properly, and also the will and determination to fight and take casualties. Although our autumn training had been focused on the specific individual and collective skills, procedures and techniques that we were likely to need in Bosnia, it had also helped build us into cohesive teams.

Putting us through a series of increasingly demanding activities had forced us all to develop and improve our capabilities. Battalion HQ had seen a significant change of key personnel after last year's Canada training, but the training we had done this summer and autumn meant that it was now more effective than ever.

We had managed to do as much as was humanly possible in the time available. Time would tell if we had got it right, but I was happy that the battalion was as well prepared for the tour as it could be.

Deployment

The battalion now had to replace the Devon and Dorsets, an operation organised as a formal 'relief in place' by Chris Booth. An advance party of commanders and key specialists left for Bosnia almost immediately after training had finished, to take over bases and equipment. Everybody else, myself included, was part of the main body. We would start moving by air from Paderborn a week later, in time to join up with our Warriors and Scimitars travelling from Germany to Split by ship.

Chris planned that the Warriors would be carried by low loaders to a British logistic base at Lipa, where they would marry up with the crews who would load the operational ammunition – a process known as 'bombing up'. Company groups of Warrior would then move by road from Lipa to Vitez. Special winter track, which improved grip on icy roads, had been developed for the Warriors and was waiting at Vitez. We were advised that this did not need to be fitted for another three weeks as substantial snowfalls were unlikely before then.

The advance party arrived in Split to find the weather balmy and a humorous reception as described in the *Silver Bugle*:

The first main body flight out to Split began only two days after the end of a well-deserved pre-tour leave of seven days. Most of the battalion had spent all their money, and were quite ready to head off to Bosnia. Going through passport control at Split was another of those surreal Bosnian experiences. Here we were, part of the much vaunted Rapid Reaction Force, having to show our passports to be allowed into Croatia. We had spent a good deal of time training for the winter conditions, so the late autumnal sunshine of the Adriatic coast was a bit of a surprise. The banners wishing 2 LI 'Merry Christmas' looked faintly incongruous when held by men in sunglasses and wearing tropical combats.

But within twenty-four hours and shortly before the arrival of the ship, snow was falling heavily inland. The winter snowfalls had begun weeks earlier than expected. The unexpected snow and ice could easily have delayed the tight schedule of vehicle movements that would allow the Devon and Dorsets to depart and 2 LI to assume their role. A key role in overcoming the difficulties and friction was played by the battalion's mechanical transport officer (MTO) Captain Paul Evanson, who showed great leadership in getting the vehicles up country.

A Company and the recce platoon arrived at Vitez as scheduled, but all the other convoys were delayed by the weather. By the time B and C Companies left Lipa, hard-packed snow and sheet ice covered the mountain roads. The most dangerous stretch of the route, from Kupres to Bugojno, became a slalom around stuck civilian cars and lorries trying to get up the hill. On the down slope, and without winter track, Warriors turned into thirty-ton sledges – in one incident Captain Mark Mortimer's Warrior shuddered out of control and slid down a road heading for the deep valley below, only to be brought to a halt by sliding into a Bosnian tank coming the other way. It is a testament to the drivers' skill that no vehicles were lost. The operation was later described in the *Silver Bugle*:

> The first taste of winter came at Lipa, where the Warriors were married up with their crews. On a high plateau, Lipa was subject to bitter icy winds that cut through the winter clothing. From here the companies were to make the journey on tracks up to Vitez and then to Kiseljak and Igman. It is a journey that would normally have taken three to four hours, but it took the Warriors anything up to fourteen. Some of the roads were covered in sheet ice, making the Warriors resemble over-sized ducks skating on a frozen pond. It was a frightening experience skating towards two-hundred-foot drops, and provided a crash course in winter driving skills for the crews. Very suddenly Split seemed a long way away.

The advance party contained a sizeable element of our Battalion HQ. Co-locating themselves with the Devon and Dorset's Main HQ in Vitez, they monitored the progress of the battalion and the difficulties the companies were facing. Travelling on the back of DROPS lorries our recce platoon had reached Vitez first. Chris Booth ordered them to deploy back towards Split straight away to monitor the move of the battalion's convoys on the planned route and to attempt to find a better route. Ian McGregor described the platoon's role during this period:

> The platoon deployed using the relative luxury of DROPS, and were delivered to Vitez avoiding, in the first instance, the nightmare of Biblical proportions that was to hinder the Warriors' arrival. The nightmare soon became reality as we were tasked to prove routes along the infamous Route TRIANGLE. Without the luxury of winter track, drivers' skills were tested to the full, and we were lucky not to lose several vehicles.

They found that Route TRIANGLE was even deeper in snow than the route being used by the Warriors. In using this route, some Scimitars, including Ian's, became trapped in deep snow and had to seek refuge at an isolated engineer camp.

Despite the delay on the routes up from Split and the subsequent arrival of a further two metres of snow on Mount Igman itself, we were able to relieve 1 D&D in time. All this sounds very simple, but for those involved, particularly vehicle commanders and drivers, the relief in place turned into a real test of skill. The whole operation only succeeded because of a considerable amount of determination by the commanders and drivers of the small columns of vehicles that crawled their way along the precarious snow- and ice-bound roads of the bleak mountains of central Bosnia.

At the end of October, A Company's advance party of officers and SNCOs took over the Mount Igman positions from 1 D&D, later described by Serjeant Hedges of A Company:

> 30 October, 0730, a wet miserable Tuesday morning. A Company Headquarters left Vitez School to recce company locations on Mount Igman. An hour's drive brought us to a sloppy, muddy mess called the Brick Factory in Kiseljak. The most prominent feature was the chimney that towered above everything with the large UN flag flying at the top. To say it needed work would be an understatement; however, the engineers were busy.
>
> Back onto the road and Route PACMAN followed by Route DOG took us to a town at the base of Mount Igman called Hadžići. Muslim, Croat and UN checkpoints gave us no interruptions. As we moved upwards on the narrow mountain track, we were taken aback by the remains of houses and cars destroyed by the years of war. Fields and hillsides were scarred by large craters left by recent NATO air strikes, and from Hadžići up to the UN area were bunkers of the former warring factions. Smoke rose from the log fires inside the bunkers in preparation for the cold winter. Eventually we arrived at a small clearing that accommodated the D&D company site: tents and ponchos. A tour of the mountain followed a brief chat with the company commander and CSM. Again the platoon locations were mainly ponchos and crew shelters.

By 2 November A Company was complete at Vitez with all its people and vehicles. Serjeant Hedges' story of the relief in place operation continues:

On 3 November the first packets moved off at 0800 hours, followed by the others at ten-minute intervals. Call sign Delta 21 started to lose track pads. We slowed the speed to a crawl and made it to the Brick Factory. A fault in the track gave us our first 'track bashing'. When the new track arrived, the heavens opened. Within one hour there were four inches of snow, which made life hell with the track. It was my birthday, knee-deep in snow, mud and grease. Lovely!

Job completed, it was onto Route SWAN into Sarajevo through the airport, Route DOG and onto the mountain. By the time we reached the UN area the snow was compressed ice. Call sign Delta 21, driven by Private McKenzie, decided to start Warrior-sledging. He came to a standstill with the front end of his giant toboggan hovering over a two-hundred-foot drop. Good character-building stuff. Corporal James gained more years in a split second than in his previous thirteen years with the battalion.

At the same time, I was making my own journey. I had planned to leave Germany on 2 November, joining our fourth flight of the main body. Together with a hundred members of the battalion I was to fly to Bosnia on a Tupolev jet chartered by the UN. The airliner arrived at Paderborn Airport, disgorged a hundred happy Devon and Dorset soldiers, and then was promptly declared unserviceable. A hundred of us returned to barracks and married quarters. Many of us, including the Barry family, found it difficult to 'unsay our farewells', as someone put it. Liz and I hired a video of Martin Scorsese's film *The Age of Innocence* and relaxed over an open fire and that delicate evocation of New York a hundred years ago.

Next day, three RAF Hercules transport aircraft flew the remainder of the battalion to Bosnia. I had lost the day that I had planned to use to get acquainted with the situation before taking over from Jeff Cook, CO 1 D&D: instead I arrived almost a day and a half later. An attempt to get a helicopter flight to Vitez failed, so I eventually travelled up in a strange convoy of assorted unarmoured vehicles. Most bizarre of all was that I and fifty others travelled up in a UN-owned luxury coach. I was expecting to find a crazed Balkan madman at the wheel, but was delighted to discover that the coach was actually driven by a genteel Dutch civilian, a reassuringly safe driver. Just as well, because we drove through a lunar landscape gleaming with reflected moonlight from the hard-driven frozen snow.

I dozed fitfully, reflecting that I had travelled straight from the lustrous colours of a glorious German autumn into a harsh and sterile winter – which might well not end until we left Bosnia in six months' time. I arrived in Vitez in time for two hours' sleep in the CO's house. This was followed by an update briefing from the staff of Battlegroup Main HQ – Chris Booth had done an extremely good job, was well on top of the situation and was loving it.

I then drove by Land Rover to Serb territory outside Sarajevo. It seemed strange to be driving on the main route into Sarajevo – subject of so much study and planning as the road we might have to forcibly open. The outgoing D&D liaison officer took me to the commander of the Bosnian Serb brigade facing Mount Igman. The commander seemed fed up with the war and very supportive of the cease-fire, but was extremely suspicious of Muslims and hostile to the Americans. The brigade had received several NATO air strikes and some shelling in September. No serious casualties had resulted, unlike other Serb brigades. Speaking to me in a disused ski chalet he said that his main worry had been that the British battlegroup would move off Igman and out of Kiseljak in order to launch ground attacks on his positions, which he could not have defeated.

We left and drove around the southern suburbs of Sarajevo. Light was fading fast but the destruction glimpsed in darkening gloom exceeded any I had seen before. On Mount Igman there was already a metre of snow. Battlegroup Forward HQ was comprised of my Warrior, a 432 command vehicle, two Land Rovers and a couple of damp tents in a disused car park. Ross Gillanders greeted me, saying: 'Colonel, I am colder than the testicles of a very cold snail crawling across a frozen lake. In fact, the last time I knew I had testicles was twenty-four hours ago.'

During my journey, B and C Companies had also been moving to their bases. Later, the *Silver Bugle* described what was happening at the same time as my move.

> The companies took over very different conditions. C Company had the relative comfort of Vitez, with its cookhouse and Corimec accommodation. B Company took over the factory of unbaked bricks, which soon resembled the Somme, at Kiseljak. The battalion had arrived. It was cold, and most people had no proper accommodation, never mind access to telephones, beer etc. Worse still, it seemed that there was nothing to do but posture and deter – the start of a long six months.

CHAPTER THREE

Roads to Sarajevo

As the Devon and Dorsets departed, I pondered on the ground and situation. Mount Igman lay just to the south of Sarajevo, with the steep dark forest of its north face overlooking the city's airport southern suburbs. These were divided between Muslim- and Serb-controlled areas. We were on a high plateau in the centre of the mountain, under the peak of Bijelsenica in a former ski resort, its hotels and other buildings burned out during previous fighting, now being used as UN bases.

The mountain overlooked Sarajevo, its airport and the surrounding suburbs, making it of key tactical importance for the battle around the city. It had been the scene of bitter conflict in 1993 when a successful Bosnian Serb offensive threatened to cut the narrow Muslim-held corridor that was the besieged city of Sarajevo's only link with the outside world. Under US threats of air strikes the Serbs had agreed to withdraw, handing a demilitarised zone (DMZ) over to the UN. In 1994 Bosnian Muslim troops had attempted to infiltrate back into the DMZ, resulting in armed confrontations and gun battles with French troops sent to the mountain to keep the factions out of the zone. In summer 1995, the British and French troops of the Multinational Brigade had moved onto the feature, from where they had shelled Serb positions and helped direct NATO air strikes during the autumn.

Now the DMZ appeared to be ignored by the Muslims and forgotten by most of the UN. Muslim forces controlled the massif, apart from the north face where a thin isthmus of Bosnian territory ran between Serb positions down to the south side of the UN-controlled airfield at the Muslim-held suburb of Butmir. Through this ran the 'Igman Road'. Overlooked by Bosnian Serb guns, it was the only way by which UN and Bosnian vehicles could reach the south side of Sarajevo airport. The route was a steep and vertiginous forest track ploughed into a dangerous quagmire by the constant passage of UN vehicles and a bewildering assortment of Bosnian cars, buses, trucks and huge articulated lorries, 'all apparently driven by kamikaze pilots', as the RSM put it. The road ended in the ruins at the south side of Sarajevo Airport, where the Bosnians had constructed a tunnel for people and supplies to pass beneath the airport and into the city proper. Control of this route was of great political and economic importance to the Sarajevo government – not least because of the dues that were charged both to commercial traffic and Bosnian civilians, who could not leave the city without permission and payment.

Route SWAN, the main road to Sarajevo through its Serb-controlled suburbs, ran from the edge of the airport to the Croat-controlled enclave of Kiseljak ten miles to the west. A further thirty miles west through Muslim-controlled territory lay the Bosnian Croat enclave of Vitez where the rest of the battalion was based.

The cease-fire was holding, although there was still a lot of firing on the front line. The battalion was now part of the Multinational Brigade, carrying out its mission of deterring violations of the cease-fire. We were the brigade's Task Force Alpha, forming the 2 LI battlegroup, along with an armoured engineer troop and B Squadron Light Dragoons (LD). Task Force Bravo was based on a French Foreign Legion mechanised infantry regiment. The brigade also had British, French and Dutch artillery. All the British components of the brigade, apart from the artillery of 19 Field Regiment, were part of the task force – more than nine hundred people, and almost two hundred and fifty vehicles, half of which were armoured. We had more combat power than any other battalion in Bosnia – faction or UN.

A Company and Forward HQ were based on Mount Igman, B Company in an old brickworks in the Bosnian Croat enclave of Kiseljak. C Company, our main HQ, logistic echelon and the LAD were based in Vitez. Mortar and MILAN sections were deployed with their affiliated companies. Each company group would spend two weeks in each location before we rotated them on to the next role. The company on the mountain guarded UN installations, including signals sites, logistic sites and Dutch radars, patrolled the mountain roads and acted as a quick reaction force for Igman. The *Silver Bugle* described Igman:

> The devastation of the confrontation line around Sarajevo Airport and the extensive minefields were a sobering introduction to Bosnia. The key problems were equipment maintenance and mobility in the wintry conditions; a temperature of minus 67°C (with wind chill) was recorded on top of the main peak. Warrior was not good in fresh snow. Winter track improved the situation, but we were not truly mobile until issued with six BV 206 oversnow vehicles. 'Celebratory' fire by ABiH soldiers was a regular occurrence and a 'celebratory' grenade was thrown close to a checkpoint.

At Kiseljak, the company escorted UN convoys to and from Sarajevo and provided the brigade reserve quick reaction force, this time to deal with incidents on the routes to Sarajevo – also the role of the huge armoured engineer tanks. These belonged to our armoured engineer troop, which had almost seventy sappers, many of whom spent their time maintaining their elderly and extremely unreliable vehicles. Based on the Chieftain tanks built in the 1960s, these were well and truly showing their age. The remaining sappers were working on Igman.

Back in Vitez, the battalion's third company was on much lower readiness, allowing time for maintenance and training. The recce platoon was split between Vitez and Igman and used for both reconnaissance and convoy escorts. They were particularly useful in the narrow back streets of Sarajevo, including those leading to the Bosnian Brewery where we purchased our fresh water. A particularly bizarre task was to escort besuited UN officials, apparently sightseeing in minibuses.

Our armoured reconnaissance squadron, B Squadron Light Dragoons, commanded by Major Bertie Polley, a charmingly well-spoken man, was based further away in Bugojno. Equipped with another thirty light armoured vehicles, organised into four troops each of three Scimitars and a Spartan, its current role was to help escort convoys. Many of the squadron had carried out at least one previous tour in Bosnia.

I took stock of the environment and our camps. In the valleys the snow was wet and shallow. In the mountains conditions were alpine. Without snow chains, wheeled vehicles couldn't move and mountain passes were littered with abandoned civilian vehicles. The amount of military traffic to the base quickly began to destroy the roads up over the mountains, which originally served a modest ski resort. The roads and mountaintop bases were maintained by UN engineers from the UK, France, Canada, Norway, Indonesia, Slovakia and the RAF. The Indonesians had never seen snow before but those operating snowploughs seemed to consider it all a huge joke. The British engineer squadron offered to accommodate both the Forward HQ and A Company in the as yet uncompleted camps that they were building. The sappers would continue to finish the camps around us. Some of us therefore had roofs over our heads and intermittent heat and light, but had to improvise cooking facilities, washrooms and latrines. This the soldiers did with great aplomb.

The Igman Company patrolled the mountain and secured positions on and around the front line. One of our forward positions was an observation post overlooking the Serb town of Hadžići, right on the front line, sandwiched between a Foreign Legion position and ABiH bunkers. Some of the craters from September's bombing could be seen, but Hadžići and the VRS positions were often swathed in mist or icy low cloud. Another position protected a British signals installation – well above the tree line and extremely cold. The most isolated detachment lived in a clearing in the forest high on a spur overlooking the front line where the Dutch Army had deployed Fire Finder radars watching for faction artillery and rocket fire.

The troops guarding these isolated sites lived in vehicles, tents, log cabins or other wooden shelters which they had to build for themselves. These varied from 'traditional' log cabins to wooden frames on which soldiers draped plastic sheeting and branches to make surprisingly effective insulation. These latter structures could be as large as a good-sized domestic garage. Having built themselves 'houses', people busied themselves making all sorts of wooden furniture. Every time I visited one of these little bases, the tenants took enormous pride in showing me their latest construction, sometimes the new field kitchen, sometimes the home-made washrooms, and most importantly the field toilets – some of which were mighty constructions indeed.

The cold weather clothes issued to complement our combat uniform were excellent, especially the Gore-Tex winter gaiters, thick pile gloves, facemasks and furry hats (universally known as Deputy Dawg hats). We also had huge Canadian-made black one-piece zipped overalls lined with fibre piling. Despite their curious label, which proclaimed them to be 'Dew Liners', they were incredibly warm. This gave us a lot of flexibility to adjust our clothing to meet the wide variety of weather we encountered. I wore green thermal underwear over which went a zipped 'Norwegian' cotton shirt, camouflaged combat trousers and a sweater, all underneath my windproof smock. I carried a loaded pistol on my belt and my pockets were full of the paraphernalia of operations. These included a penknife, metal identity disks, field dressing, maps, compass, winter sunglasses and three different pairs of gloves, of cotton, leather and Gore-Tex. We were all issued with waterproof insulated 'Matterhorn' cold weather boots, needed especially by sentries standing still outside for long periods.

The weather conditions varied from cold and dry through cold and wet to short, unexpectedly balmy conditions, which were invariably wet because the snow melted. The degree to which soldiers were exposed to the weather varied hugely depending on their jobs. Worst off were the drivers and commanders who had to endure long periods exposed to freezing snow and winds. Many used a huge 'shamargh', a great Arab headscarf dyed dark green wrapped thickly around the face, leaving only the eyes uncovered – and these protected with goggles. Everybody adjusted their clothing according to the conditions and what they were doing. I made it known that I didn't really care what people wore, as long as it was of recognisably British military pattern, serviceable and sufficient for the mission at the time. It was difficult for anyone to keep clean and our clothes quickly became covered in dust and mud, but weapons were kept clean all the time.

Mount Igman was swarming with Bosnian soldiers either manning the trenches and bunkers or using the many roads and tracks to move to and from Sarajevo. Our main base on the mountain was named Sevastopol Camp after the winter siege of the city in the Crimean War. It was neatly bisected by the main road through the ski resort. As well as UN vehicles a large number of civilians, soldiers on foot, bicycles, horse-drawn carts and ramshackle lorries used this route, as did the occasional flock of mountain sheep. Many of these people moving around the mountain were engaged in logging, farming or moving commodities to and from Sarajevo and, we suspected, organised theft from UNPROFOR.

Every second or third night there was a report of intruders attempting to steal fuel and equipment from UN positions on the mountain. Using techniques practised in Northern Ireland we raised our security profile with highly visible sentries and patrols to deter attempts to steal our supplies. The battlegroup bases on Igman never had any fuel or equipment stolen. This was not the case with other units, but inevitably many of our soldiers spent much of their time simply 'stagging on' as the slang put it – guarding bases and installations. This was a thankless and highly repetitive task that they fulfilled with stoical endurance and great humour.

Most of the soldiers took the environment in their stride. Inevitably there were one or two who needed steadying or reassurance, which their commanders supplied. This was all part of the learning curve that we were all ascending. We had anticipated this. But I had not anticipated the problem we would have with rumours, especially a few soldiers who knowingly spreading false information.

One wrote home saying he had been in a gun battle with the factions and had been injured. He explained that he was now recovering in hospital, which was why he had not written for some time. His parents were naturally very concerned and rang the Army to find out more information. Battlegroup HQ heard via the chain of command. This was the first we knew of the alleged firefight.

It could clearly be proved that the soldier had deliberately spread untrue and alarming rumours. He was disciplined and punished. The amount of gossip dropped immediately. We had learned the hard way that commanders at all levels had to prevent the spreading of false rumours and had to act rapidly to scotch those negative tales that reached their ears.

Serjeant Hedges of A Company continues his account of the adventures of his platoon:

We only had a few small problems. There were no washing facilities available, so the priority was to build our own. Serjeant Hill had already made a start with the toilets and Corporal James started with the washroom. The next day they were both up and running. The troops were so proud of them that they named them 'Jezz's Washroom' and 'Tin Shitty'. People came from as far as three hundred metres away to use them!

One Platoon had the task of guarding the Multinational Brigade HQ. Corporal Kirikmaa had the task of guarding a Dutch radar site. With the motivation of having nowhere dry and warm to sleep, his section set to work building their new home. Working around their stag, they built a small house with whatever they could beg, borrow or acquire. The Dutch were impressed and invited all the commanders including General Smith to give their seal of approval. Corporal Taylor, Lance Corporal Vaughan and their section were tasked to guard a signals rebroadcast station, a purpose-built platoon location: toilets, showers, a kitchen, sleeping accommodation – talk about landing on your feet.

The tasks complete, the main effort was to keep our outposts administered. Daily runs with mail made sure morale was high. Everyone on the outposts was more than content.

Liaison with the French Foreign Legion gave us a range on the mountain. Seven kilometres down a mud track and we were there. Left of arc was the hill to the south. Right of arc was a hill to the north. One of the best field firing ranges I have seen. Warrior, MILAN, mortars and dismounted attacks – you could see the cogs turning in the head of the company commander.

When we received a task to escort REME up to a signals installation on the 2060m-high Bijelsenica, by foot, every available man came with us. Each carried his day sack with warm clothing in case the weather turned nasty, as it did. We reached the halfway point and visibility came down to twenty metres. The wind nearly knocked you off your feet with a chill factor around minus 25°C. On our return down the mountain, Private Brown became 2 LI's Face Skiing Champion as he sped past the patrol totally out of control. He came to a halt only a couple of inches away from a seventy-five-foot drop. As he stood up, wiping the blood from his face, he wanted a photograph of himself.

On our return we began to move into Sevastopol Camp. The troops set about their tasks with renewed enthusiasm. A bunker was transformed into an all ranks' club. The floor was half mud, half tennis court; a stage and bar covered the mud; benches and stools were made and a log-burning fire revamped; a satellite TV decoder was installed. The grand opening was a quiz night run by Lance Corporal Williams and singalong with Serjeant Murray and guitar. Guests included the CO and RSM who seemed to enjoy the night.

The company slipped smoothly into a routine and liaison and friendships grew with the French, Dutch and Kiwis. Throughout our three weeks on the mountain we hosted our very own Vietnam veteran and Radio Four presenter Simon Dring and a one-hour radio special about A Company on Mount Igman was broadcast on Radio Four.

Simon Dring was a BBC radio journalist putting together a documentary about the British Army in Bosnia. I first met him as A Company were grappling with their first day on the mountain. Clad in a black 'dew liner' and camouflaged Deputy Dawg hat, he was a radiantly cheerful man, relishing every minute of a new experience. He was also battle experienced, having covered a great deal of fighting in Vietnam. Jan de Vos and I were delighted to discover that he was a close friend of legendary war photographer Tim Page, who we both admired for his photographs and his uninhibitedly devil-may-care hedonism. Simon radiated a similar but more light-hearted approach to life. He worked unobtrusively, carrying his tape recorder concealed in the folds of his voluminous black clothing. Although the battalion had an immense amount of experience of Northern Ireland, only Jan de Vos had served in the Gulf War and none of us had fought in the Falklands. That Simon Dring 'had the smell of gunsmoke on his clothes' (as one of the serjeants put it), meant that he quickly established a very strong rapport with us.

By the end of the first two weeks, our operations and base on Igman were well established.

To the west the company at Kiseljak Brick Factory were mostly living in decaying brick rooms with rotting roofs and an abundance of rats and mud. There were a few metal accommodation containers, universally known as 'Corimecs', after the initials of the Italian company that had built them, but only enough for a small proportion of the two hundred soldiers there. Chris Booth managed to arrange the move of two platoons from the factory to share Kiseljak Hotel with the Rapid Reaction Force Operational Staff. They found themselves in a large house in the grounds of the former luxury hotel – a very popular move.

The Kiseljak company did what it could to improve its austere surroundings, greatly helped by those engineers not working on Mount Igman. Gradually they made themselves less uncomfortable, even finding the energy to construct a fitness trail inside the base. The company was heavily committed to escorting a large number of UN convoys to and from Igman and Sarajevo. They had a troop of French Foreign Legion cavalry equipped with AMX 10RC armoured cars under command. Although extremely thinly armoured, the AMXs mounted a turret with a powerful 105mm gun and advanced fire control equipment. All the companies got on famously with the Legion cavalry. Serjeant Grimes of B Company wrote this account of multinational operations from Kiseljak:

> The French Foreign Legion had a troop attached to the company. Very few spoke English, although I did meet two ex-members of the Light Infantry. The company started to learn basic phases like bonjour, comment ça va? etc. However as the Legion always had an armed guard outside at night it seemed prudent also to learn the phrase ne tirez pas, nous sommes du même côté, which roughly translated means 'don't shoot – we are all on the same side!'. The phrase caused much amusement among the French who then went out of their way to learn a few English words. The Legion's hard regime often made me wonder if the guard was to prevent the would-be thief or stop the legionaries from doing a moonlight flit.
>
> On one occasion as the Guard Force for the joint UK/French Main HQ in Kiseljak I found myself sitting in on the morning brief by the commander. As the overall commander was French, all the morning pleasantries were in French, but, once everyone settled down to address the day's business, it seemed all the formal business was conducted in English and the informal in French.

Our liaison officers were hard at work getting to know the commanders of all three factions in whose areas we were operating. I had heard stories that some previous battalions had allowed LOs to dictate operations to company commanders, resulting in resentment and friction. I was quite clear that our liaison effort was to support commanders and insisted that their work was properly co-ordinated with that of the companies. Captain Sean Harris described this effort in the *Silver Bugle*:

> After twenty-four hours in Bosnia I was on my way to Sarajevo to meet my first Bosnian Serb officers. I could just about say 'hello' in Serbo-Croat; I had a lot to learn. The first couple of times I was at the Serbian Army offices in Sarajevo, I let my Devon and Dorset opposite number do most of the talking. He seemed well at ease in the company of men the world's press had labelled murderers. Soon I was on my own, and I became very adept at small talk whilst getting my point across. The trick is to learn as much as possible without giving away what you really want to know. I also learned the hard way that you do not drink the dregs of Bosnian coffee.
>
> By the end of my first month in Bosnia the road from Vitez to Sarajevo was rapidly becoming my home. During my first three months in Bosnia my trusty armoured Land Rover travelled twelve thousand kilometres. A good deal of an

LO's time is spent on the road and Bosnian driving provided amusement, and often danger. If there is a Bosnian Highway Code, then it is almost a reverse of the British one. In Bosnia it would seem to be mandatory to overtake on blind corners, especially if driving a packed coach on icy roads at night.

We came into daily contact with the civilians and soldiers of the three factions. In Paderborn we had trained everyone to use the common forms of greeting in Serbo-Croat. This did much to reduce tension and establish person-to-person contact. Many locals were keen to sell us pathetic souvenirs, military equipment or even weapons. The economy of all three factions had been devastated by the war and many people were desperate for Deutschmarks, which had become the only hard currency of any value in the country. Faction soldiers and officers would also blatantly offer large sums of money to buy our weapons. These ranged from two hundred marks for a rifle to half a million marks for a Warrior. The offers were politely but firmly rebuffed.

On Igman the ABiH and VRS both manned lines of bunkers and trenches facing each other through the steep forested slopes. Some positions were deep, warm and very comfortable, others were shallow, of slipshod construction and dank and depressing. But I saw none that would have withstood attack by our LAW 80 rockets, chain guns, Rarden cannons or MILAN missiles.

The armies could be distinguished by their clothing: VRS wore camouflage fatigues with their own pattern, whilst the ABiH soldiers were clad in a mixture of American-pattern camouflaged uniforms and civilian clothing. But all were uninterested in UNPROFOR, which they seemed to regard as an ineffectual irrelevance. The ABiH soldiers doubted that the peace would hold and confidently forecast that NATO would intervene on their side to finish the war against the VRS. The opposing soldiers in the front-line positions also seemed largely apathetic and uninterested in the war, although they professed a deep and unyielding hatred for their opponents.

Many faction soldiers were older than ours, all looking tired, dirty, undernourished and unwashed. They lived a wretched existence, subsisting on food brought from their homes and the occasional resupply of small portions of stew, delivered on the backs of exhausted-looking ponies. The camouflage uniforms, weapons and small arms were undeniably of the late twentieth century, but the faces, fortifications and much of the ambience could have come from a European war any time over the previous two hundred years.

In contrast to their soldiers, many faction officers were washed, clean-shaven and dressed in clean, properly fitting uniforms. Although I met many ABiH and VRS officers around Igman and Sarajevo I never saw or heard of a faction officer of higher rank than major spending any time on and around the front line.

All our dealings with the factions had been conducted with the aid of our 'Language Assistants' as they were formally titled by the UN bureaucracy. We simply called them interpreters. The battlegroup employed about forty, at that time ensuring that every patrol or isolated platoon had one with them. Almost all of them were women, and a significant number had professional qualifications. Many had good degrees in English, or had worked in the West. Others were students whose education had been interrupted by the war. Most had become the breadwinner in their family, the UN wage of eight hundred dollars a month being a small fortune in the battered communities of central Bosnia from which 2 LI's interpreters were drawn.

The commander's cadre had trained us how to best employ interpreters – for example by talking directly to those we were meeting, not to the interpreter. We quickly learned how to phrase statements as simply and directly as possible, talking in short statements, pausing after each 'sound bite' to allow the interpreter to translate. Inevitably this meant that meetings and discussions were lengthy, but this allowed time for tempers to cool and for us to carefully consider our next statement.

Interpreters wore British uniform, without badges or head dress. The women could not resist doing everything they could to make themselves as attractive as possible. We would often see them arrive for work having devoted hours to their hair and elaborate make-up. The cynics among us said that this was either to disguise the pallor and skin problems caused by years of stress, privation and an inadequate diet, or to find a husband with a British passport. This may or may not have been true, but on my trips to Sarajevo I had noticed that a significant proportion of women were dressed as glamorously as possible. It seemed to be a universal activity of determined young women of all three factions – possibly the only way they could defy the appalling circumstances of the war.

In the absence of our wives and girlfriends, some might have been tempted to allow the attractive female interpreters to be more than just people who translated. Leadership and self-discipline countered this.

Both the interpreters and the faction leaders were products of a society that had moved from centralised communism to civil war. The faction military commanders believed that any interpreters of a different faction represented a security risk. We knew that some off-duty interpreters were quizzed by the faction intelligence organisations. We therefore had to use interpreters in a way that respected the operational security of both the factions and ourselves. This meant not taking an interpreter from one faction to a meeting with a different faction.

Before meetings we would carefully select the interpreter for skill and ethnic origin. If necessary, they would be briefed on what we were trying to achieve (where this was not a secret). It was important to consider the body language to be used and not to let an over-helpful or devious interpreter take over the meeting – especially when, as sometimes happened, factions provided their own interpreters. Finally it was useful to debrief the interpreters at the end of meeting, getting their interpretation of the event and any nuances we might not have picked up.

2LI's interpreters provided an excellent service. A significant number of them had been hired by the Cheshires or the PWO and had experienced much fighting alongside the British UN troops. They all identified totally with the battlegroup and did their best to help us.

Early in the tour Serjeant Major Jasper identified an opportunity to play soccer against the factions. With the help of the liaison officers and interpreters and after lengthy meetings with the locals, games were organised against the local Croats from Vitez and a tournament against Bosnian Serbs in the Serb-held town of Hadžići. Both matches were described in the *Silver Bugle*:

> The game against Vitez saw the battalion team start with a display of excellent one-touch control football. This took the locals, who were semi-professional before the conflict, by surprise. It was not long before the pressure paid off. Although the locals tried hard to compete, the battalion ran out eventual 2–8 winners. The manager of Vitez applauded the battalion's win and thanked everyone for the game.
>
> Two weeks later the battalion played in a run-down sports hall in Hadžići which only eight weeks earlier had been subjected to NATO air strikes. The Serbs invited the battalion to play them in a small indoor six-a-side competition. After the formalities of exchanging regimental souvenirs, the games went ahead. It was obvious from the start that the Serbs were better prepared technically, and with the local support of around two hundred and fifty people they were too good for either of the battalion's teams. A great deal was learned from the Serbs about the indoor game. The whole day turned out to be an excellent break from the normal everyday routine and the after-match discussions showed that the Serbs were just as passionate off the field as on it. The day finished with an overjoyed Serb manager praising everyone for the efforts of bringing the two teams together in an unusual and strange setting.

Despite this bonhomie, we had little doubt that the war had been exceptionally brutal. Even if one tenth of the stories we heard from UN commanders who had served throughout the summer's fighting and from interpreters and civilian workers were true, it was quite clear that atrocity had been heaped upon atrocity by all sides.

Many faction soldiers and commanders held the attitude that all males of military age (sixteen to sixty) of the other faction were legitimate targets, whether or not they had been involved in the fighting. Prisoners were routinely tortured and killed. It appeared that the few prisoners who were kept alive were being held as human bargaining chips. On all three sides, ethnic cleansing had been accompanied by appalling atrocities visited upon women and children.

Often the character of the faction armies seemed medieval. The recent history of the British Army and other Western armies had included efforts to reduce the chances of suffering to civilians and prisoners – not only through the growing volume of international law, such as the Geneva Conventions, but also through the education and training of their commanders. The speed with which the factions had improvised their citizen armies from completely untrained personnel meant that this process had been short-circuited, resulting in armies where the restraints on looting, rape, torture and murder of prisoners were at best much looser and at worst non-existent.

In this and many other ways the faction armies presented an unpredictable mixture of highly centralised command and control with discipline was often inconsistent and indifferent. This made it all the more important that we should conduct ourselves in a disciplined and professional manner. We had to seize and maintain the moral high ground, not only for the messages it would send to the factions but also for the benefit of our self-esteem.

In the past, cease-fires had been broken by Muslim artillery attacks on Serb forces, which provoked Serb retaliatory fire. The Bosnian Government propaganda machine would avidly exploit the resulting Muslim civilian casualties. Many of the UN personnel who had seen the summer's fighting and crisis had no doubt that there were occasions when the Muslim population in Sarajevo had been fired upon deliberately by their own side in order to further tilt international media coverage against the Serbs, and gain votes in the UN security council and support in the United States. All three factions were devious, very quick to exploit any perceived or actual UNPROFOR weaknesses and would dearly love to manipulate Western troops to achieve their own ends.

The three factions had different characters. The Bosnian Croats seemed excitable, macho and Mediterranean in outlook. Many saw unity between their territory and Croatia as inevitable. The Bosnian Serbs were stubborn, defensive and more stoical and phlegmatic. They were bemused by the way that the West in general and the Americans in particular seemed to consider them the 'bad guys', but stubbornly refused to accept that their actions in Bosnia had done nothing to promote their cause. The Bosnian Muslim commanders and politicians were more than happy to play on Western consciences in order to gain an advantage over the other factions.

By now I had got to know the area around Kiseljak, Sarajevo and Igman. It was a place of strange contrasts. At first glance, the Igman ski resort appeared ready to open for business. Closer inspection showed that no ski lifts were working. During the fighting the factions had burned out those hotels not occupied by the UN. One of the larger hotels had the headquarters of the French mountain infantry battalion in cabins around it. In the centre of the hotel was the 'Igman Infirmary', a small hospital created by the French, British and Dutch medics deployed to the hill. To get there you had to go down a narrow corridor encrusted with burned and peeling paint, which opened up into what must have once been a large impressive split-level reception area, restaurant and bar. Where holidaymakers and skiers had once relaxed there was now stained concrete, burned wood and exposed beams and wires. It resembled a grandiose film set from some post-apocalyptic science fiction adventure like the *Mad Max* or *Alien* films.

Down in Sarajevo, the destruction was no less intense. A large number of UN vehicles needed to travel to and from Sarajevo. Our patrols were escorting these to and from the Croat pocket of Kiseljak along Route SWAN, through Bosnian Serb territory, including the suburb of Ilidza which lay right on the front line. The road to Sarajevo crossed no-man's-land, where the buildings were heavily damaged from the fighting. There were many land mines lying in the rubble and on the edges of the roads, most, but not all, marked off by the French UN soldiers with mine triangles and red tape. The road then split.

Turning through a French checkpoint would take convoys onto Sarajevo Airport (controlled by the UN), whilst driving straight on would lead into the government-held fringes of Sarajevo. I often travelled in both these directions, reflecting that the journey bore many similarities to the journey from West Germany to Berlin that I had made so often during the Cold War.

Around the confrontation line, buildings were little more than blasted and pockmarked silhouettes, distorted outlines of spaces that had once been homes or offices. Everywhere there were bullet holes, some small, some large. Vehicle hulks were riddled with them, paint flaking over rusted circles around small dark holes. The area was liberally sown with mines. The French only allowed the roads to be used in daylight. The resulting queues of UN and Bosnian traffic and delays gave me plenty of time for thought. I reflected that Sarajevo was the fourth divided community I had served in, the others being Sha Tau Kok, a divided town on the border between Hong Kong and China, Berlin during the Cold War, and West Belfast.

I described some impressions in a letter home:

> I went to visit the battalion of French Parachute Marines controlling Sarajevo Airport. The place has been in UNPROFOR hands since 1992, when the UN brokered a deal with the Serbs to allow it to take over the airfield for the delivery of humanitarian aid. What a set of impressions. The French observation posts and checkpoints are covered in layer upon layer of sandbags, wood and concrete. The airport has been on the front line between the two armies for more than three years of constant crossfire and shelling.
>
> All the buildings within half a mile of the airport are heavily damaged, covered with the craters of bullets and shells. Many are still standing, but only just. All the roofs are bare, burned-out timbers, skeletal frames against the dull, leaden sky. Gardens are overgrown and few trees have survived the storm of fire or the populations foraging for firewood. It is the same on both Serb and Muslim sides.

I lived at the Battlegroup Forward HQ on Igman. Days were spent visiting troops on the Mountain and the base at Kiseljak, or conducting reconnaissance in Sarajevo. I quickly learned that travelling in my Warrior was very slow. Instead I used my 'Rover Group'. One Land Rover carried me and Private Leck, my driver, another RSM and Private Ogden, his driver.

At 1830 hours daily there would be a brigade conference reviewing the day's operations and the next day's plans, lasting up to ninety minutes. I would return to Battlegroup HQ and debrief Ross Gillanders, the other staff and the company commander. I would speak to Vitez either over the French satellite telephone or on an improvised connection between our Ptarmigan secure phone and the UN satellite phones. Connections were indifferent, unpredictable and liable to be interrupted without warning, making passage of information a frustrating process.

The Multinational Brigade had a huge headquarters split between Mount Igman and Mostar. It was much bigger than a British brigade HQ, at least the same size as a British divisional HQ at full war establishment. For example, there were no fewer than twenty-two colonels and lieutenant colonels. Although the vast majority of staff were in Mostar, the forward HQ on Igman ran the operations around Sarajevo. Though the brigade was ostensibly multinational, the majority of staff were French, augmented by some British and Dutch officers. The formation was commanded by the French *General de Brigade* Soubirou, a tall former Foreign Legion officer. This extremely charismatic man was a veteran of the French wars in Chad, and of Bosnia. With great distinction and moral courage he had commanded the Sarajevo Sector in 1994. Held in some awe by all the French officers I met, he stalked through Bosnia wearing a leather jacket, a white silk scarf and a huge pistol strapped to a thigh holster.

But Soubirou was not as well supported by his HQ as it might have been. When the Rapid Reaction Force had been set up, the French took the lead in providing the HQ. But rather than use an existing formation headquarters, they assembled one from a collection of individual officers draw from peacetime jobs all over France. A British colonel, Hamish Fletcher, was chief of staff and through sheer hard work, force of personality and an unlimited reservoir of patience, tact and diplomacy kept the HQ afloat – most of the time. Even so staff procedures were based on French rather than British practice. We found them highly centralised and very slow. For example, in our Battlegroup HQ anyone could write and release a signal message – in the MNB HQ this activity was reserved for the chief of staff. Conferences and meetings, which all had to be conducted through interpreters, were incredibly slow-moving, taking twice as long as they would have done in a British HQ.

This was usually overcome through patience, good humour and the complementary skills of the French commander and British chief of staff. But when Fletcher was away from Mount Igman, at the brigade's main HQ in Mostar, the effectiveness of the Forward HQ dropped sharply. In these periods the brigade did business in a manner that often seemed the opposite of our doctrine of mission command. Orders were often vague, light on specifics, heavy on *le grand geste*, or descended to micro-management.

The brigade commander was an extremely strong personality, and a compelling leader. Often he was charming, displaying a dry sense of humour and an impish smile. He strongly identified with his soldiers, French, British and Dutch. But he seemed frustrated with the weaknesses of his HQ and had a reputation throughout French forces in Bosnia for having an explosive temper on a short fuse. Many of the French officers on the brigade staff were extremely anxious not to provoke an outburst, which they christened 'an Exocet'. This did nothing to improve the overall effectiveness of the HQ, particularly because some people were very reluctant to be the bearers of bad news.

It was therefore vital that the battlegroup should build up as good a working relationship as it could with the MNB HQ and with the other British and French units on the mountain. We needed to be able to monitor what was going on in the HQ and influence the planning as necessary. For this reason the Forward HQ stayed permanently on the mountain.

Though we had anticipated that communications in Bosnia would be difficult, we had not realised just how demanding the communications environment would be. The battlegroup was equipped with large numbers of VHF radios, which were ideal for command and control of manoeuvre operations over a small area. In the Cold War, a battlegroup might have been responsible for controlling ground perhaps six kilometres wide and ten kilometres deep. We were now operating over an area a hundred times greater. Although the well-established UN bases such as Vitez were equipped with both British and UN satellite telephones and we had a single field deployable INMARSAT satellite system, the battlegroup would have to depend entirely on its own resources for internal communication.

The minute-by-minute passage of information and orders was conducted on the battlegroup command net. This, on a single frequency was 'all-informed', with all components of the battlegroup, all our headquarters, all our bases and all our vehicles moving around the area permanently listening to it. All had unique call signs, a letter preceding a number. I was 'Zero Alpha'. The three companies were 'Hotel One Zero' (A), 'Hotel Two Zero' (B) and 'Hotel Three Zero' (C). We used large numbers of set protocols, names, nicknames and specific expressions on the net, the full jargon and conventions of military radio usage being known as 'voice procedure'.

The effect was twofold. Firstly this common approach meant that in times of stress, excitement and danger vital information could be transmitted simply and clearly. Secondly, we could all 'read' the net, allowing us to be continuously informed of the battlegroup's activities. Every time I left Battlegroup HQ I would listen to the net, monitoring our convoys and patrols as they moved about their operations. The net was an electronic nervous system, connecting all components of the battlegroup to each other, sharing all information, but, when necessary, subordinated to Battlegroup HQ or ultimately myself.

We inherited a 'multi-rebroadcast' radio net, based on a chain of rebroadcast stations positioned on mountaintops. These used two linked radios to receive a message on one frequency and retransmit it on another. With three rebroadcast stations deployed across the battlegroup area, we could use our VHF radios to transmit messages all the way from Igman and Sarajevo to Vitez. This sounds easy, but it required considerable practice to make it work. The mountains and long distances meant that VHF frequencies showed many of the characteristics of HF. Lower VHF frequencies travelled further than higher frequencies, whilst other frequencies would not work in certain areas at key times of the day. These factors forced the signals platoon to carry out careful frequency management and devote considerable time and effort to 'engineering' the net.

All our hard work and rapidly acquired expertise could not overcome the laws of physics. The mountainous terrain inevitably resulted in a large number of dead spots where transmission and/or receipt of messages were impossible. This meant that, apart from our static bases, there was no place where any vehicle could guarantee to be able to communicate with anyone else. Between our fixed bases we had an 'all informed net' but everyone else, including me as I moved round the battlegroup area, could easily miss hearing key items of information. This put a premium on company and platoon commanders regularly briefing their subordinates.

We only had three voice radios fitted with 'secure' encryption equipment allowing us to talk on formation secure radio nets. The battlegroup command net was 'insecure', which is to say that anyone with a radio tuned to our frequency could hear everything that was said on the net. We had a paper-based code system called BATCO but, despite its simplicity and flexibility, the code was time consuming to use, imposing considerable delay on the passage of information. We largely confined its use to reporting faction positions.

Fortunately Task Force Alpha had been issued with the KL43 – a simple hand-held data entry device. These were the size of a small paperback book and had a small alphanumeric keyboard and liquid crystal display. These pocket-sized devices were very user-friendly. Lengthy messages could be composed off line and only sent when the operator was ready. Better still, the devices had a cryptographic system built in which automatically encoded and decoded the messages.

With more than forty of the KL43s, we were able to create a secure data net within insecure voice nets, allowing orders and plans to be passed more securely and more quickly.

The downside was that the data messages sounded like very loud white noise. This particularly irritated Warrior crews, who had been issued with 'active noise reduction' headsets designed to reduce the high-pitched sounds of the vehicle's engine and running gear. The technology made it much more difficult to ignore the ear-piercing racket of the data being squirted through the ether. I was one of those who found this supremely distracting, but I judged it a price worth paying for the improvement in speed and security with which we could pass reports and orders.

Vitez Camp was our main base. Initially occupied by the Cheshires, it had been intensively developed since then. At its heart was an H-shaped school block, identical in appearance to countless other schools all over Bosnia. The classrooms now functioned as offices, stores and operations rooms, while the building was festooned with cables, radio antenna, satellite dishes and all the paraphernalia of modern command and control. I had a huge office in a former classroom, which was big enough to hold a meeting of fifty people.

Around the school a large village of temporary buildings had grown up, almost all Corimecs. A large cookhouse turned out a huge number of meals, which were consumed in an all-ranks dining room. It was now winter and alternating between snow and bitterly cold clear dry weather.

To prevent overcrowding and its inevitable demand on the life support systems of the camp, a large number of houses had been occupied both within our perimeter and outside it. Most of these were used for officers' accommodation. This did not mean that the officers were any more comfortable than the soldiers; in fact they were usually colder. But the officers just needed to be somewhere different for some of the time, to allow both parties an opportunity to relax and let off steam without breathing down each other's necks.

Colonel Bob Stewart had taken one of these houses for himself. Bizarrely, it was two hundred metres from the nearest part of the camp. It had already acquired a reputation amongst the British Army as 'Bob Stewart's house'. I managed to visit Vitez for a couple of days every week or so and stayed there. At this time the citizens of Vitez were preparing for the winter and I woke every morning to blood-curdling cries of distress as yet another pig had its throat cut before being butchered for the winter. Up in the mountains the villagers were doing the same, meticulously stacking firewood, stockpiling food supplies and corralling their beasts in barns. This timeless rhythm of the mountain villages had outlasted the war.

Five UN military observers (UNMOs) occupied another house. Unarmed, they answered not to the UNPROFOR chain of command, but to their own HQ in Zagreb. The party in Vitez came from Holland, Denmark, Kenya, Brazil and Argentina. All were very affable and cooperative, but it was not clear how they added value to the UN operation, particularly as they had no formal linkage to HQ Sector Southwest.

A mile away from Vitez camp was Vitez Garage, a former bus depot that now served as the battlegroup's logistic base. The two quartermasters and their logistic team were based there, as were our LAD and a large stockpile of vehicle fuel. The quartermasters organised the overall delivery of supplies within the battalion, but operations and logistics were integrated at Battlegroup HQ, where Dave Wroe worked as battlegroup logistic coordinator.

The winter weather, difficult roads, communications problems and extended supply lines created an environment that was more logistically demanding than any we had encountered before. Although the British had a well-developed national logistic system, the logistic support available to the Multinational Brigade was completely inadequate, and the brigade's logistic command and control was minimal. We fell back on the British system and our own resources. With the companies spread over more than seventy kilometres of mountainous terrain, living in harsh conditions, we all quickly learned to consider logistics from the outset of all our planning. Dave Wroe described our logistic operations in an article entitled 'You Want It When – You Must Be Joking!':

> The title of this contribution is somewhat synonymous with the cries of incredulity with which watch keepers at our 'A' Echelon greeted some of the more 'fast ball' requests from the forward-deployed companies. At times it's true to say that a more colourful greeting may well have been heard. 'Tactics is the art of doing that which is logistically possible', and we are all well aware of what that means. All very fine and Staff College, but the reality of it is you do what you can with what you have, and don't complain about the lack of what you haven't got.
>
> That is exactly what the 2 LI echelon system did, but along the way as you would expect we came across a number of problems. First of all it was the Rapid Reaction Force logistic organization based in Split, and the Multinational Brigade Forward, a predominantly French organisation based on Mount Igman. This consisted of one man, a Royal Logistic Corps major (who couldn't speak French)

and a dog; he worked back to MNB Rear in Mostar, where they had three men and two dogs! The overall control, of course, was by that mighty organisation, the United Nations, whose occasionally somewhat wayward distribution and accounting system was taken advantage of at every opportunity by the QM(M) Major Ken Kennedy.

Another task was the provision of drivers and operators for what was termed the 'honey sucker'. A necessary job, distasteful as it was. Temperatures on Mount Igman regularly dropped to twenty degrees below zero, and the MTO will dine out for a long time on the story of how the contents of one machine froze, and wouldn't empty. The enterprising Dutch operator opened the rear compartment, forgetting that he'd parked on a slope, and what hit him can only be described as the most unusually insalubrious fifty-pound ice lolly ever!

A UN bureaucratic procedure called the 'in survey' meant that the QM(T) Captain Dave Jarratt had to 'cost capture' every item of spares or equipment that came into the theatre. Around five thousand items had to be entered by hand into a register. In a thirty-one-day month, that works out at one entry into the register every ten minutes of every day of every week of that month. In cash terms, one month's cost capture was £186,545.48!

For the EME Captain Alan Mitchell, a 'B' vehicle fleet that had been in theatre since 1992 and hammered by successive units gave him and his LAD more than enough problems. A serious lack of spares available through the correct chain often had to be overcome by using the old boy net. They too provided the battle-group with an excellent service.

From my point of view our deployment showed just how important it was to have a good echelon system manned with individuals who knew how to react in a crisis. If I may be allowed to misquote again, 'never have so many depended on so few to provide so much'.

Reflections and Lessons

Even with relatively little faction activity or interference, the Multinational Brigade and the wintery mountains generated considerable friction that had to be overcome. Even the simple relief in place of one company by another could be subject to considerable uncertainty and delay, as I described in a letter home:

Today we are rotating the companies between Vitez, Kiseljak and Igman. I awoke to the heavy sound of rolling thunder echoing across the mountains, and a metre of fresh wet snow dumped overnight. This means that what should be a short, simple movement of company convoys becomes a prolonged, complicated, tiring and drawn-out operation. Our columns had to overcome problems posed by British military police (who apparently couldn't make their radios work, leaving them unable to provide the traffic control they had promised), a UN fuel tanker stuck in a ditch, broken down Bosnian Serb police cars and completely uncontrollable French convoys. All in a day's work!

All over Bosnia civilians had been preparing for winter, slaughtering pigs and stacking firewood outside houses. The battlegroup too was now prepared for winter. Our operations for the Multinational Brigade had all succeeded. In retrospect they had, in purely military terms, been relatively undemanding, particularly as the cease-fire had largely held. Of course, at the time we did not know that it was going to do so. Had it broken down, the UN Security Council could well have called the factions' bluff and mandated UNPROFOR's withdrawal. In the middle of winter and against the inevitable deterioration of the cease-fire, there would probably have been desperate attempts by the Bosnian Muslims to entangle the UN in a renewed conflict with Republika Srpska. That would really have tested us...

All parts of the battalion had the opportunity to learn from their mistakes. Although the UNPROFOR and UK chains of command provided the battlegroup with daily updates of the situation throughout the whole theatre, we had underestimated the problems of passing information from Battlegroup HQ down our chain of command to those who needed it, but we were now doing this better. Sometimes I had discovered solders not being properly briefed by their commanders. There had also been problems caused by willingness to base plans on second-hand information, without taking steps to validate the information. This was a particular problem when our troops had taken over positions from other contingents. Companies and their platoons had occasionally allowed things to be done less well than they should – particularly when our troops spent long periods in contact with the soldiers of the factions or other UNPROFOR contingents who had a different approach to soldiering. Examples included platoon outposts where sentries had not been properly posted, or where the defences were less good than they should be.

Some of these problems were due to a few commanders letting their standards slip. More often than not, mistakes and errors were caused by commanders failing to properly assess or analyse the situation they found themselves in or failing to notice that the situation had changed significantly since the original plan had been formulated. I too had sometimes been guilty of this particular error.

We had made some other mistakes. With this number of people living in very crowded conditions, there was potential for all sorts of health problems. We had covered this during training, but in mid-November one of the companies had fifty men go down with an intense, but thankfully short, bout of food poisoning. This was traced to the company kitchen and the mistake was never repeated.

We also suffered an initial surge of injuries caused by over-enthusiasm exhibited while carrying out vehicle and equipment maintenance. Vehicle maintenance in barracks in Paderborn was hard, labour-intensive work – for example, changing Warrior track (known universally as 'track bashing') involved manipulating the two-ton track in chunks of six links, each of them a two-man lift. In snow and ice this could be very difficult. It did not take us long to learn that tasks that would be done by two men on the tank park in Germany become four-man jobs in the snow, ice and gloom of the Bosnian winter.

Despite these teething problems, our fortnightly rotation of the three company groups between Vitez, Kiseljak and Mount Igman meant that all the battalion was now very experienced in operating in winter mountains, across confrontation lines and in the complex urban environment of Sarajevo. We had met and liaised with all three factions, had got used to operating in a multinational environment and had tested our language, liaison and negotiation skills. All three companies had also managed to spend some time firing on improvised ranges, so we had confidence that we could still use all our weapons effectively in the freezing and mountainous conditions. We now understood how our different types of vehicles performed on snow- and ice-covered mountain roads. We knew how to maintain our operational effectiveness in heavy falling snow, deep frosts and unexpected thaws.

This period of grappling with the intricacies of multinational command, frustrating as it was for Battlegroup HQ, had provided excellent 'in-theatre training'. At battlegroup level, we had now mastered the problems of communicating, using the command net, or whatever other means was available. Both Battlegroup Forward HQ and Main were working well and had shown themselves capable of operating for long periods without me. The companies, squadron, platoons and troops had performed well. All had problems but had overcome them.

Perhaps best of all, we had proven to ourselves that we could all 'hack it' in Bosnia, in an environment that was the real thing – much more complex and demanding than the simulations we had constructed at Sennelager. This gave everyone great confidence, which reinforced the identity and cohesion of all the teams, from vehicle crew through platoon and company to the battalion as a whole. Writing to Liz at the end of November I told her:

> There is a real sense of purpose. There are few of the corrosive and entangling distractions of peacetime soldiering in a garrison town. We are achieving more every day than we did in weeks of routine soldiering in Germany. Paderborn itself seems a million light years away – 'another country'. People are prepared to accept and assume responsibility, and willing to work till they drop. Commanders are forced to command, in all senses of the word. There is tremendous scope for initiative at every level and many are really thriving on the challenge.
>
> I am!

CHAPTER FOUR

'Burning Sky'

The battlegroup had moved into a winter rhythm, adapting ourselves and our operations to the environment. People had worked out what clothes they needed to wear in the different types of winter weather, and commanders and drivers had learned how to tackle the treacherous snow- and ice-covered mountain roads and tracks.

Vehicles now had thick patinas of mud and dust over the camouflage paint, which in Paderborn had looked so fresh and new. This dull brown layer, frosted with dirty ice, contrasted vividly with the deliciously crisp white back-drop of the mountains. It was impossible to keep the vehicles clean, but crews religiously removed the mud and dust from the large yellow radio call signs. We got used to the variable colours and textures of winter. Snow fell either as soft, puffy giant snowflakes that descended slowly, or as sharp pellets driven on piercing horizontal winds. After it had stopped falling there were layers of frozen and remelted snow draped onto the buildings and trees and huge dirty piles of ice on the sides of the roads and tracks.

We also became conditioned to the sights of Sarajevo, Igman and central Bosnia. Terrible as the destruction wrought in the suburbs of Sarajevo was, we could rationalise the damaged buildings as the inevitable result of the use of modern weapons. More difficult to accept were the empty, destroyed villages of central Bosnia, silent witnesses to ethnic cleansing. The visual impact of large villages and small towns in which every single building had been destroyed was considerable, but worse was the psychological impact. What terrible stories could these sad places tell?

Answers came from our interpreters' stories of the civil war. 'Soft' ethnic cleansing was when the occupants were told to leave, whilst 'hard' ethnic cleansing was where outright slaughter and butchery had begun straight away. How could we ever know all the multiple personal tragedies that had resulted from neighbour falling upon neighbour or from threatened or actual atrocities conducted by one of the factions? What terrible Pandora's Boxes had been opened? It was as if the savagery and primitive slaughter of medieval wars had been transported through some hole in time to the present day.

There were many of these empty, despoiled communities in western Bosnia, where the area of our operations was enlarging. Brigadier Dannatt, now commanding UNPROFOR's Sector Southwest, had established a tentative relationship with the HVO forces there. He persuaded the Bosnian Croat military to accept some British patrols, albeit with HVO escorts. National governments tied most of the UN troops in Sector Southwest to the specific areas in which they were operating. The Sector's British battalion, 1 RRF, could free up a couple of platoons to begin patrolling towards Mrkonjić Grad and Šipovo. This was insufficient to cover the vast expanse of newly liberated territory. Could I release patrols from B Squadron Light Dragoons help by beginning patrolling in the south of this area?

Brigadier Dannatt and I both approached the MNB commander for permission to do this, floating the idea through several levels of his staff. Although the simplest and most effective arrangement would have been for the squadron to work direct to HQ Sector Southwest for these operations, it became clear that this would offend the sensibilities of some in the MNB. We therefore devised a form of words stating that the MNB would conduct the operation using up to two troops of Task Force Alpha's recce squadron in a distinct MNB area of operations. We then conducted the patrols as we originally intended, but briefed up the MNB HQ as if it was their operation.

Continuing the Crimean War sequence of names we designated this as Operation INKERMAN. No intelligence was available to us concerning the forces operating in the area, and the recce troops explored a bare upland plateau completely devoid of civilians and firmly controlled by HVO units, many of which appeared to be parts of the Croatian Army proper. B Squadron's patrols were long, extremely cold and closely monitored by the HVO. The squadron identified barracks, factories and other large complexes that might make suitable British bases in the future.

These forays by B Squadron and 1 RRF were the only UN presence in the whole of western Bosnia, apart from Bihać. Here, in the far west of the country, there had been an 'enclave' of Bosnians who had spent most of the war surrounded and besieged by various Serb armies. In September, the ABiH 5 Corps had broken out and linked up with HVO forces pushing towards Banja Luka. The corps commander, General Dudakovic, a fiery leader, seemed contemptuous of the UNPROFOR battalion of Bangladeshi troops in the enclave. At the end of November a large party of ABiH troops raided the UN base at Velika Kladuša. They used threats and intimidation to overcome the Bangladeshis, swarmed all over the camp, brought up trucks and removed all the weapons and most of the supplies, leaving the UN soldiers with little more than the uniforms they stood up in.

Both General Smith and Brigadier Dannatt were furious. Here was a return to the 'bad old days' when UNPROFOR had been robbed, threatened and humiliated by local warlords. Brigadier Dannatt flew to Bihać to give Dudakovic a forcible dressing down and General Smith summoned the Bosnian deputy prime minister, telling him that despite Dudakovic's protestations of innocence, there was no doubt that the raid had been organised by 5 Corps. Events like this were deplorable in their own right, Smith continued, but especially now, because they might deter the Americans and NATO from coming to Bosnia to implement the peace. To make sure that such events did not happen again, extra British troops would be sent to the area and the British armoured infantry battalion was preparing to move to Bihać. At this the minister visibly trembled.

We were ordered to put an armoured infantry company on short notice to reinforce Bihać. A flurry of preparation took place as commanders and soldiers were briefed and vehicles and equipment prepared. I had been travelling from Vitez to Bugojno to visit B Squadron at the time, so all the work was co-ordinated by Chris Booth. By the time he briefed me over the satellite phone at B Squadron, the operation was cancelled. General Smith was satisfied that he had got the message across. Bihać would be reinforced by Fusiliers from Bugojno.

Chris suggested that the company should not be stood down until the end of the day. This would thoroughly test our mechanisms for preparing for operations at short notice. This was an excellent idea to which I readily assented – after all we were part of the *Rapid* Reaction Force. By the time I returned to Vitez, Chris had terminated the exercise and he, the Battlegroup HQ officers and the company commander were ready to debrief me on the lessons learned.

Planning for NATO Operations

Operations were being conducted against the background of the US-led negotiations at Wright-Patterson Air Force Base near Dayton, Ohio. We were pleased when the media reported progress, and were worried and frustrated when reports suggested difficulties. Hard information on the subjects being discussed at Dayton was almost completely absent. Knowing that the Americans were determined to forge a deal, I was not surprised – indeed, a media blackout was a tactic I would have used, had I been running the talks.

Nevertheless, we began to pick up several 'combat indicators' of the military arrangements under discussion. We learned that UNPROFOR was engaged in a major effort to map the front line between the Federation and VRS. A party of US officers twice flew into Kiseljak in conditions of great secrecy to brief senior representatives of the three faction armies. We had no idea of what had been said, but the visit had been impossible to conceal from our platoon guarding the UN headquarters.

We were therefore delighted when Captain Tony Allport announced to an evening meeting on Mount Igman that an agreement had been signed. Maybe it was Simon Dring's presence that spurred him to sound more serious than usual, but he began the briefing by announcing: 'Gentlemen, we have peace in our time'.

Later, I reminded him that using Neville Chamberlain's words when he arrived back from signing away Czechoslovakia to Hitler was perhaps not the best way to introduce the subject. This agreement would be the last chance for Bosnia to end its bitter and terrible war. The patience of both NATO and the wider international community was finite and implementation of the agreement would be a significant challenge for us, and a huge step into the unknown.

The first information to reach us as to how the agreement would be implemented reached us few days later. We read an interview in a Sarajevo newspaper with Mr Muratović, the Bosnian Government minister for cooperation
with the UN – the same minister who had earlier been warned about the Bihać
incident. He stated that the peace agreement would be carried out in three
stages, the first of which would be creation of a zone of separation between
the two sides, which would be controlled by NATO. In the second phase, territory would be transferred between the Federation and Republika Srpska, the
operation supervised by NATO. The third phase would culminate in the withdrawal of all the faction armies to barracks. This report could not be confirmed
by either UN or British chains of command. It and visits by American officers
to Kiseljak became the subjects of much speculation.

Speculation ended when a few days later Brigadier Dannatt summoned his
principal staff officers and all the British commanding officers to Gornji Vakuf.
He explained what he knew of the situation, the military requirements of the
Dayton Agreement and the NATO and British plans, stated his intentions and
invited his commanders and principal staff officers to contribute.

The report in the Bosnian press ten days earlier had been completely accurate.
Bosnia would be a single state, divided into two 'entities': the Muslim-Croat
Federation and Republika Srpska. There was a new constitution for Bosnia,
with a central legislature and a collective presidency. Beneath this superstruc-
ture of central government, many powers would remain with the entities,
including control of armies and police. Fifty-one per cent of Bosnia would
be allocated to the Federation, the reminder to Republika Srpska. Elections
were to be held by September 1996. Human rights were to be guaranteed and
all Bosnians were to be able to move freely throughout the country. Refugees
were to have the right to return to their original homes. All these political,
civil and economic measures were to be 'facilitated' by the international community's High Representative in Bosnia.

We were most interested in the military annex of the agreement. This
formalised the current cease-fire. NATO would deploy an Implementation
Force (IFOR) to enforce the cease-fire and faction military withdrawal from
the front line. We were given a schematic map showing the agreed cease-fire
line (ACFL) that both sides had endorsed at Dayton. There was also an agreed
'inter-entity boundary line' (IEBL) which was the final boundary between
the two entities. In many places the IEBL and ACFL were the same; in others
they diverged. In these places, territory would have to be transferred from the
Republika Srpska to the Federation or vice versa. The suburbs of Sarajevo,
currently held by the Bosnian Serbs, would be transferred to the Federation.
A large area of western Bosnia would be ceded from the Bosnian Croats to the
Bosnian Serbs. This lay in the centre of what we knew would be the British
area of responsibility.

History was littered with examples of peace treaties that had foundered
or failed on the issue of transfer of territory. Would the two factions actually
vacate the areas? How would the civilians who lived there react? What sort
of reception would NATO receive from the civilians and military? Would we

he obstructed, harassed, attacked, or met with the sort of obfuscation and deviousness to which the UN had so often been treated?

We were given a summary of the General Framework Agreement for Peace, as the Dayton Agreement was known. Later the abbreviation GFAP would be used, but throughout the tour everyone (including the factions) called it simply 'the Dayton Agreement'. I noted the key timelines were as follows:

> D Day was the transition of authority from UNPROFOR to the NATO IFOR. The cease-fire was to continue.
>
> By D+30 the faction forces had to have separated, withdrawing two kilometres on each side of the cease-fire line. All minefields were to be cleared and all foreign forces were to have left Bosnia. This measure was aimed at the Islamic mujahideen fighters who supported the ABiH, elements of the Croat Army masquerading as HVO and any forces from Serbia proper that might be inside Republika Srpska.
>
> By D+45 all faction forces were to have withdrawn from any territory to be transferred to another entity, the area to be controlled by IFOR.
>
> From D+90 faction forces were allowed to reoccupy those areas transferred to their control.
>
> By D+120 all faction armed forces were to be cantoned in barracks.

If these requirements were complied with the country would become a demilitarised protectorate of NATO. There were a host of other measures and details, which we summarised for dissemination to all commanders. This can be found at the end of this chapter.

IFOR had greater powers than UNPROFOR, including unlimited freedom of movement, and control over faction military movement. IFOR was 'entitled to use military force to ensure compliance'. It had 'the right to compel the movement, withdrawal or relocation of forces'. The IFOR commander had authority to protect IFOR and implement the peace, using 'authority without interference or permission from any party, to do all that the commander judges necessary and proper, including the use of military force'. New rules of engagement would come into force on D Day. In UNPROFOR we were allowed to use force to defend ourselves. This would still apply, but our powers as part of NATO would also allow us to use force much more proactively. The rules for this were summarised in an *aide-mémoire* issued to all commanders:

> Self Defence. You have the right to use necessary minimum force, including deadly force, employing authorised weapons to defend yourself from hostile acts and hostile intent.
>
> Use of Force for Other Purposes. Necessary minimum force is authorised to:
>> a. Defend friendly forces, persons with designated special status and property with designated special status against hostile acts or hostile intent;
>> b. Defend against deliberate military or paramilitary intrusion into designated restricted areas;

    c. Defend against attempts by hostile forces/belligerents to prevent you from
       carrying out your duties;

    d. Disarm individuals;

    e. Perform pre-emptive military operations to enforce compliance with the
       relevant provisions of the Peace Agreement.

IFOR's land component would be the Allied Command Europe Rapid Reaction Corps (the ARRC), augmented by French and US led multinational divisions and a Russian brigade. Up to fifteen thousand of the UNPROFOR troops would transfer to NATO, including the British and French contingents. The ARRC campaign plan identified the End State to be achieved:

> Within twelve months to have achieved the continuing cessation of hostilities, the withdrawal of all foreign forces as defined in the Peace Agreement and the successful separation of the armed elements of the entities along agreed internal lines, to have handed over to an appropriate structure to continue the implementation of the Peace Agreement and to have completed the withdrawal of ARRC forces from Bosnia.

Britain would lead Multinational Division Southwest, responsible for the western half of Bosnia. Almost all the British forces including ourselves were currently operating well to the south and east of this area. Western Bosnia had seen very little of the UN, which had been almost completely excluded by the factions. Most of the territory apart from the isolated Muslim enclave of Bihać had been under Bosnian Serb control since the outbreak of the war. The autumn Federation offensives had forced the Bosnian Serbs out of a huge swathe of territory, most of which had been recaptured by the HVO. In the north of the area, 5 Corps ABiH had broken out of the Bihać Pocket. Their charismatic commander General Dudakovic was intensely ambitious and had declared that he saw the cease-fire as an operational pause that would allow him to prepare another offensive to recapture Prijedor. The recent attack on the Bangladeshis at Velika Kladuša showed that he was capable of orchestrating attacks against the UN.

    There was a party of British Joint Commission Observers (JCOs) in Bihać. JCOs were highly trained volunteers. Operating in small patrols, equipped with no more than Land Rovers, small arms and long-range communications, they acted as 'directed telescopes', sending accurate reports and assessments directly to the British commanders at Sarajevo and Gornji Vakuf. The Bihać JCOs had no access to the front line. A small team of UNMOs in Banja Luka was similarly constrained on the Bosnian Serb side.

    Between Bihać and central Bosnia lay land occupied by Bosnian Croat forces, much of which was to be transferred to Republika Srpska. The Bosnian Serb population had fled and soldiers and civilians from Croatia and Croat parts of Bosnia were busy looting and burning. With the grudging agreement of the HVO, 1 RRF was patrolling towards Mrkonjić Grad, but not in any strength. As far as we could see, the truce appeared to be holding and 1 RRF was conducting regional joint commissions where Federation commanders met their Bosnian Serb opposite numbers.

Dannatt then went on to describe NATO and British plans. I noted the following:

US intend NATO operation is time-limited to one year. No US plans to put country back on its feet, but to deal with military matters and walk away.

Initially the only NATO forces will be those that transfer from UNPROFOR. Other UN troops withdraw from Bosnia.

3 (UK) Division to be framework of British-led Multinational Division Southwest – MND(SW). Could include Italian Garibaldi Brigade? Canadian Brigade HQ? Islamic battalion (Malaysian or Pakistani?).

4 Armoured Brigade to comprise 2 LI, 1 RRF, QRH (tanks!) Light Dragoon squadrons, Dutch battlegroup, light gun batteries.

From Germany: artillery – 26 Field Regiment, with new AS 90 guns. 32 Armoured Engineer Regiment will absorb existing armoured engineer troop and provide close support. 38 Regiment, in theatre already, will become divisional general support.

Combat Service Support – 2 Armoured Field Ambulance, brigade logistic squadron, forward repair group.

Brigade mission is not yet known.

Timings. Transfer of Authority UN to NATO is D Day. Not before 12 Dec.

Initial Operations – First 30 days 4 Armoured Brigade will cover whole Division area. Need to make early progress and show some substantive achievements as early as possible. Early problem will be pulling both sides apart.

Planning Assumption Establish Zone of Separation in first thirty days.

Brigade Layout – 1 RRF east, 2 LI in northwest Bosnia and Bihać.

Uncouple from MNB – 2 LI will probably have to stay until D Day. Once withdrawn, should have four days to regroup and refurbish.

Communications – Ptarmigan trunk system not before D+30. Until then work on what we have got.

Logistics – assume UN logistic system will collapse. Maximum initiative and independence for first thirty days until UK system is complete.

How do we get there from here? Intend to develop company bases in Šipovo and Mrkonjić Grad for 1 RRF. Then find bases for 2 LI somewhere.

During the first thirty days we would see no reinforcements other than some more JCO teams. The brigade would need to set the tone straight away. On D Day it would be important to demonstrate the step change from UN to NATO and to leave the factions in no doubt of our resolve. The brigade was to do this throughout western Bosnia by rapidly redeploying forces to conduct simultaneous operations throughout the brigade area. We would do everything we could to make our forces appear larger than they actually were.

Sooner or later we would be faced with military non-compliance. We would expose it, attributing blame if necessary. Initially we would use negotiation, but if this did not work we would have to use physical force to compel the faction military. If so, we would need to regroup to concentrate the greatest possible force on the problem. This would maximise the impact on the factions and minimise the number of casualties we might incur.

Finally, the NATO approach to liaison with the factions would be more structured than the UN's had been. IFOR division commanders would liaise with faction corps commanders, Brigadier Dannatt would liaise with corps chiefs of staff, battlegroup commanders would work to the faction divisional commanders and company commanders to faction brigade commanders. This would be a distinct improvement on the multiple methods of liaison used by the UN and should reduce misunderstandings and achieve consistency on the lines being taken throughout the chain of command.

During training we had frequently practised the mechanics of battle procedure: receiving brigade orders, developing a battlegroup plan and giving our own orders to the battlegroup's commanders. Every time we had done this we either had the battlegroup concentrated in a small area able to prepare for operations without distraction, or were able to receive and disseminate quick orders by radio. These were 'textbook' scenarios that had been used at Sandhurst and Warminster when battle procedure had been taught.

But we were now well outside the textbook scenario, for we were spread out over a huge area, conducting operations for the Multinational Brigade, and our headquarters was split. We would have to modify our approach. I would lead our planning effort, but since the Forward HQ was fully occupied running the forward companies, I would use the Main HQ at Vitez to lead preparation for IFOR. This would be overseen by Chris Booth and Mark Goldsack, the adjutant, who would act as a second operations officer.

We began mission analysis and the estimate process straight away. I complemented this with planning meetings with as many of my command team as I could gather around me. The first of these gathered the key officers at Vitez, to brief them on the information given me by Brigadier Dannatt. Returning to Igman, I briefed the team there. This meant that they all shared my understanding of what might be required of us. That week I did my own mission analysis and, together with Ross Gillanders and Tony Allport, began an estimate. Concurrently, Chris Booth was leading a major planning effort at Vitez.

Leaving Ross in charge on Igman the next Saturday, I led a battlegroup planning meeting at Vitez. My office was full of as many Battlegroup HQ officers as I could assemble, all the company commanders and LOs. I led them through the mission analysis and estimate, and was briefed by Chris and the Vitez team on their emerging conclusions. I was reassured that their thinking had evolved along similar lines to mine. I posed several 'what if' questions that explored how we might react to various problems, including non-cooperation or military attacks by the factions. This prepared me for the next day's planning meeting at 4 Armoured Brigade, where I took more notes:

Situation. Faction attitudes vary enormously along the front line. Area of Transfer to be handed over to Serbs by Croats now nicknamed 'The Anvil'. HVO are starting to loot factories. Croat and Muslim refugees leaving. HVO have put military bridges over several gaps blown by retreating VRS – will they remove them? Bihać now being run by RRF and JCOs. 5 Corps ABiH unused to effective UN troops.

UNPROFOR. Logistics and infrastructure collapsing.

NATO. Operation names. NATO: Operation JOINT ENDEAVOUR. UK: Operation RESOLUTE. Strong US leads on civil military cooperation, media and psychological operations. US specialist units at disposal of division.

MND(SW) Plan. Divisional composition still unknown. Canadian offer of a brigade HQ and recce squadron, but no battlegroup! Czech battalion? Islamic battalion? Therefore divisional deployment impossible to predict.

4 Armoured Brigade. Will only plan first few days in detail.

1 RRF to be responsible for east part of area as far west as west side of Anvil.

2 LI to go west. Responsible for Prijedor, Sanski Most, Bihać and all area west of Anvil. Initially with company, then joined by battery.

B Squadron LD. To work initially under direct brigade command and to advance north into Republika Srpska towards Banja Luka. Accompanied by a 2 LI Warrior platoon.

Handling Factions. Use smoke and mirrors to demonstrate capability. If they know what we are doing and what we are capable of there will be less inclination to resist, or engage in non-compliance. Allow time for message to get down chain of command. Do not surprise. Division will conduct military commission with all three faction corps commanders shortly after D Day.

Use of Force. Rules of engagement not yet received. Where possible, achieve results without opening fire.

Zone of Separation. Start by creating it where it's easiest.

Other Issues. (Less discussion, more direction than previous meeting.) R&R leave continues. US are producing authoritative 1:50,000 Dayton maps showing lines on ground. Not known when these will arrive.

Battle Procedure. Thin out from MNB to minimum safe level before D Day.

Dissemination. Consider these meeting as warning order, disseminate selectively.

Media guidelines should be disseminated to all soldiers.

This was in complete accordance with the conclusions of our planning work. We could now refine 2LI's plan and go on to consider various problems and scenarios using map exercises. Again I returned to Vitez to update the planning team. Chris was to carry on with planning and getting reconnaissance and advance parties out. I returned to Igman, updating people there and at Kiseljak who missed the planning activity at Vitez. We had begun battle procedure, warning orders and logistic preparations – although not in a way envisaged by the textbooks.

Over the next two weeks the plan was refined. I spent some time talking the concept through with battlegroup HQ officers, liaison officers, company commanders and captains. I covered the requirements of Dayton, our mission analysis, estimate and the way I saw operations developing.

A formal brigade warning order confirmed that the transfer of authority from UNPROFOR to IFOR would be at 1200 hours on D Day, which we would call H Hour. Until that time we would still be operating under the UN mandate and rules of engagement. Our mission would be to conduct peace implementation by deploying to Sanski Most and then opening and taking control of a crossing point on the main road crossing the front line between Sanski Most and Prijedor by 1600 hours on the day after D Day (known as D+1). Other tasks included providing a company as brigade reserve to be based at Mrkonjić Grad, and leaving C Company under French command on Mount Igman. Neither of these companies were likely to be released back to me for at least five days.

B Company based at Vitez could start moving before H Hour, so as to be positioned at the HVO checkpoint between Gornji Vakuf and Jajce that controlled British access to the Anvil. They would therefore be the company that would stage through Mrkonjić Grad to move onward to Sanski Most. A Company were based at Kiseljak and could not leave the Multinational Brigade until H Hour, but should be able to get to Mrkonjić Grad before nightfall. The only assets I could guarantee being able to take to Sanski Most to open the crossing point were B Company, Battlegroup HQ, the recce platoon, the mortar platoon and our liaison officers.

A detailed battlegroup warning order was issued, assigning the tasks to each company, whom I directed to begin planning for their particular missions.

All the teaching of battle procedure lays great emphasis on the holding of properly stage-managed orders groups where the commander's intent is made crystal clear to his subordinates and the arrangements for the battle are imparted to all concerned. But the battlegroup was so busy and so dispersed in the two weeks leading up to D Day that only once were we able to have a formal battlegroup orders group. Even then several key players were unavoidably absent. We gathered in a cellar at the Kiseljak Brick Factory, only to be constantly interrupted by power cuts and an advance party of American JCOs straying into our meeting. It was just as well that by this time I was confident that we had a workable plan and that all my team were 'in my mind'.

Five days before D Day the brigade held a formal orders group in its new HQ at Šipovo. I sent Chris Booth and Mark Goldsack from Vitez. A new fall of snow had descended and the journey was time-consuming and hazardous. Mark Goldsack never made it to the orders group and was eventually rescued from his snow-bound Land Rover by a passing JCO and some REME troops. The brigade orders matched completely with our concept – a product of the parallel planning process we had initiated three weeks earlier.

The troops conducting reconnaissance and advance force operations in western Bosnia were severely constrained in the routes that they could use, and were often held up at ABiH or HVO checkpoints. The attitude to these checkpoints was about to change. The Dayton Agreement gave IFOR unlimited freedom of movement and we were going to make sure that we were not held up. Brigadier Dannatt had already given a number of TV interviews where he had unambiguously stated that he would not see his troops stopped at checkpoints after transfer of authority to NATO, and the same message had been passed to the faction corps commanders.

But we did not want to kill people unnecessarily. Bosnia was a country that had moved from a communist regime to civil war and the desire to control and monitor civilian movement seemed embedded into society. We decided to give any checkpoint five minutes' grace to let us through, allowing the sentry time to telephone his superior. If at the end of the five minutes the checkpoint was still denying us freedom of movement, we would move through, using whatever force was necessary. To make sure that we deployed on our NATO tasks as quickly as possible, all armoured columns were to be to be preceded by a liaison officer travelling ahead, who would warn the checkpoint that the main convoy was coming through.

The battlegroup took this one stage further by issuing all vehicles with a card stating in Serbo-Croat that the vehicle was to be allowed through all checkpoints or force would be used. Whatever happened we were not going to allow anyone to stop our armour moving through checkpoints.

Sarajevo Deteriorates

In his final directive, General Smith explained that NATO would be conducting a 'forward passage of lines' through the UN troops, who therefore had to 'hold the ring' and keep the cease-fire intact. This required the Multinational Brigade both to remain in place around Sarajevo and to act as UNPROFOR's theatre reserve.

Throughout the war, Bosnian Government forces had held most of Sarajevo city centre. But, with the exception of Mount Igman and Butmir, the suburbs had remained in Bosnian Serb hands throughout, as had the hills surrounding Sarajevo. The Dayton map showed that Sarajevo would become united under Bosnian Government control and that the Serb-held suburbs and hills would all be transferred to the Federation. This astonished everyone – including the UN forces in Sarajevo. The Bosnian Muslims were delighted, but the Sarajevo Serbs were appalled. As far as I could see none of the inhabitants of the 'Serb suburbs' had ever seriously considered that the Pale regime might abandon them. They were now a population in a state of mental and physical shock. Many of them were desperate – some VRS checkpoint guards were in tears when the subject was mentioned. I described the situation in a letter home:

> The people living in the Serb suburbs of Sarajevo are at their wit's end. They are in terrible fear of the Muslims, who they believe want to kill them, but are very reluctant to leave their homes – especially as they have managed to hold on to these districts throughout the war. All the other areas where Bosnian Serb territory is being ceded have few, if any, civilian inhabitants. The transfer of the densely populated Serb suburbs of Sarajevo could be the first stumbling blocks on the road to peace. Whatever happens, it's going to be desperately sad. The

Serb people in the area are often very pro-British and friendly to us, especially the children. I can see no happy ending.

In the run-up to NATO operations would the Bosnian Serbs attempt to thwart the transfer of the suburbs? Might they dig in, refusing to leave, and invite NATO to evict them? Might they decide to flee and put the suburbs to the torch? Would they withdraw consent from the UN or attempt to harass our operations? Might their army attempt to sabotage the cease-fire?

The French-led Sector Sarajevo rightly saw this as a serious potential problem. The French had nominated a division HQ, then in metropolitan France, to run the south-east sector of the NATO operation and the French elements of the Multinational Brigade had been warned that they would become the nucleus of a French brigade after D Day. On Igman, the Forward HQ of the Multinational Brigade began planning Operation HORUS. This aimed to prevent the Serb sectors of Sarajevo being put to the torch by their citizens or the VRS as part of a 'scorched earth' policy. They wanted to use their two task forces – the Foreign Legion and ourselves – to secure the civil infrastructure of the Serb suburbs. The objectives were described as 'key points', and included water-pumping stations, electricity substations and the bridges that carried main roads across rivers.

Acting in the early hours of the morning Task Force Alpha could have easily seized all these places in one simultaneous strike operation. Unfortunately this was not the concept chosen by the Multinational Brigade. Their plan insisted on mounting the operation in daylight. Rather than tackling the targets *simultaneously*, they wanted to operate *sequentially*, seizing one target after another. Their plan required an exceedingly complicated series of reliefs in place on key points, governed by a rigid timetable. If it had gone ahead, one of our companies would have moved no fewer than five times, being relieved in place twice at the same target. We assessed that this approach meant that surprise would soon be lost, resulting in an ever-increasing chance of opposition, whether armed action from the VRS or resistance by civilians.

I knew that with our weapons, equipment, rules of engagement and high standard of training we could defend ourselves against any VRS attacks. I was much less happy about dealing with any civilians attempting to oppose us – perhaps by blocking roads, lying down in front of us or chaining themselves to the gates and wire fences of the pumping stations. The British rules of engagement categorically forbade the use of force against unarmed civilians who were obstructing our movements or denying us access to installations. They did not allow attacks on the faction armed forces except in self-defence or in support of a UN Security Council Resolution – and none existed to cover this operation. Some of the sites had VRS troops guarding them. We could *ask* them to leave but could not use force to compel them to hand over their positions to the UN.

I knew that the French took a different attitude to these things than we did, for example deploying land mines to protect their positions, despite the UNPROFOR rules that forbade this. But it was quite clear that the operation was outside the rules of engagement for British forces. Although we could employ our weapons to defend ourselves or save lives, we were not allowed to use lethal force to defend or seize property. If the plan were for a simultaneous strike in the small hours of the morning, it could have been carried out so quickly as to pre-empt any military or civilian reaction. But the Multinational Brigade HQ's plan seemed so complex, slow, ponderous and inflexible that it positively invited the VRS and Bosnian Serb civilians to oppose it.

I put my concerns to the officer leading the planning, the Multinational Brigade's new British chief of staff – a colonel who had recently arrived in Bosnia. The original batch of British staff officers who had been with the Multinational Brigade since May had returned home and had been replaced by newcomers. Gone was Hamish Fletcher with his dry humour, lightness of touch, understanding of the complexities of multinational operations, and, most of important of all, his rapport with the brigade's commander. His successor was a different character. We did not see eye to eye about this operation. No, he politely but forcefully told me, he did not agree either with my analysis of the weaknesses of the plan or with my concerns about rules of engagement. It was about time, he told me, that people started doing as they were told, instead of continually arguing about orders.

In his capacity as the commander of all British forces in Bosnia, Brigadier Dannatt had to refer to the Joint Headquarters at Wilton any plan involving British troops in 'operations of a novel, contentious or risky nature'. Without positive clearance from him, I would have to refuse to allow the battlegroup to participate in Operation HORUS. I did not want to do this if I could possibly avoid it, for playing my UK 'national red card' would probably destroy our working relationship with the Multinational Brigade, but I was not going to commit the British troops under my command to an operation that my British superiors would not have supported.

After the inevitable communications difficulties and delays I managed to explain this to James Everard, the UK brigade chief of staff, on the MENTOR phone. James confirmed that I was right to have expressed my concern on the issue. Brigadier Dannatt would get the new Multinational Brigade chief of staff to Gornji Vakuf to explain our rules of engagement to him.

Advance Force Operations

Over the crackling and tenuous satellite telephone link James changed the subject. Brigadier Dannatt had persuaded the HVO commander in Mrkonjić Grad to sign an agreement giving us access to potential bases in this area. Time was short and we needed to get our people into Mrkonjić Grad tomorrow, to prepare an abandoned bus depot for use as our forward logistic echelon. At the same time the brigade signal squadron would need protection as it set up the new HQ in a hotel in Šipovo. Could we deploy an advance force to protect the HQ of 4 Armoured Brigade as it set up, and to develop the looted bus depot into a base?

I thought for a moment. Clearly, here was a task that would help get the British NATO operations off on the right foot. Clearly also, the HQ of the Multinational Brigade, ever more concerned about Sarajevo and Operation HORUS, would be unsympathetic to any formal request to release parts of the battalion back to national command.

'In theory', I replied, 'this is well within Op INKERMAN, albeit conducted with infantry platoons rather than recce troops. However, if I ask the MNB chief of staff, there is little chance that he'll agree. Our forces at Vitez are at six hours' notice for MNB operations. Since troops in Šipovo and Mrkonjić Grad can, in theory, get back to Vitez in six hours, the Multinational Brigade doesn't need to be consulted.'

I called Vitez and spoke to Chris Booth, Mark Goldsack and Dave Wroe. We quickly discussed the options. The evolving plan for our NATO operations meant that A Company would move from Kiseljak to become the brigade and divisional reserve based initially in Mrkonjić Grad, while B Company would leave Vitez to lead the battlegroup move. B Company should therefore provide the platoon for Šipovo and A Company the platoon for Mrkonjić Grad.

I had taken a calculated risk by neither seeking the Multinational Brigade's consent nor informing them of the operation. The risk was justified, but in order to reduce the chances of the secret being disclosed, we christened the operation 'Operation INKERMAN Part 2'.

Our advanced forces deployed into western Bosnia, moving through deep snow. David Livingston's platoon guarded a devastated hotel in Šipovo that the brigade signal squadron began to develop into the new Brigade Headquarters. Everything that could be moved had already been looted and fittings had been ripped out, including every single component of the hotel kitchen. As they guarded the hotel, soldiers saw house after house burning, all of them put to the torch by Bosnian Croats.

The efforts to turn the derelict bus depot into a usable base were masterminded by Captain Martin Bellamy and the regimental quartermaster serjeant, WO2 Wilson. They found the base littered with blood, animal carcasses and human excreta. It was so badly damaged by artillery fire that it was far from certain that a habitable base could be created there. The location was a long way from the rest of the battalion, accessible only by roads made dangerous by snow and ice, and communications were extremely difficult. Bellamy and Wilson oversaw the cleaning up of the depot and its preparation for occupation by the rest of the battlegroup.

At the same time we were reconfiguring our logistics. For all we knew, we would be fighting to enforce the peace from the outset of NATO operations and we could not afford to wait for ammunition and other supplies to be brought up from Vitez. We moved as many supplies to Mrkonjić Grad as we could, whilst simultaneously ensuring that all vehicles were as fully stocked as possible. In the cramped muddy bases at Vitez and Mrkonjić Grad the soldiers of Echelon worked long and hard to organise our supplies.

Meanwhile permission to conduct a battlegroup reconnaissance had been negotiated with both the HVO and ABiH. Chris Booth led a recce party out on a long journey through the Anvil and on to Bihać, before looping back through Sanski Most and Klju, giving vivid impressions of the area that was being variously christened 'the Wild West' or 'the Badlands'. Accompanied for part of their journey by a BBC camera crew, they were given an escort by HVO military police. The party saw at first hand that the Bosnian Croats were systematically looting any industrial, commercial or agricultural equipment from the area.

North of Bihać they found the UN base at Cazin to be a huge complex capable of accommodating the entire battlegroup, but far away from the front line. Guarded by a small party of Fusileers, the camp contained a helpful patrol of JCOs that lost no time in showing Chris the area. The ABiH already occupied most of the buildings that would make good bases and Chris had great difficulty in finding buildings we could use.The return journey back through the Anvil was illuminated by light from houses being burned by the Bosnian Croats, another demonstration of malice against the Bosnian Serbs who would eventually reoccupy the area. Captain Sean Harris was left behind in Bihać commanding a small advance party.

Simultaneously the signal platoon began to extend our VHF rebroadcast net all the way to Sanski Most. As a first stage a rebroadcast station was established on a hill above Gornji Vakuf. The platoon's efforts to establish further rebroadcast stations were later described in the *Silver Bugle*:

> WO2 Thirlwell departed with Serjeant Hodgson and a crew to provide communications from Sanski Most to the rebro network, which now stretched to Gornji Vakuf. The journey proved to be quite eventful for the party of an FV432 and two Land Rovers. The 432 broke down after ten kilometres and was replaced by a Spartan. One of the Land Rovers broke down while resupplying Corporal Belshaw's rebro at Gornji Vakuf and had to be abandoned there. The Spartan developed a coolant leak on the route to the final destination. The remaining Land Rover broke down halfway up a mountain, and had to be towed by the Spartan as far as it could.
>
> Eventually heavy snow made the journey impossible to complete so the intrepid signallers bedded down for the night. Unfortunately snow continued to fall, cutting off the crews. The signallers were finally rescued by Serjeant Rutherford and his boys in the recce platoon, who threw a track on arrival, which the signal platoon lads put back on. They decided to stay on the mountain for a further night; the next morning found their journey back to civilisation delayed after Serjeant Rutherford's Scimitar ran out of petrol. Once again the recce platoon were saved by the signal platoon. Who rescued whom, you may ask.

Whilst deploying and administering this chain of rebroadcast stations, WO2 Thirlwell, the platoon second-in-command, had so many adventures and narrow escapes that people compared him to Harrison Ford in the *Indiana Jones* films. He was quickly christened 'Raider of the Lost Rebro' or 'Harrison Rebro'.

The Final Days of UNPROFOR

House-burning had now begun around Sarajevo, as Bosnian Serb families started to leave the area. Groups of angry-looking youths would gather on road junctions in the depressing housing estates of Hadžići during the dark winter afternoons. Verbal abuse and the occasional rock would be directed at passing UN vehicles. With our experience of long hot summers of rioting on the streets of Belfast this seemed like small beer, but we decided to steer clear of any confrontation with angry civilians.

Sector Sarajevo and the Multinational Brigade commander became more and more focused on the Sarajevo suburbs. General Bachelet, the French Sector commander, emotionally told the media that the Bosnian Serb civilians should not be abandoned to their fate. Paris was unhappy with this and Bachelet was called back to France 'for consultation'. He did not return to Bosnia.

NATO advance parties began to arrive and ARRC staff officers started to take over Kiseljak Hotel from UNPROFOR. Extra British and American specialist troops reinforced the JCOs, the only NATO combat troops to arrive before D Day.

The ARRC and UNPROFOR HQ ordered that the Anglo-American JCO headquarters should be set up in the Kiseljak Brick Factory. Although this had the potential to overwhelm the base's limited infrastructure, the British JCOs brought with them their own logistic support, including an excellent quartermaster and more cooks. They also had a section of Gurkha soldiers to help guard the camp and willingly pitched in to help with its administration. A headquarters brimming with computers and high-tech communications equipment was quickly constructed in some cellars – christened 'the Batcave' by 2 LI. A communication detachment with Ptarmigan arrived and plugged our company into the system, vastly improving our ability to communicate with Kiseljak. Best of all, the JCOs' quartermaster had his own budget and was able to spend money on improving the base in ways that had been denied to us. Within a few days of their arrival, the JCOs and A Company were getting on famously and making the best of a very Spartan base.

We kept the Multinational Brigade forward HQ well informed of the situation. The new chief of staff had looked into the issue himself and was satisfied, he told me. While this had been going on, the brigade commander had been at Mostar – presumably engaged in planning his IFOR operations. Five days before D Day he returned to Igman. Angrily proclaiming that no one had told him about the JCOs moving into Kiseljak, he descended on the base and inspected it. A British officer in the HQ had warned me that, for some reason, the brigade commander was very unhappy with the JCOs being in the base. Sensing trouble I made sure that I was at Kiseljack that day. Soubirou walked round the base, meeting French and British troops. He was polite and tight-lipped. Matters deteriorated when he demanded that the JCOs leave the base, The British JCO commander, a Green Jacket lieutenant colonel, patiently explained the situation but to no avail, and he and I were subjected to a loud harangue. This ended with the JCO commander being peremptorily ordered to leave the base, which he refused to do without orders from his commander – who was the ARRC Chief of Staff.

I was then taken to one side. 'You have been disloyal', the brigade commander told me. 'You have let me down. I have no confidence that you are loyal to me. This must not continue. I shall now go to the UN HQ and have this decision reversed.' The force of this chastising was greater than I had ever received from any British officer in my military career. I had no doubt that if I had been a French officer I would have been sacked on the spot.

Why had this happened? Was it because he wanted to establish French control over the Kiseljak base before transfer of authority to NATO? Or was it because of different British and French perceptions of the role of a chief of staff – who I had wrongly assumed was totally in his commander's mind?

As the general drove away in his jeep, Jan de Vos and the JCO commander emerged from the shadows. They regarded the whole scene as a huge joke, which immediately restored my morale. I was later told that the Multinational Brigade commander had failed to persuade UNPROFOR to reverse the decision, returning to his HQ on Igman, where there was, it was said, a frank exchange of views in the headquarters...

The JCOs remained in the base.

My morale further improved on our return to Igman when Ross Gillanders briefed me on a rugby match played in Sarajevo between UN troops and a Bosnian Muslim team from Zenica, a large industrial town in central Bosnia. Ross Gillanders led a contingent of British and French rugby enthusiasts in a small convoy of Land Rovers and VBLs to the stadium in Sarajevo to watch.

The match started promisingly enough. The first sign of trouble was the arrival of Kate Adie, the TV journalist. This caused much mirth and general hilarity, with the English speakers calling out her name and an outbreak of Mexican waves in the crowd. This, Ross said, was when things started to go wrong. Zenica took exception to one of the referee's decisions and walked off. It required no little cajoling to get them back onto the pitch. Zenica then engaged in a number of illegal substitutions of players; the game quickly degenerated into a shouting match and scuffles broke out. The event was abandoned. We were all amused, but once we had finished laughing, we began to wonder whether this was a bad omen for the impending implementation of the peace.

By now we had developed a taste for peculiar and unusual events. A new phrase was coined: 'Bosnia Bizarre'. Those with a natural ability to tell jokes were learning to recount their adventures in a way designed to raise the maximum number of laughs.

On the day before D Day, we painted out the small UN badges on our vehicles and removed the UN number plates, replacing them with standard British Army plates. 'IFOR' was stencilled in large white letters on the side of all our vehicles. We also painted on the silhouette of a small bipedal rodent, the Jerboa – the historic 'Desert Rat' badge of 4 Armoured Brigade, whom we would rejoin on D Day.

Extract From Letter to Liz, 17 December 1995

Life has had more than its share of frustrations – but I think I have been managing to rise above most of them.

Today, my morale was restored, as was my sense of humour and confidence. Firstly, I managed to have a face to face with Brigadier Dannatt and his staff. After the friction and temper tantrums of the Multinational Brigade, this was a breath of fresh air. The British Army may not be perfect, but it is a lot, lot better than some of the others here. I left in an optimistic mood, and was further cheered up by being able to get a helicopter flight from Brigade HQ to Mount Igman – thus saving myself an exhausting four-hour road journey.

We have just had a very successful visit by the Archbishop of Canterbury. The first we knew of the proposed visit was the arrival at Sevastopol Camp of someone claiming to be the British Ambassador. He was dressed in a shabby anorak – his appearance described by Captain Mark Mortimer as 'down-market trainspotter'. Mark was convinced that this was a British aid worker taking part in some elaborate practical joke. It was only when he checked the man's credentials and put in a confirmatory satellite telephone call to the British embassy in Sarajevo that he was convinced that it was not a joke.

Rex Sartain organised the visit brilliantly. Firstly, he had the Archbishop and his wife travel up the mountain in the turret of a Warrior. Secondly, he had all his soldiers sitting and standing on Warriors in the maintenance hanger for the visitors to meet. At the end of the visit, the Archbishop was persuaded to climb onto one of the Warriors and his wife onto another, and, at Rex's enthusiastic urging, we sang Christmas carols. The Archbishop said a few well-chosen words, declaimed a simple but direct prayer, blessed us all and wished us luck.

Our forthcoming NATO operations mean that will have to change roles quickly, refurbish ourselves and move long distances to take part in the British operations. This is happening around Christmas, so be prepared for many, if not all, of us to be unable to contact our families. Don't be surprised if this all happens in a blaze of publicity from both national and international media.

There will be a step change in the way we operate. There will be a much more robust approach and the emphasis will switch from compromise to unambiguous implementation of the peace agreement. Those who do not comply with the agreement will be made to. We may have to use force if the factions oppose the NATO mission. If this were to happen, we would do everything we could to reduce the risk to ourselves, but there would always be a chance of things not quite going as planned. This would be when I would really start earning my pay.

This is not exactly cheerful reading, but I am sure we are as well prepared as we can be. I have complete confidence in everyone's motivation, training and in our equipment. I know that you and little Jamie will continue to be my lighthouses in what could be a quite rocky and storm-dashed voyage.

Ops 3000

13 Dec 95

MILITARY IMPLEMENTATION OF THE PEACE AGREEMENT

1. It is essential that all commanders have a thorough understanding of military aspects of the peace agreement especially:
   a. What the former warring factions are required to do.
   b. What IFOR is required to do and the powers it will have.

2. <u>Military Aspects of the Peace Agreement</u>. Company Commanders have already been issued with a synopsis of the peace agreement. To aid dissemination of this a summary of the relevant military aspects is at Annex A. This is to be read and understood by all officers.

3. <u>Rules of Engagement</u>. Rules of engagement are being disseminated separately. All soldiers are to be issued with and understand the 'Gold' card. All commanders are to have a thorough understanding of the 'White' card. This is to be achieved before Transfer of Authority from UN to NATO.

B W BARRY
Lt Col
CO

<u>*ANNEX A TO*</u>
<u>*OPS 3000*</u>
<u>*DATED 13 DEC 95*</u>

<u>MILITARY ASPECTS OF THE PEACE AGREEMENT</u>

1. The FWF have agreed to fulfil the military aspects of the agreement and those regarding the status of NATO personnel. The following points are the important issues. The 'entities' are the Federation of Bosnia-Hercegovina and Republika Srpska.

2. The purpose of the general obligations placed on the parties is to:
   a. Establish a durable cessation of hostilities.
   b. Support and authorise the IFOR.

<u>Cessation of Hostilities</u>

3. The parties shall:
   a. Refrain from offensive operations.
   b. Cease firing or emplacing weapons or patrolling forward of their own lines.

c. Maintain civil law, disarming armed civil groups less police by TAO+30.
d. Permit freedom of movement.
e. Avoid reprisals/responses to violations.

Withdrawal of Foreign Forces

4. Forces not of local origin are to be withdrawn by signing of Peace Agreement (PA) +30 days.

Redeployment of Forces

5. The redeployment of forces will take place in three phases:

  a. Phase 1

    (1) By TOA+30 forces are to be withdrawn behind Zones of Separation (ZOS) which extend 2km either side of the Agreed Cease Fire Line (ACFL). No forces less IFOR may remain in ZOS.

    (2) Obstacles

      (a) Mines and other obstacles in ZOS and other areas vacated are to be removed by TOA+30.

      (b) All minefields and obstacles in B-H are to be marked by TOA+30.

    (3) Registration
        All military personnel living within the ZOS are to register with the nearest IFOR Command Post (CP).

  b. Phase 2
    Where the Inter-Entity Boundary (IEB) does not follow the ACFL:

    (1) In areas of transfer withdrawing entity must vacate and clear the area by TOA+45.

    (2) In areas of transfer incoming entity must not put forces into areas until TOA+90.

    (3) IFOR will have right to provide military security in areas of transfer from TOA+30 to TOA+91.

    (4) Once areas are transferred, new ZOS will be established by IFOR.

  c. Phases 1 and 2 General Rules

    (1) IFOR are to supervise the marking of ACFL and ZOS, IEBL and its ZOS.

    (2) IFOR entitled to use military force to ensure compliance with:

      (a) Removal of forces from 4km ZOS by TOA+30.

      (b) Vacation of areas of transfer by TOA+45.

      (c) Invasion of areas of transfer before TOA+90.

      (d) Failure to keep weapons and forces out of IEB ZOS.

      (e) Violation of cessation of hostilities.

d. *Phase 3*

   Confidence building measures will be:

   (1)   *Forces and heavy weapons are to be withdrawn to barracks by TOA+120.*

   (2)   *Forces and weapons which cannot be accommodated are to be demobilised by TOA+120.*

   (3)   *IFOR has the right to compel the movement, withdrawal or relocation of forces.*

Notification

6.   *On the establishment of a Joint Military Commission (JMC) the parties shall give details of mines, unexploded ordnance, booby-traps, wire and other obstacles and hazards and safe-lanes.*

Deployment of IFOR

7.   *IFOR shall have the right to:*

   a. *Monitor and help compliance by all parties.*

   b. *Authorise and supervise selective marking of ACFL and ZOS and IEBL and its ZOS.*

   c. *Establish liaison with local civil and military and international organisations.*

8.   *IFOR shall:*

   a. *Help create secure conditions.*

   b. *Assist organisations accomplishing humanitarian missions.*

   c. *Assist the UNHCR.*

   d. *Observe and prevent interference with the movement of the civil population.*

   e. *Monitor the clearing of minefields.*

9.   *Comd IFOR has authority without interference or prior permission.*

10. *IFOR has right to observe, monitor and inspect any forces.*

11. *Air and Surface Movement*

   a. *IFOR is to have complete and unimpeded freedom of movement by air, ground and water. IFOR has the right to billet and manoeuvre and use of any facility. IFOR is not liable for any damage caused by combat or combat related activities.*

   b. *There is to be no military air activity without the permission of the IFOR. Comd IFOR is the sole authority for the rules for the use of IFOR.*

   c. *Comd IFOR has the authority to promulgate rules for the control of surface military traffic.*

    d. *IFOR can utilise means and services that it requires to communicate and has unrestricted use of the electro-magnetic spectrum.*

Use of Force to Compel Compliance

12. *The agreement states that 'the Parties understand and agree that the IFOR Commander shall have the authority, witout interference or paremission of any Party, to do all that the Commander judges necessary and proper, including the use of military force, to protect the IFOR and to carry out the responsibilities listed above.'*

13. *Comd IFOR will have the right to decide on military matters relating to the safety of IFOR or compliance.*

Prisoner Exchanges

14. *The parties shall release and transfer without delay all combatants and civilians held.*

Cooperation

15. *The parties shall cooperate fully with all entities involved in implementing the peace settlement ...*

Timelines

17. See Appendix 1 for a summary.

APPENDIX 1

TIMELINES

Serial	TIME	ACTIVITY
1.	D-3	All air early warning, air defence or fire control radars are shut down.
2.	D+30	All forces in Bosnia which are not of local origin withdraw.
3.	D+30	1. All armed civilian groups, less police, disband. 2. Parties withdraw behind ZOS. 3. Parties remove or destroy explosive devices in ZOS, mark all explosive devices in B-H and others as required by IFOR. 4. IFOR to provide military security in areas of transfer. 5. Parties inform JMC of deployments within 10km of ACFL. 6. Parties release and transfer all prisoners held.
4.	By D+45	Areas of transfer are to be vacated by occupying entity.
5.	By D+90	Incoming forces allowed to enter areas of transfer.
6.	D+91	IFOR ceases to have right to provide military security in areas of transfer.
7.	D+120	1. Parties withdraw forces and weapons to cantonment areas/barracks. 2. Parties demobilise forces that cannot be cantoned. 3. Parties inform JMC of all forces and weapons in B-H.

CHAPTER FIVE

'Start!'

I wake early on 20 December. Lying in my sleeping bag as Sevastopol Camp comes to life, I wonder what the next few days will bring. The work of our recce parties, advance force and B Squadron mean that we are well poised, with a quarter of the battlegroup conducting preparatory operations. We have done this without upsetting the Multinational Brigade commander. Our NATO operations will hit the ground running.

This is as well, as there is precious little time between Transfer of Authority, at 1200 hours 20 December, and the deadline for opening WHITE FANG, 1600 hours 21 December. I have twenty-eight hours to move the two hundred and fifty kilometres from Sarajevo to Sanski Most. We must then demonstrate a strong IFOR presence in the Sanski Most area, while 1 RRF does the same to our east, and B Squadron, with an armoured infantry platoon, moves north into Serb territory.

The French have told us that they will not be making any changes to any of their practices at their checkpoints and will not allow any earlier access off the mountain. I therefore have time to bid farewell to C Company, congratulating them on their work so far and explaining what the rest of the battlegroup will be doing. They are no longer our main effort, but they will not be forgotten. I do not know when where or how they will return to the battalion, but am confident they will do well. I conclude by wishing them a happy Christmas.

Self-consciously, I pose for a team photograph with the RSM and our drivers. At that stage we do not know what adventures we are going to have, or whether we will all make it to the end of the tour.

The mountain is still several inches deep in soggy, wet snow and the road to Hadžići is treacherous. Two aggressively driven French jeeps overtake on a blind corner. They are still painted UN white, but have the word 'IFOR' casually applied in small black letters. Do I recognise two of the French soldiers in the back vehicle as bodyguards? I see a black-gloved hand. Is that a glimpse of the white silk scarf? Is it the Multinational Brigade Commander waving? Does he know it is me? These are the only French forces that I see this morning that display any indication of the change from UN to NATO.

This makes me reflect on the Multinational Brigade. Despite its achievements of August and September, I have to agree with one of my captains who assesses that it is 'well past its sell-by date'. The brigade seems an example of how not to organise a multinational formation. Its effectiveness has been limited by the ad hoc nature of the headquarters and the highly centralised way in which it has done business. It successfully co-ordinated the shelling around Sarajevo in September, but this was an operation planned over the preceding months and executed from secure fire bases against static targets, with no retaliation or counter-battery fire by the Bosnian Serb artillery. The evidence I have seen from the planning for Operation HORUS makes me strongly doubt whether the brigade could have managed manoeuvre operations in a fluid and dynamic situation.

I recall the difficulties we had reconciling the brigade's focus on Sarajevo with our British preparation for IFOR. These are similar to, but greater than, the problems that emerged as we 'played' a similar scenario at the brigade and Battlegroup Trainer back in Sennelager, two months earlier. The changeover of British staff in the Brigade HQ three weeks ago has given them little time to get up to speed, and they see things differently to us. Perhaps I could have done more to keep them informed or win them over to my point of view, but I cannot see what. It is just as well that Operation HORUS was not called so I have not had to play my British 'red card'.

Many of the brigade's problems seem to stem from the speed with which it was thrown together. If countries really want to combine their troops under multinational military formations, it is essential that they are properly worked up, trained and experienced and have a properly constituted headquarters. Otherwise they will result in a whole that is less than the sum of the parts.

I am relieved that those events are now definitely behind me. By moving to 4 Armoured Brigade, we will return to a properly constituted military organisation that knows how to get the most out of us. The two months with the Multinational Brigade have been intensely frustrating. Now my only frustration is that I am not up with the leading column of B Company as they cross into western Bosnia to execute a new mission under a new mandate and working for a properly 'joined up' Brigade Headquarters.

A Company's Warriors are all lined up at the Kiseljak Brick Factory, waiting for midday when they can start moving. All have 'IFOR' freshly painted in huge white letters over the slabs of Chobham armour. The little UN flags are all replaced by large Union Jacks. 'We brought one for every vehicle over from Germany in our freight', Jan de Vos tells me. He and his company are in fine form, delighted to be seeing the back of the Brick Factory and looking forward to a new challenge. Their only regret is that they are leaving their friends in the Foreign Legion cavalry and the JCOs with whom they have established excellent working relationships. The company is also delighted to learn that they will not only qualify for the UNPROFOR medal, but will also earn the new NATO campaign medal.

On to Vitez School. For the first time the vehicle park is empty. So is the school building. Mr Matthews takes our Land Rovers to refuel and I stroll around the unfamiliarly deserted corridors. Although the operations room is manned, the rest of the building is quiet. I check the arrangements for the residual presence that we will leave in Vitez. Most unusually, there is no queue for the telephone call boxes – an effect of the base being almost empty. I call my wife, my brother and my parents, and wonder when I will be able to speak to them again.

At noon we cut the UN badges from our arms and drive on to catch up with the battlegroup. It is unexpectedly warm and the snow is melting fast. In Gornji Vakuf, we enter the spectacular gorge formed by the River Vrbas. There are enticing glimpses of ruined medieval castles and isolated hilltop villages. We are waved through ABiH checkpoints. The depth of the gorge makes communications difficult, but we can hear snatches of conversation on the battlegroup net. Everything seems to be going well.

On to Jajce. I have heard much of this town with its medieval walled fortress, and of the importance that many Bosnian Muslims had placed on it as a symbol of their identity. The biscuit-coloured fortress ramparts glow in the afternoon sun. I come upon two broken-down mortar platoon vehicles, waiting for recovery. The crews tell me how HVO soldiers manning a checkpoint had been determined not to let B Company's column through until the last possible moment before noon.

On into the Anvil, the area under Bosnian Croat control to be handed over to the Bosnian Serbs. It is a gloriously sunny afternoon, the temperature well above freezing, and the south-facing slopes are alive with rivulets of meltwater. The area is an upland plateau with few towns or hamlets. There are many signs of recent battle: destroyed and abandoned vehicles, minefields, trenches and bunkers, expended ammunition cases and boxes and an abandoned VRS artillery position with the ground around it torn and mutilated by Federation counter-battery fire. Almost all of the buildings, apart from those commandeered by the HVO, are vandalised and stripped of all furniture and fittings. I can see no civilians, only a few snarling dogs, furtively investigating the abundant piles of rubbish. It is an apocalyptic scene.

I pass through the mountain town of Mrkonjić Grad, spectacularly nestling on the edge of a narrow gorge, amongst a ring of rounded, wooded summits. It is completely empty, save for a few HVO troops and vehicles and a small factory with a few of the Fusileers' vehicles outside it. The bus depot compound here is full of the battlegroup's armoured vehicles and soldiers. There are more people in green berets and more of the battalion's armoured vehicles in one place than I have seen since the Sennelager exercise. Although only two thirds of the battalion are present, it is an extremely impressive sight.

I have an intense feeling of déjà vu. The large blue sheds of the depot, apart from battle damage and evidence of looting, appear identical to the vehicle sheds at Suffield in Canada, and the yard of the bus depot has an atmosphere similar to the end of BATUS training eighteen months earlier. Morale then was high, with everyone pleased with the results we'd achieved on the prairie. Morale in Mrkonjić Grad on 20 December is even higher, with a palpable 'edge' to the atmosphere. We are all delighted to be back as a formed body of men, amongst our friends and colleagues. Everyone is conscious that none of the promised American or French reinforcements have yet entered Bosnia and the British tanks and heavy artillery will not arrive for another three weeks.

Until then 2 LI will be the most powerful single battalion-sized unit anywhere in Bosnia. We are delighted to be taking the initiative, after three years in which the UN has been well and truly messed around by the factions; and even more pleased to be doing so in a familiar British military environment.

One soldier sums it up when he says, 'Sir, it's ----ing awesome'. In my diary I write: 'EXHILARATING!'

In a development as bizarre as it is typical of Bosnia, General Wilsey, the UK's Joint Commander, arrives in the midst of the battlegroup. He seems to get a good impression. As he is about to leave, he summons one of his staff and presents me with a brace of freshly shot pheasants as a Christmas gift. I am truly dumbstruck. 'Sir, I think you were gobsmacked', a serjeant major tells me.

Battlegroup HQ is working out of its command vehicles, just as it has done on training in Canada and Germany, the only difference being the lack of the concealing drapery of camouflage nets. Mark Goldsack is running it with his usual good humour. The battlegroup net is working well, and we can talk to all our sub-units, from C Company left on Igman a hundred and fifty kilometres to the south-west through to our advance party in Sanski Most fifty kilometres in the opposite direction. The brigade secure radio net is not working, but we can use our satellite telephone to reach Šipovo – when the line is not engaged. Mark is clearly in his element, and finds the lack of brigade communications a minor complication that is of note more for its amusement value than its effect on battlegroup operations.

Steve Noble briefs me on the media arrangements. We have a journalist from the West Country local papers, CNN, the American satellite station, an agency journalist and two photographers, one from *Newsweek* and one from *Time* magazine. We are particularly impressed with the CNN team's communication equipment, which lets them transmit reports straight to the CNN centre in Atlanta. The agency journalist, a Frenchman, has a large briefcase containing a portable computer and satellite telephone. Since arriving in Mrkonjić Grad he has already transmitted reports to Paris. These modern, compact, robust and effective communications belonging to the media seem a generation ahead of ours, in both capability and reliability.

Dave Jarratt shows me our logistic base. He is full of praise for the work that Martin Bellamy and RQMS Wilson have done in developing it into our springboard for operations in western Bosnia. There is already an improvised cookhouse producing meals for the queue of hungry Light Infantrymen and sappers. It is a pleasure to stand in that hot, sweaty, steamy room and see so many familiar faces smiling and joking with friends and colleagues who they have not seen for some time. The high morale in the cookhouse is an intense boost to my own morale.

I chat to Chris Booth, who has obviously relished his time in command of the battlegroup. So far the move has gone well but the plan for the next day's move is more complicated. There are two routes available. The first route is a long journey, to the east through Bihać and then due north and west for Sanski Most. Reconnaissance shows it is a reasonable road and all the bridges and culverts could carry a thirty-five-ton Warrior. The problem is that it could take the best part of a day to move a force of Warriors along it. We have christened this option the 'SAFARI Route'.

The other route is a northward drive along the main road from Klujc to Sanski Most. It already has a name from UN days: Route PHOENIX. The route crosses the River Sana, where the bridge has been blown up by retreating Bosnian Serbs. The ABiH have subsequently crossed the river by constructing a lightweight floating pontoon bridge. The problem is that our recce party assesses that this bridge will not take vehicles of more than ten tonnes – indeed, if a vehicle of more than that weight attempts to cross, it will sink the bridge, which rules out any attempt to cross it with a Warrior.

The engineers have a plan to get our Warriors across the river using bridge-laying tanks. The river is too wide for a single tank-laid bridge – no fewer than three are required, overlaid upon each other supported by trestles, the whole being known as a 'triple combination' bridge. There is sufficient engineer equipment for just one attempt at the crossing.

This option is the current plan. It is vital that the bridge goes in on time; otherwise the Warriors will not be in Sanski Most in time to open the crossing at WHITE FANG. A vast amount of snow has melted today, up to a metre and a half in places, and the streams and rivers are swollen to higher levels than we have ever seen. This bodes ill for the bridge across the Sana.

Brigadier Dannatt arrives. He has watched the opening of BLACK DOG and has followed B Squadron's advance north to Krupa. The squadron with a B Company Warrior platoon has successfully advanced halfway to Banja Luka and is now harboured up in a village. He has with him Hamish Macleod commanding 39 Engineer Regiment, bringing disheartening news. The River Sana is flowing too high and too fast for the armoured engineers to complete their combination bridge.

The silver lining to this dark cloud is Major Jonathan Passmore, the engineer squadron commander, who has already ordered his engineers and the battalion's recce platoon to find alternative routes that might bypass the bridge. These attempts have identified a new route, a track along the east bank of the Sana. A patrol from the recce platoon has just driven along the route. The ABiH are using the track as a supply route. Warriors can get along most of the route, but there are plenty of choke points where a broken-down or immobilised Warrior could completely block the track.

The critical point is a wooden bridge across a stream that will certainly collapse if a Warrior attempts to cross it. Just to the side of the bridge is a site where it might be possible for Warrior to ford the stream. It is deep, close to the maximum depth that Warriors can ford. It will require a full assessment by an engineer recce party, probably some preparation, and will certainly need to be marked. There are a couple of engineer sections from Jonathan's squadron who could work overnight. Would I like to have this done, or do I want to move around the SAFARI route?

The Brigadier has been listening to all this. Gently, he tells me that he doesn't mind how I get to Sanski Most, or in what order my forces arrive. He is more than happy for the Warriors to take the SAFARI route through Bihać, but the Sanski Most crossing point must be opened by last light tomorrow.

The Brigadier departs and the Battlegroup HQ planning team assembles in a dingy office. Steve Noble has with him the journalists and TV crews. We identify three options.

We could send the whole force on the SAFARI route via Bihać. Although the route is proven and capable of taking Warriors it is so long that, for us to reach Sanski Most in time to conduct the WHITE FANG operation, we will have to leave in the next couple of hours. We do not relish a night drive with tired vehicle crews along an unfamiliar route, nor our vehicle crews arriving at Sanski Most exhausted – especially with our force levels being so low and the prospect of subsequent enforcement operations in an unfamiliar area.

The second option is to move the whole force along the new route. As with the previous option, we are moving a single balanced force of a company's worth of Warriors with MILAN and mortars in one group. If the factions pose difficulties this could be invaluable as we have guaranteed firepower, indirect fire, command and control and plenty of Warriors to protect the lighter armoured vehicles and soft-skinned trucks and Land Rovers. There are significant disadvantages: the uncertainty of the route, the chance that the Warriors will not successfully get across the ford, and the proximity of the route to the front line. Indeed, not only do we have little idea of the exact location of the front line, but also some of the maps we have been given showed the route as crossing the front line in several places.

The final option is to split our force into two columns. A 'light column' of the light armoured vehicles and Land Rovers would use the pontoon bridge route. It would have rifles and machine guns, but its only heavy weapons would be the cannons of the Scimitars. A 'heavy column' of all the Warriors would use the new route along the River Sana. This is an unorthodox option for grouping forces that we have neither considered nor practised before. It has the advantage that if movement on one route fails, we could continue with some force down the other route. The most likely problem we can foresee is some difficulty on the newly identified route. If we cannot get Warriors along it, we can always send them the long way around the SAFARI route.

The discussion that leads to these options is fast moving and multifaceted. I lead it, ensuring that no one in the planning team who has something to contribute is left out. I then sum up what I think are the advantages and disadvantages of each option.

'Anything I've left out?' I ask.

Silence.

'I favour the third option. I think the light column has the best chance of reaching Sanski Most in time. Therefore I will go with that column, as will Main HQ. The battlegroup second-in-command will go with the Warriors, including the Battalion HQ Warriors. We'll call this the heavy column. Clearly, this plan depends on the ability of the engineers, working through the night, to improve the route and prepare the Warrior ford. We will therefore have to confirm that the new route is passable in time to change our plans if necessary.

If the sappers don't succeed and the new route can't be used, the back-up plan is for the heavy column to go round the SAFARI route. I want to have battle-group quick verbal orders in an hour. I'm off for a quick meal; I'll be back in half an hour to tie up any further details and prepare for the orders.'

I am unaware that, half hidden by the throng of Battlegroup HQ officers, at the back of the room is our huddle of attached journalists, chaperoned by Steve Noble. Larry, the CNN team leader, tells me, 'Gee, Colonel, I've been on a lot of operations with the US military and they just could not react so quickly to such a radical change to the situation.' He mutters happily about this for the rest of the evening. Steve becomes more than a little bored with his repeated comparisons between 2 LI and various US units that Larry has accompanied on operations.

Leaving Mark Goldsack to organise the orders, I wander to the kitchen to thank the mixed team of Light Infantry and engineer cooks, bumping into Paul Baker, the brigade deputy chief of staff, who has come to visit our logisti-cians. Since we still have no workable communications with Brigade HQ, I invite him to attend our orders so that he can bring Brigadier Dannatt up to date on our plans.

The orders group is short and to the point. After I give the mission, con-cept of operations and key tasks, Mark Goldsack and Chris Booth explain the necessary co-ordinating instructions. As these are explained, I watch the tired dirty faces of those receiving the orders. In the stuffy, dark, ill-lit room many wear frowns of concentration as they scribble into notebooks or write on their maps.

With the flickering yellow glow of hurricane lamps and dim rays of electric torches, I have another intense flash of déjà vu. The scene is almost identical to an orders group in a hut on a training area in North Germany almost eighteen months earlier. At that time I had just assumed command of the battalion and was unsure both of the personalities of my subordinates and of my ability to command this powerful but complex organisation. After the orders, as com-manders and Battlegroup HQ officers chat, confer and exchange light-hearted banter I am filled with an immense confidence in them all. This is immensely exhilarating, but also immensely humbling.

The commanders disperse. I fall exhausted onto a camp bed in a cramped disused office. Chris Booth and I listen to the BBC World Service news, where the NATO operation is the top item. As it describes 'three powerful British armoured columns' heading north and west from central Bosnia we both grin broadly, in my case from a desire to hide any embarrassing signs of the naïve pride I feel.

Most of the battlegroup catch a few hours rest. Jonathan Passmore's engi-neers work through the night to improve the crossings on the route along the River Sana, christened 'Route BUGLE'. After four hours of fitful sleep I wake, and am told by Jonathan Passmore that the ford can definitely take Warrior. Vehicles crossing the streams will have to exercise great care when crossing. There are still plenty of places where a breakdown or a minestrike could lead to the route being blocked.

Just as dawn is breaking I follow the heavy column departing from the Bus Depot, the road shaking under their weight. Our route out of Mrkonjić Grad is marked by British military police, all wearing body armour and helmets, no longer UN blue but with British camouflage patterns, their Land Rovers no longer white but painted green and black. The whole brigade will be wearing helmets and body armour for the foreseeable future. I travel with the light column, through a misty dull grey morning, across a spectacular high plateau and then into a huge open valley full of clouds and curtains of mist. The routes of the two columns diverge. We pass villages where all the houses are burned out or blown up. In the grey rain this is a chilling reminder of ethnic cleansing.

The River Sana is even more swollen than we expected. The road bridge across the river is completely destroyed, large slabs lying askew on the river-bank. The ABiH bridge is a Russian-pattern single pontoon, covered with mud, and attached to the river bank by a multitude of cable and ropes. As my Land Rover crosses, the bridge pitches and yaws alarmingly. Muslim engineers run out onto the bridge, furiously gesticulating and holding up their hands to stop the remaining IFOR vehicles of the light column. Several of us race forward, weapons ready, hyped up with adrenaline, to remind them that they can't obstruct IFOR.

'No, no', they say through the interpreter, 'we are worried that your vehicles are going too fast.' I can see for myself that the combination of armoured vehicles and the swollen fast-flowing river is testing this small floating bridge to its limits. I order that all our vehicles should be led over by the vehicle commander on foot and tell the Muslim engineers this. They seem mollified.

Steve Noble arrives with the journalists. I give an impromptu interview and leap into my Rover for the rest of the trip to Sanski Most. As we drive north, the landscape opens out to a wide flood plain. Arriving in Sanski Most exactly on schedule, our 'base' is no more than a single large shed, a low block of half a dozen offices, a damp muddy field and a perimeter fence. While I wait for the heavy column's arrival I chat with Captain Sean Harris and B Company's advance party. Everything is on schedule. As the column of Warriors comes in to the camp I mentally congratulate the engineers who worked through the night to make the route passable.

After a quick meeting to co-ordinate arrangements with Sean Harris and the JCOs, B Company deploys to secure and control the cease-fire line crossing point WHITE FANG. Back in October at Brigade and Battlegroup Trainer, we had thought through the problem of establishing a presence at a crossing point on a cease-fire line. The exercise had posed a number of problems, which seemed to get more and more challenging as it progressed. We finally agreed that, at the end of the day, so long as we put a vehicle on the cease-fire line and opened a route between the two sides, we had achieved our mission. That is exactly what we now do to establish the first crossing point at WHITE FANG.

Stuart Mills, the company commander, has all the resources he needs and a sound plan. I therefore monitor the operation, but from a short distance behind the leading troops. In Canada, this was where I positioned myself when one of my companies was conducting an attack on the prairie. Driving forward I pass a mortar section deployed in fire positions around a roadside junction. Monitoring the operation on the command net it is clear that although we are prepared for confrontation, everything is going well. A VRS officer hands over his checkpoint to B Company, shakes Stuart Mills' hand and then walks away.

I drive forward, passing a Muslim checkpoint, where the ABiH soldiers are putting land mines they have just lifted from the crossing into boxes. The Muslim soldiers wave me through with a smile. As I arrive I meet the CNN team departing, immensely satisfied with everything they have seen and hurrying off to Sarajevo where their controllers from Atlanta want them next.

Stuart shows me the Serb checkpoint, a bunker built into the side of the road. Although reinforced with timbers and breezeblocks, it would be unable to withstand our LAWs, Milan missiles or the cannon and machine gun of our Warriors, let alone our mortars. This is nothing new, many bunkers on both sides of the line on Mount Igman being as pathetic, but without its Serb defenders the bunker seems lifeless and hollow, like a discarded ice-cream wrapper.

Brigadier Dannatt arrives to see things for himself. At that moment a Mercedes estate car appears from the north (Serb territory!). The elderly couple are affluent Bosnian Serb refugees who speak good English. They have come from Prijedor, where they are lodging with relatives, having fled their house, which was on the front line. Have they been back? No, they say, the Bosnian Serb Army has previously stopped them at the checkpoint, but now the checkpoint has gone they can visit the house – it is only fifty metres down that side road, would we like to come with them?

We follow and inspect a perfectly adequate four-bedroomed house – albeit with every single piece of furniture stolen. All the fittings that could possibly be removed have been taken. The couple told us that soldiers – 'our own soldiers' they shrug ambiguously – have looted everything. They are delighted that 'NATO has finally come to end the war' and offer the house as a base.

I see Stuart talking to another couple in a car, Bosnian Serb emigrés who have driven from Paris to see their former home in Sanski Most. Can we escort them there? Stuart patiently explains that we can't escort individual civilians, and, as the Muslim checkpoints are still in place around Sanski Most, we don't recommend they make an attempt yet. The couple reluctantly accept this.

I return to Sanski Most, where our base has already been christened 'the Mud Factory'. Lieutenant Pete Chapman's platoon is providing local security. He describes their move into Serb territory and their first day's work:

> We approached the checkpoint for the first time. I was still wondering whether we would have to force our way through when a sleepy Muslim recruit appeared and hastily raised the barrier, but not high enough! He began to tug at the wooden pole as if every second wasted would increase the chances of us firing at him, until it came away in his hands. Still too narrow. The bricks were flung to one side and, with the hut the only intact item left, we entered the HQ. It felt

like being royalty – everyone stood and stared, as this was probably the first time that they had seen a Warrior. As we parked up, the rear vehicle traversed his turret to the rear, causing an old lady to drop her bags in fright and lose her footing in the snow.

There are many features of a move into the unknown, not least of which is the effect that a Warrior can have on an uninitiated population. Others are more daunting, such as the initial contact with a hostile soldier, or more historically significant, which can be measured by the quantity of press cameras present. However, one of the most challenging was the initial effort to find that most basic of requirements, somewhere to live.

We divided into groups to clear out the warehouse. The first people in were the engineers, who reappeared, eyes glazed, a few minutes later carrying an anti-tank mine, several different calibres of ammunition and a live artillery shell. Next in went the riflemen appointed as temporary butchers, with the unbelievable task of tying the dead pigs to Land Rovers to be dragged outside. Finally, there were the cars, which to the disappointment of a few had already been deprived of their car radios. To my surprise I had a large number of volunteers to help me with this task, all of whom appeared uncannily skilled in rolling cars onto their roofs before attaching them to Land Rovers to be dragged away. Not for the first time we were doing something that can hardly be called soldiering, yet it was an essential step towards the creation of a camp and unexpectedly enjoyable at the same time.

When we first arrived in Sanski Most it was hard to gauge the reaction of the local population to our presence. When a shot went whistling over the head of an unsuspecting corporal, it was naturally assumed that the local military were having a go. The alert state went up and we prepared for an attack, until a grinning grandfather biked up to the front gate with his well-worn hunting rifle, and proudly announced that he was our deadly sniper! No one discovered what he was doing or why, but his intentions were not as hostile as originally thought. We were becoming used to a culture that accepts the sound of gunfire as a daily occurrence.

At our base the armoured vehicles have turned the ground into a sea of deep, dark, glutinous mud. At least everyone has a roof of some sort over their head, with Battlegroup HQ in a small brick building and everyone else in the single large shed. Both buildings are filthy and damaged by fighting. Fortunately our logisticians have obtained sufficient tents for everyone in the shed to have canvas between them and the roof and have access to some kind of heater. The cooks have already set up a field kitchen inside the hangar and through some miracle of organisation we have sufficient tables and chairs for an impromptu dining area.

Outside the shed a work party has installed some water heaters, and buckets and canvas screens are used to make a toilet area. This at least gives people an illusion of privacy but will require a daily work party to dispose of the excrement by burning. I have the power to authorise 'Payment for Work of an Objectionable Nature', an allowance to those involved in handling human bodies or waste. The sum of money is small but it at least goes some way to showing the soldiers involved that the Army recognises the distasteful nature of what they have to do.

CHAPTER SIX

The Mud Factory

The next day, my diary reminds me, is my wedding anniversary. I hope that the cards I posted to Liz two weeks earlier have reached her. This is the first Christmas we have spent apart in eleven years of marriage. I have been incredibly lucky, for most of my contemporaries in the infantry have had far more separation from their families than I have – as is the case with most of the battalion.

I have no time to be homesick. Today, the main effort is a patrol by B Company towards the Bosnian Serb city of Prijedor. For the moment, the mortar platoon will deploy to provide a potential umbrella of covering fire under which all of our patrols will work. The recce platoon will probe along the road to Bosanska Krupa on the Muslim side of the line looking for ABiH headquarters and possible sites for new bases. The Mud Factory is too small for Battlegroup HQ, B Company and the recce platoon, and we need bases for A Company, B Squadron and the artillery battery.

I drive into Republika Srpska, north through WHITE FANG, waved on by B Company's soldiers. I encounter Serb checkpoints manned by Serb police in their distinctive 'blue lizard' camouflage uniforms. I pass three of the mortar platoon's vehicles parked in the centre of the road, hatches open and tubes pointed to the sky. We wave at each other as I slowly weave my way through the chicane formed by the three vehicles, positioned in the middle of the road so as to avoid any mines that might be buried in the surrounding fields.

This brazen deployment, right in the open with no camouflage or conceal-ment, is the antithesis of the way our mortars have previously deployed on training for war fighting where concealment is a high priority. Here, we are positioning mortars where they can not only provide covering fire to our troops, but can also be visible to the local soldiers and civilians. This is the way we will use our mortars and artillery from now on.

Prijedor shows few signs of war, apart from a general shabbiness and dilapi-dation. The JCO team led by a staff serjeant have already made contact with a major VRS headquarters on the outskirts of the town, believed to belong to 43 Infantry Brigade. The formation commander, a colonel, has done little to hide his incomprehension of how he should deal with such low-ranking emissaries. He is refusing to divulge his troop dispositions until the senior IFOR commander for his area comes to *his* headquarters. Initially he wanted this to be General Jackson, but he has now grudgingly accepted that the IFOR 'procovnik' would be acceptable.

We drive to an industrial estate on the outskirts of town. All the factories are inactive. The HQ is sited in a driving school – still decorated with quaint pictures of family saloon cars driving along idealised Yugoslav roads. 'It's a bit like something from the Janet and John book of Bosnian motoring', Sean Harris says as we drive up. A JCO tells me, 'By the way Colonel, they don't allow anyone to park inside the compound.' But as our column of Land Rovers arrives a military policeman directs that 'the Procovnik' park in the visitors' parking bay. The rest of the party shake their heads in amazement.

Inside the building the walls bear a bizarre mixture of posters – half road safety and half Bosnian Serb military propaganda. Even the most taciturn JCO finds it hard to suppress a grin. The colonel's office is surprisingly small. I am given a huge soft armchair and the rest of our party somehow manage to squeeze in: Sean Harris, four assorted interpreters, three VRS officers and three extremely bulky JCOs, all in a tiny office, which was already full of chairs and tables.

If this was a gathering of 2 LI officers, it would be impossible to pack everyone into such a small place without laughter, jokes and the sparkling banter that characterised the start of so many planning meetings and orders groups in Paderborn, Canada and central Bosnia. Here the body language of the Serb colonel is rigid and extremely stern. My initial introductions and pleasantries fall on deaf ears. This is the hardest faction leader I have had to deal with so far. Using the notes I made on Mount Igman I rehearse IFOR's role:

> We are NATO, not UN. New, robust rules of engagement. Powerful, combat capable force. Military capability to implement Dayton peace agreement.
>
> Leaders of entities signed agreement, on the behalf of communities. We have been invited in to implement the agreement. This has to be passed right down the chain of command. If at local level a commander or group does not want to abide by the peace agreement, we have capability and rules of engagement to allow us to enforce it. Really hope it doesn't come to that. But if it does, we will not shirk our responsibilities.
>
> Currently equipped with Warrior, light tanks, artillery, support weapons. Armed helicopters and NATO strike aircraft available. Challenger main battle tanks, engineer tanks and heavy artillery on the way from England.

I explain our dispositions, glossing over our relative weakness without actually telling any lies. Giving the colonel a map marked with our locations seems to relax him. After a bit more coaxing he sends for a map of his own and unfolds it over his desk. I can remember enough Warsaw Pact map marking from my Cold War intelligence training ten years earlier to decipher the military calligraphy that overlays the contours and green forests on the map.

I ask the identity of the units on his flanks. He refuses point blank to divulge them, saying that he has no knowledge of the layout of the troops on either side of his formation. Repeated attempts to elicit this information are met with repeated refusal. I change tack. What is the big thick black line that so neatly splits his area into two halves, one east and one west? 'These are my two subordinate sectors', he states, and points out where the sector HQs are located.

'Where are the minefields?' I ask. 'There are none marked on the map.' For the first time, a flicker of surprise and emotion crosses his face. Has my ability to read his map unbalanced him? Apologetically he offers to produce a minefield map the next day. By now the ice is broken and standing around the map we have a wide-ranging and frank discussion.

As we leave, I ask why my Land Rover was directed to park inside his compound when the rest of our vehicles are outside. Smiling broadly, he looks me in the eye and says, without a trace of irony, 'Procovnik is Procovnik'. I have the feeling he understands more English than he has let on throughout the meeting.

Meanwhile, B Company are dealing with a noncompliant ABiH checkpoint. A party of Royal Engineers in a Land Rover are turned away outside the town. They report this to B Company, who send two Warriors to the site. With an interpreter, they demand the attention of an officer who appears, apparently quaking in his boots. The barriers are rapidly lifted.

A Military Commission

The next day, 23 December, was the first meeting of the divisional military commission. General Jackson had summoned the corps commanders of all the faction armies in the British division's area. I had suggested to Brigade that A Company be deployed along the approach routes to the meeting to help create an impression of strength. I had already warned off Jan de Vos that he should be prepared to do this. Brigadier Dannatt agreed.

Although I was not invited to the military commission, the meeting would provide a useful opportunity to catch up with A Company and brief Jan de Vos on events in the battlegroup area. Overhearing me discuss this at Battlegroup HQ a liaison officer asks me to act as escort for General Alagic, the commander of 7 Corps ABiH, from Sanski Most to the site of the meeting at the Balkana Motel. I agree to do this.

Arriving at the Sana Hotel in the centre of Sanski Most, I met the divisional liaison officer, Captain Tom Mallinson. We waited for Alagic in the bar of the hotel – dark and gloomy, reeking of harsh Balkan tobacco, thick coffee and sweat. This combination of impressions was to become one of my overriding memories of meetings with Bosnians of all factions.

A huge Bosnian Muslim colonel with an impressive beard introduced himself as Colonel Mesanovic, the 7 Corps deputy colonel with special responsibility for cooperation with IFOR. A great bear of a man, he was brimming over with enthusiasm and could not be stopped from giving me a complicated account of how he was personally responsible for arranging all aspects of the corps implementation of IFOR. From an apparently bottomless leather briefcase he produced sheaves of documents, most in Bosnian, some in English and a few in both languages. I was impressed to see what he called a 'soldier document', already issued, he claimed, to each Bosnian soldier, explaining the role of IFOR and its powers.

Tom Mallinson arrived to tell me that Alagic had appeared and was waiting for us in his staff car – thus sparing me from exhausting my limited repertoire of Bosnian military flattery. We assembled a bizarre convoy led by my Land Rover, followed by two camouflaged Bosnian Land Cruisers and finished by the RSM's armoured Land Rover. We had exactly two hours to be at the Balkana motel – some eighty kilometres to the south-east. This I now realised, was going to be extremely demanding. We sped along the road south from Sanski Most. Rattling uncomfortably along Route BUGLE we drove behind the ABiH front line, through an area crowded with Bosnian Government forces. All the buildings were occupied and covered with graffiti. Some of this was propaganda, but other inscriptions signposted the way to headquarters. We could see dishevelled and scruffy troops, some ignoring us, others leering.

Stopping outside Klujc, I met Alagic, a short pugnacious man with several days' grey beard growth and penetrating eyes. Here, Alagic told me, he would wait to be joined by General Dudakovic, the commander of the Muslim 5 Corps from Bihać. 'Colonel, up ahead is a Croat checkpoint', he told me. 'They make many difficulties for my soldiers and for civilians who need to travel across their territory. Remember, Colonel, you are travelling with two generals of the *Armija* to a very important meeting. You are responsible for our safe passage.' He looked disposed to lecture me further, but at that point Dudacovic arrived, and backslapping and embracing his comrade-in-arms seemed to take priority over our conversation.

I returned to my Land Rover and pulled away, worried. The Bosnian Croats had a history of making difficulties for Muslims, both military and civilian, attempting to move through Croat territory. Ahead, I could see the checkpoint erected by the Croats on the edge of their territory and a queue of civilian vehicles at least half a mile long waiting to pass through, all heading in the same direction as us. Were Alagic's words intended as a warning? I thought of several incidents in the past, especially the assassination of the Muslim vice president inside a French armoured vehicle in Sarajevo in 1992. Or was Alagic, a notoriously difficult character, attempting to unsettle me, knowing that I would find his statement worrying?

Whatever Alagic's intentions, time was against me, for if I took my turn in the vehicle queue I would never arrive at the military commission in time. So, employing a technique I had seen Bosnian senior officers employ at their own checkpoints on Mount Igman, I told Leck to overtake the column of waiting vehicles, put his foot on the accelerator and his hand on the horn, and drive straight through the checkpoint. If the Croat soldiers or police attempted to stop us, we were to keep going. Behaving like the escort for a Third World *presidente* had the desired effect, although several times we had to force oncoming vehicles off the road. At one point we had to stop because of the number of Bosnian soldiers and civilians who wanted to personally groot Alagic. Seeing the throng around his car, I could not help thinking of the Italian-American supplicants around the Corleone brothers in Francis Ford Coppola's *Godfather* films.

We now had only an hour to travel across the Anvil. For the only time in the tour I told Leck to drive fast, to get to the military commission on time. Fortunately there was little traffic on the roads, much of the ice and snow had melted, and the Bosnian Croats waved us through the rest of their checkpoints.

As we sped through the open landscape, I reflected that I had made a serious error of judgement. Important as the military commission was, getting faction corps commanders to the meeting was a tactical task, more appropriate to a liaison officer and escort party than a battlegroup commander. I had fallen into the trap of taking charge of a small tactical operation that was the business of my subordinates, and, as my worries at the Croat checkpoint illustrated, I had neither planned nor executed the task particularly well. I had failed to anticipate the potential problems that might arise at the Croat checkpoint – which I should have countered by positioning a force of at least platoon size there, able to forcibly hold the checkpoint open if needed. I had also missed the opportunity to line our route with such armoured vehicles as we had. I had underestimated both the importance and potential difficulty of the situation and resolved not to make similar mistakes again.

We passed our echelon base at Mrkonjić Grad and turned into the deep gorge of the River Vrbas. It was a dark day, the sky glowering with steel-grey clouds. The road north to Banja Luka clung to the sides of the huge, gloomy gorge. I passed several of A Company's Warriors, parked in places that maximised their visibility to anyone using the road. I hoped that my two Bosnian generals were impressed. I was.

The Balkana Motel was almost completely destroyed, its large car park occupied by 4 Armoured Brigade's tactical HQ of armoured command vehicles shrouded in camouflage nets. Attached to the large elevated antenna were the brigade flag of a large black desert rat and the most enormous Union Jack flag I had ever seen. Major Jan de Vos and Lieutenant Will Hogg were in the turrets of their Warriors. Elated, I climbed up and spent a happy five minutes comparing notes on our operations so far, and laughing and joking with them and their vehicle crews. We watched General Jackson arrive, a tall, gaunt and impressive figure in a maroon Parachute Regiment beret, strolling purposefully into the meeting.

Returning to Mrkonjić Grad, I stopped and watched A Company return to base. A sudden gap in the cloud sent fleeting shafts of sunlight across the landscape and against a backdrop of burned and looted houses the huge white 'IFOR' slogans seemed to glow with authority. An artist could not have contrived a more spectacular sight. Perhaps the company felt some of the drama of the scene, or perhaps morale was high, for there was no shortage of smiles, waves of greeting and cheerful salutes.

The company's Warriors were filthy, covered with dust and mud and streaked with diesel and oil. Their turrets, stowage bins and hulls were cluttered with the impedimenta of operations, including air marker panels, rolls of barbed wire, tools and ration boxes. Nevertheless, the call signs had been cleaned and all the newly painted desert rat symbols and 'IFOR' initials had had the dust and dirt scrubbed off. Many of the crews' uniforms were coated in dust and oil, but their rifles and pistols remained spotlessly clean.

Jan and I compared this with the appearance of the faction soldiers. Both the HVO and the ABiH used US-pattern combat fatigues with their own insignia. Many soldiers, particularly the ABiH, also wore items of other uniforms, including French, British and German combat clothing. A number also sported civilian gloves, boots, hats and cold-weather jackets, especially ABiH soldiers, who appeared to have fewer resources than the HVO. Many of the soldiers and civilians showed the effects of three years of war, including loss of teeth and hair, bad breath and skin ailments. Our uniforms were equally if not more dirty, but they were of a standard pattern, we were shaved and well fed, and our weapons were clean and ready to be used.

A Mine Incident

As I was travelling to the military commission, B Company heard an explosion to the east of Sanski Most. Shortly afterwards Brigade told Battlegroup HQ that a Royal Engineers vehicle had run over a mine in that area. There were serious casualties. B Company immediately sent their Quick Reaction Force of two Warriors commanded by Lieutenant David Livingston to assist. He was quickly on the scene with the battlegroup's Royal Engineer Explosive Ordnance Disposal (EOD) team. They found that there were two Land Rovers, one blown up, one intact. David takes up the story:

> The first Land Rover took the full force of the explosion and was destroyed. The crew sustained severe blast injuries to their lower limbs but miraculously both survived. They were lucky. The Land Rover had actually already passed six anti-tank mines, with anti-personnel mines laid around to deter tampering, and detonated a seventh anti-tank mine. A helicopter was tasked for casualty evacuation and the two injured men were carried out of the danger area, carefully following the Land Rover tracks to a site where the helicopter could land. IFOR's policy on mines clearly stated that mines should be lifted by those who laid them. However in this instance British troops and equipment were still at risk so Royal Engineers cleared the remaining mines on the roads.

This is a short and self-effacing account of a dangerous, long and cold afternoon. The ABiH soldiers at the scene were helpful and seemed genuinely concerned for the British soldiers, claiming to have tried to attract the attention of the engineers by waving at them, to stop them driving onto the mines. The uninjured Land Rover crew who had not been evacuated confirmed that they had indeed seen ABiH soldiers doing this.

The engineer patrol had entered our area without either informing or consulting us. We were incredulous to discover that they were carrying out a reconnaissance of routes that might be suitable for Challenger tanks. The maps they had with them were very poorly marked. The senior member of the party was a Territorial Army officer who seemed to have only just arrived in Bosnia. They were very lucky that David and his platoon were on the scene so quickly, immediately taking charge of the incident, aiding the casualties and organising medical evacuation by helicopter. David had stabilised the situation, acting with calm composure that all involved found immensely reassuring.

Later, I saw the carcass of the Land Rover that had driven over the mine. Most of the vehicle forward of the passenger compartment had ceased to exist, leaving jagged petals of metal twisted outward. In the dust on the outside of the vehicle someone had scrawled the words, 'The Royal Engineers Christmas Cracker'.

This was the first mine incident of the IFOR operation.

Christmas Eve

In the meantime I had attended a conference at Brigade HQ, in a hotel at Šipovo. As far as we could tell, all three factions were largely complying with the military requirements of the Dayton Agreement, but attitudes were completely unknown in much of the brigade area. In the area of transfer from Bosnian Croat to Bosnian Serb control looting had been thoroughly organised, including the stripping out of all industrial, agricultural or domestic machinery that could be moved. Šipovo town had been systematically looted and then vandalised by the HVO. With the only light coming from IFOR vehicle headlights and the smouldering embers of buildings that had been fired by the Bosnian Croats, the town was an apocalyptic scene. Most buildings had been looted and vandalised. There were no civilians to be seen. Rubbish and detritus was everywhere and the water mains had burst, flooding the main streets.

Returning to the Mud Factory on Christmas Eve, it became obvious that conditions were extremely squalid and overcrowded. Stuart Mills identified a disused mining facility about three miles west. It was very dilapidated but had hard standing, a large shed in better condition than the Mud Factory and some offices and storerooms. Chris Booth gave B Company and the recce platoon permission to move out there.

First our Explosives Ordnance Disposal team checked the complex for mines and booby traps. Then B Company went to work. The complex, now christened 'the Mine', was full of wrecked cars and lorries. The REME unceremoniously towed these to the edge of the base, where the accumulated pile of rusting and corroded vehicles came to resemble a scrap yard. A large shed contained a huge pile of blood-caked bandages and dressings, and walls and floor were covered with the congealed remnants of what had once been a considerable amount of blood. As soldiers donned thick rubber gloves and boots to clear out the building and make it fit for use by the company, they noticed small chunks of frozen flesh, bits of limbs, body parts and other pieces of apparent human tissue. It seemed most likely that this shed had been some kind of medical post. Had this been where doctors patched up the wounded before despatching them to the rear? This seemed the most likely explanation, but this deep-frozen charnel house was a sobering reminder of the realities of war.

While B Company moved and prepared the Mine for occupation, the recce platoon was busy patrolling to the west of our area. The platoon and its commander Ian McGregor were in their element as they were working on their own. My orders to them were to patrol the area west of Sanski Most and south of the cease-fire line in order to demonstrate an IFOR presence, locate faction formation and unit HQs, and assess possible IFOR bases.

Later Ian wrote in the *Silver Bugle*:

> The change to IFOR brought the platoon some real challenges. We led the move into the unknown, and soon found ourselves knee deep in mud at Sanski Most, but with a real recce job to do. Leaving Vitez meant losing phones, showers and heating but the patrol tasking more than made up for it. We often found things that shocked. There was large-scale evidence of looting, and bodies were located at previous battlefield sites.

Our patrols saw plenty of evidence of war, not only the shell holes, discarded ammunition and military debris from recent fighting, but also signs of civil war and ethnic cleansing dating back to the break-up of Bosnia in 1992. On the Federation side of the front line, whole villages were empty and had been comprehensively looted, either by retreating Serbs or the advancing ABiH or both.

Most disturbing was the number of villages and isolated houses that had been destroyed, not, it seemed, as a result of fighting, but burned or demolished as part of ethnic cleansing. Houses were burned out, with gaunt timbers poking at the sky. Others had been blown up, with the explosion clearly having come from the interior of the house. In many cases, plants were growing inside the buildings, not only weeds and grass but also saplings and bushes, indicating that the destruction had taken place some years earlier, probably when Bosnia imploded in 1992. Apart from the former Bihać pocket, our area was either Serb-held territory or territory from which the Serbs had been expelled by the Muslims a mere three months earlier. So most of this ethnic cleansing seemed to have been directed against Muslims and Croats.

Unsurprisingly patrols discovered human bodies. Many were wearing uniform and appeared to have been soldiers killed during the autumn fighting. We also found body parts and macabre remains, like the throat, windpipe and pair of lungs one patrol observed dangling from a bush on the bank of the River Sana. Some of the body parts we saw could have come from animals struck by artillery fire or who had detonated mines. Others were clearly human in origin, apparently from soldiers and civilians killed during the autumn fighting.

We could see no direct evidence of war crimes or atrocities, but to be certain, Division sent the commander of its military police, the Provost Marshall, up to the battlegroup to give an independent assessment. If he decided that there was evidence of war crimes, he would have the evidence professionally recorded. After spending a couple of days with us and a freezing night in the Mud Factory, he concluded that none of the bodies or groups of bodies we had discovered was anything other than 'fortunes of war'.

We were unsurprised, mainly because our patrols could see all the evidence of battle for our own eyes. During our training we had considered how we might deal with the aftermath of war crimes. Nothing that we found or saw during this period appeared anything more than unfortunate soldiers against whom the 'fortunes of war' had turned, or luckless civilians who happened to get caught in the crossfire. Most of us who discovered the pathetic human remains found them repellent – for not only did the bullets, shells and shrapnel literally rip the bodies apart, but the destruction of mortal flesh inevitably reminded us of our own fragile mortality. But as far as I could tell, this was not a morale problem – merely a part of our job.

Planning

But I could tell that morale was definitely being eroded by conditions at Sanski Most where the mud at the Mud Factory, was thicker than ever. Compared with Šipovo and the camp at Mrkonjić Grad it seemed very squalid, but the battlegroup would reduce its operations to a minimum on 25 December, in order to allow the maximum number of people to celebrate Christmas. It would also let us all relax after four days during which both people and machines had been at full throttle.

Straight after Christmas we would need to give fresh direction to the battlegroup. I gathered the planning team around a wooden table and spent the morning conducting the estimate and making plans for our new mission.

We had to implement the military aspects of the Dayton Agreement in the westernmost part of Bosnia. It was a huge area, which had seen little or nothing of the UN. As we went through the familiar checklist for mission analysis and the estimate, I could see that all the Battlegroup HQ officers relished the task.

As B Company and the recce platoon were seeing for themselves, much of the Muslim area had recently been captured from the Serbs. It had been heavily looted, subjected to ethnic cleansing and mass movements of population. It was effectively lawless, as a constant rattle of gunfire around our camps testified. The part of Republika Srpska that we had patrolled seemed in contrast relatively civilised and prosperous, but we had already found traces of ethnic cleansing carried out several years before. So far on both sides, however, many soldiers and civilians seemed to welcome IFOR and all the military commanders we had encountered seemed prepared to cooperate.

Our role should be to reinforce their military compliance with the peace agreement. We would do this by being seen to be impartial, and by persuading them that we could provide sufficient security for them to take the risk of lowering their military guard.

We planned our operations in three 'core functions', of finding, fixing and striking. Clearly we had an awful lot of finding to do. The only information we had about where the faction armies actually were was a single hand-drawn map of the front line that had been bequeathed to us by the UNPROFOR Bihać Area Command, together with the locations of the Muslim 5 and 7 Corps HQs. Everything else we had to find out for ourselves, by patrols and liaison.

If we found the factions, and 'fixed' them by promoting compliance and deterring non-compliance, we would only need to be *prepared* to strike. So 'fixing' meant targeting the will and capability of the warring factions in order to deter non-compliance. It was important that the factions and the civil population could see that we had the ability to strike decisively – either to defend ourselves or to enforce the Dayton Agreement. If there were any infringements of Dayton we would issue a formal protest immediately and be prepared to act as robustly as the situation required.

All our operations would be conducted within an integrated framework of deep, close and rear operations. Deep operations would aim to shape the opinions of the military and the civil population in favour of compliance. We would do this by liaison at every level from myself downwards. Military commission meetings would be used to explain to the faction military what we were doing, what they were required to do and how we expected to see them implementing Dayton. Liaison and commissions would inform the military commanders, but we also needed to get the message across to ordinary soldiers and civilians on both sides, about IFOR in general and what we were doing in particular. We needed to locate local newspapers and radio stations to get our message across more widely. We would encourage contact between the factions on the front line, including body and prisoner exchanges and mine-clearing operations. The battlegroup had nothing to hide from anyone, so our operations would be transparent and open.

Our close operations would be based on three principles. Firstly, deploying our forces in a way that maximised their exposure to the faction armies and civilians in order to instil confidence. Secondly, verifying that the factions were complying with the military requirements of Dayton. Thirdly, clearly demonstrating our ability to use force to compel compliance if necessary.

This meant we had to monitor what was going on and maintain our presence on the ground, operating equally on both sides of the confrontation line. Currently we only had B Company, the recce platoon and Battlegroup HQ. Within a week A Company and B Squadron would return to our command and an artillery battery would join us. How should I deploy them and configure the battlegroup? The best option seemed to be that B Company should not move base, but should continue to work in the ABiH 7 Corps area on the Muslim side and in Serb territory immediately opposite. They would be in the east of our area with B Squadron in the centre and A Company on the west. All would operate on both sides of the cease-fire line. This would help demonstrate our even-handed approach and would help promote liaison and problem-solving across the front line.

As our only access to Serb-controlled territory was WHITE FANG, we needed to open more crossing points, to improve our ability to deploy throughout this huge area. This would not be easy. We still hadn't been able to confirm where the front line was and we knew little about either faction's command structure.

We also needed to protect ourselves and to sustain ourselves logistically, activities the Army calls Rear Operations. Although IFOR had very wide-ranging powers, it would be necessary to keep as much of the consent and cooperation of both military and civil communities as possible, without interfering with our operations. There was nothing to be gained by creating unnecessary friction.

We would protect ourselves by retaining the initiative and dominating the ground. The priority was operations and the only fortifications would be the presence of whatever armoured vehicles happened to be at the base. We chose to construct the bare minimum of defences at each base, simply to deter the theft of stores and equipment. This meant that bases never appeared to be over-fortified or under siege, giving local civilians and the military confidence. It also meant that the occupants of the base could focus on operations, diverting minimum resources to security. We did not want to show a defensive attitude. If someone shot at us, we would shoot back. If we were shelled, we would go out and find the artillery piece or mortar, kill the crew and destroy the weapon.

Developing the plan and supporting staff work took Battlegroup HQ the afternoon and evening – the officers huddled around the maps and hurricane lanterns spread around two tables in the small, cold, dark room where we did our planning. Once I was satisfied that the operations officer and the rest of the team had enough direction to allow them to produce a written operations order I ended the meeting, and walked into the shed of the Mud Factory. It was ten o'clock at night. Most soldiers were already asleep, but a few were drinking tea and coffee, quietly talking in low voices. I chatted for a while, admiring the impressive Christmas tree that had somehow been erected. It was decorated with Christmas baubles largely improvised from wrappings of presents people had received.

I was the only person to have my own room, but it was more like a prison cell: a square box maybe two metres on each side, which, despite Private Leck's valiant efforts with a kerosene heater, never seemed to get warm. Amazingly, the factory contained some relatively undamaged furniture, and I had been given a desk and a very battered old wardrobe. About half the glass in the window was still intact and the remaining empty panes were now covered with transparent plastic sheeting. A folding metal and canvas chair and my camp bed completed the furniture.

The only adornment was a huge piece of graffiti on the south wall of the room. It showed two enormous rabbits mating. The size of the rabbits, each four or five feet long, was not the most offputting feature, nor was the word 'SEKS' with which the artist had thoughtfully captioned the picture, nor the grossly exaggerated genitals of the rodents. It was more that each rabbit seemed to have fur covered in the spots of a leopard and ferocious jaws with an incongruous array of long jagged teeth, like a caricature of the enormous shark from *Jaws*. It was, I explained to visitors, clear evidence that the Bosnians had been experimenting with genetic engineering and planned to release giant man-eating mutant rabbits upon their opponents. No one took this seriously, but at least it gave me a conversation point for breaking the ice with visitors.

Too often on exercises and in Northern Ireland, I had experienced the results of sleep loss – both on commanders and on myself. Sometimes I had become so exhausted that my effectiveness had been significantly reduced. I had no difficulty with pushing others and myself on short, intense, exercises, or when the operational situation really demanded it. But a six-month tour in Bosnia was different – I had a responsibility to the whole battlegroup not to allow myself to become unnecessarily tired. From the start of the tour, I had been determined that my head should hit the pillow, or whatever served as a pillow, by eleven o'clock in the evening.

Despite the conditions, I achieved this every night in the Mud Factory. On Christmas Eve I fell into my sleeping bag to the sounds of Puccini's *Tosca*, which my short-wave radio had picked up on a Croatian station, and then flicked over to the reassuring sounds of Big Ben and the BBC World Service Radio news. It already had reports of Christmas celebrations. As with every other evening I spent in the Mud Factory, I fell asleep to the sounds of long bursts of automatic gunfire in the distance. In a strange way the sound of various Bosnians firing their Kalashnikovs around us seemed a form of background music to the December evenings in Sanski Most. We joked that if they were shooting so far away from us, they were at least not shooting *at* us.

'Merry Christmas Everybody'

I was up early on Christmas morning. Our excellent satellite communications detachment had rigged up telephone extensions to allow everyone to make a call home during the Christmas holiday, using old packing crates and sheer ingenuity to convert the tiny vandalised washroom of the factory into three minuscule telephone booths. I knew that these would become extremely busy, so at seven o'clock, I telephoned my quarter in Paderborn. Liz was only half-awake and a little bemused to be receiving a call so early. As I spoke, I found it difficult to imagine the contrast between the damp, muddy base and the warm dry comfort of our married quarter. I found it particularly frustrating that I would not be able to spend the day with my two-year-old son – missing the first time he would appreciate the fun. It was almost a relief when I reached the five-minute limit of my Christmas call.

By the time I had finished the lines had already become very busy and, for the next few days, people would have to wait for hours for a connection.

Despite this frustration, almost all of the battlegroup managed to get through to someone in England or Germany at some time. I let officers and warrant officers use my room for calls home.

Next on the agenda was the officers and warrant officers taking 'gunfire' to the troops in their beds. Lugging the containers of this traditional brew of tea, whisky and rum into the tents and dispensing cups to sleepy soldiers was hugely enjoyable, particularly to see the many Christmas cards and decorations which were proudly displayed in every tent.

I then retired to my room. I had a small bag of Christmas cards and gifts from friends and family that I wanted to open in private. Many cards showed paintings of Biblical scenes. I could not help thinking of how the Christmas story might be portrayed by setting it in Bosnia in the 1990s. The country had certainly seen plenty of Old Testament vengeance and retribution. I had no doubt that the Massacre of the Innocents had sometimes been horrifically brought to life. What Bosnia really needed now was some New Testament humility and selfless reconciliation.

More mail arrived. I was touched to receive Christmas cards from Princess Alexandra, the regiment's deputy colonel in chief, General Guthrie, chief of the General Staff, the head of the Army. He wrote: 'To Ben and all members of the battalion, thinking of you all at this crucial moment in the history of the Balkans'.

Steve Noble had a bag of cards addressed to the battalion or to 'a British soldier in Bosnia'. Helping him open them, I was even more touched to find a card to the battalion signed by Light Infantry veterans of the Korean War living in Sunderland. I had visited Korea and knew that the mountains were jagged, the summer was hot and humid and the winters were bone-chillingly cold. We were far better equipped and sheltered than British soldiers had been in that bleak theatre of war. It was humbling to receive a card from four of our regimental forebears who had operated in a country with a similar mountainous climate, who probably fought for their lives with far less of the comfort and technology we took for granted.

We had a church service for B Company the JCOs and the division liaison officer and his crew from Prijedor. I gave a short reading and Nick Cook, our padre, produced a snappy sermon. Some of us found singing the familiar carols an emotional test, for the tunes triggered too many memories of previous Christmas celebrations with friends and family. Christmas lunch was again served to the private soldiers and junior NCOs by the serjeants, warrant officers and officers. I wore a Father Christmas red hat that I had been sent by my brother and a garish Santa Claus badge, complete with flashing red light on the nose. Through some excellent anticipation and sheer hard work the quartermaster and WO2 Stemp, the Master Chef, had ensured that all of our bases had a traditional Christmas lunch of turkey, fresh vegetables, all the trimmings and Christmas pudding. Later I learned that 2 LI managed to have more British soldiers eating a proper Christmas lunch than any other British unit then in Bosnia. Given the enormous strain on the battlegroup and brigade logistic systems imposed by our redeployment west, and the conditions in which the cooks were working this was no mean achievement, and had an excellent effect on morale. There was a tremendous atmosphere around the wooden tables and benches crammed with soldiers.

I made a short sharp speech, telling everyone that I, like them, was missing my kith and kin. We should be satisfied with our work in UNPROFOR, and the first four days of NATO operations had gone really well so far. I concluded by leading the officers, warrant officers and serjeants in toasting the health of the soldiers and corporals. I then privately said goodbye to Mark Goldsack, the adjutant, who was being posted to command a company in our First Battalion. Much of the success of our initial NATO operations was due to his work as a second operations officer. Johnny Bowron, his successor, had a hard act to follow.

I had to be at Mrkonjić Grad in time for the Christmas supper that A Company and Echelon were having. As I drove across the Anvil, I was struck by how little IFOR traffic there was. Brigadier Richard Dannatt had directed that the brigade should allow the maximum number of soldiers the opportunity to celebrate Christmas. It certainly seemed that this had been done.

At Mrkonjić Grad, I helped serve Christmas dinner, again to the same high standard. Soldiers seemed amused by my hat and badge. Someone had an enormous ghetto blaster playing a tape of Christmas music. Slade's loud brash song 'Merry Christmas Everybody' with its anthemic chorus brought a wild cheer. A Company had organised a game of charades after the meal. Inevitably I had to take my turn and drew *The Bill*, the television programme about a London police squad. I mimed a policeman arresting someone, which worked. After a hugely amusing game, Jan and his officers insisted that I help them eat some Stilton and drink some port that had arrived in Christmas presents. This I did, enjoying their company and relaxed banter. It was the first time I had seen them all together for over a month – a reflection on the diverse nature and far-flung location of the tasks the battlegroup had been performing.

CHAPTER SEVEN
'Across the Great Divide'

We needed to establish formal liaison channels between NATO and the faction armies as conduits for the passage of information. Experience had shown that liaison by commanders and liaison officers played a key role in nipping potential problems in the bud. During UNPROFOR operations, liaison with the factions had often been poorly co-ordinated, with faction commanders receiving visits from many different UN liaison officers and commanders. This 'revolving door liaison' reduced unity of effort, and the British Division was determined to do better by adopting a more structured approach. General Jackson liaised with corps commanders and Brigadier Dannatt with faction corps chiefs of staff. I had to deal with faction divisional commanders and my company commanders would deal with brigade commanders.

Boxing Day saw the first Brigade Military Commission meeting at Šipovo. Brigadier Dannatt would be in the chair and the factions would be represented by the chiefs of staff of each corps, or 'Operations Group' in the case of the HVO. The two British battlegroup commanders and the artillery and engineer commanders would attend 'in the cheap seats'. We would know exactly what had gone on at the meeting, which would help make sure that the factions got the same message at every level of command.

The meeting was brisk and conducted in a businesslike manner. From the outset Brigadier Dannatt made it clear to the factions that they must comply with the military provisions of the Dayton Agreement. We were there to see that they did so. If they didn't comply, they could expect us to use force. The faction delegations were subdued, but both the HVO and ABiH delegations gave the impression that they would be taking every opportunity to whinge – if we give them any.

During the drive back to Sanski Most, I noticed that a hard chill had set in. The unexpectedly balmy weather, which had caused so many problems by melting the snow, had ended. By the time I reached the Mud Factory, it was bitterly cold and snowing hard. The Factory was muddier than ever.

Finding the Factions

Since we had arrived in Sanski Most our operations had been constrained by a lack of information about the factions. Without knowing where their units, formations and HQs were, we could not assess their degree of compliance. Unless we had knowledge of their front-line positions or minefields, we could put ourselves at unnecessary and avoidable risk. The profession of soldiering is, of course, all about risks, but one of the most important functions of a commander is to make sure that unnecessary risk is minimised.

We had arrived in the area with little information about the faction armies other than a few HQ locations that had been identified by the JCOs and liaison officers. We had a couple of out-of-date air photos of Sanski Most. Requests for air and satellite photos of other key towns and of the front line were never met. The same applied to requests for information concerning faction air defences – although NATO had kept the area under surveillance for three years.

I had been given just two copies of the new US-produced 1:50,000 scale 'Dayton map' that showed the authoritative positions of the Agreed Cease-fire Line and Inter-Entity Boundary Line. But the rest of the battlegroup was still using the less accurate and out-of-date 1:100,000 scale maps issued for UN operations. Onto these the user had to copy by hand the two Dayton lines and the UN-mapped front line. All commanders in the battlegroup down to lance-corporal needed a set of maps, and a huge amount of hand copying had to be done – with a high probability of errors resulting.

Brigade were giving us regular briefings concerning the overall situation in their area and we could hear the reports from the Fusileers to our east over the command net, but there was no other intelligence or information available to us. We therefore had to use our patrols and liaison officers to go out and find out where the factions were.

The key information was the location of faction military HQs, from brigade down to company. We were not yet seeking to get onto the front line. Not having established which faction formations were responsible for what areas made this too dangerous until we had more accurate information. Indeed, Brigadier Dannatt had firmly directed that front-line patrols were only to be conducted with the factions in attendance.

Patrols were being conducted by a pair of Warriors or Scimitars. We remained quite cautious at this stage and the mortar platoon was still used to create an umbrella of potential indirect fire. At some risk, liaison officers attempted to identify HQs further afield. Given the objective to separate the faction troops at D+30, I directed that our operations should be limited to the immediate area of the front line within fifteen kilometres of Sanski Most. The recce platoon were also tasked to identify locations, such as disused factories, barracks or warehouses, which might be suitable for bases. In this they were singularly unsuccessful, as all the suitable facilities were already occupied by faction troops, whose need for shelter from the winter weather was the same as ours.

Patrol commanders would be given a route or an area to conduct a reconnaissance in, to establish faction locations and attitudes. Initially there was a lot of hit and miss in our targeting, but we soon gathered sufficient information to be able to focus our patrolling a lot more precisely.

We were aided in this by the ABiH's practice of liberally daubing buildings with graffiti. Some of this was slogans, propaganda and insults to the Bosnian Serbs, but there were also directions to units and headquarters. This allowed our patrols to locate ABiH brigade HQs almost as soon as they entered the formation's area. Where this did not work, our patrols would simply ask faction soldiers whom they encountered where their units or HQs were located.

The vast majority of these enquiries were usually met with stupefied amazement, followed by a refusal to give any information without explicit permission from their superiors. But occasionally a faction soldier or officer would be more cooperative, offer some clue, or let slip a piece of information from which we could derive some intelligence which we could use for more accurate targeting of other patrols or liaison officers.

Command, Control and Communications

I commanded the battlegroup, while Battlegroup HQ controlled and co-ordinated operations on my behalf. In all our war-fighting training, I had used a mixture of personal contact with my subordinates, seeing what was going on for myself, and listening to or talking on the battlegroup radio net. I would be well forward, often just behind the leading squadron or company. When necessary I could exert personal influence. Battlegroup HQ, sited in a central location further to the rear, used the radio net, the Ptarmigan trunk communication telephone and, when time allowed, written orders and instructions to control and co-ordinate.

Co-ordination and supporting functions were dependent on communications, particularly if a high tempo of operations was to be maintained. Without accurate and timely communications, our tempo would reduce to that of the British Army in the First World War. As the factions' speed of decision, action and movement seemed to be at the same level of the British Army of 1916, maintaining a high tempo was one of the ways that our small force could give the factions the impression it was larger than it was. It also gave us the flexibility to quickly concentrate overwhelming force as a response to incidents. Without communications, we would be unable to achieve our mission.

I was spending most daylight hours visiting the factions, patrolling the area in my Rover group or otherwise on the road. In war, Battlegroup HQ would usually have been a small complex of armoured vehicles parked closely together around a canvas awning. Signallers, warrant officers and officers would crouch in the back of command vehicles listening to radio headsets, talking into microphones, writing into logs or marking information on maps. The work of the components of the HQ – the command vehicle controlling the battlegroup net, the artillery and mortar command posts, the engineer cell, the logistic officer and the intelligence section – all needed to be integrated into a whole. The small size of the HQ aided in this, making passage of information easy, although it would have been easier without the incessant noise of generators and vehicle engines. I used the battlegroup second-in-command to co-ordinate and integrate the work of the HQ – effectively acting as battlegroup chief of staff.

We could also set up the HQ away from its vehicles – something we might have done in war if we had needed to operate from buildings, cellars or bunkers. We did this now in Sanski Most, moving the HQ into a corner of the Mud Factory, occupying two small rooms with armoured command vehicles parked alongside. We had set up an operations room in an office, with the intelligence section and logistic cell sharing a disused shower and changing room. A larger room had our attached Battle Group Engineer Operations Officer (BGEOO) with his huge store of maps and ever-increasing collection of minefield traces in one corner; the rest of the room was used for planning and meetings. The HQ gave us only a slightly larger area than if we had been working from our vehicles, but we had more headroom and were able to make the working area a little cleaner and warmer.

Although we were only commanding a company, the Recce Platoon and some mortars, the headquarters team had to work hard to overcome a considerable amount of frustration and friction resulting from difficulties with our communications. Of course, our doctrine of mission command was designed to allow commanders at every level to work around the inevitable problems arising in war and I had complete confidence in the officers and serjeants of the companies and platoons. But our tempo of operations was being reduced by the time taken to pass information. In addition, any casualties we might take might not be reported and then evacuated as quickly as they should be.

We knew that there was a huge amount of high-technology strategic communications equipment linking the NATO HQs, as well as the UK Joint Headquarters at Wilton. Staff officers at these locations had no shortage of video-conferencing facilities, computers, faxes, photocopiers and all the other paraphernalia of the information age and modern business practice. But the 'information revolution' seemed to slow down at brigade level and it ran out of steam almost completely at Battlegroup HQ. In the Mud Factory we had four laptop computers, a couple of which were usually broken or clogged with dirt, and a single compact photocopier, which received a tremendous battering as it travelled around Bosnia. Miraculously it kept operating.

Company HQs commanded and controlled their platoons in ways little different from practice in the Korean or Second World Wars. Working from their vehicles or looted and abandoned buildings, they kept written logs of radio transmissions and marked information by hand onto maps stuck together with adhesive tape or glue. The only piece of command equipment unfamiliar to infantry companies fighting in the 1940s or '50s would have been the pocketbook-sized KL43 data entry device, which reduced the time to format and encode messages.

Platoon commanders and serjeants led their patrols from the turrets of their armoured vehicles, using insecure radios, paper codes or scribbling orders into a pocket notebook by torchlight. The inside of their turrets would be festooned with cards showing radio call signs and codes, folded maps, pens, pencils and marking pens – all held in place with a combination of bulldog clips and elastic. All these items would be dirty, oily and either dusty or wet, depending on the weather outside.

Our battlegroup command net continued to work through a network of mountaintop rebroadcast stations deployed by the Signal Platoon. These consisted of one or two communications vehicles and were manned by a couple of signallers for weeks on end. The signallers seemed to enjoy this tedious job on these lonely, vulnerable, desolate and windswept locations.

As it had in our war-fighting training, the signal platoon provided an outstanding service. We had direct communications both with C Company on Mount Igman and with the recce platoon now working to the west of Bosanska Krupa. This was a distance of almost two hundred and fifty kilometres over mountainous terrain, using five rebroadcast stations. The signal platoon had practised this with great skill in the first part of the tour, albeit over one-third the distance.

If one of the rebroadcast stations stopped working for whatever reason, this could disrupt the chain, and break it into two parts. We had a high-frequency (HF) backup net, but the winter weather and technical characteristics of HF made this even less reliable than our VHF net. Despite the expertise and dogged determination of our signallers, the net would 'go down' regularly, anything up to half a dozen times a day. Fortunately, these interruptions usually only lasted about ten minutes, but no one could ever predict when they would happen, except that the net always seemed to collapse just as someone had some important information to pass. We had learned to work with these problems over the previous seven weeks but the increased size of our area doubled the difficulty. That the interruptions in the net were no greater in our NATO operations than in our UN operations was a significant achievement by the signal platoon.

We had to use the brigade command net to communicate with the rest of the other units in the formation and the brigade HQ. This also used a number of rebroadcast stations, established by the signallers of the Brigade Signal Squadron. It was 'secure', all stations using encryption devices to scramble the signal in order to conceal our conversations from the factions who we knew would try to eavesdrop on our transmissions. This net had two problems. Firstly the encryption units added a degree of complexity and unreliability to the radios, especially when connected together in a rebroadcast station. Secondly the Brigade Signal Squadron had not had the opportunity to practise multiple rebroadcast nets in the way we had. Not surprisingly this led to significant initial problems with the brigade command net. Down times were more frequent and longer than on our nets – often between a third and half of the day. In addition the quality of the net was often extremely poor, making it very difficult to understand what the other person was saying. Simple messages that in training might take a minute to pass could take five or even ten times as long.

Battlegroup HQ had a single satellite telephone. Unlike the compact satellite phones used by journalists, this was bulky (so large that it required a complete eight-tonne lorry to carry the equipment, aerial dish and protective dome), extremely fragile and not very easy to use. The NATO forces, UN and humanitarian agencies, media and the factions all used satellite phones on the same network, all trying to access the same satellites. Consequently it could often take up to an hour to get a connection, let alone make a successful call – which depended on a line being free at other end! We had two more of these devices, one deployed to Echelon and one with C Company, which we were in process of reallocating to A Company.

The saving grace was the Ptarmigan trunk communication system, which used a combination of radio relay and satellite terminals to produce a kind of secure telephone service. Eventually, 3 Division's Signals Regiment would establish a full divisional trunk communications network, but the bulk of the Ptarmigan equipment was on the ships coming from the UK and would not be in place in western Bosnia until late January. In the meantime, a skeleton Ptarmigan network had been deployed. We had been given an 'Airmobile Ptarmigan Detachment'. Commanded by a young but extremely competent Royal Signals officer, this team carried a satellite terminal and some Ptarmigan equipment in a Land Rover. They connected us into the Ptarmigan network and could access civil telephones worldwide. At night we allowed those who had yet to make their Christmas call home to use the system.

Medical and Logistic Problems

If we had been at war, the evacuation and treatment of casualties would have taken second place to the fulfilment of the mission. But we were not at war. I knew that any unnecessary casualties would do nothing to promote NATO's aims, and might have undermined support for our work. The difficulties with communications worried me greatly. If we took casualties, would company and Battlegroup HQ learn about them quickly enough? Would we be able to orchestrate evacuation by road or helicopter to the medical facilities at Bihać or Gornji Vakuf quickly enough? I could not be sure, given the state of the winter roads and the winter weather, which often precluded helicopter evacuation.

I tried to make sure that I did not show my worries to my subordinates, but I redoubled my exhortations to Stuart Mills and Ian McGregor not to take any unnecessary risks. I also made sure that Battlegroup HQ was absolutely clear that, should we take any casualties, passage of information about them and arranging and conducting their evacuation would be the main effort, taking precedence over all other activities. We had used the same principle in Northern Ireland.

At this stage, the Ptarmigan system could not support the Single Channel Radio Access (SCRA), a secure mobile telephone. This meant that there was no way of directly communicating with brigade logistic units, except over the difficult and congested brigade command net, or by going to see them. This made co-ordinating our logistic effort considerably more difficult. Our KL43 data entry devices were extremely useful for sending logistic information within the battlegroup, but there was no way of linking them to the brigade net or the satellite phone in order to send messages as electronic data.

Both Dave Wroe, the logistic co-ordinator forward in Battlegroup HQ, and Dave Jarratt, the quartermaster in Mrkonjić Grad, found it difficult to talk to each other and virtually impossible to talk to the logistic units responsible for our support. In addition, the Royal Logistic Corps logistic support detachment, which was supposed to act as a link between the quartermaster and logistic units with radios on the logistic net, had yet to move from Vitez. Somehow these problems were overcome, largely through the battlegroup's logistic officers spending an enormous amount of their time travelling to talk to each other and the logistic support units.

As if the friction imposed by unsatisfactory communications was not enough, we were also gravely concerned about our logistic situation, particularly fuel and spare parts, which were in very short supply. As more troops and vehicles joined the battlegroup and as wear and tear took its inevitable toll, these shortages could become major limitations. The most critical problem was a shortage of fuel. On three separate occasions in late December and early January we thought that we were about to run out. I had to reduce the intensity of patrolling to make sure that operations did not grind to a halt and that we had sufficient fuel left to be able to evacuate casualties. We instituted emergency measures to ensure that the battlegroup got the fuel it needed. Captain Paul Evanson did not wait, as he was supposed to, for fuel to be delivered to the Battlegroup Echelon, but sent his fuel-carrying vehicles to the Brigade Supply Area to collect petrol and diesel as soon as it was available. We had fuel flown to the battlegroup, swinging precariously in nets under giant Chinook helicopters, all the way up from the logistic base at Split on the Croatian coast.

We learned that the fuel shortage was caused in part by the division's logistic units having to cope with the same kind of communications problems as us. The large distances, poor roads and winter weather were also putting a considerable strain on the elderly fuel tankers travelling from Split to the division's units. All this was against the background of the division moving itself into Bosnia with many logistic assets yet to arrive at this stage.

Between Christmas and New Year, we were managing to overcome most of the problems most of the time. It was a time of great frustration for those responsible for our logistics. Dave Wroe was working flat out, often to the point of exhaustion, to arrange the logistic support that would sustain our high tempo of operations. Dave later described our logistic operations:

There were shortages of every commodity except rations and ammunition. Everything we needed, they said, was on ships approaching Split. Was it, we all wondered, on the Marie Celeste?

The solution to the logistic nightmare was to play every known card in the deck to get what we wanted. Initially the greatest problems facing the G4 chain was without doubt the Petrol Oil and Lubricant (POL) supply. Lines of communication extended from Vitez to Mrkonjić Grad to Sanski Most to Bihać. Blizzard conditions and a route that became a hundred and eighty kilometre slide with no safety bars was no joke, particularly when it was mostly done at night.

The considerable effort that we had put into logistic training during the previous eighteen months had really paid off. We were also fortunate that the seven weeks of operations in the winter mountains around Sarajevo had taught us logistic lessons aplenty, especially the need to consider logistics from the outset of all our operational planning.

Captain Paul Evanson, assisted by Serjeant Major Anderson, his deputy, was leading resupply convoys in atrocious weather over the treacherous mountain roads to ensure that the battalion remained properly supplied. The logistic vehicles were continually travelling to and from their base in Mrkonjić Grad across the Anvil. This huge empty area was still garrisoned by the HVO, and Bosnian Croat soldiers and civilians were still looting buildings. The desolate landscape held plenty of evidence of war and ethnic cleansing. It was littered with the discarded paraphernalia of war including shells, ammunition boxes, bandages and other military detritus. Under the lowering winter skies and in the chill wind, the plateau could be profoundly depressing. Writing in the *Church Times* Nick Cook, the battalion's chaplain, described his journeys across the Anvil, which he saw as a kind of material Hell:

> All the houses along the way were trashed, burned and looted; cars were wrecked and possessions strewn in the gardens. Everything was smashed, torn, burned. There were no signs of life – not a single living soul; no dogs, nor other animals. This was not some blitzed region where aerial bombardment had laid everything waste; though just as disturbing, that might have been easier to understand. Along the roads anything in the least useful had been ruined. Roofs were damaged and every single pane of glass was shattered in every house, every shed, every building in the towns and villages.
>
> From a distance, each hamlet or town gives the impression of civilisation. As you draw near though, your hopes are dashed; it's another false reflection of normality. Everything that at a distance seems useful is, on closer inspection, damaged. If you stopped there would be nothing to sustain you in that frozen wilderness – so you keep moving.

I also took in these sights as I travelled around the area. But my mind was on other things. I was greatly concerned by the difficulties of logistics and especially of communications. The battlegroup was further away from the British logistic bases and from medical support than other part of the division. We had already learned that it could be difficult or impossible for helicopters to get through the clouds and freezing fog that so frequently covered the mountains between us and their operating bases at Gornji Vakuf and Split.

If the situation had deteriorated and the factions had ceased to comply, logistic and medical risk would have constrained our operations. This we could have coped with, provided that we had the initiative and were not taking casualties. My biggest concern, however, was the difficulties that would result if the battlegroup incurred any serious casualties. If so, would the combination of inadequate communications and bad weather make it more difficult or impossible to evacuate casualties – particularly if the cloud was too low to allow helicopters to reach our positions?

Deliberately, I did not share these concerns with others. The only way to reduce the risk of what we were doing to the minimum would have been never to leave our base in Sanski Most. This, of course, would not have achieved our mission. It would also have considerably increased the risk of factions being unimpressed by us, and our capability to reinforce compliance, or to deal with non-compliance. We would also have been unable to deter or prevent any attacks on us. All three factions showed contempt for weakness and would take advantage of it at every possible opportunity. I had seen too many contingents in UNPROFOR whose operational approach was so defensive, cautious and minimalist as to have no effect on the factions. This meant that these contingents became marginalised, vulnerable to intimidation by warlords, a danger to themselves and a net drag on the effectiveness of UNPROFOR.

I was determined that this would not happen to us. Therefore I consciously decide not to pass my concerns to the company commanders or lower. Excessive caution could paralyze junior commanders' initiative. So my role would be to make sure that that I and the HQ provided the best possible planning, command and control to the battlegroup, in order to maximise the chance of success and minimise the chances of casualties arising as a result of miscalculation, avoidable confrontation, or inadequate planning. Over this period, as I mulled over this difficulty of achieving the balance between risk and mission success, I often reminded myself that this is what I was paid to do.

'Bondi Beach'

We needed to promote liaison and give the armies and civilians more exposure to IFOR. One way of doing this was to establish platoon bases. These would be in disused houses or other small buildings and would be opened and closed as the tactical situation required. The brigade had already begun to use the phrase 'manoeuvre basing' to describe these concepts.

We managed to do this sooner than I expected, due to B Company turning two problems to their advantage, creating an opportunity which they then exploited. The story began with the minestrike by the Royal Engineers' Land Rover on 23 December to the east of Sanski Most (described in the previous chapter).

On Christmas Eve, at the same place, a Serb position directed machine-gun fire towards the Muslim line. A formal letter of protest written by General Alagic, the 7 Corps commander, was handed to the IFOR Divisional Liaison Officer. The letter also complained that Bosnian Serb troops in the area had been improving existing trenches and bunkers and building new defensive positions. Some time was spent deciphering the obscure ABiH map references, for 'position TT 4372', as the Serb position that had fired was called, conformed to no system of map references that we knew of. We needed to investigate this cease-fire violation as soon as possible, and it seemed best to bite the bullet and to get on with it before the trail grew too cold.

Stuart Mills put his LO, Captain Toby Ellwood, onto the task. He and the JCOs worked hard in Serb territory to establish just what unit was responsible for the area. After much patient negotiation, B Company arranged for a meeting to be held in no-man's-land. The JCOs would bring the Serb battalion commander from the east, B Company would provide security and Toby Ellwood, escorted by David Livingston's platoon, would bring the Muslim commander. David deployed his Warriors to cover the site of the minestrike, to respond to fire from either side. David takes up the story:

> We were keen to get the two opposing commanders together in the middle to sort out the problem that had caused the letter of complaint and instil respect and trust. After discussion with both sides it was established that the minefield had been laid by the Muslims. They stated that we had cleared all their mines. The Serbs claimed not to have laid any at all. However, we still had three hundred metres of snow-covered track to clear to the Serb side. I decided the risk was acceptable and started to move down the track in my Warrior. We stopped several times for me to dismount and check suspicious lumps in the snow, all the time being watched tentatively by both sides. The route, as the commanders had said, was clear and we linked up with the JCOs on the Serb side.
>
> Having cleared the route it was then up to us to coax both opposing commanders into no-man's-land. They were put into the rear of the JCOs' Land Rovers, which in turn were escorted by Warriors from my platoon. Once in the centre I deployed riflemen to provide a close inner cordon round the group while the two Warriors sat close at hand, traversing their turrets menacingly, as the liaison officer and JCOs conducted the negotiations.

The Serb commander admitted that the machine-gun fire had come from his position. He explained that, far from improving their positions, his soldiers were attempting to dismantle them. The wood and metal that had been used to shore up the trenches and bunkers would be extremely useful for a multitude of non-military purposes. The Muslim commander accepted this. David's troops were delighted to see no animosity between these two officers, who were easily persuaded to shake hands at the end of the meeting. David observed:

It was a strange moment as the two commanders who had been fighting each other for so long met, discussed and resolved a problem, shook hands and then returned to their respective sides, all under close protection of British soldiers.

David's willingness to expose himself to danger by accompanying the Muslim commander into the zone between the two forces gave both sides great confidence in the security that IFOR was providing. This was practical leadership, of the highest order.

I was elated to learn that B Company had been able to turn two setbacks – the mine incident and the cease-fire violation – into a major success. Opening this additional crossing point would improve our ability to get patrols onto the Serb side of the line. I wanted to have a permanent IFOR presence there, to increase our visibility and deter any malcontents on either side from laying mines to close the crossing.

Stuart Mills anticipated this. He had already got David Livingston's platoon to take over a derelict house next to the road. Toby Ellwood christened the crossing 'BONDI BEACH' after the Australian surfers' paradise – the name standing for warmth, warm water, constant sunlight and bikini-clad beach beauties; all notably absent anywhere in Bosnia.

We were all living cheek by jowl, either in cold, overcrowded and uncomfortable bases like the Mud Factory or Sanski Most Mine, or out of our vehicles. It was a real test of morale and leadership for seven or eight men to live continuously in and around a cramped armoured vehicle. To minimise aggravation and friction required self-discipline, limitless patience and a real sense of humour. Using empty houses as platoon bases relieved the pressure on B Company's main base at the Sanski Most mine. The BONDI BEACH house had no windows or doors and only a few fragments of furniture. Soldiers painted the name 'BONDI BEACH' in letters four feet high on the bare unplastered breezeblock walls, together with large red tropical palm trees. Lance Corporal Credland described how his platoon made the building habitable:

The building we had to make our home was a detached house in the middle of the ethically cleansed village of Sassina. Rooms didn't have any windows or doors. We began sealing the 'envelope' (surveyors' terminology) of the building. This consisted of wedging timber slats into the window void, cut to length using a rusty bow saw. Plastic sheeting was then nailed to the frame and then cut to size. The frame was finally sealed by using vast amounts of brown masking tape. Quality of finish varied considerably, from double glazing down to 'that will f---ing do'. Next priority was the door. Rugs were nailed to the existing frame. In view of the weather, possibly the most important pieces of kit were the wood fires that are in constant use throughout Bosnia. One appeared in every room.

The cookhouse was run by Corporal Shelley and Private Socks (a scraggy mutt of the four-legged type). Dinners were a big favourite with everyone.

Having filled up on all-in dinners day after day, inevitably the time would come when the excess would require disposing of. With health and hygiene a priority, the toilet was sited opposite the kitchen. It initially comprised a chair with the bottom smashed out and a black bin liner, but we progressed onto a 'Gucci' plastic thunderbox and soft bog roll.

We were fortunate to have a natural spring. A cast iron bath was propped up on bricks and six-foot pickets to allow a fire to be lit beneath it. We also constructed a shower. A metal trough was positioned midway between the basement wall and a showerhead attached at one end. A cement mixer was then filled with wood and used to heat the trough. Temperature control was a nightmare for both bath and shower.

The company used the crossing point to gain access to a huge hinterland of Bosnian Serb territory to the east of the front line. It was a network of hills, woods streams and small villages. Tracks were constricted, narrow and twisting, and the company had great difficulty getting Warrior down some of these routes. In one case a 5 Platoon patrol moving along a farm track became bogged in. The ground was so soft that it took over a week to recover the Warrior concerned – a causeway had to be built over the soft ground before the vehicle could be pulled out.

Assembling the Full Battlegroup

With just B Company, the Recce Platoon, some liaison officers and two JCO patrols, the battlegroup was far too thinly spread for its tasks. Our area of influence was limited to WHITE FANG, Sanski Most and the area around Bondi Beach. The recce platoon and our LOs were working further afield, but the effects they could achieve were very limited. The small size of the battlegroup and the need for all forces to be covered by the mortar platoon meant that we could not give much of an impression of overwhelming military capability, limiting our ability to deter or challenge non-compliance. We had anticipated this risk, but were relieved when Brigade HQ confirmed that we would shortly receive the battery of light guns that had come off Mount Igman. C Company, also off Igman, would relieve B Squadron Light Dragoons, allowing them to move to us, and A Company would be released from its reserve role by New Year's Eve. This was good news, but we needed to receive these new forces properly and make the best possible use of them as soon as they arrived.

The artillery battery was first to join us. We had been warned that they were arriving several times, but they had not appeared. It was therefore no surprise when, without warning, half the battery arrived by helicopter, guns and vehicles dangling precariously as under-slung loads beneath Sea King helicopters, now with aggressive green 'tiger stripes' painted over the previous coating of UN white. The other half arrived later by road, followed by the battery commander, and finally an order from the chain of command telling us to expect their arrival.

The battery had six 105mm light howitzers, the same type of weapon that had been used to bombard the Argentine defenders of the mountains around Port Stanley and more recently had shelled the Serbs around Mount Igman. The battery had an Arctic warfare role, had trained in Norway every winter, and was well accustomed to operating for prolonged periods in cold mountains. As well as an impressive array of specialist Arctic tents, cookers and survival equipment, the battery was lavishly endowed with Volvo BV 206 over-snow vehicles. As we had left our UN provided BV 206s behind on Mount Igman, we were especially pleased to see these vehicles. Most of them were used as prime movers for the guns, but the battery commander and the three forward observer parties also had them.

These forward observer parties had the same role as our own mortar fire controllers, but were commanded by captains. They had excellent surveillance and target acquisition equipment, principally the OTIS thermal imager, more powerful than our hand-held Spyglass thermal imaging sights. Each team also had a ground surveillance radar, known as MSTAR. Falling snow and some types of rain and fog could defeat binoculars, image intensifiers and thermal sights, but the radar could watch people and vehicles moving through all these conditions. Like the mortar fire controllers, the forward observers were trained to control both artillery and mortar fire, to make the most of this impressive array of surveillance devices and to co-ordinate fire planning. The battalion had practised all of this in our war-fighting training in Germany and Canada, and during the pre-Bosnia training in Sennelager.

We therefore welcomed John Turp, the battery commander, with open arms. I had not worked with John before, but I knew that he would be trained and practised in the co-ordination of all 'offensive support': artillery, mortars and ground attack aircraft, including producing and then executing an integrated fire plan in support of battlegroup operations.

I lost no time in explaining what we were trying to achieve, how we were trying to achieve it and how I thought that he and his battery might help. I explained that, given the high level of compliance showed by the factions so far, reinforcing compliance and deterring non-compliance would be the first priority. We would only need to fire the guns and mortars if this did not work. Therefore I wanted John to expand the indirect fire umbrella covering our patrols, being prepared to fire at any time. Guns and mortars were to be deployed where they could be seen by as many locals and military as possible. This would increase the impression of our strength on the ground. The battery's deployments would be considered as patrols and fully integrated with the work of the rest of the battlegroup. Finally the dedicated artillery communications would provide a way of passing information and messages that could provide much-needed backup to the battlegroup command net.

John was a large, tremendously cheerful man, who quickly gained the confidence of Battlegroup HQ and myself. But on this first meeting he seemed taken aback and a touch surprised to receive such a detailed concept for his artillery. Was I treading on his toes, or was he surprised at the depth and detail of our planning? If the former, would this lead to problems integrating his battery into the battlegroup? Events were to show my fears were groundless.

Quicker than we had been told to expect, B Squadron in Banja Luka were tasked by Brigade to move to a base in Prijedor to work for us. A Company was also being released from their Brigade reserve role to rejoin the battlegroup. I planned to make them responsible for the western part of our area, from the Croatian border eastwards. We had yet to find a suitable base close to the front line, so I ordered them to move to Ćoralići Camp, a former UN base near Cazin, north of Bihać. The company would move along Route BLUEBIRD. This would take the company column through the centre of Bihać, the location of the main headquarters of the Muslim 5 Corps, commanded by the notoriously difficult and truculent General Dudakovic. I wanted him to see more than twenty armoured vehicles travel through an area which had previously seen no IFOR activity.

As soon as the company was ordered to move, Jan de Vos and the advance party set off for the Mud Factory to get an update brief. The main body of the company moved separately to Ćoralići Camp under the command of Captain Martin Bellamy. Their route was more than a hundred and fifty kilometres through high, windswept plateaus and constricted passes. Fresh snow was falling onto the road's layers of hard, compacted ice, making it difficult for drivers to maintain control. The plan was to complete the whole move in daylight, but progress was so slow that darkness fell before the company was even halfway to its destination. Some of the vehicles at the back of the convoy were unable to cross the higher, more exposed mountain passes as the snow had become so thick that further movement in darkness would have been extremely dangerous. Martin had them wait for daylight before continuing.

After several hours of darkness, the Warrior in which Martin was leading the move broke down on a narrow mountain road near Ostrozac. There was little room to pass the vehicle but, ignoring any attempts to slow him down, a Bosnian truck attempted to squeeze by the Warrior anyway. An irresistible force met an immovable object and the truck became well and truly jammed between the Warrior and the side of the mountain, completely blocking the route. Having summoned a recovery vehicle from the back of the column, Martin dismounted to assess the situation. The blockage of the route quickly resulted in a large number of Bosnian civilian and military vehicles forming themselves into traffic jams on either side of the obstruction.

Within minutes Martin was surrounded by extremely angry locals, all jostling, insulting and threatening him. Tempers were running high, and the general chaos was increased in quick succession by a wedding party (all drunk) and by a coachload of Muslim soldiers returning from the front line for New Year's leave (some armed and most drunk). Just as Martin was wondering whether things could get any worse, a soldier told him that a car carrying a pregnant woman in labour had joined the traffic queue.

It took three hours to clear the blockage, during which Martin and his soldiers received much drunken advice from soldiers and armed civilians who vented their frustration by firing their weapons over the stricken vehicles. Eventually the blockage was cleared and the situation was resolved peacefully, but the incident had been greatly at risk of sudden deterioration. Martin showed remarkable coolness in withstanding the considerable pressure from the irate Bosnians, defusing the situation and preventing it from worsening, while also finding time to give clear and concise accounts of the situation over the radio.

The incident illustrated the considerable difficulties of moving vehicle columns. The weather, the poor state of the roads, the drunkenness and obduracy of many of the Bosnians using them and the appalling standards of Bosnian driving and vehicle maintenance all had great potential to cause delay, friction and significant risk. No journey in Bosnia could ever be treated as routine if the considerable inherent friction and risk were to be overcome, all convoy moves had to be treated as major operations, thoroughly planned and controlled.

Friction and risk were also increasing at the Mud Factory – the result of overcrowding and the poor conditions of the base. The whole complex was deep in mud, and the road leading into the complex had disintegrated. The Battalion HQ staff were beginning to look distinctly tired and flat. The newly arrived gunners of our artillery battery wore noticeably cleaner uniforms and curious little camouflage caps, called 'combat caps', that I thought the British Army had abandoned at the end of the 1970s. They told me that these floppy caps were 'much better than berets in Norway'.

The gunners had brought their own cooks and support personnel, but the arrival of sixty more soldiers meant that the Mud Factory was again creaking at the seams. On its own, the Factory would have been just sufficient for the main body of the battery, but putting it together with Battlegroup HQ served to emphasise just how unsuitable the place was as a headquarters. I was increasingly concerned at just how much effort Battlegroup HQ was putting into overcoming the inherent problems of the location. People were getting tired, irritable, run down and worn out, and there was a resulting increase in mistakes and problems of co-ordination. Living and working conditions were still better than if we were working out of armoured vehicles, but only just. We needed to get a move on to find a better location for the HQ, before the morale and effectiveness of Battlegroup HQ fell below the minimum safe level.

The chain of command had told us that we were not to exercise IFOR's right to 'use any facility' by occupying bases without the consent of the local authority, so as not to forfeit civil consent or attract accusations of interfering with economic reconstruction. It was just as well that we had already worked out for ourselves that forcibly seizing factories, bus stations or barracks, no matter how dilapidated they were, would create greater problems than it solved. But this made it more difficult to find a new base for Battlegroup HQ.

Meanwhile B Squadron was moving into the Prijedor area and was offered a number of potential bases by the town's mayor. They selected the impressive modern Prijedor Hotel, right in the centre of the town, overlooking the River Sana. This twelve-storey building would be big enough for both the Squadron and Battlegroup HQ.

The next day, 28 December, Battlegroup HQ formed up on the road outside the Mud Factory, waiting to move, with the various cells operating from the back of command vehicles. I went to the hotel with the advance party. Here we discovered that the Prijedor authorities had second thoughts and now refused us the hotel, apparently on direct orders from Pale, the Bosnian Serb capital. A long, very cold and frustrating morning and afternoon were spent attempting to reverse this decision, unsuccessfully. Bertie Polley was tasked to find somewhere else for his squadron and our HQ to go to.

The advance party returned disconsolately to the Mud Factory, but I found myself at the JCO house in Prijedor, chatting with the JCO commanding officer and the company commander of the JCOs working in the British sector. Both were old friends and they brought me up to date on operations elsewhere in Bosnia, outside the battlegroup area. This added useful collateral to the information that had been coming from both the chain of command and the BBC World Service.

Leaving the JCO house in the late slanting sunlight of that bitterly cold afternoon, I saw an evocative scene. In front of me was a large open space where several railway tracks converged. The low afternoon sun threw the dark tracery of tracks over the hard grey snow and ice into sharp relief. The huge yard was crowded with people, maybe five hundred of them, all dark and bulky silhouettes swathed in long thick clothes to keep out the piercing cold. Many were clutching luggage, some huge suitcases and others boxes and bags. There were a few children, all huddled with their families.

I thought of photographs of population movements in the Russian Civil War and the film *Doctor Zhivago*. I didn't know whether they were refugees, people travelling around Republika Srpska, Muslims and Croats forced out of Prijedor by ethnic cleansing, or any combination of these. I did not have the time to stop and ask, but, as our small convoy sped past, I thought that whoever they were, they would have tales of suffering and deprivation to tell me. At the very least we owed them our efforts to make sure that the fragile peace we were establishing had the best possible chance of success.

Bertie Polley had been offered a school at Donja Ljubija, south-west of Prijedor. It lay at one end of a relatively prosperous and affluent village. A hundred metres along the same road lay a small disused factory of some kind, which Bertie had also been offered. The RSM and I looked it over, and immediately assessed it to be eminently suitable for Battlegroup HQ, especially as the school had a huge tarmac playground, which was more than sufficient to hold all the vehicles of both B Squadron and Battlegroup HQ.

The next day I drove west from the Mud Factory to visit A Company. The RSM and I stopped in Luisci Palanka, a deserted and looted small town, finding it empty save for a few scowling ABiH soldiers. We wanted to see for ourselves another empty school that the recce platoon had identified as a potential Battlegroup HQ location. Under dark and lowering skies against a bitterly tearing wind, swirling with sharp hard crystals of snow, we inspected yet another school built to the same design as Vitez. The building itself was intact, but its contents, fittings and furniture had been comprehensively looted and vandalised. Most of what remained had been smashed. The dismal state of the school was probably due to the actions of both retreating Serbs and vengeful Muslims. Yet again the children would lose out, I reflected.

Ćoralići Camp was a revelation. Extensively floodlit, it was based around a huge mineral extraction complex. Enormous hoppers and cylinders stood like turrets of some medieval castle, standing sentinel over Corimec accommodation units and dwarfing A Company's dark ice-encrusted Warriors. There was ample electricity and hot water. The base had been home to UNPROFOR's Bangladeshi battalion and already held the advance party of the Canadian Brigade HQ. A Company already had most of their Warriors out on patrol identifying faction positions, and were beginning to build up a fair picture of the Federation forces. So far his patrols had met great interest from the Muslim commanders. Some stated that they were relieved to see us – and when would our forces begin operating on the Serb side opposite them?

A Company's operations were considerably limited by geography. The first constraint was a part-demolished bridge in the Muslim town of Bosanka Krupa, which lacked the strength to take Warrior. The only other bridge that could carry Warrior across the River Una was some fifteen kilometres further back. This split the Federation side of his area into two sectors and made it hard to shift armoured infantry platoons quickly between them. Just as serious was the lack of any crossing between Federation and Bosnian Serb territory in his area. Finally, Ćoralići Camp, although better than any base the company had yet occupied, was much too far from the front line.

Jan and I drove through the ruins of the riverside town of Otaka and along the west bank of the River Una, along the Muslim front line overlooked by Serb positions amongst the low hills on the other side. Jan had already ascertained that the track was clear of mines, but it was too narrow for Warrior. Our convoy of Land Rovers felt distinctly naked and vulnerable, relying for security on the orange marker panels, Union Jacks flying from our radio antenna, and the white IFOR initials painted so boldly on the sides of the vehicles. Our body armour, helmets and the thin metal of our Land Rover offered little protection. Like it or not, the only way to show an IFOR presence on this part of the front line would have to be Land Rovers and Scimitar moving along this route under the weapons of both sides. Unlike some other risks, this was one we would have to accept.

Returning to Sanski Most, I met one of A Company's platoons parked in a roadside layby. The fronts and turrets of the four Warriors were coated with wind-compacted snow and ice, turning them into a solarised negative picture of themselves. Bulky figures swathed in dew liners, parkas and huge gloves were busying themselves checking wheels, lubrication and track links. The commanders and drivers wore anything they could to keep their faces warm without reducing their ability to see, including the Army issue facemasks, green head-overs and arab shamarghs dyed green. Most of the platoon was huddled in the backs of the Warriors, drinking tea. Morale was as high as it could be.

Morale was not so high back at the Mud Factory. Our failure to get into the Prijedor Hotel had been intensely disappointing, particularly since everyone was well aware that the Mud Factory was now the battlegroup's worst base. Even the platoon living between the front lines at BONDI BEACH was less uncomfortable. Chris Booth's recommended that the best course of action was for the headquarters to move to the garment factory at Donja Ljubija.

The next day, New Year's Eve, Battlegroup HQ finally left the Mud Factory. In our war-fighting training we had practised moving our HQ extremely quickly, swapping control between the main HQ and a smaller 'step-up' HQ. If necessary my forward tactical HQ could also assume control. Any one of these three components could assume control of the battlegroup within minutes of coming to a halt and could configure vehicles, set up tents and be fully concealed under camouflage nets within fifteen minutes. Here things were different. Because of the number of vehicles detached as rebroadcast stations, we would have to improvise a 'step-up'. Setting up and taking down the airmobile Ptarmigan satellite station and the civilian satellite telephone would take most of the day.

I went to Ljubija early and watched the long column of Battalion HQ vehicles wind their way into the school car park. Standing in the street outside, I was approached by two young men, each with girls on their arms, all swathed in heavy coats and hats. In English, halting at first but getting increasingly confident, they enquired who I was. I explained that I was the Procovnik commanding the British IFOR troops between Bosanska Gradiška in the north and Ključ in the south and between Bihać in the east and Prijedor in the west. This was received with sharp intakes of breath.

'In that case, sir, we must invite you to join us. It is New Year's Eve and we are having a family party. We must welcome you to our village.'

In the streetlight and the large slow-falling snowflakes, with their wide-eyed girlfriends, they looked so *normal* that I had to steel myself to mumble vague excuses as to why I could not attend. I returned to Battlegroup HQ to find that occupation of the garment factory had been badly executed. I expressed my displeasure to the officers involved. Afterwards, as I watched the exhausted signallers setting up their equipment, I realised that I had underestimated just how bone-tired all the headquarters personnel were.

After satisfying myself that we had communications with the two companies and the squadron, I relaxed and walked amongst the officers and soldiers putting together camp beds and unfolding sleeping bags amongst the tables and machinery of a large sewing room. Somehow, the CQMS had obtained enough beer for everyone to have a couple of bottles. We all stood around talking and drinking until the midnight time signal came over the BBC World Service. There was much cheering and friendly goodwill from the soldiers of Battlegroup HQ, all of who seemed to want to shake my hand and offer me a drink. Exhausted, I eventually made my excuses and collapsed into my sleeping bag.

CHAPTER EIGHT

'Badlands'

I allowed the headquarters a later start on the morning of New Year's Day and treated myself to the unexpected luxury of simply lying in bed, thinking about the extraordinary turn of events that had brought us to north-west Bosnia. I also contemplated the next few weeks. Here we all were on the first day of a new year, conducting peace implementation on the mainland of Europe – an operation that five years ago none of us would have considered. We now had just over two weeks before the separation of forces. We still had a lot to do.

NATO estimated that there were up to a hundred and fifty thousand faction soldiers in our battlegroup area. We had about seven hundred men and would be very thinly spread. For example, B Company had forty kilometres of the cease-fire line that ran through wooded and hilly country, reminiscent of the Welsh Borderland, including hills as large as the Black Mountains. On the Bosnian Serb side of the line the company had to monitor three brigades (varying in size from four hundred to four thousand men), a major training area, logistic installations and lines of communications. On the Federation side, there was the most of the ABiH's 7 Corps including the corps forward HQ, a divisional HQ, eight brigades, and corps and divisional troops. We had also discovered a concentration of several thousand troops, logistic units and training facilities in the hills to the north-west of Klujc. Even with the eight Scimitars of the recce platoon under command, Stuart Mills had only two hundred men and twenty-two armoured fighting vehicles to monitor approximately fifty thousand armed men in an area of over a thousand square kilometres. A Company and B Squadron were faced with a similar ratio between themselves and the faction forces in their areas.

Brigade HQ had set a deadline of withdrawal of the faction forces from the Zone of Separation by D+25, the withdrawal to be verified by D+30. This would require us to develop good working relationships with both armies. We still needed to create an impression that we were stronger than we were, which would involve being present all over our area. There would also be much to be gained by organising joint VRS/ABiH mine clearance operations, and joint IFOR/faction patrols to mark the Zone of Separation. Throughout all this we would need to ensure IFOR's freedom of action and continue to identify the military structure of the factions.

We would achieve this by being flexible and imaginative in the way we moved forces around. Martin Bell of the BBC had asked Brigadier Dannatt if his tactics were all 'smoke and mirrors'. As far as I was concerned, the more smoke and the more mirrors the better.

The faction armies employed some modern technology, including Cold War-era tanks, mortars and artillery, but their attitudes and general level of military capability seemed similar to mass armies of the First World War. We knew that they had some sophisticated communications equipment, including radio relay and satellite telephones reaching to corps and in some cases divisional, HQ. But further down their chain of command, we saw far fewer radios. Much use was made of telephones by the front line brigades of both sides.

By British standards, their command and control was highly centralised. Many commanders were suspicious of IFOR. If we had been at war, we would have wanted to exploit this; indeed, we would have been attacking our enemy's command and control systems. Here, we wanted the factions' command and control systems to work in harmony with ours. Great care had to be taken to strike a balance between enthusiastic exploitation of opportunities by sub-unit commanders, and allowing the factions time to be briefed by IFOR, understand our intentions and pass information amongst themselves. It was essential to maintain the initiative without 'frightening the horses'.

The young officers who acted as company and battalion liaison officers were playing an important role. They spent their days visiting faction commanders and headquarters, as well as local mayors and village elders. Captain Sean Harris described their work:

> Following D-Day the battalion LOs spent their time passing on the CO's very clear point of view to the factions. We often travelled on our own. On a regular basis we were demanding to see brigade commanders and higher to tell them how they were to behave. We found that sometimes what appeared initially to be a ridiculous strategy was very effective. This was brought home to me while we were trying to gain information on the military equipment held by an ABiH brigade. I was attempting to skirt around the subject of armour held by the brigade, hoping to get the information by guile. I found, to my amazement, that the best approach was to produce an armoured vehicle recognition handbook. The commander then proudly pointed at the pictures telling me how many he had of each vehicle. The information he gave me was later proven to be entirely truthful.

The other way of gathering information was by patrolling. Patrols would usually be a pair of armoured vehicles, usually led by a platoon commander or platoon serjeant. Initially our lack of information meant that patrols would be tasked with simply finding out what faction forces were in a particular area, but as we gathered more information they were more precisely targeted. The attitude of the factions varied considerably from brigade to brigade. Most were pretty compliant, but a significant number were hostile and uncooperative. Patient negotiation by the patrol commander, often with the help of a company or battlegroup liaison officer, would usually gain us some sort of cooperation, it only grudging and ill-natured. We often had to make it very clear that we were prepared to press on regardless and would force our way through if necessary.

Those patrols that needed to approach the front line would begin at the relevant faction brigade HQ. The patrol would then move up to faction battalion and company HQs, seeking to verify the locations and strengths of their troops and the exact locations of their front-line positions and minefields. Patrol commanders would do their best to get their armoured vehicles on to the front line, but in the hills or mountains that covered much of our area, this would often be impossible. The patrol commanders would then dismount and, with a protection party, move forward on foot.

We used Warriors for most patrols, but we exploited the lighter weight and greater cross-country mobility of Scimitar and Spartan by tasking them to patrol especially steep, narrow, muddy or ice-covered tracks. Land Rovers would be used to patrol particularly difficult terrain. Fitted with snow chains and with an experienced and confident driver, these had even more mobility on snow- and ice-covered mountain tracks than Scimitars and Spartans.

Serjeant Grimes of B Company wrote this account of patrolling:

Working with the former warring factions proved to be more difficult than I first expected. I had a simple task: 'Find out who is in this area'. I initially adopted the wrong approach. I went in my two Warriors with my interpreters, thinking all I had to do was to stop at the first bunker and speak to the commander and all would be clear. How wrong could I be?

As we approached total chaos erupted. One man was frantically talking down a field telephone as about ten others swarmed round. I asked who the local commander was, to be met with blank faces and looks of total distrust. Their structure gave no responsibility to anyone under the rank of captain, so to be asked questions by a serjeant was beyond their understanding. I then asked them to show me their locations. As they studied my map with interest my expectations rose. However any hope of finding the position was dashed as a soldier raised the map and proudly proclaimed that he had found his house. I learned nothing from them of a military nature but I did find out most of them were married and had about five children each – a great intelligence coup!

Knowing now that the only way anything gets done in the Bosnian army is if a high-ranking commander attends, I arranged a meeting with the battalion commander via their brigade liaison officer for the following day. Unsure of how I would be received, I set off with mixed feelings. On arrival I was made to wait outside and then shown in; the battalion commander sat at a large table, while the interpreter and myself were shown chairs opposite. A long silence followed with an uncomfortable atmosphere, then the questions started. How old was I? How long had I been in the Army? Had I been in Northern Ireland?

Satisfied with the result of this interrogation, we could get down to the day's business. Telling a senior captain battalion commander, equivalent to a lieutenant colonel in our Army, what I would like him and his troops to do initially went against the grain, but I soon became accustomed to it. Even when we had agreed in principle what had to be done, everything still had to go up to his brigade for approval.

Listening to commanders' accounts of their patrols, I was often struck by the huge contrast between our decentralised and devolved method of operation and the highly centralised style of command in the faction armies. Much responsibility rested on the heads of our young officers and serjeants. For them and the corporal vehicle commanders, patrolling involved spending most of their time in the turrets of their vehicles. Here, surrounded by maps, pencils and marker pens held to periscope shrouds by rubber bands, they were festooned with their radio headsets and harness. Close to hand would be the ubiquitous plastic wallet holding the paper codes for radio communication and the KL43 data entry device. To see what was going on around them and to assist the driver, whose vision was very limited, they had to crouch or stand with much of their head and torso exposed. In the winter weather, this was no fun, and commander, driver and gunner would be swathed in layers of warm and waterproof clothing. Even so, they always found it cold – a deep, penetrating and enduring cold that the constant supply of cups of hot tea and coffee made by the vehicle crew and passed to them could only temporarily allay. But they were all very keen to get to grips with patrolling and dominating their areas.

I wanted to see for myself what was going on. I would spend the day driving around our area, eager to see the situation and the ground for myself. It was good for the factions to see that the battlegroup commander was out and about, moving around the area in an unpredictable fashion and liable to appear anywhere without notice. I was trying to complicate the calculations of any of the faction military who were thinking about non-compliance. We knew that all the factions monitored our communications and had sufficient English speakers to understand much of what we were saying. It would be no bad thing if their signals intelligence units listening to the battlegroup and company radio nets concluded that we had two headquarters, mortar, artillery and air control nets, secure data transmissions and a satellite link to the Ptarmigan secure system. We were confident that they could neither decipher these latter transmissions nor penetrate our BATCO paper codes.

I wanted to meet and be seen by faction soldiers and commanders on both sides. They needed to understand that we were different from their own armies. I also wanted to talk to civilians, to find out what they knew and thought of the Dayton Agreement, IFOR and the other factions. Most of the soldiers and civilians on both sides welcomed the end of fighting and wanted to get on with their lives. They had usually little idea of what was going on outside their town, village or particular small part of the front line and were hungry for information about what was happening in the rest of Bosnia. There remained considerable distrust of the other factions.

I would also visit our bases, sometimes warning them of my arrival, sometimes not. More often I would drive to whichever part of our area of responsibility took my interest. It was important to keep all the battlegroup's commanders on their toes. I was not trying to catch people out, but all my experience in training had convinced me that knowledge that the commanding officer could appear unexpectedly at any time or place, ready to praise or criticise, reinforced commanders' determination to keep standards up. I had a well worked up and perfectly capable team in Battlegroup HQ, in whom I had total confidence. The Sewing Factory held no attractions and it seemed important to make the most of the scarce hours of daylight to get out and see for myself what was going on. As our forces were so thinly spread, the RSM and I in our Land Rovers were helping to increase the battalion's visible footprint on the ground. The RSM and I conversing, drinking coffee or slivovitz with soldiers or civilians was just as much part of the battlegroup operation as a patrol by two Warriors.

I therefore spent most of the daylight hours on the road with the RSM. We would drive on the roads and tracks on both sides of the front line stopping to talk to civilians, faction military or our own troops. My companions in the vehicle would be Private Leck, an interpreter, the battlegroup command net, with its constant background wash of reports, messages and information, and my thoughts. I often encountered our patrols, Warriors, Scimitars or 432s carefully negotiating the lonely winding roads. I would stop and chat. The vehicles would be black with ice and mud, and the commanders and drivers frozen to the bone. They were always in good humour, never complaining about the cold, the difficult roads or the lack of contact with home.

Opening More Crossing Points

We now had a good feel for the practicalities of patrolling in our area. Vehicles of all kinds could make reasonable speed on the main road network connecting Ključ, Sanski Most, Prijedor and Bos Krupa – provided that the snow and ice were not too thick. Elsewhere, most of our area was criss-crossed by a network of dirt tracks linking the farms and villages. Progress on these was very slow, even for our most agile vehicles: the Scimitars, Land Rovers fitted with snow chains and the artillery battery's over-snow vehicles. Patrolling on these tracks, which up to now had largely been used by tractors and horse-drawn carts, required commanders and drivers to make finely balanced judgements. What was the best way to tackle a particular route? At what point did the risk of bogging in, or of track collapse, become so great as to justify turning back?

This meant that patrols moved very slowly. As our only front line crossing points were near Sanski Most, the centre of the battlegroup area, it was extremely difficult to patrol the large amount of territory to our western and southern flanks. This made it still more important to get better access across the front lines.

On their own initiative, B Company opened another crossing in the middle of their area. They had organised several meetings between VRS and ABiH commanders on a track in a deep valley near a school that was being used as a forward outpost by some Bosnian Serb soldiers. The track was not mined and B Company was able to take over the small school for use as a platoon base. They also wanted to give it the name of somewhere hot and sunny so the crossing was christened 'MALIBU CORNER'.

Even with this success, the battlegroup needed more crossing points opened. B Squadron and A Company each needed one, and the difficulty of the terrain in B Company's area meant that they needed another one too. But the country was laced with marked and unmarked minefields, as if several necklaces of lethal pearls had been flung casually onto a map. Brigade HQ was planning the co-ordinated opening of routes across the confrontation lane. Although the Dayton Agreement made it clear that all minefields were to be lifted by the forces that had laid them, there was in reality no way to physically compel the factions to do this. To open the extra crossing points, we had to persuade the factions that it was in their best interests to lift their mines, to better allow IFOR to play its role. The factions would only do this if we gave them the confidence that their mine-lifting parties would be protected by our troops. They also needed to be assured that the other side was lifting their mines at the same time, and that we would ensure that their opponents did not take advantage of this cleared route.

The commander of 4 Brigade's close support engineer regiment, Lieutenant Colonel Peter Wall, masterminded the planning, persuading the faction corps chief engineers to conform to his plans. Brigade having obtained this high-level agreement, the battlegroup would actually run the operations. We selected the crossings to be opened and negotiated with the faction engineers and brigade commanders. This involved much patient work by our LOs and the battlegroup engineer officer.

Once we had got both factions to agree, troops would be tasked to provide military security. This required not only close protection for the mine clearance parties, but also visible positioning of armoured vehicles on and around the front line, in positions where they could deter any attempt to fire on the clearance parties. Mortars and artillery would be deployed on both sides of the front line to provide an umbrella of indirect fire protection over the area of the operations. Finally, the Royal Engineers would provide expert Explosive Ordnance Disposal (EOD) teams for the particularly dangerous task of monitoring and supervising the mine clearance by the faction engineers.

The first crossing point selected for a deliberate route opening operation was in B Company's area. The operation would be under the tactical control of B Company, with Serjeant Fyfvie's EOD team splitting to provide detachments with the engineer parties from both sides. Since this was the first deliberate route-opening operation since the opening of WHITE FANG, I made it the battlegroup main effort. B Company would split, with half its forces protecting the Serb mine clearance party working from the east, the other half the ABiH troops clearing from the west. The mortar platoon would deploy to the Serb side of the line and the artillery battery would provide indirect fire cover from the Muslim side.

That morning was bitterly cold. I drove south from Ljubija and down the main road to the site of the crossing. Stuart Mills had arranged a rendezvous (RV) point where those joining the operation would report and get clearance to come forward. This was the junction of the main road from Sanski Most to Klujc with the farm track leading up to the crossing point. B Company had a pair of Warriors and their REME vehicles positioned there. Standing at the side of the road around an abandoned petrol station and an ethnically cleansed village were several hundred ABiH soldiers. A spur road to the west of the petrol station led to some kind of small factory. ABiH flags and a cluster of roughly camouflaged vehicles indicated some kind of ad hoc barracks.

The artillery battery had deployed at dawn to fields directly opposite the Muslim base. The gunners learned that they were inside a concentration area where troops withdrawing from the front line were assembling prior to a troop rotation, all waiting for buses to take them back to central Bosnia where they were going on two weeks' leave. Some went out of their way to tell us how impressed they were to see our guns and our Warriors, particularly the howitzer that John had deployed in the shattered remains of a roadside restaurant.

I received a radio message. Brigadier Viggers, the British artillery commander, was in a helicopter on his way to me. He had arranged an urgent meeting with an ABiH officer at our RV and we were to provide security. The number of IFOR troops, vehicles and artillery around the site meant that this was not a problem! Further planning was interrupted by the arrival of his Lynx helicopter. Viggers briefed me that the RRF battlegroup had discovered a major Bosnian Serb training area within five kilometres of the frontline. The VRS were planning to train on the area, conducting a large-scale firepower demonstration for the cadets of their military academy in Banja Luka. General Jackson was still making his mind up about whether this training should be allowed to proceed, but we needed to explain what was happening to the chief of staff of 7 Corps ABiH, who was on his way here.

He was due in five minutes. We needed somewhere to have the meeting. If we'd had half an hour's notice, we could have set up a forward headquarters with some command vehicles and Warriors and had the meeting there. B Company headquarters was forward controlling the route-opening operation, and the Land Rovers and BV 206s of the battery were insufficient. The houses in the area were full of shifty-looking ABiH soldiers. As the ABiH party approached and was greeted by the brigadier I noticed a still-burning fire that had been left by the Muslim soldiers. Around it were scattered a filthy and mutilated teddy bear and four children's sledges. Clearly the soldiers had been sitting on them to keep warm. Why not use them, I thought. All my meetings with Bosnian military commanders so far had been in their headquarters, all of which were in comfortable warm offices – the antithesis of so many of our orders and planning meetings and the opposite of the conditions endured by their soldiers on the front line. I sat our brigadier and the two ABiH officers on the sledges around a pathetic fire, in the middle of the front garden of one of the trashed houses. It was a pretty cheerless place for a meeting.

Neither the brigadier nor the ABiH officers had brought an interpreter with them, so Magda, my interpreter for the day, sat with us. Mr Matthews kept us from being interrupted and Private Leck brought me a vacuum flask of coffee. I passed this around the group, wondering what the two Bosnian Muslims thought of British Army instant coffee, which was so much thinner and weaker than theirs. Sipping from the single small cup, they betrayed no emotion and passed no comment on the lukewarm beverage. They also passed no comment on the brigadier's explanation about the Bosnian Serb training. They knew about the training, they told us; after all the facilities the VRS were using were former Jugoslav Army ranges. The chief of staff was disposed to give us a long diatribe about Bosnian Serb war crimes, which the brigadier very sensibly deflected. I concluded the meeting by giving a short brief on our battle-group activities, which elicited no comment. The meeting was over, my flask of coffee was empty, and we were all shivering. The Bosnian officers departed north in their Land Cruiser and Brigadier Viggers left by helicopter.

I moved forward to the crossing site to see for myself how the operation was going. At the end of a steep and narrow farm track were Warriors, poised to give protection or fire support as required. Stuart Mills had a good grip on the operation. The chief engineer of the Bosnian 7 Corps was there. A small precise man, he was immaculately turned out in a brand-new combat uniform. The squad of Muslim engineers was also in clean new uniforms, but all wore bright blue ski gloves and American baseball hats emblazoned with the legend 'CHICAGO'. They had a detailed and accurate record of where ten anti-tank mines were located. They found them in the snow straightaway and quickly lifted them. The good news was that this boded well for future mine clearance operations with the ABIH. The bad news was that the Bosnian Muslim mine records confirmed that they had laid anti-tank mines on all the remaining roads and tracks that crossed the front line. It also appeared that the Bosnian Serbs had done the same.

We inspected the mines as the Bosnian engineers cleaned earth from them and carried the devices to their vehicles. It was ironic that, having removed the mines, the ABiH could stockpile them, but there was nothing in the Dayton Agreement to stop them doing so.

Unfortunately, there had been less success on the Serb side. Their engineers had been late arriving at their agreed RV with B Company. The tracks leading to the crossing site proved to be extremely narrow and covered with ice. A decision was taken to split the party into a fast group of Scimitars, Land Rovers and Serb trucks and a following slower group of Warriors, but even so the lighter force made very slow progress. Eventually the Serb troops gave up and B Company was unable to cajole them into going any further forward. Peter Wall departed, grimly determined to ensure that the Serb engineers did not give us such problems again.

All this was watched by a BBC TV news team led by the veteran journalist Martin Bell. He was highly respected by the British forces, having accompanied the UK armoured division during the Gulf War, and had been wounded at Sarajevo airport during the initial stage of the Bosnian civil war in 1992. His team filmed our operation and interviewed Peter Wall. Next they interviewed the 7 Corps chief engineer who stated: 'It is only because of confidence in IFOR that we are able to do this.' This was heartening positive feedback that the thinking behind our clearance operation was sound.

I was interviewed by Martin Bell, who quizzed me about the size of the mine problem in the area. I explained that we had a hundred and fifty kilometres of front line, most of which was mined. He then questioned me about whether I had sufficient forces. I side-stepped this loaded question and shifted discussion onto the level of cooperation between us and the faction armies. The report was subsequently transmitted on BBC TV news, the first British television coverage of the battlegroup's NATO operations.

Moving Forward

A Company was also hard at work patrolling, and attempting to get a crossing point opened. The ABiH 5 Corps regarded Jan de Vos as the senior IFOR commander in their area and invited him to the Bosnian Army's New Year's Day parade in Bihać. IFOR policy forbade fraternisation with the factions which was not directly concerned with the military implementation of the Dayton Agreement, but I thought that Jan's presence at the parade and subsequent reception could help him meet key commanders and staff from 5 Corps. It would also give us some extra visibility to the military and civilians in Bihać town.

Jan had a particularly bizarre New Year's Day. The ABiH mounted a parade of about a thousand troops. Although the men of 5 Corps might be equipped with the usual rag-tag mixture of uniforms and weapons, they had a battalion of well-maintained tanks. Jan was told that the vehicles were 'all captured from the Serbs'. Though the majority of Bosnian commanders and officers welcomed the cessation of hostilities, they would have no hesitation in resuming their offensive against the Serbs should the Dayton Agreement fail. They had sustained the defence of the Bihać Pocket for two and half years and then broken out and evicted the VRS from the swathe of territory from Bihać in the west to Sanski Most and Ključ in the east, and they had enormous confidence in both their combat skills and their commander, General Dudakovic.

Jan was introduced to Dudakovic, who looked directly into the British officer's eyes and said: 'We are both professional officers. If I have to, I will kill you without hesitation.'

Pausing momentarily , Jan replied:

'General, many have said that to British soldiers, but all have subsequently deeply regretted doing so.'

Silence fell, as Bosnian and Briton stared at each other. Awkwardly, Jan's hosts moved him on. After the reception the commander and officers of a brigade based in Cazin took Jan back to their headquarters to 'properly celebrate New Year'. The brigade's idea of celebration consisted of drinking enormous quantities of slivovitz brandy and firing vast amounts of ammunition skywards. At one point the conversation turned to the soldiers' wives and families. Suddenly Jan's host picked up a telephone, spoke to an operator and asked Jan the telephone number of his house in Paderborn. Within a few minutes Jan was speaking to his bemused and disbelieving wife Kate, with the Muslim officers offering all sorts of drunken New Year's greetings to her in Serbo-Croat and broken English.

In the next few days the company's patrols enjoyed great success in locating, meeting and getting alongside all the ABiH brigade commanders in their sector. The commander of 511 'Glorious Mountain' Brigade was a particularly striking character. He wore a mixture of American combat uniform and black leather motorcycle clothing, had a vast Afro haircut, a red bandana and two ear-rings. He told Jan that one ring was for 'the men I have lost in the fighting', and the other 'for my lost youth, which I have spent fighting'. Despite his unconventional appearance he was an effective leader and clearly had the respect of his men. A Company instantly christened him 'the rock 'n' roll brigadier'.

Ćoralići Camp was too far from the front line. If, as I hoped, A Company eventually opened a crossing point to increase access to their assigned sector of Republika Srpska, they would need to deploy in strength into Bosnian Serb territory very quickly. If we failed to open a crossing point, I would order the company to deploy half their strength on the Serb side by taking a round trip through WHITE FANG and Prijedor. Either way, the company could not afford for its patrols to waste so much time travelling between Ćoralići and the front line area.

As I was musing over this, Brigadier Viggers told me that Division was worried about Bosanska Krupa. Intelligence suggested that tension between Muslims and Serbs was much greater here than along the other parts of the front line for which we were responsible. As there were few battlegroup patrols Serb-side in this area, I could not contradict the assessment. This spurred me to action, and I told A Company to move their main base to a factory in Bosanska Krupa. To help make an impact, and to give the company additional light vehicles that could cross safely the damaged bridge in the centre of Bosanska Krupa, I sent them the recce platoon and a troop of three light guns.

I invited Martin Bell to bring his BBC News team to battlegroup. He was amazed to see how we had crammed Battlegroup HQ into such a small building. Downstairs we had a cookhouse, offices and stores, while upstairs we had an operations and briefing complex. The intelligence section was ensconced in a large cupboard. People were living and sleeping in offices, cupboards and rooms full of sewing machines and cutting tables. We showed Martin the building by torchlight, as a power cut was in progress, and went on to have a long and enjoyable meal, illuminated by candles and enlivened by his stories of the Bosnian civil war.

The next day, we took Martin around the Serb area between Ljubija and BONDI BEACH so he could capture on film the freedom of movement and access we were achieving in Republika Srpska. I also showed him the base's improvised bath, suggesting that he film it. he agreed, and the soldiers based at BONDI BEACH were delighted to light a fire under the bath, fetch water in buckets from the pump and find a volunteer to sit in it. The soldier concerned was interviewed in the bath, stark naked except for his helmet. Stuart Mills then arrived, telling us that B Company had arranged a meeting between Muslim and Serb commanders at MALIBU BEACH fifteen kilometres to the south, and suggesting that the BBC should film that. Martin left to do so. I made my farewells and departed for Ljubija.

Two Shootings and an Interview Without Coffee

On the battlegroup net, A Company reports an incident at their base in Bosanska Krupa. Shots have been fired, striking the top of the building. The company reacts immediately. Warriors deploy to fire positions on the perimeter of the base, traversing their turrets, and soldiers dash to pre-designated fighting positions. The artillery troop's guns adopt fire positions at the corners of the compound – deploying in the open with the guns ready to engage targets by direct fire over open sights.

Within minutes Flight Lieutenant Mark Jacklin is delivering an extremely forceful protest to the headquarters of 511 'Glorious Mountain' Brigade in the town. The brigade 'security officer', a huge, muscular man wearing dark sunglasses, comes to the company's base. He is forcefully told that the shooting is unacceptable and that measures must be taken to deter any further such incidents.

A Company show him the building from which the shots came. Muslim soldiers and police enter the building. A civilian with a rifle is apprehended, disarmed and forcibly arrested. Looking terrified he is marched off to a police car. Police and military commanders profusely apologise to the company commander, who gets the distinct impression that the gunman will be lucky to escape with his life.

As this incident draws to a conclusion, I am approaching WHITE FANG, thinking that today is Orthodox Christmas Eve. For the last few days, the Muslim checkpoint barrier has been left up, a healthy sign of relaxation of tension. This time the barrier is down. However, it is not Muslim soldiers standing in front of it, but two IFOR Land Rovers and two French Army officers. What are they doing? As I pull up, a British cavalry officer emerges from the checkpoint. I imagine that he is either conducting liaison with the ABiH (and if so, why do I know nothing about it?), or the Muslims have stopped him at the checkpoint for some reason. Either scenario is bad news, so I harshly ask him what is going on. He tells me he is a Division HQ staff officer. There has just been a shooting at the IFOR checkpoint just to the north and 'your solders have just ordered us out of the danger zone and told us to stop people going forward'.

Even as he finishes his sentence I am leaping back into the Land Rover, telling him to open the barrier and Leck to drive on. I curse to myself. I haven't heard anything about this on the net. Why not? Is a firefight still going on? Have we taken casualties? There's only one way to find out, which is to get to

WHITE FANG as soon as possible and see for myself. I shout to the interpreter sitting in the back of the vehicle to make sure that the first aid box of bandages and shell dressing is ready. I then send a short report over the radio:

'Hello Zero and Hotel Two Zero, this is Zero Alpha. Possible Contact Shooting at WHITE FANG. I'm moving there to acknowledge. Over.'

'Zero Roger, all stations less Hotel Two Zero, minimise, Hotel Two Zero acknowledge over.'

'Hotel Two Zero. Roger Out.'

We are now halfway along the stretch of road between the ABiH checkpoint and WHITE FANG. A soldier is running towards us, sweating and out of breath. His name is Private Mitchell and he tells me that WHITE FANG came under machine-gun fire from a VRS position. He and some others fired back. There's no firing now, so he is going back to the Muslim checkpoint to check the people in the two IFOR Land Rovers are OK and to warn any other vehicles coming from the south. Despite displaying a very high level of adrenalin, he is articulate and remarkably composed. I tell him to crack on to the Muslim checkpoint as he had intended and thank him for a good brief.

We drive on to WHITE FANG. There are two Warriors with hatches closed down, both menacingly traversing their turrets, and the Spartan belonging to the Tactical Air Control Party. While the RSM parks our vehicles, with his armoured Land Rover outermost, I quickly speak to the RAF flight lieutenant and Serjeant Parkin.

They tell me that about half an hour ago a Serb position to the north fired a rocket of some sort which exploded in the air. This was probably a rocket-propelled grenade. Serjeant Parkin sent a patrol of four infantrymen along the road to the north to investigate.

They had hardly got a hundred metres north of WHITE FANG when bursts of heavy machine-gun fire hit the road around them and the wooded bank just above their heads. Muzzle flashes were seen coming from a Serb bunker about eight hundred metres to the north. The Spartan returned fire with its machine gun, but it had a stoppage after firing a few bursts. Private Mitchell turned to face the direction of the firing point and, ignoring his own safety, immediately returned fire with his rifle while the remainder of the patrol withdrew behind the hard cover provided by armoured vehicles. He kept firing until all other members of the patrol were safe and the firing from the Serb position had ceased. At the start of the firefight, both the Warrior crews had engines running, and by the time they had realised what was going on the firing had stopped. Mitchell noticed that a British Land Rover was approaching the position from the south. Heedless of his own safety he dashed into the open and diverted the vehicle into a safe area.

It seems that about thirty rounds of machine-gun fire have fallen around our positions. Between Private Mitchell, who emptied a full magazine of thirty rounds at the bunker, the Spartan and other soldiers, we have returned at least twice as many rounds.

The RSM sends a full report to Battlegroup HQ and B Company while I assess the situation. The rules of engagement allow us to fire at faction positions If they are firing at us or preventing us carrying out our mission. This is not happening now, but the two Warriors lay their turret weapons onto the bunker from which the fire came and are ready to reply with chain gun and cannon fire. The Spartan has a laser marker to designate targets for attack by NATO aircraft, which is also laid onto the bunker. The flight lieutenant has been talking on his satellite radio to the air support organisation and we should be able to summon up an air strike fairly quickly, if we need to.

What could happen next and what should we do? If there is more firing, we have sufficient firepower to take on a few bunkers. However we are over-looked by many Serb front-line positions. If a full-scale firefight erupts we don't have enough firepower to overmatch their bunkers. Therefore we need more armoured vehicles, cannon and MILAN missiles, in sufficient strength to deter further attacks and to quickly neutralise any firing that takes place. We need to be able to use mortars and artillery, which will require mortar fire con-trollers and an artillery forward observer. The weapons should be deployed in locations where they will be highly visible to the factions. It would help to have Lynx helicopters moved up to the battlegroup area, for recce, armed action with their TOW missiles or evacuating any casualties, and we need fast jets in the sky above WHITE FANG to show that NATO is not taking this lightly.

I tell B Company and Battlegroup HQ to arrange this. I am quite happy to be divulging my intentions in clear over the battlegroup command net. If the Bosnian Serbs are listening to our transmissions they will be in no doubt that we mean business. Both headquarters have obviously been thinking along similar lines, and tell me that it will take at least half an hour to get more Warriors to WHITE FANG. B Squadron offers a troop of Scimitar, which should get here in thirty minutes. Although the Scimitar are less imposing and less well protected than Warrior, I accept the offer with alacrity, but stipulate that they should return as soon as WHITE FANG is reinforced with extra Warrior.

Meanwhile, none of the Warriors at WHITE FANG can talk to B Company on their radio net. Our Land Rovers' radios can contact both B Company and Battlegroup HQ. The company commander, Major Stuart Mills, was conduct-ing the meeting at MALIBU CORNER to the south. B Company HQ tells me that he has already handed the meeting over to Captain Toby Ellwood in order to get to WHITE FANG, but it will take him at least an hour to arrive. I decide to take command of the incident, remaining at WHITE FANG until the company commander arrives.

This takes care of the near future and the close operation. Reinforcing the position and deploying mortars and artillery should show VRS that if they want to cause trouble, we can give it back with interest. Morale at WHITE FANG seems sky high and I notice a huge amount of cheerful banter going on between the RSM and the soldiers.

What should we now do to further the deep operation and make sure the Bosnian Serbs don't do this again? I summon Major Ian Baker, the chief liaison officer, to the radio. He is already tasking liaison officers to deliver formal protests to the VRS headquarters in Ljubija and Prijedor. We decide that once WHITE FANG is reinforced I should return to Battlegroup HQ, where we should summon the local Serb commander for an 'interview without coffee'.

I have been impressed with Ian and Ross Gillanders' handling of the situation. The RSM grins, saying, 'Sir, it looks like you are really enjoying yourself'. I am! The adrenalin rush, the cheerful determination of the soldiers and the quick response by Battlegroup HQ, B Company and B Squadron make a heady cocktail.

I am about to reply to the RSM when I see two recce platoon Scimitars approaching from the south. Great, I think, a recce section commander has been listening to the net, used his initiative, cut short his patrol and come to reinforce us. The vehicles are closed down, but I am astonished, then dumbfounded, to see that instead of stopping, they speed right past us – so fast that neither the RSM nor I can read their call signs. What is going on? I call on the battalion command net.

'Hello unidentified recce call sign moving through WHITE FANG, this is Zero Alpha. Stop at once and talk to me as soon as possible, over.'

I repeat this message several times but the Scimitars speed north and there is no reply on the radio. Furious, I order Battlegroup HQ to contact them somehow, if necessary by breaking in on the Recce Platoon's own radio net.

I am still fuming about this when I am delighted to see six of B Squadron's Scimitars and Spartans appear from the north. The commanders are enthusiastic, and delighted to have been sent to the scene of the action. Shortly after, additional B Company Warriors arrive, as does the company commander in a battered and mud-covered Land Rover. I explain to him what has happened since I arrived and that I want us to maintain our high-profile reinforcement of WHITE FANG and the area around it for at least twenty-four hours. This should not involve everyone sitting around getting bored. Provided that there is sufficient strength at the crossing point to overface the Serb bunkers, there is plenty of scope for moving forces to dominate the area around the crossing.

Returning to the Ljubija I go straight into planning with Ian Baker. I am concerned that, although the fire on WHITE FANG ceased, we have no evidence that any of our return fire actually hit the Bosnian Serb position from which the fire came. We know that the VRS brigade responsible for the area is 43 Infantry Brigade. We have identified their main HQ in the driving school outside Prijedor and a forward tactical HQ about a mile south of us in Ljubija proper. We will not be fobbed off with liaison officers or staff officers, but insist on the brigade commander. Protest notes have already been delivered to both HQs and Ian has summoned the brigade commander to us at the Sewing Factory.

The meeting will be stage-managed to show our extreme displeasure and that, unlike the UN, we will not be messed around. Warriors and Scimitars move into position around Battlegroup HQ as a show of force. The biggest and toughest-looking Battlegroup HQ soldiers are posted on guard outside and inside the building. All are armed to the teeth. We will all use strongly assertive body language: no smiles, no handshakes, no small talk, no exchange of pleasantries or compliments, plenty of firm, unflinching eye contact. This is not a meeting, but a one-way expression of displeasure to the VRS, to deter them from allowing such events in future.

The Serb commander is collected from his HQ by a troop of Scimitars. We would have sent Warriors, but the streets are too narrow. Ian meets them at the gate. The VRS delegation is over a dozen in number, half of whom are clearly bodyguards. We cause consternation by refusing to allow in anyone other than the brigade commander, one staff officer and one interpreter – armed only with their own pistols, which must be unloaded. They object. Ian tells them the alternative is to have the meeting in the back of a Warrior.

I am watching from the shadows inside the front door of the factory. As this discussion takes place, there is a power cut, the whole village goes dark, and soldiers switch on torches and light hurricane lamps. Leaving the bodyguards and hangers-on at the gate, watched by heavily armed IFOR soldiers, the party is brought forward to the entrance. Two things surprise me.

Firstly, the Serbs have with them a female interpreter. Nothing unusual about this, but I have already already met her, working as the JCOs' main interpreter! Clearly she is serving both sides – suggesting she may be in the pay of the Bosnian Serbs. I raise my eyebrows at the RSM; he nods and makes a mental note to have the JCOs informed of this straight after the meeting.

Secondly, the Serb commander is not the man who was in charge during our meeting ten days earlier in Prijedor. He was present at that meeting but only as a non-speaking subordinate. I ask myself, are we being fobbed off with a supporting actor? I come out of the door and say:

'I require to see the commander of 43 Brigade. You are clearly not the commander of 43 Brigade that I met in Prijedor ten days ago, but one of his subordinates. Why has he not come?'

As this is translated, confusion and apprehension appears in his face. There is hurried conversation between the two VRS officers and the interpreter. Replying through the interpreter, they tell me:

'The man you met was the commander of Operations Group 10. We are the commander and staff officer of 43 Brigade headquarters in Ljubija. We are one of the two sectors of Operations Group 10, whose commander you met in Ljubija. Surely you knew this?'

Ian Baker and I exchange glances. Over the last week we have become increasingly confused as to which VRS units belonged to what formation and exactly how their subordination worked. It isn't that the Bosnian Serb battalion and company commanders have been uncooperative with us about their own units and locations, but they have all refused to divulge information about the sectors to their flanks. Ian and I nod to each other, for this simple statement fits the facts much better than any of the theories produced by the Intelligence Section. I find it difficult to keep myself from smiling, but swallow hard and remember the soldiers at WHITE FANG and their narrow escape from injury.

I tell the VRS officers that I accept their explanation and they should follow me to our meeting room. We take them past yet more soldiers lining the route in helmets and body armour and holding loaded weapons, the only time I have ever allowed any loaded weapons inside the HQ. We enter a prepared room, bare apart from a table, with a map taped to the surface, and a few chairs. The brigade commander attempts to shake hands and offer pleasantries. I refuse to shake hands, cut him short and tell him to listen to me. I give a short and factual account of the firing incident, including my own role in it and finish by asking for his explanation. He seems quite bullish and has neither explanation nor apology. I tell him:

'This is the first time that British IFOR troops have been shot at and we are extremely disappointed that one of your positions did this. It is only luck, forbearance by the soldiers at the crossing point and the fact that the fire ceased that prevented our troops from engaging and destroying all the bunkers involved. You should be under no illusions about our combat capability and willingness to use it. Even now, every one of your bunkers and trenches there has been registered for engagement by cannon, anti-tank missiles, mortars, artillery and NATO jets.

'You have until 1800 hours the day after tomorrow to deliver to this headquarters a full written explanation, together with your plan to make sure that such an incident never occurs again. Tomorrow at 0900 hours, Major Mills the company commander and all the British IFOR soldiers involved in the shooting incident will be at WHITE FANG. They will be prepared to cooperate fully with your investigation, for example by showing you exactly where the bullets fell and the target they engaged with return fire. We will accept no excuses. Do you understand? Are there any questions?'

There are no questions. I indicate that the meeting is over. They leave, tight-lipped and looking very unhappy. I recall that tomorrow is Orthodox Christmas Day.

I go back to the Battlegroup HQ planning room to debrief all those involved in the meeting. I am surprised that as well as Ian Baker, all the liaison officers are gathered to meet me, all smiling broadly. The meeting had been held in a small room we have created by partitioning a large one with wooden boards and blankets. Unbeknownst to me, most of Battlegroup HQ has overheard me giving the Serb commander what became known as 'the interview without coffee'. Not only have the liaison officers trained extensively to swallow their pride while dealing with difficult and obstreperous commanders from all three factions, but they have also experienced much obfuscation and friction from Bosnian officers and from 43 Brigade in particular. The 'interview without coffee' I have administered is a wish come true. In addition, Paul Sulyok has had many frustrating experiences with the VRS whilst taking UNPROFOR convoys in and out of Goražde, including being detained as a hostage. He is in a state I can only describe as mild ecstasy.

As if by magic, a bottle of whisky appears from somewhere, and there is much convivial retelling of tall and amusing tales from the battalion's adventures since November. The adjutant says that he has briefed Captain Mick Garner, the families officer in Paderborn, about the incident and the crucial news that none of the battalion has been hurt. News of the shooting is already being carried on the BBC World Service and I call Liz on the satellite telephone to reassure her as well. She is unfazed and our conversation turns to domestic issues, a warmly reassuring injection of normality.

Returning to the operations room, I am briefed that over in Bosanska Krupa, A Company has deployed sniper teams and Warriors using night sights to deter or defeat any other shooting at their base. There has been none and the town is quiet. As I stumble to my camp bed, I recall that I have not followed up the problem with the Recce Platoon. I am too tired to do so now. But I know that Battlegroup HQ will have done so. The problem may simply have been poor radio communications. Or it may have been an error of judgement by the patrol commander. In the latter case, the commander will have lost a great deal of face by being criticised over the radio net by myself. Knowing that the platoon commander will deal with it, I let the matter rest. As I am reviewing these events in my mind the electricity comes back on. This, I think, is a good omen.

The Morning After

The next day was a brigade orders group. I drove south to WHITE FANG, passing our mortars set up in the middle of the road south from Prijedor and a troop of light guns moving into position. This would have shown the VRS party heading to WHITE FANG that our indirect fire weapons were capable of going into action at very short notice. At WHITE FANG there was a huddle of a dozen VRS officers and a tall imposing man in an elegant woollen overcoat. I recognised him as the Bosnian Serb officer I had met in Prijedor, the commander of Operations Group 10, whom I had confused with the commander of 43 Infantry Brigade. The officers stood at WHITE FANG itself, deep in discussion with Stuart Mills and the B Company soldiers who had taken part in yesterday's incident.

Later, Stuart Mills told me that the VRS delegation was extremely high-powered. The commander of Operations Group 10 had returned from his parents' house in the Serb suburbs of Sarajevo, driving through the night to arrive at WHITE FANG in his own car. The officers had paid close attention to the accounts of the participants. They had been extremely apologetic, almost over-anxious to please and desperately keen to avoid any more exchanges of fire between IFOR and themselves.

They had then all investigated the bunker indicated by our soldiers. Stuart noticed an elderly and bespectacled soldier in ill-fitting but brand-new combat clothing, with no insignia or badges of rank. He had been asking questions of the other VRS officers, but not of us.

The bunkers were empty, but this civilian picked up a number of expended ammunition cartridges. A heated discussion then took place between the Serb officers and this man, who Stuart now believed to be a weapons specialist or forensics expert. Stuart could see that the VRS battalion commander responsible for this bunker was being given an extremely hard time by the brigade and divisional commanders.

The next afternoon a written note from 43 Brigade's commander was delivered to the Sewing Factory. It had a short apology and a pretty limp explanation of the incident. Nevertheless I was satisfied. The VRS had taken our demands very seriously. We had indications that the battalion commander concerned had been severely punished, for what we believed was probably the actions of a bored soldier venting his frustration at being on duty on Christmas Eve – not that this made firing at NATO any less serious. Our assertive and no-nonsense approach, although a gamble with an element of bluff, had paid off. The VRS had lost an enormous amount of face. There would be little sense in rubbing their noses in it and Ian Baker let 43 Brigade and Operations Group 10 know that we would not hold a grudge about the incident against them – provided there was no repetition.

The thoroughly satisfying outcomes of the two shooting incidents raised our morale. In this, there lay danger. I made a note to discuss this at the next orders group. We had to be very careful not to cross the line from asserting our rights and duties under Dayton into being overbearing, hectoring and bullying, which would risk destroying the respect that the factions had for us, as well as eroding civil and military goodwill.

The next day, our families and friends in England and Germany watched BBC TV news report the shooting and broadcast Martin Bell's report, filmed the previous day. He called us 'a stage army, exiting stage left from Serb territory, to immediately appear stage right in a Muslim area'. How right he was.

Private Mitchell had played a decisive role in the incident. He had only joined the battalion from recruit training in September, two months before the tour. By choosing to stand his ground and return fire, he exposed himself to danger while covering the withdrawal to safety of the other soldiers. He then had the presence of mind to not only turn back the IFOR Land Rovers, but also to give me an extremely accurate briefing on the situation. This independent action, instantly taking responsibility for a problem and sorting it out without waiting to refer it up the battalion's chain of command, was something I had sought to inculcate in all ranks. It was in stark contrast to the command philosophy of the faction armies. Lieutenant Peter Chapman described their *modus operandi* and his participation in the follow-up to the shooting:

A feature of the former warring factions that is hard to get acquainted with is their concept of rank, and the centralised, communist-style method of decision-making. Simply put, every decision is made at the highest possible level, which can be infuriating. The British Army prides itself on delegating responsibility down to the lowest level, so it comes as a shock to turn up at a faction Battalion HQ and suggest a joint patrol, only to be informed that their battalion has to clear every joint patrol in advance with its Brigade HQ. The disadvantages of this system are that proportionately fewer people know what is going on, leading to a slower dissemination of information, although once you have found the right commander you can be sure that everyone beneath him will follow his lead.

The rank hierarchy is an important part of the faction structure, partly because of the strict delineation of responsibilities, but also because it does not have a 'normal' age-related basis. This is especially true in the Muslim Army where, since former Yugoslavian Army soldiers are few and far between, professional training and combat experience have far more influence on rank than white hairs. Thus it is entirely normal to meet a twenty-eight-year-old Muslim brigade commander with a forty-year-old battalion commander, who has platoon commanders aged twenty-five and fifty-five. But just as we have difficulty adjusting to their rank structure, so do they in coping with ours. In particular, it has long been recognised that captain is the minimum rank needed to liaise successfully, and as a lieutenant I spent my first few meetings merely proving I was familiar with details of the Dayton Agreement and capable of independent action. Once I had proved my credentials and responsibilities, I was treated to more information and accorded more respect, although two incidents provide example of the difficulties the Serbs had in coping with our system.

The first occurred at the investigation into a firing incident, when rounds originating from the Serb side of the line had landed at the feet of British soldiers on a checkpoint. The apologetic Serbs were leading the investigation, and I was charged with overseeing it, but when introduced to the local brigade commander I stuck my hand out – and was completely ignored! Clearly as a mere lieutenant, I did not merit the honour of shaking a colonel's hand, although at the time I took it far more personally, as about twenty people saw me get the ultimate snub

The second was when I was unable to introduce my Warrior serjeant to the local Serbs in person. His first trip to their HQ was on his own. They simply did not believe a serjeant could know as much as an officer, let alone command the platoon while I was on R&R. Their confusion was complete when he said he had thirteen years more experience and was better paid than me, and he had to go through a lengthy interrogation about the Dayton Agreement before they even started to take him into their confidence.

We were lucky indeed to have soldiers and commanders who relished having responsibility devolved to them and who had the ability to operate for long periods of time with minimal supervision.

CHAPTER NINE

Darkness at the Edge of Town

I had been so preoccupied with the aftermath of the shooting that I had hardly noticed the effect of the Serbs celebrating Orthodox Christmas. But now we could not ignore the constant fusillade of 'celebratory' fire – weapons ranging from pistols through Kalashnikovs to heavy machine guns being fired skywards. The distinctive 'crump' and shock transmitted through the ground told us that hand grenades were being thrown. By now we had all become quite blasé about this. As none of the ordnance being expended seemed to be coming in the direction of our bases or patrols, we took no particular action. Interestingly, there was no 'celebratory' fire at all coming from the VRS front-line positions – it seemed that the message I had delivered the previous evening was getting through.

We now knew that in our area we had the following military formations.

VRS Operations Group 10, 1 Krajina Corps. Headquartered in Prijedor, with two brigades, one of which was 43 Brigade in Ljubija, now extremely compliant after the shooting incident.

VRS 2 Krajina Corps. Headquartered in the village of Celopec, this formation had been heavily battered in the Federation offensives, and had a logistic base and a few weak brigades. Despite its apparently limited combat power, it still held almost a third of the VRS frontline in our area.

ABiH 5 Corps. Main HQ in Bihać with forward HQ in Jasenica. At least eight brigades were spread along the front line. We believed that there were reserves and corps troops based in barracks, particularly in Bihać. Intelligence suggested that these included a brigade of Bosnian Croat HVO troops that had fought alongside the rest of the overwhelmingly Muslim corps. There was a battalion of tanks, captured from the Serbs, or exchanged for cash or black market commodities during the various cease-fires around the Bihać pocket.

ABiH 7 Corps. Detached from the main body of 7 Corps in central Bosnia was a forward headquarters in Sanski Most, a divisional HQ in Klujc, eight brigades and corps and divisional troops.

Military Commissions

We wanted to use military commission meetings as a way to communicate with faction commanders and staff officers in an IFOR-controlled environment. Many meetings between UNPROFOR and the factions had deteriorated into long-winded arguments around the table. We intended that IFOR military commissions would be firmly controlled so that they did not become forums for dogmatic posturing or get distracted by red herrings. It would be essential to prepare the meeting thoroughly beforehand and to stage-manage the events.

B Company had conducted a number of extremely successful bilateral meetings with the two Serb brigades subordinate to Operations Group 10. In the aftermath of the WHITE FANG shooting incident, we had given these formations considerable direction. Holding a military commission for them would be unnecessary. The other three corps in our area were a different matter. The company and squadron commanders and I had not met all the brigade commanders – indeed, we were not yet confident that we knew exactly where all the brigades were. I directed Ian Baker to arrange military commissions with the ABiH 5 and 7 Corps and the VRS 2 Krajina Corps.

In each case, we accepted the corps' invitation to have the meetings at their HQs. Ian and his team sorted out arrangements beforehand. All of the company and squadron commanders would be present, as would the battery commander and BGEOO, so that the faction commanders and staff officers would be able to identify, meet and recognise the IFOR officers with whom they might have to deal.

I chaired the meetings and did most of the talking. After the meeting, we would encourage the faction commanders and staff to continue discussions informally. The three commission meetings were very successful. We came to realise that they were not just meetings, but an integral part of our close and deep operations. Although they were not battles, they were set-piece engagements of the faction military, requiring as much preparation as a battlegroup as any operation we might conduct in war.

The first commission was held on 3 January with 7 Corps ABiH in the restaurant of the Hotel Sana at Sanski Most. All the corps brigade commanders attended, accompanied by Major Klosman, the corps 'operations staff officer' who had accompanied the Chief of Staff to the meeting with Brigadier Viggers a week earlier. Also present was the corps Chief Engineer who had so admirably organised the ABiH sappers at the same day's route-opening operation. I used these notes:

Introduction. Self & home team.

IFOR replaces UNPROFOR. Clear mission to implement military annex of Dayton. Agreement was the product of much negotiation. Treaty is non-negotiable in this forum. We now have to make it work. Will require effort, perseverance common sense and willpower.

Hope all will comply, but WE HAVE NO ILLUSIONS. Have robust Rules of Engagement and combat capability to enforce if necessary.

IFOR Deployment, Operations & Basing. Explain:
Our composition and locations. Heavy artillery and tanks arriving soon.
Helicopters and NATO air power available.
Liaison structure: JCOs, Division, Brigade, Battlegroup and Company LOs.
ALL OPERATING EQUALLY ON BOTH SIDES.
Freedom of Movement. IFOR needs it to do its job. OK so far.
HQ Locations, Units and Weapons. We respect your security BUT need to be able
  to contact your HQs. IFOR will need full locations of all your units and heavy
  weapons within 10km of ZOS by D+25.
Cease-Fire Violations and Protests. Aim will be to solve any problems ASAP at as
  low a level as possible – BUT we will take a dim view of bogus protests.
Foreign Forces. Advisors, freedom fighters, volunteers must all leave NOW.
'Celebratory' Fire. Have been exposed to your troops and civilians firing weapons
  in celebration – for example festivals, coming off the front line and drunken
  parties. UNPROFOR put up with this. We will not. Refuse to believe that you
  cannot control your soldiers. Fire falling on or near our position will cause us
  to use force to defend ourselves. IT MUST STOP.
Mines and Mine Clearing. No new mines may be laid. You must lift all of yours.
  IFOR monitors, supervises and assists by providing security. We require
  minefield maps from you. My chief engineer will co-ordinate this with your
  chief engineer.
SEPARATION OF FORCES.
Next major Dayton milestone. Why? Will reduce tension by taking both sides out
  of sight of each other, reducing opportunities for incidents. 2km back from
  front line. IFOR commanders using satellite equipment are arbiters. I have
  authority to adjust up to 50 metres. Where ZOS crosses roads/tracks we will
  mark with yellow poles. You can help in two ways:
Identify your new positions to us as soon as possible. Declare them to us and we
  will check locations – using satellites if necessary. This should prevent embarrassing mistakes.
Tell us your plans. Then we can monitor as they happen and provide maximum
  security. YOUR SECURITY WILL BE RESPECTED.
Our Plans. Maximum presence close to front line ON BOTH SIDES. Artillery and
  mortars will cover whole front line and ZOS from depth positions. Helicopters
  and jets above. We will verify withdrawal.
Zone of Separation. Once created, NO WEAPONS OR MILITARY EQUIPMENT
  OF ANY KIND ALLOWED. IFOR will prevent occupation or reoccupation by
  any armed people or groups. Not to be confused with civil policing or law and
  order which is not IFOR responsibility. Civilians have freedom of movement
  in ZOS – provided they are unarmed.
Any Questions?

There were no questions or comments from any of the brigade commanders
but after the formal meeting there was much discussion, standing round the
map drinking thick, lukewarm Bosnian coffee. Seven Corps operated in a
highly centralised fashion. The real authority was quite clearly held at Corps

HQ, with all the brigade commanders being extremely deferential to the two staff officers present. The corps' plan to withdraw from the Zone of Separation had been written, but it would not be disseminated to the brigade commanders until just before the operation.

The second meeting was with 5 Corps ABiH at their forward headquarters at Jasenica. Of the four corps that we were dealing with, this appeared to have the most professional command set-up. Unlike the other corps, their HQ was guarded by smart, alert sentries wearing helmets. For the first time in Bosnia we saw camouflage nets in use, draped over communications vehicles. The room used for the meeting was clearly a functioning part of the headquarters. Hanging on the walls were a large number of maps showing 5 Corps' dispositions down to platoon level, their artillery, minefields and, most interestingly, their assessment of the positions and deployment of the VRS forces opposing them. Not only did they accurately depict their own dispositions, but they also had a very accurate idea of where the VRS positions were located – and in considerably more detail than we did. I wondered if this departure from the usual Bosnian paranoid attitude to divulging their dispositions showed that we had their confidence.

Jan de Vos introduced me to the commander that A Company had christened the 'rock 'n' roll brigadier' – a Bosnian major with an Afro hairstyle and a black leather motorbike jacket over his combat fatigues. Another major was a woman, the only time that I ever met a female officer in any of the faction armies. After the meeting we sat down to a simple lunch. After the first course, brigade commanders began to slip away, so that by the end of the meal only the 2 LI and corps staff officers were left. The commanders were off to brief their subordinates on the outcome of the meeting they had just attended, as the corps commander had insisted this was done immediately. This seemed to be genuine and my impression of 5 Corps as having the most professional attitude of the four corps in our area was reinforced.

The final commission was held with the 2 Krajina Corps at Čelopek, this time in a village restaurant. This meeting was notable for the respect with which all the VRS officers treated Serjeant Major Blue, the leader of the Prijedor JCO team. As we still had no crossing point in A Company's area, the JCOs had been patrolling much of this corps' territory. At the meeting, I emphasised the difficulties caused to us by not having a front-line crossing point in their area. This made 2 Corps the only VRS Corps in our divisional area not to have a crossing point.

The military commissions seemed to galvanise 5 Corps and 2 Krajina Corps into action, for within two days arrangements were made to open a route between the two formations. We selected the village of Arapuša, which the map showed to contain the only other metalled road directly crossing the front line in our area. By now our drills for these operations were well practised. A Company were in charge, working from the south with the ABiH engineers, while B Squadron accompanied the VRS forces in from the north. The artillery and mortars again deployed in highly visible positions alongside the major routes to the crossing points and on both sides of the front line.

The crossing point was opened on 9 January. Unusually, the road into the village was wide and I could pass A Company's Warriors, which lined the crest of the large natural bowl containing Arapuša, a long village straggling between the VRS trenches lining the northern rim and the ABiH bunkers along the southern rim. Jan de Vos was forward, commanding the operation from his Warrior less than fifty metres behind the 5 Corps sappers. I joined him, tucking my Land Rover behind the bulk of his Warrior just as both factions' engineers lifted the mines from the exact positions shown on their records.

Just ahead, we could see Serjeant Fyvie, the EOD team walking right behind the ABiH engineers as they checked the road. A party of VRS engineers were working in the opposite direction towards them supervised by Fyvie's second-in-command. Both groups of sappers were wearing helmets and protective eye shields and using long sharp-tipped metal probes to prod the track for unrecorded mines – under the close supervision of our two EOD experts, who accompanied the faction engineers throughout this dangerous task. Should the faction engineers have stumbled on an unmarked mine, or accidentally initiated one whilst attempting to lift it, the British engineers would have been very close to the resulting explosion.

Both parties confidently approached each other, prodding to a common meeting point. Although the faction engineers hung back separated by some ten metres, fidgeting uneasily, Fyfvie lost no time bringing together the officers who had accompanied each faction party in the middle of the crossing point. We went forward to see this unprecedented meeting for ourselves. By the time we arrived, the small huddle of IFOR and faction engineers were deep in discussion. There was no tension, Fyfvie explained, because all the officers were former Jugoslav National Army military engineers. My interpreter told me that they were busy discussing how they would lift the remaining mines from their respective front lines.

I was elated and sent for the bottle of whisky that nestled in my rucksack. I congratulated the faction engineers on their efforts and explained who I was. The Bosnian expressed of amazement that so senior an IFOR officer should appear on the front line immediately after a crossing operation. After some light-hearted small talk, and much quaffing of whisky, I had to depart for Šipovo where a Brigade orders group was to take place. As I made my apologies to the engineers and left, I asked the two senior officers from each faction if they would shake hands. They did so without hesitation. I left Arapuša in high spirits.

Dark Mines

I drove to Šipovo, spooning out a 'boil in a bag' meal that Private Leck had thoughtfully prepared at Arapuša. My mood was darkened by a report from Battlegroup HQ that a party of journalists had arrived at our HQ seeking stories about mass graves of Muslims that were alleged to lie in the mines at Ljubija, just south of our bases in Donja Ljubija.

In December, our only exposure to the issue of alleged war crimes had been the bodies and fragments of bodies that our patrols had chanced upon, all in Federation territory. There was no evidence to suggest that these forlorn human remains had been caused by anything other than fighting. But in early January, a senior Muslim officer had requested a private interview with me after our military commission with 5 Corps. His story was that in the September offensive 5 Corps had entered the southern part of the mining complex at Ljubija, but had quickly been beaten back to the current front line by an unexpected VRS counterattack. In the short time that they occupied the mines, they had found evidence of mass graves of Muslims, evidence that he claimed was corroborated by testimony from escaped Muslim prisoners. Using a large-scale map he indicated a number of mine workings just north of the front line.

At this stage, the chain of command had offered no guidance about how to deal with allegations of war crimes, let alone how to handle such detailed information about the potential sites of mass graves, which could yield hard evidence. We reported this particular allegation up the chain of command. Back down came the IFOR line:

> The investigation of war crimes is a matter for the International Criminal Tribunal for former Yugoslavia (ICTY). IFOR is fully committed to supervising the implementation of the military tasks specified by the Dayton agreement, which helps foster a secure environment within Bosnia. NATO is going to use IFOR neither to conduct investigations into war crimes, nor to directly assist the ICTY.

We were to forward all allegations or evidence of war crimes up the chain of command, who would pass the information to the ICTY, who would use it as they saw fit. I made sure that this 'line to take' was briefed down the chain of command throughout the battlegroup.

The International Tribunal was based at The Hague. In January 1996 its permanent presence in Bosnia was a single liaison officer in Sarajevo. We were told that it would be some time before the ICTY began fieldwork in Bosnia in earnest. Over the next few days, similar allegations of mass executions at Ljubija were made to us by a number of different sources, a high proportion of which appeared to be bona fide. There were many detailed reports that the mines had been the sites of repeated cold-blooded executions of Muslim civilians, that the bodies had been fed into the mining complex's rock grinding and crushing machinery, then buried in the deep open-cast pits, some flooded, that abounded in the Ljubija area.

We collated these reports in Battlegroup HQ. This was not an issue we could ignore. So we needed to deter any guilty parties from attempting to tamper with the evidence, but only to do so without prejudice to our priority task – which remained implementing the separation of forces. And we needed to know if any journalists chose to see the area for themselves. B Squadron stepped up patrols in the Ljubija area, including patrols at night. We tasked helicopter patrols to overfly the area. The helicopters saw nothing unusual. The mining complexes were close to the front line, which we knew to be heavily mined by both sides. Our ability to patrol the complex was limited by the high threat of mine strikes. If, as 5 Corps alleged, the ABiH had advanced into the mining area and been forced to withdraw, there was a considerable land mine threat to patrols that ventured onto new routes.

The area was covered with open-cast mines, all sited in high hills covered with snow. Clouds and mists made flying over the area extremely difficult, and we could not achieve anything like complete surveillance coverage of the area from the air or ground. We found no evidence at all that either confirmed the allegations or suggested that any Bosnian Serbs had any special interest in the area. Indeed, the whole mining complex seemed inert and lifeless. Almost two months had elapsed since the signing of the Dayton Agreement, allowing plenty of time for war criminals to cover their tracks.

On several occasions, the RSM and I took our Land Rovers on patrols around the area. The huge, echoing, empty pits, the cold wet snow over the brutal wounds of the enormous excavations and the great, dark metal skeletons of the mining machinery, like the bones of malevolent dinosaurs, gave the whole complex a chilling air of depression. These gaunt, forbidding shapes of dark metal and the detail and verisimilitude of the allegations made it extremely easy to believe that there was 'no smoke without fire'.

The British and international media became interested in the allegations and we began to receive enquiries from journalists. Many considered the story sufficiently newsworthy to travel from Sarajevo – a long and difficult journey across the length of the country in the depths of winter. They were extremely inquisitive and had many detailed and probing questions. What did we know about the allegations of war crimes? What were we doing about them? Had we taken any witnesses under our protection? Why were we not securing the mines to prevent tampering with the evidence? Why were we not excavating the mines and diving in the lakes to find evidence? Why were we not arresting those responsible for the killings? Would we provide escorts for the journalists to visit the sites of the killings?

We handled all these questions as politely and courteously as we could, but firmly and patiently stuck to the IFOR press line. We would not provide escorts for the journalists, and strongly advised against leaving routes known to be clear, because of the high danger of encountering 'a mine in a mine'. This phrase was the only aspect of the story that ever raised a smile.

As time went on, some determined and persistent journalists attempted a different approach. Sometimes they would flag down passing patrols or directly approach our outposts to elicit comment on the Ljubija mines. The young officers who were questioned managed both to stick to the IFOR line and to remain polite and good-humoured under some very persistent interrogation. Representatives of the *Guardian* and *New York Times* asked for interviews with the commanding officer. Captain Steve Noble gave them detailed briefings and I spent a long time discussing our operations. Towards the end of these lengthy interviews, questioning subtly shifted to the issues of war crimes and the specific allegations of Ljubija mines. Again, I stuck to the IFOR line, even though the questioning became extremely persistent.

Reports of the allegations appeared in British and American newspapers. Most were accurate but some were exaggerated and others included text that bore no relation to the facts as we understood them. A report in the *New York Times* of 11 January stated:

> Senior British commanders stationed in the mining town with NATO forces say that British patrols sometimes find corpses, usually badly decomposed, only to have the bodies whisked away by the Bosnian Serbs, often within hours. They speculate that some of these bodies are from executions carried out this fall by paramilitary forces led by Zeljko Razaslovic, known as Arkan. Others, they say, may date back four years to one of the earliest waves of ethnic killing in the Bosnian conflict.
>
> 'Everyone seems to be in a hurry to cover their killings', said one senior British commander, who asked to remain unidentified. 'There are bodies all over this place. We go in to houses and find floorboards ripped up and holes in the basement. They are working very hard.'

To my knowledge, no one in the battlegroup gave any such interview. A charitable interpretation might be that the 'quotations' were made up, but reflected some of the sights of area around the front line, the bodies of dead soldiers and the comprehensively looted houses. An uncharitable interpretation would be that the quotation was a complete fabrication.

By the time I saw a faxed copy of the newspaper a week had passed and the attention of the media had moved on to other matters. We decided we were lucky to receive so little adverse media comment and took no action.

At the same time, we learned more about the long and dark trail of war crimes throughout Bosnia. We knew that many of the faction military considered all men of military age, which was universally taken to be sixteen to sixty, to be legitimate targets. There was clear evidence that some faction commanders and many paramilitary groups, including Arkan's notorious 'Tigers', were happy to execute prisoners without compunction. We heard other stories of the routine abuse of such prisoners as were taken. Finally, the ethnic cleansing of the villages could not be hidden. Although many media reports proclaimed the Bosnian Serbs to be the sole perpetrators of these crimes, we heard more than enough evidence to become convinced that both Muslims and Croats had performed plenty of evil deeds.

The nature of the allegations, the constant questioning by the media and the fact that we were living on the edge of the area where these killings were supposed to have taken place made it extremely difficult to remain unemotional and detached. It was quite possible that Bosnian military personnel with whom the battlegroup was dealing had blood on their hands. Many of us wondered about this – asking ourselves all sorts of questions; how many Bosnian officers sitting round the table at a military commission were war criminals? How many Bosnian politicians and local officials, like the mayors we were dealing with were accomplices to war crimes? As the snow melted what evidence would come to light?

Whatever my conscience might tell me about this, I knew that getting on with implementing the peace had to be the priority, for if the peace broke down, more soldiers would die and more war crimes would be committed. We had no powers to arrest faction commanders 'on suspicion' of having committed a war crime. There was neither British nor international legislation to allow us to do so. Like it or not, the faction commanders and political leaders must be treated as innocent until either proven guilty or indicted by the International War Crimes Tribunal.

All three factions were accusing each other of having committed war crimes. British troops in Central Bosnia in 1992 and 93 had seen with their own eyes very strong evidence of Muslim and Croat atrocities. There had been plenty of coverage in the media of both the appalling treatment of prisoners by the Serbs and the alleged massacres after the fall of Srebenica. But here in Ljubija, all the allegations were being made against the Serbs.

Even if they were all true, we still had to remain impartial in our treatment of the factions. Whatever the strength of the allegations and our own emotions, siding with the Muslims against the Serbs would be a threat to both our impartiality and our ability to focus on our primary military tasks. I directed that those involved in handling this issue must neither become personally involved nor do any more than the minimum required by our orders. I had to be blunt and brutally frank, offering sympathy but little comfort. Maintaining the IFOR 'line to take' and refraining from getting involved in actively investigating these allegations was a moral challenge which we had to face head on, like it or not.

During our time in Ljubija we never discovered any physical evidence of war crimes. In Battlegroup HQ we often discussed the possibility of pursuing war criminals. It seemed to us that it would be very difficult to balance justice and peace. After the Second World War the victorious Allies had conducted the Nuremberg trials, finding senior German officers and politicians guilty of crimes against humanity. We had no doubt that serious crimes against humanity had been committed in Bosnia, but with none of the entities being either victor or vanquished, it was going to be more difficult to investigate war crimes and hold the perpetrators to account. It was also clear that if the ICTY simply investigated crimes conducted by the Bosnian Serbs, it would be very difficult to uphold NATO's impartiality.

On more than one occasion we were asked how we could bring ourselves to meet with people who we thought could well be war criminals. If the question were put, as it often was, by visiting journalists, I would simply quote the IFOR line.

If the question were put privately by British Army or NATO personnel, I would reply that dealing politely with people suspected of terrible crimes but who were still at large and had not been arrested, was a skill the Army had learned over the years in Northern Ireland. For over twenty five years soldiers and officers had patrolled the Province's towns and countryside constantly coming into contact with people suspected of having committed terrorist crimes, including the murder of soldiers. But the British Army operated within the law and people could only be arrested under due process of law.

The emotions arising from hearing detailed and highly disturbing allegations of war crimes might make us want to take justice into our hands, but this was the business of the International Tribunal, not ourselves. We were professional soldiers, and our training had emphasised from the outset that we operated within the rule of law. In Northern Ireland this was domestic UK law, in war it would have been the Geneva Convention and laws of armed conflict. Here in Bosnia, it was the Dayton mandate, our rules of engagement and the international agreements that set up the International War Crimes Tribunal at The Hague. They had their job to do, and we had ours. Establishing a lasting peace would at least prevent future war crimes.

Fortunately our junior commanders seemed rarely, if ever, directly troubled by this issue. For example the Recce Platoon, which was cheerfully getting on with patrolling. Their Scimitars and the REME Samson recovery vehicle that supported them had each by now clocked up at least twenty thousand miles since they arrived in Bosnia. They were particularly useful on narrow snow and ice-covered tracks over which Warrior could not travel. Ian McGregor, the platoon commander, wrote in the *Silver Bugle*:

We conducted operations from various locations, moving on average every three to four days. Everywhere we moved, we seemed to miss the showers. Most of us had not had one since December, and by mid-January we were all pretty unsavoury. Morale remained high in spite of the constant sub-zero temperatures. Corporal Moses suffered a dose of frostbite, and was asked by an attached medic if he had 'been exposed to the cold'! As I write he is awaiting the answer as to whether he'll be able to count to four or five on the fingers on his right hand.

Working for B Company, we were at our busiest proving routes for Warrior and locating the positions of both warring factions. This was to ensure that the rules agreed in Dayton were not being broken. Vehicle recognition was used on a daily basis. Lance Corporal Shickle, a definite 'trainspotter', who many of us feel would be perfectly at home on the platform of a railway station wearing an anorak, showed an almost unnatural affinity for finding faction equipment, as did Corporal Young, who located a VRS missile site that NATO had not found.

Private Kelsall consistently managed to appear as a walking 'oil change', and could easily top up a gearbox by wringing his jacket out. Private Wilks started many letters to 'pen-pals' by saying: 'Bosnia is OK, I can hack the hardship . . . it's the kids that get to me.' He had some success! Lance Corporal Dooler is unrecognisable unless cowering in the candlelight over a bluey to the missus. Lance Corporal Potter was similar: his mother's welfare parcels remain a legend, as does the fine Christmas cake.

Heavy Metal

British vehicles, stores, ammunition and equipment were now arriving at Split. Seven ships and two hundred and fifty aircraft sorties had brought eighteen hundred more vehicles (two hundred and fifty of them armoured), two and a half million litres of fuel, four thousand tonnes of ammunition and thirty thousand tonnes of other supplies. The first elements to reach the brigade were the tanks of the Queen's Royal Hussars (QRH). Based in Catterick, they had sailed from the north of England in a huge Ukrainian ferry. On 11 January the battlegroup received two troops of Challenger tanks, all mounting powerful 120mm guns, outperforming all our other direct fire weapons. They also had excellent thermal imaging sights, superior to any other thermal imagers available to the battlegroup. The tanks had even greater protection than that afforded by the Chobham armour plates on the Warriors. These characteristics, together with the vehicles' size and noise, considerably impressed the factions.

But there was a price to be paid. Firstly, the tanks' size would make it impossible for them to negotiate some of the steeper and narrower tracks. The weight of the tanks, double that of Warrior, made them too heavy to cross many of the local bridges. The weight also meant that the tanks could cause significant damage to the unmetalled farm tracks that made up a high proportion of the routes we needed to use in and around the front line. Finally, the tanks incurred a significant logistic bill. Not only did each tank consume over three times as much diesel as a Warrior, but they were also significantly less reliable. Fortunately the QRH were deploying their own fuel vehicles to assist in keeping the tanks topped up, and the half squadron to join us had been accompanied by a huge Challenger Repair and Recovery Vehicle with its crew of REME experts. Armoured engineers would lay tank bridges on crossings south and west of Sanski Most; without these the tanks would not be able to reach the southern parts of the A Company or B Squadron areas.

I went to WHITE FANG to watch the first troop arrive, carried up all the way from Kupres on the backs of huge tank transporters, the combined load being more than a hundred tonnes. The tank crews were in high spirits and seemed to be delighted to be with us. One troop had a serjeant commanding whilst the other was led by a lively young officer, Lieutenant Rupert Greenwood, who seemed to already know all the platoon and troop commanders in the battlegroup. Over the next few days, both troops did exactly what the company and squadron commanders asked of them, as well as coming up with numerous ideas and suggestions of their own.

Although the QRH were far from complete in Bosnia, they spared no effort in making sure that the tanks with us were properly supported. The role of the squadron commander was critical in this. Sensibly, he chose not to attempt to direct the employment of his tanks, for I had company and squadron commanders who were doing that perfectly adequately, but spent his time co-ordinating the logistic support necessary to keep three tanks continuously on the road. I could not have asked for better support.

I was also extremely pleased with the way that the light gun battery had integrated into the battlegroup. Major John Turp had quickly become a valued member of my team, accompanying me on my trips around the battlegroup area. The forward observers had also similarly got alongside the company and squadron HQs. When weather permitted we moved artillery by air, slinging guns, ammunition and vehicles below Sea King or Chinook helicopters, increasing their visibility to Bosnian military and civilians. Finally, we had successfully used the battery to rapidly reinforce threatened or sensitive areas, as with the aftermath of the WHITE FANG shooting.

Minestrike

While I was visiting the artillery battery at the Mud Factory, one of our vehicles struck a mine in the south of B Company's area. The reports over the battlegroup net announced that there had been no casualties, which was reassuring. At B Company's base, Captain Peter MacFarlane briefed me that patrol comprising a Recce Platoon Scimitar and Mortar Platoon Spartan had been travelling along a route between the two front lines. They had seen from our copies of the 7 Corps ABiH mine maps that the route was clear, and had been told so by ABiH soldiers; nevertheless the lead vehicle, the Spartan, had struck a mine. Those in the vehicle were suffering from mild shock, but, miraculously, were otherwise unscathed. The crew of the Spartan were now sitting on top of the Scimitar, which was not moving because the crews had seen at least half a dozen other anti-tank mines in the area.

Battlegroup HQ advised that the EOD team could not be at the location before darkness. Since the soldiers were out of immediate danger, they would have to remain where they were until first light, when B Company would organise a clearance operation. I accepted this, but was worried that, stuck in the middle of no-man's-land, they were vulnerable to shooting attacks by ill-disciplined soldiers from either faction. I could imagine how isolated the stranded soldiers felt and I wanted to make sure they knew that they had not been forgotten. The mortar platoon and artillery battery were tasked to deploy to the area and to fire illuminating rounds to deter attacks. A helicopter patrol was also tasked to overfly the stranded vehicles during the night. In the darkness, the faction military would not know how many aircraft there were and whether or not they were armed.

Next morning, B Company mounted a large-scale clearance operation, for which the 7 Corps Chief Engineer turned up. His minefield records were neat and tidy but inaccurate. The clearance operation needed the services of the full EOD team. Seventy-eight anti tank mines and forty-nine anti-personnel mines had to be cleared before the damaged Spartan could be recovered. These particular mines were not marked on the ABiH mine maps, but the soldiers manning the trenches and bunkers clearly knew they were there.

Stuart Mills investigated the incident. The patrol had no interpreter with them and had conversed with Muslim soldiers in pidgin English and sign language, forming the impression that the soldiers were telling them the route was clear. As a result the patrol had blundered onto mines that they could have avoided. Although I was extremely unimpressed with the way the patrol had got themselves into the mess, my discussions with the two vehicle commanders convinced me that they had had to call on their reserves of endurance to spend the night on top of their small vehicle in the minefield. I was also impressed with their eagerness to resume normal patrolling straight away. Most impressive of all was Stuart Mills' quietly sympathetic but firm leadership, instrumental in quickly restoring their shaken morale in order to allow them to resume operations.

We had narrowly escaped having three soldiers killed. I had Stuart Mills brief the Battlegroup Orders Group on the lessons from this incident, and directed that all movement in the Zone of Separation was to be restricted to cleared routes, routes recently travelled by IFOR or clearly used by faction military or civilian traffic.

Maps and Snapshots

The battlegroup is visited by the British commander of the Allied Rapid Reaction Corps (COMARRC), Lieutenant General Walker. His helicopters fly in to MALIBU CORNER, the B Company platoon base in an isolated schoolhouse. The General seems genuinely interested in what we are doing, asking me what he can do to help the battlegroup. I reply that he could get us more of the American-produced Dayton maps with the Inter Entity Boundary Line and Zone of separation printed on them. Even now, the battlegroup, although well provided with reproduced pre-war Yugoslav maps, doesn't have enough Dayton maps for every patrol, let alone sufficient to give to the faction commanders we are dealing with. COMARRC tells me that this is a repeated refrain from his visits to the French and American divisions, as well as British troops. He is puzzled, as his staff are telling him that there is no shortage of maps. Later I learn that he went on to ask the ARRC staff about this. A number of senior officers then write to COMARRC claiming that there is no shortage of Dayton maps. There is no significant increase in the number of Dayton maps available to the battlegroup for another month. We manage somehow using a photocopier and lots of Sellotape.

We are now using three different types of maps. The factions have given us a few original Yugoslav survey maps, marked with their positions and minefields. These are very clear and detailed, but lack the NATO grid system.

Our British topographical engineers have copied these maps, overprinting them with several different grid systems. Although the maps are useful, the clear colours of the Yugoslav originals have faded in reproduction and the maps are now covered with several overlapping black and blue grids, thus making detail much harder to discern.

All our vehicles and commanders are using these maps, but the 'Dayton maps' arriving from the US are from a completely new survey. As well as showing the definitive location of the IEBL and ZOS, they are very clear and accurate, apparently having been compiled from a fresh aerial or satellite survey. The only problem is that the survey appears to have been conducted in the summer, as the maps show streams where there are now wide rivers and raging torrents.

I reflect that having to use three different map editions, all showing the terrain in different ways, all accurate only at the moment they were made, and all with different advantages and disadvantages, is a microcosm of our operations. Not only are we dealing with three factions, each with different characteristics and agendas, but we also have to grapple with a vast flood of information coming into the company and Battlegroup HQs through many different channels of communication. This deluge of information is of highly variable accuracy and reliability.

Just as we need all three types of maps to form the best mental picture of the ground, so we need to assess and fuse the information reaching us to make as accurate a picture of what is going on as we can. Even so we are using a rule of thumb, that 'things are never quite as good or as bad as they seem'.

I visit A Company at Arapuša, the town containing most of the company's armoured vehicles. A second tank troop arrives, as does Captain Paul Evanson leading a logistic column and a much-needed resupply of fuel. The only area definitely clear of mines is the single narrow street, those buildings occupied by A Company and a few areas of concrete to the side of some of the houses. The conflicting requirements to move the tanks through the town, to refuel all the vehicles and to maintain the security of Arapuša has immense potential for friction, which could result in a dangerous military gridlock. Without fuss Paul Evanson, A Company's Serjeant Major and the tank troop serjeant control the operation. As Jan de Vos and I grab a sandwich and talk, we yet again marvel at the culture of our Serjeants' Mess, which allows our warrant officers and senior NCOs to assume responsibilities that in other armies would not be devolved below officers.

I visit one of B Company's platoon houses. We have brought up a sack of mail. The RSM gives this to the platoon serjeant, who immediately sorts the parcels, letters and 'blueys' and starts distributing them to the soldiers. The regular arrival of mail from home makes a real contribution to morale, as does the supply of British newspapers, even though both are taking up to six days to reach their recipients.

Off-duty soldiers amuse themselves playing cards and listening to music on portable tape and CD players. Battlegroup HQ and each company have a satellite TV system, but these are not available to the platoon houses. People spend a lot of time reading and writing letters. Living out of armoured vehicles and in the platoon bases puts a real premium on tidiness, a sense of humour and self-discipline if people are not to rub each other up the wrong way.

We all try to begin each morning with the reassuring ritual of washing, shaving and cleaning our boots. Weapons are kept as clean as possible, but most of the battalion have not had showers for more than two weeks, instead having to use 'a bird bath' (washing from a bowl of water). Much of our clothing is filthy.

By strange coincidence passing through B Squadron's area I often seem to meet the same patrol of Scimitars. Commanded by Sergeant Tribe, their Scimitar is notable for having a teddy bear strapped to the top of the turret. The bear has been there since Christmas and is now looking more than a little bedraggled. The ever-cheerful Tribe and the members of the patrol find these chance encounters with me a huge joke. Every time I encounter them there is more and more banter and bonhomie. Despite long hours spent with their upper bodies exposed to the freezing air and petrol fumes of the vehicle, the Light Dragoons are enjoying their work.

I encounter another patrol whose broken-down Spartan is blocking the road. REME is on the way, but the patrol needs assistance to unblock the road by moving the Spartan to a lay-by further along. We cannot afford the risk of using the verge of the road, which may be mined. The RSM adds the impressive horsepower of his armoured Land Rover, while I stop and talk to some farmers patiently waiting to pass with horse and carts full of manure. I explain that I am the Procovnik in charge of the IFOR troops. They have heard about us, but seem amazed that I am talking to them.

One tells me that the only Bosnian Serb officer who talks to civilians is General Mladić. He is their war hero, who saved Republika Srpska in its hour of greatest need, and they are willing to forgive him a great deal because of this. I question them about this. Do they mean forgiving him the loss of so many Bosnian Serb soldiers in his battles, the eventual loss of much of Western Bosnia to the Federation, the NATO air strikes or the atrocities he is said to have presided over? At this, they fall silent, then change the topic of conversation.

I discover some beautiful countryside in A Company's area. The low, rounded hills are covered with a mixture of pine and deciduous forest and interlaced with a network of clear streams and flat open meadows. Everywhere there are tiny wooden watermills, all of which are carefully marked on our maps. I have no doubt that in summer the countryside will be idyllic, probably very similar to the Lot in France. Away from the front line the countryside is largely unspoiled, but my enjoyment of this is ruined by suddenly encountering a large ethnically cleansed village on the Bosnian Serb side of the line. It is utterly uninhabited, every building either burned out or blown up. The place is redolent with a sense of terrible crimes.

We are fed up with snow. When it falls, the snow covers everything, adding a temporary coating of false beauty, but as it melts the illusion of softness is stripped away. In many of the ruined towns and villages, the snow on the burned out rafters and charred timbers produces a stark image – like an abstract painting or an over-exposed photograph.

Just inside Bosnian Serb territory, about two kilometres from the front line, the RSM and I pass a VRS brigade headquarters. Parked next to it is a civilian bus. There is nothing new about this for soldiers of all three factions are moved in such vehicles. What is strange is that children aged between eight and ten are getting off the vehicle. Straggling along the road to the north is a column of perhaps forty children and a few adults. Intrigued, we stop and ask one of the adults what is going on. A middle-aged man tells us, with some pride, that this is a school field trip to study plants and wildlife. The children appear happy and relaxed, as are their teachers. I am astonished. It is the most 'normal' sight I have yet seen in Bosnia.

CHAPTER TEN

'This Hard Land'

The crossing point at Arapuša had been nicknamed GREY CAT. This was chosen not only to continue the BLACK DOG, WHITE FANG series of names, but also because of the saying, 'in the dark all cats are grey', a phrase frequently used by young officers bantering about their amorous adventures. A Company had exploited the opening of this crossing point to get forces into their part of Republika Srpska, with two platoons working in Serb territory from a patrol base in the settlement.

The village straggled for a mile on both sides of the road across no-man's-land. Surprisingly, most of the houses were neither damaged nor looted, probably reflecting the haste with which the occupants had fled. A Company moved two platoons to the village to use it as a base from which to launch patrols across the front line. Serjeant Oldfield described how they did this:

> We took over the houses within the village and made them into our homes for the next couple of weeks. The main aim was to get wood burners into each room. We made washrooms and a dining room for the platoon; one of the houses became a cookhouse and was named 'Sad Café. The cooks who were attached to the company were absolutely brilliant with the resources they had.
>
> We received orders from Major de Vos to find out exactly what was happening in the local area. We visited all the local commanders and asked them to show us all their positions. They showed us and also made us very welcome with coffee and a strong chaser. The local commanders were not able to read a map: all information was logged and then sent up their chain of command. The next few weeks were spent visiting the local battalion positions and meeting soldiers.

Many of the company had not had any access to telephones since they had left Vitez at the beginning of January. At Arapuša, Serjeant Bain used the Clansman high-frequency radios of the company to contact the British Telecom station at Portishead. This link through 'Portishead Radio' connected into the UK telephone system. This was highly successful, enabling people to contact their loved ones. The company christened it Operation DORIS.

Nestling as it did in a huge natural bowl between the two front lines, the base was exposed and vulnerable. Nightfall saw firing from positions on both sides. Initially it seemed that bored and ill-disciplined soldiers were loosing off a small amount of sporadic fire. Over successive nights firing increased, bursts of machine-gun fire falling on the village. The platoons took cover and manned the Warriors. Although the firing appeared to come from the Muslim positions, the actual firing point could not be seen. Our rules of engagement did not allow the company to return fire unless they could identify the place from which the firing came.

The next night, several bursts of sustained heavy machine-gun fire were directed against Arapuša from the ABiH front line. Bullets struck the buildings and fell among the A Company positions. Jan de Vos was already driving from Bosanska Krupa to Arapuša in his Land Rover. As he and his driver came down the hill into the village, they saw what Jan – in a moment of tired absent-mindedness – thought were 'coloured lights' floating past them. His rather more alert driver disabused him of this notion, pointing out the spectacular effect was, in fact, heavy-calibre fire passing around them, as they sped down to the relative safety of the village buildings. As soon as he reached the village, Jan issued orders for the return of fire. Another long burst of machine-gun fire came from a bunker about a thousand metres to the south and east. The firing point was identified by a Warrior gunner, Private Foster, who could clearly see the flashes coming from the muzzle of the machine gun using the image intensifying night sight. Foster fired two cannon shells. Both hit the centre of the bunker, the impact producing showers of vivid red sparks, clearly visible from the village. The noise of the cannon blasts was of a completely different order of magnitude to that of the incoming machine guns: the entire valley reverberated as the two thunderclaps rolled back from its sides, dying away in strange hissing echoes.

Interviewed later by *Soldier* magazine, Foster modestly described the incident as follows:

> There was a little buzz as we waited. When we were fired on again, I instinctively put two armour-piercing rounds into the positions. There was no more firing after that.

The valley fell quiet. There was no subsequent firing seen or heard by A Company along the Muslim/Serb front line that night, or any other nights.

A Company had both neutralised a position that had been firing at them and cowed the remaining positions on both sides of the front line into ceasing fire. Because of this success, the potential danger of moving along the ill-defined routes that straddled the front line and the abundance of mines in no-man's-land, I decided against immediate reinforcement of the company in the dark, but ordered the tanks and artillery to move to Arapuša at first light. In the morning Jan de Vos and I would deliver another 'interview without coffee' to the ABiH brigade commander responsible for the positions that had been engaged by A Company.

The next morning Arapuša and the surrounding hills are enveloped in swirling mist. Jan and I drive to the crest of a Muslim-held hill overlooking the village from the Muslim side. With the RSM and a small protection party of some A Company soldiers, we meet the Muslim brigade liaison officer. He leads us up a short track that curves along the hill. A similar-sized party of ABiH soldiers and officers emerges from the mist heading towards us. Like us they are carrying rifles and wearing helmets. The commander is introduced. I fix the officer with eye contact, state who I am and deliver an unequivocal statement of IFOR's displeasure and willingness to use whatever force is necessary both to defend ourselves and to implement the peace. It is similar to the interview I had given to the VRS brigade commander after the WHITE FANG incident. As the one-way conversation progresses the Muslim commander looks increasingly sheepish and spends more and more time looking at his boots.

He has no questions and we turn to go. The mist has cleared and we can see Arapuša in the middle of this immense natural bowl. As we walk down the hill, the RSM tells me that he'd been 'a bit worried'. The Bosnian soldiers accompanying the ABiH officers had looked extremely uneasy and more than a little trigger-happy. Fearing the worst, the protection party had discreetly prepared to get Jan de Vos and me out of trouble, if necessary by using force against the Muslim soldiers. Safety catches had been eased off rifles, grenades had been readied for throwing and targets had been allocated.

I am thanking him for this when there is a swelling rumble of heavy armour. The troop of tanks appears on the main road from the south into Arapuša, closely followed by guns and vehicles of the artillery. Glancing back up the hill we see the Muslim commander and his troops staring open-mouthed. Neither the guns nor the tanks had been to Arapuša before, and my expression of displeasure was being strongly reinforced. I had not specified when reinforcements were required at Arapuša, but through sheer good luck, they were arriving at exactly the right time. Jan, the RSM and the soldiers accompanying us all exchange broad grins.

There was no more firing, either around Arapuša, or on any part of the cease-fire line controlled by A Company. Two amusing stories emerged after the incident. The senior officer in the village at the time should have been Lieutenant Will Hogg. He was however, quite properly, camping out with his driver some miles away guarding their Warrior, which had shed a track and could not be repaired before daybreak. In a remark typical of the enthusiasm of all ranks at this stage, he commented on his intense frustration at listening over the radio to the sequence of events, without being there to participate. His platoon did not quickly let him forget that he had been 'absent without leave' for their first firefight of the tour.

Some days later Jan returned on a routine visit to inspect the positions. Sergeant Patterson was in temporary command, with all the officers away on other tasks. Jan was somewhat surprised to see the armoured Rover group of General Jackson, the NATO Land Force commander, parked up, with assorted bodyguards and staff officers busying themselves. As company commander, he would normally have expected to be aware of any such visitor. Looking up at the balcony of the house the platoon was using as a base, he was amused to see the general and Sergeant Patterson standing leaning together on the iron balustrade, both smoking. They were animatedly discussing the incident, with Sergeant Patterson punctuating his gestures by stabbing the cigar at the distant hillside bunker where the firing had come from. As Jan watched, Patterson handed his rifle to the general, who used the sight to inspect the bunker. It looked for all the world like a pair of senior executives reviewing a land deal. Jan wisely decided to drive on by, leaving the two clubmen to their cigars in the spring sunlight, wreaths of smoke drifting around them.

A Company's operations continued. Corporal Oldfield, who returned to the battalion from a training posting arriving in A Company the day after the shooting, wrote this account of his activities as a section commander during this period.

The platoon's patrol base was a house, which they had made into their home. There were wood burners in each room, a cooker and table and chairs, comfortable considering the conditions. I was briefed by the platoon commander, Captain Welch, on the tactical situation in the area. The previous night 3 Platoon had been involved in a firefight, returning 30mm rounds into a position. Needless to say, the firefight ended there.

I was told that I would be leading a four-man foot patrol into the Zone of Separation and meeting the local battalion commander who would nominate one of his company commanders to show me his position in the area.

After checking the patrol to make sure we had everything for the task ahead, we left in the back of the Warrior and headed for our meeting. We arrived and met up with the battalion commander, who invited us in for coffee. After about twenty minutes, the company commander took us up to his positions. The patrol met numerous soldiers, all of whom were friendly; we saw a few positions, all of which were unoccupied. Most of the soldiers were living in the houses, and most still had AK47 rifles and grenades. Some of them invited us in for coffee and we spoke a few words of their language with the help of the phrase book. Their company commander then took us up to the confrontation line and showed us the rest of his positions. Our patrol had all their kit on while the company commander carried nothing, not even a weapon, so we found the going extremely difficult, especially uphill. Believe me, there were some difficult hills.

We said our goodbyes to the company commander who said we were his friends and could come back anytime. We were picked up and headed back to Arapuša.

Separation of Forces

All these events were leading up to the separation of forces, which the Dayton Agreement required to be complete by D+30. Brigadier Dannatt had directed the factions to complete their withdrawal from the four-kilometre-wide Zone of Separation by D+25, so that the final five days could be used to verify that the forces had separated and deal with any problems.

So far, the faction armies' compliance with the Dayton Agreement had been largely passive – they had just acquiesced in NATO deploying and moving. This would be the first military milestone of Dayton that actually required the faction armies to become active, to begin the demobilisation and demilitarisation of the country. Achieving this physical separation of forces would take the two sides out of line of sight of each other and thus reduce the opportunities for cease-fire violations and contribute to the lowering of tension.

There were potential problems, principally the residual hatred, fear and mistrust between armies who had been only recently ceased hostilities. Withdrawal is the most difficult land operation, as the withdrawing force is at its most vulnerable to any attack. So we had to give each side confidence that IFOR could provide security for them whilst they withdrew, so that their opponent could not attack. We continued to do everything we could to reassure both sides, patrolling in as many places as possible, constantly moving tanks, mortars and artillery around and briefing all the commanders we could on both sides. During the five days leading up to the separation of forces, we deployed as much strength as possible around the front line.

The faction forces had far fewer maps than we did and far fewer of their commanders and soldiers seemed capable of reading them. This could cause friction in the separation of forces and, we suspected, could well be used an excuse for non-compliance. To pre-empt this problem, it was decided that NATO troops would mark the boundaries of the Zone of Separation wherever it crossed a road or track. Six-foot-long metal pickets painted Day-Glo orange would be the markers. At Battlegroup HQ we were worried that the factions might make mischief by moving the marker pickets, so we gave each one a unique serial number and used our satellite navigation systems to fix and record their exact position with great accuracy. This process was described by Corporal James:

> First things first, painting huge numbers of 6ft pickets a sexy shade of orange. We then located the Zone of Separation (ZOS) locations, recorded these by use of the Magellan satellite system and hammered them in
>
> One problem we encountered immediately was the factions' incompetent map-reading skills. On numerous occasions they had troops and equipment further in the ZOS than they should have, due to poor map reading. Once proved wrong, by the use of our maps and the Magellan satellite navigation system, there was no problem.

Both factions asked us for permission to send military traffic along roads and tracks where they crossed the ZOS. Some of the routes they wanted to use just clipped the ZOS by a few hundred metres, requiring faction military traffic to make lengthy detours. In every case we said no and firmly stuck to this line, despite a large amount of special pleading by faction commanders. B Company's conversation with a 7 Corps ABiH staff officer on this subject was revealing. After about half an hour of arguing the case to use a particular route with the company commander, the Muslim officer suddenly relaxed and smiled. Stuart Mills asked why he had kept on at this issue for so long. The ABiH officer replied: 'We were testing you. If you gave in to us, we would have no confidence in your ability to say no to the VRS.'

There had been a major thaw during the last few days. Suddenly both faction armies wanted to use the unexpectedly fine weather to clear more of their minefields. They requested that we protect them while they did this. We agreed and patrols deployed to cover the faction sappers as they went about this dangerous business. Our mine clearance experts from the EOD team attended all these operations, to assess whether or not the factions were doing it properly.

We were impressed with the obvious motivation and sense of urgency displayed by many of the Bosnian sappers. Quickly the mine clearance operations gained a momentum of their own. Suddenly we were finding it difficult both to supply troops to cover all the faction mine-lifting parties and to sustain our operations supervising the separation of forces. We managed both tasks, but only by reducing the size of all our patrols and protection parties to a pair of vehicles. Although this disrupted the plan we had carefully crafted for deploying troops to cover the withdrawal from the ZOS, I reasoned that putting Warriors and Scimitars close to their sappers would give the factions more confidence in us. It would also give us up to date information as to which routes around the front line were clear of mines, increasing our freedom of manoeuvre in no-man's-land.

The clearance operations were inherently risky. Luckily the battlegroup had not suffered any casualties from mines – so far. But simply moving and operating on the steep, narrow, muddy and icy tracks on the front line was dangerous enough. This was graphically brought home during a B Squadron operation to cover a VRS mine-lifting party. On a narrow track one of the Scimitars rolled over, landing on its side wedged against a house and crushing a Bosnian Serb soldier. Pinned by the legs, he was badly injured and needed medical attention from a doctor before he could be evacuated.

Battlegroup HQ despatched our doctor, Major Russell Overs, and a medical team to the site of the incident at the extreme west of B Squadron's area. By chance, A Company had a Warrior patrol led by Serjeant Bain near the area. While the Light Dragoons dug the victim clear and applied first aid, Bain moved quickly to the site of the accident. The casualty was still not stable and was losing too much blood to guarantee his survival until the medical officer arrived. Helped by Corporal Furminger, the patrol second-in-command, Bain inserted an intravenous drip into the casualty's arm in order to start replacing the lost blood. This was not an easy thing to do in a classroom, let alone a muddy Bosnian field. The task was made doubly difficult by the cold weather conditions and the advancing state of shock of the casualty. Luckily Bain and Furminger were successful.

Russell Overs and his team arrived shortly afterwards. Pausing only to congratulate Bain on successfully inserting the drip and keeping the casualty alive, the medics set to work to fully stabilise the man. Russell assessed that he needed urgent evacuation to a hospital, and Bain started making the arrangements to get him out. It soon became apparent that despite clear weather at the minefield, the British helicopters based far to the south could not get over low cloud covering the mountains of central Bosnia. The casualty would have to go by road to the British field surgical team at Ćoralići Camp near Bihać. As he was a Bosnian Serb, we would need to conceal his movement from the Muslims. The simplest way to get him to Ćoralići would be inside one of the Warriors.

This was quickly arranged and Russell Overs accompanied the party to keep the injured man alive. Later that night when Russell returned to Ljubija, he briefed me that the actions of our commanders had been the single biggest factor in the casualty's survival. Our training in advanced first aid had paid off. We could be confident that our patrols could indeed supply a sufficiently high standard of first aid to care for any serious casualties we might take.

The battlegroup was now operating at full throttle with the maximum number of vehicles and patrols deployed on both sides of the front line. A faction brigade commander expressed his amazement to me that we managed to get so many Warriors up such narrow, steep and muddy farm tracks. I was amazed too at the way patrols in the great hulking thirty-ton armoured vehicles managed to negotiate these routes. They were operating right at the edge of their skill and sometime beyond it.

For example, while an A Company Warrior was patrolling near Arapuša, the narrow muddy track beneath it suddenly collapsed. As a result the vehicle stopped with a severe tilt to one side, overlooking a steep slope, with only one track remaining on the route. It would need great skill to extract the vehicle from its predicament. Private Lister, the driver, volunteered to stay in the vehicle alone throughout the subsequent recovery operation. With exceptional coolness and expertise, he managed to manoeuvre his vehicle to a safer resting-place with the aid of members of the REME Section. This was at great personal risk to himself as he was faced with a potentially lethal drop to one side of the vehicle. Lister was a driver with exemplary skill, courage and coolness, but he was not unique. All the battlegroup's drivers had by now clocked up huge mileage under both UN and NATO flags. Johnny Bowron later described driving in Bosnia as 'like nothing we have driven before' and 'a real test of nerve, rather like adventure training, to drive in some of the conditions'.

Most of the routes we had to use were in hills and mountains, with many narrow bends, blind corners and vertiginous drops at the roadsides. The snow and ice, particularly compacted black ice, exacerbated the difficulties, as did the frequent descent of fog, cloud or thick snow. The war meant that most routes had received little or no maintenance other than from UNPROFOR engineers – who of course had been completely absent from western Bosnia. Our constant movement of heavy armoured vehicles – Warriors, Challengers and AS 90s – was damaging the road surfaces still further.

If this were not challenging enough, Bosnian vehicles and drivers reinforced the danger. Cars and trucks, both military and civilian, showed the effects of four years of war and no maintenance. Brakes were especially poorly maintained. Many vehicles showed no lights at night. Drivers were uniformly aggressive, often overtaking blind on the bends of mountain roads. Many were drunk. Horses and carts belonging to farmers or refugees used all the roads, moving slowly but unpredictably. At night none had lights. The cart driver would often be dead drunk, fast asleep or both – even in broad daylight. We often compared driving in Bosnia to a bizarre video game.

Inevitably accidents occurred. Immediately after D Day a signal platoon Land Rover commanded by WO2 Thirlwell went over the side of the road near Mrkonjić Grad, and slipped down fifty feet of sheer drop before coming to a stop. Mercifully the crew were only cut and bruised but the vehicle and the valuable communications equipment it was carrying was destroyed. None of these accidents were due to mechanical defects on our vehicles. The drivers, the platoon Warrior Sergeants, the company fleet managers and the REME all took great pride in the long hours they devoted to keeping the vehicles serviceable.

During the separation of forces our operations reached a climax, with the whole of the battalion monitoring and checking the withdrawal of the factions, or participating in mine clearance. Our patrols were successful in marking the outer limits of the Zone of Separation with two-metre metal pickets painted in Day-Glo orange, and I came across an ever increasing number of these as I toured the area.

The evening before the separation of forces a Bosnian Serb commander pays an unexpected call on A Company at Arapuša. The officer is the 'chief of staff' of 2 Krajina Corps – a Serb colonel who appears to be in charge of the remains of that formation. Jan de Vos is astonished to be told that the basement of a large, previously uninvestigated barn in Arapuša is full of extremely expensive machine tools. These have been there since 5 Corps ABiH forced the Bosnian Serb forces to retreat during the autumn battles.

As the building lies outside the part of the town that A Company is using, the troops have not investigated it – to avoid mines and booby troops. But Jan de Vos is shown a large room full of heavy-duty lathes, grinders, cutters and various precision machine tools. The Serb claims that they came from a factory that was in Republika Srpska. When the front line stabilised after the 5 Corps offensive had run out of steam, the machines were effectively trapped in no-man's-land. Now the Serbs want to retrieve the tools and move them back into Republika Srpska. The officer demands IFOR allow them to so do.

The Serb states that since the building is a hundred metres on their side of the agreed cease-fire line, and thus is in their territory, they can do what they want. And what they want to do is to send some Army trucks to recover the machinery.

Jan's initial reaction is disbelief. Is he really being asked to adjudicate on ownership of some pretty tired-looking industrial tooling? His second reaction is to settle where the barn actually is, using the system regarded with awe by many of the local soldiers – unsurprisingly, given the average standard of map reading.

If the entrance is in Serb territory, he intends to advise them that they are welcome to do what the hell they like with the equipment – provided, of course, that there is no military involvement. With something of a flourish, he puts his GPS satellite navigation system down next to the barn, and sets it to average its position readings for the next ten minutes (this averaging function increases the accuracy available). He is therefore rather irritated when it produces a result that places the barn, the animated Serbs and himself all squarely within the hundred yards or so of ground that is covered by the thickness of the centre line on the US-produced Dayton Agreement maps. At this point the Serb officer announces his intention of simply taking the machinery. Jan cannot allow this to be done by Serb military personnel and equipment.

The Serb officer takes this very badly, for he believes that even if the goods lie on the Muslim side of the line, they still belong to Republika Srpska. Jan is adamant that A Company is not going to allow access. There is much discussion and argument, but no meeting of minds. Eventually negotiations break down, with the Serb insisting that they will ignore us. If we succeed in stopping their vehicles they will set fire to the building, in order to deny the material to the Muslims.

Jan de Vos reports this. We are in what could become a no-win situation. Clearly we can prevent Serb troops from crossing the cease-fire line. But since the Dayton Agreement explicitly endorses freedom of movement for civilians throughout the territory of all the Bosnian entities, we have no explicit power to prevent Serb civilians from crossing the line and removing the equipment. But do the machines actually belong to the Serbs? Their story is, on the face of it, plausible, but we are unconvinced.

It is quite possible the equipment was looted from a factory on the other side of the line. There is an outside chance that the equipment was placed there by the Muslims. Do the Muslims know about the equipment? Probably not but we cannot be sure. What if the Muslims find out what the Serbs are up to? Will they try to interfere using force? Or will Muslim civilians attempt to obstruct the Serbs?

We cannot know what the answers are to any of these questions. But it is quite clear that we must not allow forces of either side to cross the cease-fire line. What we also know is that with tomorrow being the day when the forces separate, we cannot afford to allow the situation to get out of hand.

We have no secure speech communications to A Company, so I use the KL43 data device to send an encrypted message to A Company at Arapuša. It confirms that Bosnian Serb troops are not to cross the line, and that the company are to prevent them from doing so, using force if necessary. Jan de Vos deploys his troops to blocking positions to ensure that they can deny the Bosnian Serb military the ability to cross the cease-fire line. I turn in, expecting to be woken as a confrontation develops.

But the night is quiet. The next day is the deadline for the separation of forces. We make an all-out effort to deploy the maximum number of patrols. Some of these are joint foot patrols with the factions, allowing their more cooperative commanders to show us that the bunkers, trenches and fortified buildings that lie both in the ZOS and that commander's sector have indeed been abandoned by their troops. Other patrols deploy to roads or tracks leading back from the front line, where they can monitor the factions moving off their positions, but prevent them returning. The reception given by the factions to our patrols varies enormously – from silent, sullen, unashamed hostility to friendliness.

In B Squadron's area a troop commander monitoring the withdrawal of one of the faction brigades is surprised to be asked to sign for the entire formation's fighting positions. In a number of places the factions continue their efforts to lift land mines. A VRS operation to do so lifts three hundred mines, but a VRS soldier is injured after standing on a mine. The casualty is evacuated through the VRS medical chain.

British helicopters are making an all-out effort to provide air patrols. Overhead fly Lynx helicopters from 3 Division's aviation regiment. We are tasked by Corps HQ to use one of the enormous RAF Chinook helicopters for another patrol. The requirement is for soldiers with local knowledge and up to date marked maps to investigate the area up to ten kilometres from the cease-fire line. The massive aircraft produces a distinctive 'thwack' noise from its twin rotors and can be heard all over the front line.

Halfway through this busy morning the A Company is again contacted by the Bosnian Serb commander. He is insisting on recovering the industrial machinery. Jan de Vos fears a confrontation and would like me to reinforce the message that the Bosnian Serb military may not cross the line.

I drive to meet him. The quickest route to Arapuša is through Republika Srpska. Approaching the Bosnian Serb front line from behind, I see several military trucks and an assortment of Serb soldiers and officers waiting just north of their front line. I assess that the party is waiting to recover the machinery. In Arapuša, Jan de Vos and I confer with the chief of staff of 2 Krajina Corps. I tell him in no uncertain terms that although there is no objection to civilians removing the equipment, no military personnel will be allowed to cross the line and, after today, no military personnel will be allowed into the Zone of Separation.

So, I conclude, this applies to those military vehicles assembled behind their front line and to anyone wearing uniform or carrying weapons. The conversation is over and the Bosnian Serb leaves. He does not return. The Bosnian Serb forces make no attempt to move into Arapuša – neither on that day, nor during any of A Company's remaining time at Arapuša.

Just after he leaves, a party of Bosnian Muslim officers from 5 Corps ABiH arrive at A Company. They are clad in clean new combat uniforms and, unusually, are all wearing steel helmets. They have come to ask A Company's permission to withdraw from their trenches and bunkers.

I leave A Company, for I need to see other parts of the battlegroup area for myself. Battlegroup HQ tells me over the radio that the Zone of Separation withdrawal is apparently complete. Our extensive patrol effort has successfully monitored the faction movements. To confirm that the withdrawal is complete, joint foot patrols with factions are ongoing.

Simultaneously there is a resurgence of media interest in the alleged mass graves of Ljubija. Reporters and television news team from ITN, ABC, Serb

TV and Czech TV turn up at main gate of Battlegroup HQ, demanding to know what we are doing about the allegations of atrocities. All are given the standard IFOR line that any information is passed up the chain of command to be forwarded to the international war crimes tribunal. ITN interview our tactical air control officer and attempt to elicit adverse comment about this, but he sticks to the NATO line and convincingly acquits himself.

Meanwhile planning for our future operations goes on. HQ Company conduct a reconnaissance of possible new base locations in Banja Luka. We also are short of interpreters and need more urgently. Major Ian Baker interviews fifty potential interpreters at a local hotel. Five are chosen.

Brigade HQ contact me on the satellite telephone. In northern Bosnia US troops are beginning to destroy all the trenches, fortifications and bunkers left by the faction soldiers. Engineer tanks are bulldozing some and explosives are being used to demolish others. The chain of command asks whether we should attempt to do the same.

I advise not. Firstly, attempting to do this in our sector will increase risk of mine strikes – particularly as we know that unmarked mines have been liberally sown between the two front lines. Secondly, as the ABiH and VRS pulled out they removed almost all of the timbers, pit props and metal that were supporting the sides and roofs of their bunkers. Most of the structures have collapsed leaving little more than shallow pits filled with loose earth. These would offer little or no protection against incoming fire, considerably reducing their value. Thirdly, if the situation does deteriorate and the factions attempt to defend their territory, it could well be easier to deal with them if we know the positions they might be attempting to re-occupy. Finally we need all our scarce engineer resources for mine clearing, route opening and essential life support work on our bases.

The idea is not pursued any further.

A Problem With Mujahideen

At four in the morning the next day a curious message came from Brigade. Division HQ required us to send an armoured infantry company to control a party of a hundred and fifty armed and dangerous mujahideen at the village of Koprivna, north of Bihać. This was to be done immediately.

After some backward and forward dialogue from battlegroup to brigade and division, it emerged that, unknown to us, this group of so-called 'armed Islamic extremists' had previously been monitored by the Bihać JCO team, with security provided by Canadian military police. They were all under the command of the Canadian Brigade HQ in Bihać. There had been some kind of confrontation that had resulted in Canadian troops being threatened by the mujahideen. The detail of the incident was not clear. It was never explained why we had not been told of this operation being conducted in our area of responsibility, but there was no time for recriminations. Whatever had happened, the result appeared to have been that the mujahideen were now

Training and preparation for the tour involved long hours spent on the range. Captain Mark Mortimer and Major Rex Sartain with C Company's Warriors on the firing ranges at Sennelager. (Author)

A Warrior platoon on Mount Igman. (Author)

A Sentry tries to keep warm with a an improvised brazier. (Author)

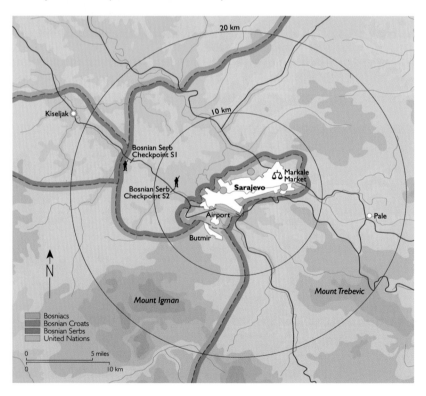

The Sarajevo area in November 1995, showing Kiseljack, Mount Igman, the then Bosnian Serb capital and the boundaries between the factions. The urban area of Sarajevo suburbs is greater than shown, including suburbs to the east and west of the city, then occupied by tens of thousands of Bosnian Serb civilians. The Dayton Agreement ceded Serb territory west and north of Sarajevo to the Muslims, causing the tension described in Chapter 4. (© Osprey Publishing)

Above left: A Warrior commander keeps the Bosnian winter at bay. (Courtesy Sergeant Hedges)

Above right: The driver of an FV 432 on Mount Igman. (Author)

Two FV 432s of the Mortar Platoon are refuelled by the MT Platoon on Mount Igman. (Courtesy Jan de Vos)

Soldiers patrol to a Bosnian bunker on Mount Igman. The Bosnian soldiers are not sober. (Courtesy Jan de Vos)

Captain Tom Welch stands amongst the tents at Kiseljak Brick Factory. (Courtesy Jan de Vos)

Serjeant Grimes (arm raised) and his crew take advantage of a break in the weather to 'track bash' at Kiseljak Brick Factory. (Author)

A Foreign Legion armoured car followed by a Warrior escorting a convoy into Sarajevo. (Author)

Battle-damaged houses on the front line in the Sarajevo suburbs. (Author)

Above left: Brigadier Richard Dannatt, Commander Four Armoured Brigade. Now General Sir Richard Dannatt, Chief of the General Staff. (General Dannatt's collection)

Above right: Logistics. Our ration store in a metal shipping container on Mount Igman. (Author)

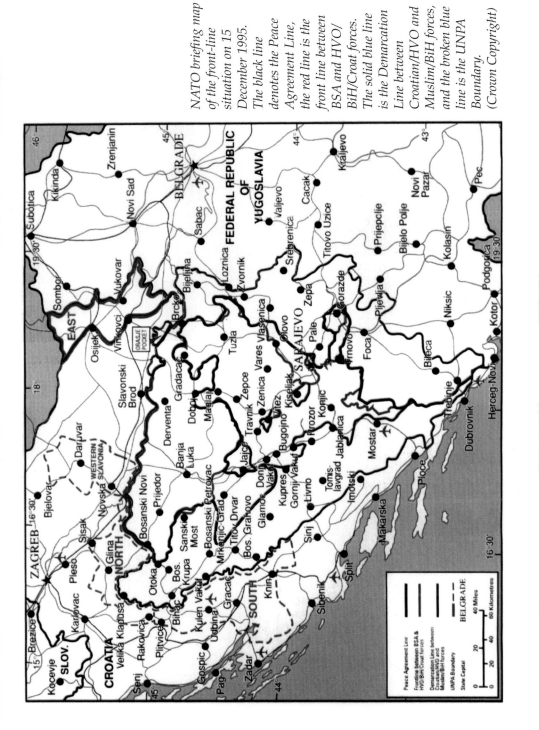

NATO briefing map of the front-line situation on 15 December 1995. The black line denotes the Peace Agreement Line, the red line is the front line between BSA and HVO/ BiH/Croat forces. The solid blue line is the Demarcation Line between Croatian/HVO and Muslim/BiH forces, and the broken blue line is the UNPA Boundary. (Crown Copyright)

A Company lined up at Kiseljak on 20 December 95 D Day waiting to move west at 1200 hours. (Author)

The Scimitars of B Squadron Light Dragoons in Mrkonjić Grad on D Day, waiting to begin their advance to Banja Luka. (Crown Copyright)

21 December 95. Negotiating the opening of the WHITE FANG crossing point. From left to right; Major Stuart Mills, Bosnian officer, interpreter, Captain Sean Harris. (Silver Bugle)

Royal Engineer's Land Rover damaged by running over a land mine. (Silver Bugle)

Having cleared the crossing point at the site of the mine incident, B Company established a platoon base, nicknamed BONDI BEACH between the Muslim and Serb front lines. (Author)

The Recce Platoon gathers around a Scimitar for orders at the Sanski Most 'Mud Factory'. (Author)

Christmas Lunch at the Mrkonjić Grad Bus Depot. (Courtesy Jan de Vos)

Ethnic Cleansing. A mosque destroyed by Bosnian Serbs. (Author)

January 1996. Houses on the front line. One has been destroyed, the other covered with military graffiti showing it to be used by 501 Brigade ABIH. (Courtesy Jan de Vos)

A 105mm light howitzer is lifted as an underslung load by a Royal Navy Sea King helicopter. January 1996. (Crown Copyright)

A Bosnian soldier poses next to a looted house. (Courtesy Soldier *Magazine)*

The ABiH anti-personnel mines removed by their sappers. (Author)

Four Platoon's Warriors force their way through an un-cooperative ABiH checkpoint outside Sanski Most. (Soldier Magazine)

Freedom of movement having been restored, the Bosnian sentry settles his differences with Major Stuart Mills. (Soldier Magazine)

Soldiers of B Company in the disused school used as a base at MALIBU CORNER. (Soldier Magazine)

Captain Guy Avery (fifth from right) and Major Jan de Vos (third from left) with Bosnian officers. (Courtesy Jan de Vos)

A Light Dragoons' Scimitar on patrol. Left to Right: Lance Corporal Everest, Ted the Bear and Sergeant Tribe. (Soldier Magazine)

Separation of Forces (1). Lieutenant Pete Chapman (right) confers with a Bosnian Officer. (Silver Bugle)

Separation of Forces (2). Soldiers check that front-line trenches have been abandoned. (Courtesy Jan de Vos)

Private Mitchell, who played a decisive role in the firefight at WHITE FANG described in Chapter 8. (Soldier Magazine)

Private Foster, the Warrior gunner involved in the firefight at Arapusa described in Chapter 10. (Soldier Magazine)

The mining installations at Ljubija, scene of alleged war crimes. (Author)

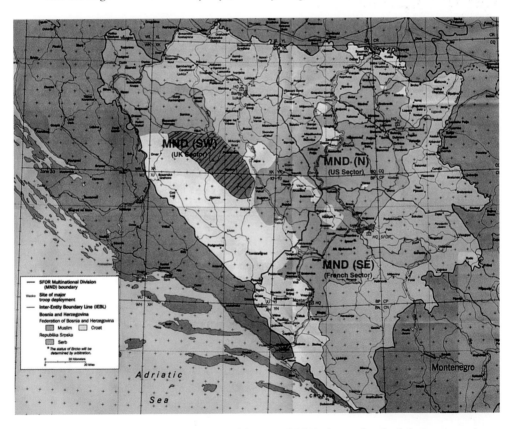

This 1997 map made after IFOR had become SFOR shows the shaded area around Mrkonjić Grad (the Anvil) that was transferred from Croat to Serb control (and all the Serb suburbs of Sarajevo transferred from Serb to Muslim control), following the Dayton Agreement. The map also shows the sectors allocated to each of IFOR's three multinational divisions. The areas occupied by the three factions at the end of 1996 are shown: Serbs in pink, Croats in yellow and Muslims in green.

Kulen Vakuf seen from the hills to the South. (Silver Bugle)

Lieutenant Colonel Nigel Beer prepares to negotiate with the factions on the bridge at Kulen Vakuf. Heavily armed Bosnian Croat paramilitary police can be seen at the far end of the bridge. View from the turret of a Warrior covering the bridge. Incident described in Chapter 12. (Silver Bugle)

A few minutes later. Bosnian Muslim paramilitary police moved onto the bridge whilst Nigel Beer and David Livingston's party can be seen negotiating between the two factions in the middle of the bridge on the right-hand side. (Silver Bugle)

A heavily armed foot patrol in Kulen Vakuf, carrying sniper rifle and GPMG in addition to SA 80 rifles. Lieutenant David Livingston is second from the right. (Silver Bugle)

Reinforcements arrive, Challenger tanks and Scimitar reconnaissance vehicles of the Queen's Royal Hussars and Lynx Helicopters of 3 Regiment Army Air Corps. (Crown Copyright)

The C Company Warrior incident described in Chapter 12. (Silver Bugle)

A Challenger tank of the Queen's Royal Hussars passes empty shell cases and other detritus left over from the fighting. February 1996. (Crown Copyright)

Bosnian Serb self-propelled artillery concentrated to the south of Banja Luka.
(Silver Bugle)

An AS90 self-propelled gun belonging to 127 Battery Royal Artillery. (Author)

A Warrior Observation Post Vehicle blown up by a mine in the Zone of Separation. Awaiting rescue, the crew could not set foot on the ground. (Silver Bugle)

Opening Banja Luka Airport (1). One Platoon guards the airport entrance. The three dismounted soldiers wearing helmets are all volunteers from the TA Parachute Regiment. (Silver Bugle)

Opening Banja Luka Airport (2). A Spartan and FV 432 of the Mortar Platoon deploy. (Author)

Opening Banja Luka Airport (3). A Chinook lifts a Spartan Armoured Vehicle off the tarmac at Banja Luka airfield as part of an inaugural visit by the first fixed wing aircraft there. (Crown Copyright)

A Company acting as Brigade Reserve for the re-occupation of the Anvil by Bosnian Serb forces. Orders being given in the concentration area. (Soldier Magazine)

Having been ordered to Sarajevo to help evict non-compliant Bosnian forces from the Zone of Separation A Company move to Kupres. (Soldier Magazine)

Getting the message across. The author briefs refugees in Banja Luka. (Silver Bugle)

Scimitars of the Light Dragoons cross the Hungarian pontoon bridge over the Sava. (Soldier *Magazine*)

Light Infantrymen relax in a platoon house. (Author)

A patrol of Light Dragoons (Soldier Magazine)

Human remains discovered by B Company. April 1996. (Crown Copyright)

Bosnian refugees return home. Each horse has a pornographic picture on its forehead.
(Silver Bugle)

Return to Normality (1). Children in an upland village. (Courtesy Rupert Witherow)

Return to Normality (2). With the advent of Spring weather the Battlegroup receives large numbers of official visitors. Here the Minister of Defence Michael Portillo, General Mike Jackson and the author all look jolly pleased with themselves. (Author)

All our operations depended for success on the British soldier. (Author)

considered too dangerous to be contained by military police. It emerged that the actual requirement was for a company HQ and two platoons, including Warrior, to 'monitor and contain' a group of about a hundred mujahideen soldiers. These were living in an otherwise empty village north of Bihać, while awaiting transport to Zagreb from where they would return to their home countries. The force would be placed under command of the Canadian Brigade HQ in Ćoralići.

We knew that in September 1995 a confrontation between a 1 RRF patrol and a group of mujahideen soldiers had resulted in one of the Islamic soldiers being shot dead. The mujahideen had declared a blood feud against the British. Once IFOR arrived, the Americans stated that they considered the 'armed Islamic extremists' a great threat to their security and were determined that they should leave the country.

Ross Gillanders had some difficulty in getting a clear idea of the situation, a mission and the forces required. The instructions we were getting from the chain of command seemed unclear and incomplete. Ross got no clearer answers to the questions he was asking the chain of command on my behalf. This gave me little confidence that the operation had been well thought out. I was worried that unclear orders could lead to troops deploying without a proper idea of what the situation was or what they had to achieve. This meant that an experienced commander was needed on the ground, so I directed Jan de Vos to take charge of the force to be despatched at least twenty-five kilometres from the rest of A Company.

There was a degree of urgency implicit in the pressure we were under to sort the situation out. Accordingly Jan left as soon as he could for the Canadian base. The drive was on unusually open territory. Keen to find out what was going on, he instructed his driver, against all speed limits, to get there as fast as he could. A Warrior is capable of touching seventy miles an hour on metalled roads, and Jan soon huddled down in his command seat, face frozen in a bitterly frosty morning, with the Warrior bellowing through small villages and deserted fields.

After linking up with the Canadian brigade HQ back at Ćoralići, Jan and his force deployed north to the scene of the incident. After providing some support to the JCOs who had been successfully containing the situation, he deployed his troops in positions watching a village. A hundred mujahideen soldiers and some Bosnian Muslim civilians occupied it. Some ABiH soldiers and police were present. To Jan it appeared that there was little threat to anyone from the mujahideen, who were due to be bussed to Zagreb. From there they would fly to destinations that included Islamabad, Riyadh, Tunis and Bradford, England.

Jan came under quite strong pressure to take a troop of 105mm howitzers under command. He initially dismissed this, as he had no intention of shelling a village full of civilians, and felt that 30mm cannon was a sufficient threat to enforce his wishes. Nonetheless, a half-hour 'discussion' followed on the radio, with brigade and divisional staff insistent that he take an artillery observation party under command, so that if required he could shell these fierce Muslim warriors into compliance. Watching from his vantage point on a hill, he could see them being brought food from the houses. In the end, not wanting to alienate all the staff above him who appeared to believe that a jihad might be brewing below him, he accepted the artillery observers.

When they arrived, he used them to reduce the number of periods his soldiers had to be on duty, and had them ostentatiously deploy their target acquisition radar on the hill, with a view to discouraging any night time activity by the mujahideen. There was no more mention of artillery barrages.

Land/Air Operations

Meanwhile, all the components of the battlegroup were reporting success. From the most westerly platoon patrol of A Company through the recce troops of B Squadron to the most southerly platoon base of B Company the message was the same: the faction military had abandoned all their bunkers, trenches and defence lines. True, there were isolated incidents where faction soldiers, armed police and even armed civilians had attempted to enter the Zone of Separation, but all of these were successfully turned back by our troops.

The weather had been clear and we had received some helicopters. None of the airborne patrols had found any faction military in the ZOS; they had concentrated particularly on areas of high mine risk that I could not allow patrols to enter. The lines of trenches and bunkers on both sides had previously been full of soldiers, many staring up at our helicopters as they flew over the front line. Now the fighting positions were empty. The rectangular black trenches, bunkers and weapon pits lacing the hillsides and forests reminded me oddly of black beads on a long necklace draped over a green and brown sweater.

With the clear skies, we found it particularly frustrating that there were no NATO jets visible or audible in the skies above the battlegroup area. From the outset of our IFOR operations both Brigadier Dannatt and General Jackson had been extremely concerned that the division was very thinly spread throughout the British sector. The brigade and battlegroup tactics of constantly moving forces around, 'manoeuvre basing', forward deployment of artillery and mortars and frequent high-profile use of helicopters had been designed to create an illusion of greater strength than we actually possessed.

But we wanted to use the NATO jets to help reinforce the impression of IFOR robustness, capability and presence. In the final months of the UNPROFOR operation NATO jets had only flown at altitudes of ten thousand feet or greater. At this altitude they were totally inaudible and, save for the occasional vapour trail, invisible to the naked eye. We repeatedly requested that from D Day onwards, the NATO aircraft should come down below ten thousand feet, where they could be seen and heard by the factions.

Yet despite the step change in Western land operations in Bosnia, the NATO air component, 5 Allied Tactical Air Force, based in Italy, was insisting that all jets continued to observe this minimum altitude of ten thousand feet. Although a considerable number of sorties were flown over Bosnia by NATO jets based in Italy, the only evidence that we and faction soldiers and commanders had of this extensive and extremely expensive operation was a few sightings of contrails.

The apparent inability of the NATO air component to make itself visible to the factions generated much criticism from within the battlegroup. This was particularly the case after the shooting incident at WHITE FANG when battlegroup and brigade requests for NATO jets to provide 'air presence' were repeatedly denied. To those of us on the ground, it seemed a strange posture, given that IFOR was operating throughout the British sector with no serious challenges to our freedom of movement.

C Company had established a presence in the very centre of the remaining Bosnian Serb air defence network in Banja Luka. They and the JCOs were reporting no evidence of any activity on the part of the VRS air defence system. Army, RAF and Navy helicopters were flying all over the British sector at altitudes well below ten thousand feet, with no evidence of any hostile attitude or deeds by the factions. Those of us who had been on Mount Igman during September's air strikes could also remember seeing American A10s diving on the Bosnian Serb positions around Hadžići. They had been coming well below ten thousand feet to fire their cannon.

The final irony was that, to reduce the threat from faction anti-aircraft missiles, the Dayton Agreement forbade the factions from operating any air defence radars. This of course meant that many of the NATO aircraft flying above ten thousand feet would not only be invisible to the naked eye, but undetectable by any of the faction military forces. How this was to reinforce IFOR's posture of deterring non-compliance was never made clear.

Battlegroup HQ officers were scathing about the apparent difference in attitude towards force protection being displayed by the IFOR land and air components. They understood that minimising the risk to NATO was important. But they felt that if the same defensive logic was applied to our operations on land, we would neither cross no-man's-land between the faction front lines, nor even approach to within three hundred metres of any faction soldier armed with a rifle.

As one officer said: 'If the IFOR land operation adopted the same force protection policy as the air operation, it would have been unsuccessful.'

I was unable to disagree.

Relief in Place

Before D Day there had been considerable uncertainty concerning the eventual configuration of the British-led Multinational Division Southwest. We knew that the tanks of the Queens Royal Hussars and another squadron of Light Dragoons would join the division, as would a Dutch mechanised battlegroup. Apart from the remaining British supporting troops and JCOs, there was no hard and fast information of any manoeuvre troops joining the division, apart from a possibility that a brigade of Pakistani troops might be allocated. This was something we were looking forward to, as the brigade was reported to contain two battalions of the Baluch Regiment, with whom we had a regimental affiliation. We knew them to be extremely hospitable and cookers of huge gourmet curries, and wanted to renew our association.

It soon became clear that the Pakistanis would instead deploy to the UN force in Eastern Slavonia, on the border between Croatia and Serbia. A mechanised battalion of the Czech Army was to join the division at the end of January. The Canadians were providing a brigade headquarters, a reconnaissance squadron and a mechanised company, but no battlegroup headquarters. Finally, the Malaysian battalion from UNPROFOR currently based around Jablanica would eventually join the division. This would take a considerable time. Yet even when fully reinforced, the division would have considerably fewer troops than the other two divisions, despite having a much larger area to cover. General Jackson therefore planned that the final configuration of the division would be as follows:

Two Canadian Multinational Brigade would cover the west of the divisional area. This would comprise the Czech mechanised battalion, with a British artillery tactical group; the Queens Royal Hussars Battlegroup, with a British tank squadron, B Company 2 LI and the Canadian mechanised company; and a Canadian armoured recce squadron working independently.

Four Armoured Brigade would cover the east of the divisional area. This would comprise 1 RRF, the mechanised battalion, headquartered in Mrkonjić Grad, including the reinforcing squadron of Light Dragoons and a tank squadron from the QRH; 42 BLJ, the Dutch mechanised battalion, headquartered in Sisava; and 2 LI, headquartered in Banja Luka, once we were relieved by the Canadian Multinational Brigade.

We would hand over to the Canadian Brigade, but initially only our Battlegroup HQ and support company would move on to Banja Luka, to reinforce C Company. The Czechs were yet to arrive and we would have to leave behind A Company and B Squadron. They would cover the Czech AOR, working direct to the Canadian Brigade HQ. Once the Czechs were in place, these two sub-units would be released back to us. B Company was to remain in Sanski Most, as part of the QRH Battlegroup.

There is a standard doctrine for handing over an operational area between one unit or formation and another, known as 'relief in place'. We used its associated procedures in passing our responsibilities to the Canadians. We worked up a plan which I put to their commander, Brigadier Jeffries, who was content. This involved 2 LI continuing to run operations up to the last possible minute. It was important that the factions did not realise that our move would significantly reduce IFOR force levels until the QRH and Czech battlegroups were complete. To achieve this, it would be 'business as usual' until the afternoon when our HQ closed down. Our move to Banja Luka would be spread over a whole day, travelling in small packets of two to four vehicles, using as many different routes as possible, to give the impression that we were simply conducting more patrols than usual. But the patrols would not return to Ljubija. In this way, the first the factions would know of our departure would be when the Canadian, Czech and QRH liaison officers called on them.

We handed the Sewing Factory over to B Squadron, who would in turn hand it over to the Czechs when they appeared. B Squadron and A Company had by then been joined by detachments of Canadian signallers with both secure radio and satellite telephones connecting them with the Canadian HQ. Both sub-units continued to operate as they had under 2 LI command. For B Squadron this posed no particular problems, but A Company were still split, half the company 'wet nursing' the mujahideen and the other half monitoring the company's sector of the front line.

Exchanges of People

In the meantime, WHITE FANG had established itself as a major crossing point between the Federation and Republika Srpska and was being used a convenient place to arrange meetings between both sides. On a number of occasions B Company had been asked to arrange for prisoners to be released from one faction to another there.

I had joined B Company for one of these, spending an intensely cold and frustrating afternoon in the 'sanitised environment' that the company had created for the International Red Cross, who were in charge of the exchange. Half a dozen young Swiss men and women sat in sumptuous, well-equipped and comfortable Land Cruisers, occasionally muttering into radio microphones. I attempted to engage them in conversation, but they were uncommunicative to the point of rudeness. Almost all of our soldiers and officers at WHITE FANG were dirty, imperfectly shaved and clad in uniform that had not been washed for weeks, while the Red Cross personnel looked clean, smart and well rested. I supposed that their much vaunted neutrality, and much higher pay than that of the other international agencies working in Bosnia, explained their attitude.

A collection of reporters and camera crews turned up on the Serb side. I walked up to talk and offered myself to be interviewed. There was some astonishment that I should do so and I was in turn astonished to find that the assembled media included not only Bosnian Serb journalists, but also reporters from Belgrade and even Zagreb in Croatia. Eventually the Red Cross people finished mumbling into their radios, curtly told us that the operation was cancelled and sped away in their well-heated vehicles.

There had been many such attempts to persuade the factions to release prisoners, but all had failed. While Battlegroup HQ was moving to Banja Luka, Stuart was asked to arrange for yet another exchange. This time the Red

Cross was absent but the UN High Commission for Refugees, civil police and civilian officials from both sides were present. It quickly became clear that the accumulated distrust and friction on both sides was making the organisation of the exchange extremely difficult, so Stuart stepped in, took over the running of the exchange and, using his company, made it happen.

Stuart and his soldiers were astonished when both sides produced a considerable number of civilians to hand over. Many were old and infirm and most were distressed and confused. All had pathetic bundles of clothing and personal possessions. Some were so old and decrepit that they could not move from the seats of the buses in which they had arrived without assistance. In total the Bosnian Serbs 'released' a hundred and seventy civilians and the Bosnian Muslims a hundred and fifty-five civilians and a hundred and ten VRS soldiers.

Stuart believed that he was witnessing the reciprocal deportation of civilians of the 'wrong' ethnic group, who had probably been summarily evicted from their homes. This was ethnic cleansing by another means. However, the civilians were too frightened to stay in the territory of the dominant faction and preventing the 'exchange' would probably have created a greater evil than it alleviated. Stuart described the operation as his most distasteful few hours in Bosnia.

Two Minor Incidents

As Battlegroup HQ was moving out from Ljubija, an A Company patrol in the Zone of Separation became involved in an incident as unexpected as it was typical. Lance Corporal Lathan, who was filling a full corporal section commander's post, commanded the patrol. Six Muslim policemen travelling in two cars approached his Warrior. Dismounting, Lathan informed them that under the terms of the Dayton Agreement they were not allowed to cross the cease-fire line. The policemen became highly aggressive and threatened to drive across the line. Lathan's response was to block the road with his Warrior. Doing this he noticed that the police were also carrying five rifles. Faction weapons of any kind being forbidden in the ZOS, Lathan ordered the police to remove the weapons from the Zone immediately.

The police got out of their car and became highly agitated. Lathan rapidly found himself surrounded by increasingly abusive and threatening policemen, who began to gesticulate and point their weapons at him. Faced with a situation that was rapidly going downhill, Lathan ordered his Warrior gunner to turn his turret in the direction of the police.

As the cover of the weapon sight on the Warrior was raised, the policemen's attitude instantly changed. They immediately placed their weapons on the ground. Lathan and his men then confiscated the rifles and the police quickly withdrew in the direction from which they had come.

Lathan had been under no little pressure during a rapidly deteriorating situation in which there was a direct threat to his and other soldiers' lives.

He was quite clear in his mission and stuck to his task, applying the principle of minimum force appropriately to prevent the incident degenerating into violence. He not only succeeded in preventing a violation of the Dayton Agreement but also defused a dangerous confrontation. We were fortunate indeed to have such capable young commanders.

Meanwhile, A Company troops were still monitoring and containing the village occupied by mujahideen north of Bihać. Two Warriors were being used to keep the village under surveillance, watching the mujahideen soldiers – who seemed to be spending most of their time playing football. Although the mujahideen normally appeared relaxed, the Muslim police and soldiers in the area were distinctly jumpy.

Twice a week small parties of mujahideen were leaving for Zagreb in mini-buses, escorted by both Bosnian police and Canadian military police. Jan de Vos had left them in no doubt of our resolve, at the same time doing what he could to reduce tension.

On 28 January, the force closest to the mujahideen was a platoon commanded by Serjeant Patterson – the platoon commander being away on R&R. That afternoon, two Hungarian reporters arrived on a pre-arranged official visit to interview British soldiers involved in the operation. Twelve Muslim policemen intercepted the Hungarians, showing great hostility to the journalists in what appeared to be a crude attempt to intimidate them. Sergeant Patterson decided to deploy a Warrior either side of the police, both to deter mujahideen intervention in the incident and to prevent an attack on the reporters by the police, who were heavily armed with assault rifles. As his troops did this, Patterson saw that the police had by now manhandled the press and confiscated their cameras. Patterson placed himself between the two parties and retrieved the equipment. The police responded by cocking their weapons and pointing them at Serjeant Patterson, who ignored them.

Things quickly got worse as ten ABiH soldiers arrived at the scene and it quickly became apparent that all the police and soldiers were drunk and very belligerent. A policeman prepared a rocket launcher and aimed it at one of the Warriors. Serjeant Patterson ordered his gunner to traverse the turret to point at the police. He directed the press to shelter at the rear of his vehicle, before demonstrating to the policemen that they should allow the journalists to pass through. The police backed down, allowing the press and the Warriors to move back to the original platoon positions.

Throughout this delicate and hazardous episode, Serjeant Patterson remained interposed between the police and the reporters at great personal risk to himself. At a number of occasions, including the police cocking their assault rifles and the preparing for firing of the rocket launcher, Patterson would have been fully justified in using lethal force to neutralise a direct threat to himself and his troops. But by holding his nerve and dominating the drunk and excitable soldiers and police, he had defused an extremely tense situation without having to open fire. Had he done so, I have no doubt that the police would have all been killed or wounded by our soldiers, but there would have been a chance that the mujahideen soldiers would have been drawn into the shoot-out. This would have resulted in the failure of the mission to monitor and contain, and could have threatened the plan to return mujahideen soldiers to their country of origin.

Patterson was typical of the battalion's sergeants, who could take charge of such dangerous situations and through sheer force of personality resolve them without loss of life. I was very lucky to have such subordinates.

CHAPTER ELEVEN

'Strange Town'

We had left C Company behind on Mount Igman. Shortly after Christmas they had been released from the Multinational Brigade and moved to Banja Luka as the northern company of the 1 RRF Battlegroup. Their southern boundary was the front line between the Bosnian Croats and Bosnian Serbs which delineated the northern side of the 'area of transfer', the so-called 'Anvil'. The company was responsible for a huge piece of real estate, larger than the county of Wiltshire. It was bounded in the west by the 2 LI Battlegroup area, in the north by the international border between Bosnia and Croatia along the River Sava and in the east by the US-led Multinational Division North. Rex Sartain proudly pointed out that his company area was larger than any brigade area in the American division's sector! Rex therefore decided to concentrate on the VRS front line and the area to its immediate north, leaving the rest of the area for subsequent IFOR operations. The commander of 7 Platoon, Second Lieutenant Tom Harper, described the company's early operations in Republika Srpska:

> With the change from the UN to IFOR came new rules of engagement and an entirely new operational requirement. C Company found itself allocated an area entirely in Bosnian Serb territory. Given the vast area to be covered and the need for an extensive and consistent liaison structure, platoons were allocated Areas of Responsibility (AORs).
>
> Seven Platoon's boundaries matched exactly those of the 'Famous 16 Krajina Motor Rifle Brigade' – a seventeen-kilometre front. The 16 Brigade proudly boasted that they had never lost a square metre in battle and wherever the fighting was difficult they would be found. They were last in the Posavina Corridor before moving to Banja Luka. The Commanding Officer of 16 Brigade (equivalent roughly to a UK Battlegroup) was Lieutenant Colonel Dragan Vukovic, twice wounded in the conflict, who liaised directly with Major Rex Sartain. This left the three battalion commanders (equivalent roughly to a UK company group) liaising to platoon level. Sixteen Brigade also provided a liaison officer, Captain Zec, who had spent twenty-two years in the Yugoslav Army.
>
> The run up to D+30 on 19 January, the date the factions withdrew either side of the cease-fire line to form the Zone of Separation, kept the platoon busy as it attempted to acquaint itself quickly with the new area. In fact the first patrol

found a previously undiscovered anti-aircraft battery. There was also a large training area and camp full of tanks and APCs. Being so close to Soviet-type equipment felt very odd!

Given the size of the frontage, the need to break the platoon area down further into section areas became apparent. Second Battalion's area, covered by 1 Section under Corporal Lindley, was the most heavily populated with two hundred and fifty-nine civilians living in, or planning to live in, the actual Zone of Separation. When three more Warriors, from the Milan Section commanded by Serjeant Bramwell, were attached, they quickly teamed up with 1 Section to cover the whole Battalion area. The First and Third Battalions were covered by Corporal Hayward commanding 3 Section and Serjeant Stewart commanding 2 Section. Having found accommodation in deserted houses, the soldiers started developing a friendly rapport with the locals. In the few days remaining until D+30, the main effort was to mark the ZOS with orange six-foot pickets, using satellite navigation to place them accurately on all main routes. On D+30, the withdrawal of forces went very smoothly.

The Metal Factory

C Company found a base in an enormous metal factory on the north-west outskirts of Banja Luka, On arrival they discovered that, apparently undetected by NATO intelligence, the factory had been used to conceal a large number of Gazelle helicopters and a large number of support vehicles. As the company moved into the factory, NATO allowed the helicopters to be flown to the VRS helicopter base at Zaluzani, to the north of Banja Luka.

While Rex and his platoons concentrated their energies to the south of Banja Luka, Mark Mortimer, the company second-in-command, grappled with co-ordinating and sustaining the company's far-flung operations. Mark also worked to establish a *modus operandi* with the Metal Factory's manager. The building was an enormous square hangar, some four hundred metres along each side. In its dark cavernous interior the looming bulks of milling machines, cranes and derricks dwarfed Warriors and trucks. Mains electricity was still connected, although both it and the running water were extremely unreliable.

C Company devoted a minimum of resources to the direct protection of the base. Armed sentries were posted at the two entrances to the factory, with a Warrior at the main gate, and patrols checking the mile-long perimeter fence. Both Muslims and Serbs had repeatedly told us that this lack of overt fortification of our bases gave them great confidence in our impartiality and capability. They were derisive about other IFOR national contingents who turned their bases into huge muddy fortresses. This was just as well, as we needed to use our engineers not for fortifying the Metal Factory but to make it habitable.

The complex had been offered to us on a 'care and maintenance' basis: an understanding that we would allow the factory to be maintained so that it could eventually be reactivated. Although this limited our freedom of action, it committed the factory authorities to looking after the facilities we were using. Rex had got his people into rooms with solid roofs, doors, windows, very occasional electricity and running water. C Company had opened the factory's canteen, a large modern building capable of seating two hundred people. For the first time since D Day, I found some of our cooks working from something approaching a proper kitchen.

The factory authorities employed a force of fifty civilians to maintain and clean the facility. C Company had arranged for many of these to work in the kitchen. Others worked on the factory's power and water supplies. Many of these men wore items of Bosnian Serb military uniform – because they had no other work clothes, they explained. Having paramilitary engineers and labourers working in the base added a further strange touch to our already unusual environment. We fed them lunch – the alternative being lower work rates and a higher risk of theft.

We had learned that the capacity of a base was not usually limited by the space available, but by how well its infrastructure could support the troops living there in terms of feeding, sanitation and heating. Overcrowding the base beyond the carrying capacity of the infrastructure laid us open to risks, particularly from illness and accidental fires.

Banja Luka had an extremely irregular supply of mains electricity and some running water. Our other bases had no electricity, running water, heating or lighting. Since D Day, equipment for bases had been in short supply, as were engineers to help improve conditions. Although all ranks achieved an enormous amount by hard work and improvisation, the lack of campaign infrastructure such as portable toilets, heaters and washing units meant that we spent much of the tour living in spartan and uncomfortable conditions. It was lucky that the soldiers and commanders of the battlegroup were so robust.

Although the Metal Factory looked impressive, much of it was uninhabitable. The parts we could use for accommodation were filthy and insanitary. We filled all the rooms, but still had more than a hundred people living in tents inside the building. In that huge dark metal cavern the cold seemed to have a ferocious intensity all of its own. We had just enough electric or paraffin heaters to give one to each inhabited tent or room, but these seemed to make little difference to the freezing atmosphere. Those who spent January and February in Banja Luka will never forget the long, intensely cold nights. We were all desperate to keep warm. Some were tempted to take risks with unauthorised heaters and modifications to the electrical supplies, posing real risks of starting a fire. The NCOs living in our small tent city earned their pay in preventing this.

It quickly became the least popular base in the battlegroup – so much so that signal platoon soldiers volunteered to serve on the hilltop rebroadcast stations, rather than in Banja Luka. The least uncomfortable soldiers in the battlegroup were those living in the isolated platoon houses on the front line.

A major factor helping to keep the cold at bay and thus sustain morale was the high standard of food prepared by our chefs, often matching that achieved in barracks in peacetime. This was a source of great pride to us all. Directing the catering effort was WO2 Stemp RLC. He and the cooks responded magnificently to the constant changes of company and platoon locations, allowing the battlegroup to concentrate on the mission and not on the problems of feeding and rationing.

Another Estimate

The day after we arrived in Banja Luka we began the estimate process anew. I deliberately included Rex Sartain in this, for we were taking over his operation and he had the local knowledge we lacked.

We would continue to monitor and, if necessary, enforce VRS compliance with the military aspects of the Dayton Agreement. This already required the complete inactivation of all air defence systems, especially radars. By D+120 all the faction armed forces had to be withdrawn to barracks or cantonments.

Although the withdrawal of the armies from the Zone of Separation had gone well, the large number of minor incidents and the immense latent hostility and suspicion on all sides provided plenty of evidence of potential problems. Previous peace agreements in Bosnia and elsewhere which had achieved a cease-fire had all failed to achieve any substantive disengagement on the front line. There was no room for complacency. We would have to give everyone sufficient confidence that the war was over and that IFOR could prevent any return to armed conflict. This would encourage the civil and military leadership to participate fully in this countrywide demobilisation.

Almost all battlegroup operations had been in and around the area of the front line. Other than movement, logistics and some liaison work, little activity had taken place further than ten kilometres from the cease-fire line. The same applied to C Company's patrolling. Apart from the location of barracks in Banja Luka, we had no information or intelligence at all concerning the area to the north, east or west of the town. Neither air photographs nor intelligence from NATO air forces was available.

We identified that our area was the military heartland of Republika Srpska. So we should demonstrate an IFOR presence and monitor all military activity throughout the area, not just in what we were coming to call the 'ten kilometre zone'. We would need to identify all the VRS units, formations, barracks and installations. Doing this would put us in the best possible position to monitor and then confirm the withdrawal of the VRS to barracks as it happened.

For the moment we only had C Company and the recce and mortar platoons, but A Company and B Squadron would join the battlegroup once the Czechs were up and running in the Canadian Brigade area. We had left our friends in 19/5 Battery, but would shortly be joined by the battery commander and forward observation officers of another battery. A troop of Challenger tanks from the QRH would join us, once that regiment's deployment was complete.

A and C Companies would each cover the forward area between the ZOS and Banja Luka, with a frontage of about twenty kilometres of cease-fire line each. Since C Company had built up so much local knowledge and contacts, it seemed sensible for them to be left in place as much as possible. They would be south and west of the city, an area containing a large VRS barracks, range complex and training area. A Company would take over the area south and east of the city, relieving the two platoons of C Company whose territory it had been. Once B Squadron returned, they would take over responsibility for area to the north of the city, up to the international border with Croatia.

A Company had been operating very intensely over the previous three weeks. Men and machines were worn out. Our logistic base at Mrkonjić Grad was now reasonably developed and less austere than the Metal Factory. We therefore put all the platoons of A Company through a three-day refurbishment period at Echelon where they maintained their Warriors, their equipment and themselves. B Squadron, on return to the battlegroup, did the same.

I would use the recce platoon to reinforce the two armoured infantry companies, using the lighter Scimitars to complement the larger, heavier Warriors. I regrouped the mortar platoon, taking the sections away from the companies. The platoon had been handicapped by having to work with a fleet of extremely worn out vehicles and the amount of maintenance and sheer hard work required to keep their fleet on the road has been a source of great frustration. Now they would be used as battlegroup troops, both 'in role' to augment or replace artillery cover and or to provide patrols.

Operations in Banja Luka

Banja Luka was a large town or small city of more than three hundred thousand people, including many refugees and displaced persons. I saw signs of a wartime siege economy. Many houses and buildings were without electricity and there were few working traffic lights. Many people seemed to be spending time either standing around aimlessly, or carrying pathetic bundles about. Some seventy thousand displaced persons lived in houses and flats from which Muslims and Croats had been evicted. Many were totally dependent on their families and/or humanitarian aid dispensed by the few relief organisations working in Republika Srpska.

It was the largest conurbation of Republika Srpska and an economic, political and social hub, containing large Bosnian Serb camps and other military installations. These included a Corps HQ, a military academy and a camp on the north of the town that had sufficient sheds and hard standing for at least an armoured brigade. The Bosnian Serb Air Force had their headquarters in the town and the 'Kosmos Factory', an electronics plant, was jam-packed with air defence radar equipment. North of the town was Zaluzani, which held their remaining helicopters. Further north was Banja Luka Airport, the civil facilities on one side appearing completely intact as did the military airbase on the other side, which held the Bosnian Serbs' few jet fighters.

Despite the war, ethnic cleansing and successive waves of refugees, the town still held a few thousand Muslims and Croats, together with their religious leaders, a Catholic bishop and a Muslim mufti. The population appeared more cosmopolitan and a touch less embittered and illiberal than many we had encountered. A contributory factor could have been the lack of fighting in the immediate vicinity of the city, with NATO missile strikes having been the only direct attacks on the town. There were a considerable number of factories and industrial installations on the fringes of the town. All were silent. We assessed that it represented a political and military centre of gravity of western Republika Srpska.

How we handled the town and its population would have a direct influence on civil and military attitudes throughout the battlegroup's area and beyond. We needed to give the townspeople something to lose if the factions went back to war. We should do everything we could to encourage a return to normality. 'Normal' towns and cities, even in former Yugoslavia, do not have heavy concentrations of NATO troops and armour barracked within their city limits. It was essential for us not to be seen as an army of occupation.

We would have to make sure that our activities caused the minimum inconvenience to the city. I decided to make Banja Luka a distinct area of responsibility within the battlegroup, commanded by Ian Baker, the Chief Liaison Officer. He would coordinate all our activities in the town from liaison through to logistics. We would attempt to restrict unnecessary heavy armoured vehicle movement in the town.

I called on the mayor of the town. He seemed bored and disengaged, probably because he had already had a large number of IFOR callers, from General Jackson to the JCOs. I found it more productive to talk to ordinary civilians.

We were sent IFOR newspapers and leaflets intended for distribution to the local population. These were received with great enthusiasm by the people of Banja Luka. I made sure that my Land Rover always carried some to hand out to civilians. In the centre of the town was a large open-air bus station where people were always waiting, either to travel or to meet arrivals. The first time I stopped there I had only a few newspapers and leaflets to distribute. These ran out in less than a minute and a crowd of curious and expectant men quickly surrounded me. All were refugees, some, but not all, from the 'Anvil', the area to our south that was due to be transferred from the Bosnian Croats to Republika Srpska. All were hoping to move to the area, either to repossess their homes or to find somewhere new to live – the latter because they were refugees from the Serb Krajinas or some part of Bosnia now in Federation territory. All were full of questions. What was the threat from the Croats? What would IFOR do to protect them? How would they eat? How much destruction had there been? What was the threat from mines? Was the area safe for children? Would IFOR help transport them and their belongings?

I tried to answer these questions as best as I could, being frank and cautious, but not, I hoped, so pessimistic that I would put them off returning to the Anvil. I was a week away from the start of my leave in the UK and found their worn, tired faces and the few remaining sparks of hope in their eyes almost unbearable.

Operations South of Banja Luka

South of Banja Luka C Company had naturally concentrated on the immediate area of the front line. Now we needed to explore the rest of our area to locate and then monitor troops wherever they were. We needed to achieve maximum presence on the ground to deter infringements of the Dayton Agreement. We also had to verify the details of the military dispositions submitted by the VRS.

The area was a high rolling plateau, divided into two halves by the steep sides of the gorge of the Vrbas River. The roads and tracks were poor and in the snow and ice it could take three or four hours to travel the thirty kilometres from Banja Luka to the south-east corner of our area. Indeed, A Company quickly christened the twisting, tortuous road to Skender Vakuf 'The Road to Hell', a nickname that stuck for the rest of the tour. The companies established platoon bases amongst areas that were initially crammed full of VRS troops. Sites used included derelict houses, disused rural medical clinics, deserted schools and even an abandoned restaurant. For the platoons this was a satisfying role; commanders relished being anything up to two hours' driving time away from company HQ, thriving on the independence and devolved responsibility.

The VRS welcomed this presence. Most soldiers were only too anxious to get out of uniform and civilians were delighted to have IFOR troops in their villages. Seven Platoon's account of these operations continues:

> The civilians were very concerned about their safety now that their soldiers were no longer present to protect them. The platoon began extensive patrolling with unarmed VRS guides to ensure the ZOS was clear of any military factions. This was a very intense period. With amazingly clear and warm weather, many unfinished mine clearances and other disposal tasks were able to take place. Tasks included overwatch of body exhumation, which turned out to be a sheep carcass; overwatch of minefield clearance by unarmed VRS engineers; and handing out IFOR newspapers.
>
> The few days remaining until D+45 (3 February 1996) were spent preparing for the civilians who were expected to return to areas recently vacated by the Croats under the Peace Agreement. Lance Corporal Butcher also had an exciting moment when he confirmed, with satellite navigation, that a manned VRS position was inside the ZOS. He confiscated four weapons and various munitions.
>
> A troop of Challenger tanks from the Queen's Royal Hussars, commanded by Lieutenant Rupert Greenwood, arrived just prior to D+45. The tanks worked closely with the platoon by helping to provide an observation post and check point with Lance Corporal Judd and his vehicle on the 'Golden Mile', a main route within our area.
>
> The expected 'mass exodus' did not occur. However, a rather right-wing Bosnian Serb colonel initially refused to let an 'undisciplined', 'leaderless' group of about fifty civilians pass into the Golden Mile. From D+45 the platoon began to concentrate on verifying the clearance of all heavy weapons from the

ten-kilometre zone while maintaining the integrity of the ZOS. The platoon also continued to develop relations with the locals, Private N Oakley being a favourite of Mr Savanovic, mayor of the town of Sarici. The locals also helped the platoon with free firewood, the occasional slivovitz and Turkish coffee.

The platoon worked off a four-day ration and water supply and a forty-eight hour fuel replenishment. This along with constant demands for post, chocolate and fresh rations kept the platoon serjeant, Serjeant Lovell, very busy indeed. The constant use of the Warriors left the drivers, Privates Shingler, Thurlow, Williams and Blewett, with few spare moments. Long days and patrols aside, everyone enjoyed the interaction with the civilians and soldiers. We all learned a great deal about a very different culture and military organisation. Working with the VRS to see the Dayton Agreement through and also seeing civilians return to their homes made this the most productive and rewarding part of the tour.

By now the artillery tactical group of 127 (Dragon) Battery, equipped with AS90 self-propelled guns, had joined us. They were old friends, who had served with the battalion on a Northern Ireland tour two years earlier. More importantly, they had accompanied the battalion during its month on the Canadian prairie in August 1994 and had joined in other war fighting training since. We had established an excellent mutual rapport.

Major Piers Tucker, the battery commander, had served in Bosnia in early days of UNPROFOR as General Morillon's military assistant. He and Morillon had been taken hostage at one stage, and Piers' actions had earned him the Military Cross. An extremely intelligent and articulate officer, he had given me stalwart support, making a huge contribution to battlegroup planning.

His battery's guns were based to our south in a disused slaughterhouse in Jezero. It was little more than a shell and had absolutely no facilities at all. The guns therefore alternated between their base and high-profile deployments into the battlegroup area. Since they were not firing in anger, Piers offloaded some of the ammunition carried on his DROPS lorries and offered them to our hard-pressed logisticians – giving us much-needed additional lift capability at a time when we still did not have sufficient logistic assets. This initiative was typical of the unselfish and generous way in which the battery supported the battlegroup.

The battery had three Forward Observation Officer (FOO) parties, all equipped with the Warrior Observation Post Variant (OPV). The vehicle had a sophisticated electro-optical system that integrated a very powerful thermal imaging sight with a laser rangefinder and an electronic navigation system, the whole being in turn integrated with the artillery BATES computer system, making the Warrior OPVs extremely useful surveillance platforms. Piers had a fourth Warrior, a Battery Command Vehicle (BCV). In war fighting this allowed him to accompany me as we planned and conducted the manoeuvre battle. We had spent many happy hours doing so in Canada and Germany. Here the situation was different. Piers therefore employed the BCV as if it were an OPV, allowing deployment of two artillery patrols of two Warriors each, improving our flexibility.

I watched the battery's first move to a fire position in C Company's territory. It was an impressive organisation – six enormous AS 90 self-propelled howitzers, larger than Challenger tanks, each accompanied by a huge eight-wheeled DROPS lorry and half a dozen other support vehicles. The battery made a column over a mile long, winding across an open, windswept upland plateau. The VRS soldiers who watched the guns move into fire positions shook their heads in wonder.

Unfortunately we lost one of their Warriors when it ran over an anti-tank mine in Seven Platoon's area. The vehicle was badly damaged and immobilised, but there were no serious injuries. The Warrior had been carrying a driver, signaller and two forward observation officers, patrolling in order to familiarise themselves with routes in 7 Platoon's area. It had got lost in fog and driven into an unmarked minefield.

Seven Platoon's commander was in Banja Luka receiving orders, the platoon serjeant was on leave and Corporal Stanley was in charge. He moved quickly to the scene of the incident, immediately warning the essential medical and explosive ordnance detachments. He cleared the company radio net of unnecessary traffic and gave regular reports as the incident developed. Throughout the clearance of the remaining mines and recovery of the crew and vehicles he remained firmly in command. The calm and confident manner in which he dealt with the incident was immensely reassuring to the crew of the Warrior who, although surviving unharmed, were severely shaken.

Far to the south the division had been reinforced by another reconnaissance squadron of Light Dragoons who were operating in a huge swathe of Bosnian Croat territory south of the 'Anvil'. Shortly after our mine incident, a Spartan of theirs struck an anti-tank mine. Desperate attempts were made to rescue the victims and to extract the surviving Scimitar and its crew from the minefield as darkness was falling, but all three crewmen were killed.

Although the squadron was not under our command, we all felt the loss most keenly. It made me realise how lucky we had been. The battlegroup had been involved in three mine strikes. Vehicles and equipment had been destroyed and people had been injured and severely shocked, but everyone involved had lived to tell the tale. The Light Dragoons' loss was desperately sad.

Some weeks later, the *Daily Telegraph* newspaper carried an interview with the parents of the young officer who had been killed in the mine strike while commanding the patrol. I was struck by their unselfish and stoical view of their son's tragic death. Their quiet dignity and uncomplaining acceptance of the cruel hand that fate had dealt them seemed to be the same concept of duty that contributed to the way in which so many members of the battlegroup put up with harsh conditions and other privations as they carried out their missions. This concept, together with the mutual responsibility that we all owed each other to carry out our tasks, applied at every level from two-man vehicle crews up to the battlegroup as a whole. Without these simple qualities, that many outside the Army seemed to consider old-fashioned and potentially corrosive of civil liberties, we would not have been able to survive in the Balkan winter, let alone carry out our missions.

Nowhere was this truer than in our signal detachments. These consisted of a few soldiers headed by a corporal, working either from a vehicle or an improvised operations room. This was a high-pressure responsibility which all of them executed with enormous professionalism. Whilst I was renewing my acquaintance with C Company, I got to know their signals detachment very well. Key to its success was the leadership of its commander, Lance Corporal Pritchard. The distances he managed to operate over far exceeded the normal operating ranges of company radios, and he often succeeded when no one else could manage, in conditions that defeated other outfits. Huge responsibility rested on the shoulders of Pritchard and the other signals detachment commanders. They all made an outstanding contribution. C Company's signal detachment also included an extremely able volunteer from the Territorial Army Parachute Regiment, Private Boxall-Hunt, an eternally cheerful signaller who did wonders for morale of the Company HQ.

The company had ten other TA soldiers, including a self-employed carpenter who was invaluable in helping to repair, maintain and improve many of the externally dilapidated and ramshackle buildings that the company had used. These and all the other TA officers and soldiers who had volunteered to come to Bosnia with the battalion were all completely integrated into their companies and platoons.

They were all performing well and most of us had ceased to draw any distinction between them and the regular comrades in arms. Although we had a sizeable contingent from the TA battalions of the Light Infantry, two thirds came from the Royal Green Jackets, Parachute Regiment and Wessex Regiment. All these now identified with 2 LI – indeed the Parachute Regiment soldiers were wearing green berets, and identified with them as well as with their much loved red berets. We were very well supported by them all.

Operations North of Banja Luka

The ground north of Banja Luka was much flatter and more open, much of it low-lying agricultural country with dark, rich soil and a complex artificial irrigation system. There was an extensive road network and far fewer derelict buildings. The whole area appeared more prosperous and much less affected by war than any part of Bosnia we had yet visited.

There had been no previous IFOR contact with the Bosnian Serb military in this area. With the exception of the location of the VRS air bases at Zaluzani and Banja Luka Airport, the chain of command could not supply us with any information concerning the faction military. B Squadron would simply to have to go out and find the factions. Because the information vacuum was greatest in this area, I allocated them most of the few helicopter recce patrols available to us.

B Squadron set to work with vigorous enthusiasm. They quickly discovered a significant number of VRS forces still in battle positions facing Croatia. The single bridge over the River Sava at Bos Gradiška had been demolished, its central span dropped into the river. The south bank of the river Sava was strongly defended, with the great levee fortified with trenches every twenty or thirty metres. In the towns, buildings facing the river and Croatia had been turned into fighting positions. Further south there were more units deployed in depth facing north and apparently guarding the main approaches to Banja Luka. It was only six months since the Croat offensive against the Serb Krajinas to the north.

Halfway between the Sava River and Banja Luka B Squadron discovered a complete VRS anti-tank brigade. Equipped with both guided missiles and anti-tank guns it was screening Banja Luka from any successful crossing of the Sava by Croatian armour. The brigade was delighted to see B Squadron, their officers telling ours that 'now you IFOR troops are patrolling between Banja Luka and Croatia we can go home'. This they did. The brigade's officers and soldiers seemed to be recruited entirely from the students, staff and professors of Banja Luka University. They wanted to return to their studies quickly, and invited Bertie Polley to a memorable demobilisation lunch just before the last of their positions was abandoned.

This was in stark contrast to the VRS Brigade based in Srbac right up in the north-east corner of the battlegroup area. They were initially very hostile to B Squadron who reported their first meeting as follows:

OC B SQN VISIT TO HQ SRBAC BDE 04 FEB 96

Major Polley, Captain Frost, Lieutenant Elwell and Lieutenant Van de Pol visited HQ Srbac Brigade. On arrival at 1100 we were greeted by Colonel Suvajac and his officers. The colonel was extremely drunk, and found it difficult to speak without slurring his words. We all had coffee and slivovitz in his office, and he repeatedly stated that we should not fear the Serbs and that Major Polley would be his friend forever. Maj Polley gave the Tank Captain (Captain Babic) a trace of B Sqn LD Area of Responsibility (1:50000) The Colonel then stated that he would only speak with Major Polley if the IFOR interpreter (Sanja) was present. He said he loved her and would pay us eight hundred Deutschmarks per month for her services. Maj Polley diplomatically avoided this issue and finalised plans for the day.

The Colonel and his officers escorted us on a guided tour of various positions within his area. This included visits to the River Sava overlooking the town of Davor in Croatia, a T55 tank and MT-12 gun location.

We were invited to lunch in a restaurant and spoke at length with Capt Babic about numerous subjects. He used to be a teacher in Banja Luka, and had a very good command of the English language. He has asked if it would be possible to look at a Challenger tank, as he had studied all NATO tanks.

Colonel Suvajac was still keen to try and engage Maj Polley in polite conversation. He had stated that he would arrest us so we could stay with him until the following morning, but was so drunk that he fell asleep after forty-five minutes. Capt Babic assured us that this was only a joke, and that the Colonel was so drunk because he had been told on 3 February by the International Red Cross that seventeen of his soldiers had been killed in Tuzla prior to a prisoner exchange. The lunch was a very friendly affair, and we left at 1530 hrs.

The visit was successful, marred slightly by the difficulty in discussing serious subjects with Colonel Suvajac. We were extended many courtesies, and thanked the colonel and his officers for being so open with us. The visit was reported on local TV in Banja Luka and was said to be a great success.

This bizarre incident provided plenty of amusement. The Adjutant and I had both needed some light relief, as we had to deal with a serious breach of discipline. Four Brigade's policy was that drinking would routinely be limited to two cans of beer per person per day. Johnny Bowron described how the policy was applied.

These cans mentioned in the policy were the UK variety, not the local ones, which are larger, stronger and cheaper than ours. Beer was being bought from the locals at a cheaper price that the NAAFI was selling it. It quickly became a rule in 2 LI that purchase or consumption of local beer was outlawed. Additionally drinking in the small outposts was completely banned. Drinking was only allowed in designated bar areas and not in accommodation or work areas.

Our soldiers were not angels and we had one or two disciplinary problems in January, all results of soldiers drinking Bosnian brandy or slivovitz that they had purchased from the locals. The individuals concerned were disciplined. Unauthorised purchase of any kind of alcohol from the locals was immediately banned (it was an oversight not to have banned it from the start of the tour). Word soon got out around the battalion and we had only one other incident of misbehaviour.

This involved a corporal from the recce platoon and an attached RAF officer, both discovered in the early hours of the morning attempting to sneak back into the Metal Factory base. Both were drunk.

The incident was well handled by the corporal in charge of the guard, and a formal disciplinary investigation was convened. The two individuals claimed that the incident had its origins in some work the recce platoon with the RAF Tactical Air Control Party attached had been doing in B Squadron's area. They had made contact with a number of previously unknown VRS minor units and logistic installations. At one location the VRS commander was not present, but the VRS soldiers claimed that he could be found in a particular nightclub in Banja Luka. The corporal and the officer then chose to 'borrow' a Land Rover that evening. Between leaving our camp and returning five hours later in a drunken state, they claimed to have been searching the nightclubs, bars and cafés of Banja Luka for this elusive VRS commander.

Even if their story was true, they had broken the rules on drinking, had got drunk, had broken standing procedures about vehicle movement, had been out of radio contact with the battlegroup for five hours and had failed to let anyone else know where they were or what they were doing. A less charitable, but more likely, explanation was that both men had concocted a flimsy excuse to attempt to go drinking and searching for female company in Banja Luka.

We were very lucky that the incident had not become more serious. With the agreement of the senior RAF commander in Bosnia the RAF officer was relieved of his appointment and sent straight back to the UK to await formal disciplinary action. The other man, a corporal, had recently joined us from our First Battalion already under a cloud. He was punished with a significant fine and returned to the UK.

As I signed the disciplinary paperwork for the case of the corporal and the RAF officer, I reflected that so far in the tour, there had been remarkably few disciplinary problems. Positive leadership at all levels and a battalion regime of 'zero tolerance' of misconduct meant that there were very few disciplinary problems serious enough to warrant my attention.

The winter could have an interesting effect on people and organisations who had come to the theatre of operations with a peacetime or 'jobsworth' attitude. The demands of operations, the minimal infrastructure and the harsh conditions would make such an attitude worse. The question I used to ask myself was something like this: 'Does that group of people have the morale and leadership to rapidly switch from what they are doing to peace enforcement, using war fighting techniques, and are they prepared to take serious casualties?'

When I asked that question about parts of the battlegroup, I was always satisfied. Some other sub-units and people I had seen had given me some doubt.

I had to do everything I could to make sure that my soldiers were as well looked after as possible, but achieving the mission had to come first. It was important that soldiers were not allowed to get into a mindset about their 'rights' to receive mail and three square meals a day. The chain of command, quite rightly, needed to fight any drop in standards of service to the soldier, but it could not be allowed to prey on their minds. Getting this balance right was not easy, but given positive leadership, it could be achieved.

We were largely getting the balance right, but although morale was extremely high overall there were some troubling indicators of a few unhappy people. Just a couple of days before, a soldier employed as a company storeman had attempted suicide by shooting himself in the face. Fortunately he had only shot himself through his cheek and was remarkably lightly injured, but his company was shocked. He was a quiet likeable individual who had distinguished himself as 'an uncomplaining hard grafter', as his company commander put it. Investigation showed that he was engaged to be married at the end of the tour, and appeared to have become depressed by being unable to talk to his fiancée by telephone. He was one of the first soldiers to go back to England on R&R in December, and the prospect of another three months in Bosnia may have reinforced his depression.

'Welfare' telephones that would allow soldiers to call UK and Germany from Bosnia had repeatedly been promised to us. None had arrived and no one in the battlegroup had had any access to such phones since Christmas. For many, the inability of most personnel to contact friends and family by telephone was the biggest single negative morale factor. The single free call at Christmas had been made long ago. Platoons all had high-frequency radios which could call a UK radio station near Bristol who would connect the radio to the British or international telephone system, but this was an extremely expensive option.

Fortunately the Banja Luka metal factory had just been connected to the Republika Srpska PTT and we had four telephones that could make international calls. I therefore dedicated one of these to 'welfare' calls, aiming that everyone in the battalion should get a single five-minute call a week. The phone was hugely oversubscribed and I instructed that anyone with any personal or family problems was to be given access to a PTT line, INMARSAT or Ptarmigan as quickly as possible.

However successful these measures were, the root problem of the attempted suicide had been that a quiet and self-contained individual working in an extremely demanding yet isolated job, had become worried and depressed, and we had not picked up the signs. The sorry story demonstrated the need to keep an eye on personnel employed in jobs that required them to work on their own. During intensive operations, it was too easy to miss the telltale signs of stress.

This incident suggested that we were not looking after our soldiers as well as we should. We needed to pay more attention to those who had taken leave early, who could be particularly vulnerable to stress later on in the tour. I briefed the company commanders about this as soon as I could.

In Sanski Most and Ljubija, we had been exceptionally busy and working with overstretched brigade and battlegroup communications systems. Both our pace of operations and our success required me to tolerate a certain lack of finesse in our *modus operandi*. I was now worried that our own internal passage of information was not as effective as it should be. Back in January, I had become so concerned at this that I had ordered the formation of the 'Bugle Express', a pair of vehicles that visited all our locations each day, taking mail, orders, reports and other information. This represented such a diminution of our thinly spread combat power that the ops officer and others advised me strongly against it – but I had overruled them.

One of the principles of mission command is unity of effort. To achieve this it is essential that all elements of the force understand both the situation and the commanders' intent. During our UN operations, passage of information had been good and we had been able to monitor events throughout the former Yugoslavia. There had been a considerable period of time after D-Day when it had been very difficult to find out what was going on outside our brigade area. During January and much of February the principal source of timely information about events outside the brigade area was the short-wave broadcasts of the BBC World Service. It was worrying to see satellite television reports of

IFOR's struggle with the difficulties of the transfer of Sarajevo's suburbs from Bosnian Serb to Federation control, whilst hearing nothing about the issue coming down our chain of command. When we were engaged in discussion about the issue, we struggled to be able to put forward the IFOR 'line'.

Now with a smaller area and a more mature communications infrastructure, lack of timely information was a source of weakness. Not knowing what was going on had negative effects on morale and could have led to inappropriate responses to unforeseen problems. At times it resulted in the factions receiving contradictory messages from different levels of command, causing confusion and giving the factions a legitimate excuse for procrastination. This made it more difficult to achieve unity of effort.

On a conventional war-fighting battlefield, the battlegroup's horizons would have been limited to the enemy it was engaging and the forces it might fight in the next few hours. Now the battlefield was the minds of all the Bosnian people in our area. Their attitudes could be influenced by events happening on the other side of the country – reported very quickly by the Bosnian and international media. We needed to have the highest possible standard of 'situational awareness'. Instead we were relying on our analysis of World Service and satellite television news to replace information, analysis and prediction that should have been flowing to us down the chain of command.

Brigadier Dannatt was most sympathetic when I summoned up my courage and went to see him to state politely that we needed more information passed to us about what was happening throughout Bosnia. Matters improved very quickly. However it was also essential that we put our own house in order, and we took concerted action to do so.

CHAPTER TWELVE
A Hard Return

'Missing'

Despite the excitement of the tour and the high morale of the companies and platoons, all of us had moments when we felt low. I found the lack of quiet and privacy particularly trying. All our bases constantly rumbled with vehicle engines, the rattle and screech of armoured vehicle tracks and the sounds of people coming and going at all hours – all combining to produce an environment of constant noise. Sometimes when driving around, I would direct Leck to stop at an isolated place. Making some excuse to the crew, like 'I'm taking this map to have a look at the ground', I would walk up the road until out of earshot from the vehicles, and allow my senses to feast on the landscape and relative quiet. I'm sure that they saw through my excuse, but were too polite to question me.

My personal low usually occurred when I returned at night from Brigade HQ to Battlegroup HQ. This was not due to any negative morale at Šipovo – far from it, for contact with Brigadier Dannatt and his staff always had an invigorating effect – but to the interminable night journeys by road. With virtually no street lights, little road traffic and few road markings it was as if we were travelling down an endless black tunnel. At night there was usually less traffic on the radio net, adding to the tedium of these immensely monotonous journeys, but Leck and I had to maintain our alertness, if only for our own safety. The trips were too bumpy to do any work and by the late evening I would be too tired to concentrate much on operational planning.

Inevitably my mind would wander. I would think of my family. Often I would recall the words of songs with themes of loneliness, separation or travelling. These would include Bruce Springsteen's songs: 'Drive All Night', 'Wreck on the Highway' and 'Valentine's Day' with its haunting lines:

> I'm driving a big lazy car rushin' up the highway in the dark
> I got one hand steady on the wheel and one
> hand's tremblin' over my heart
> It's pounding baby like it's gonna bust right on through
> And it ain't gonna stop till I'm alone again with you...

> They say he travels fastest who travels alone,
> But tonight I miss my girl mister tonight I miss my home.

There was the more recent 'Missing' by Everything But the Girl. Against a sparse acoustic and sampled beat, Tracey Thorn's voice repeated the haunting refrain:

> I miss you, like the deserts miss the rain...

All of us missed our families and our friends. We knew that they missed us. Many wives, Liz included, found Sundays the most difficult – reinforced by the rigid German laws forbidding Sunday opening of shops. Most had friends from whom to draw support, and Liz was lucky to have so many good companions amongst the families living in our little estate of Army houses. Even so, with husbands and fathers away family life became more difficult and less enjoyable. Executing the comfortable rituals of Sunday lunch turned from fun to a chore and the day seemed to drag on interminably. It was as if our families had become temporary widows and orphans.

The simple physical separation was exacerbated by difficulties keeping in touch, particularly the lack of access to telephones. The internet was unknown to us. We all could write home for free and people could send free letters to us, provided that they were written on the special blue-coloured free air letters known as 'blueys'. These took between three and seven days to travel to and from Bosnia. I imagine that by the standards of our forefathers fighting in the two world wars this must have seemed a lightning service, but most of the battalion had grown up used to communicating not by letter but by telephone. Perhaps our ability to compose letters had atrophied, but most of us were much better on the phone than in writing. No one found this easy and many found it very difficult. At the end of January I described this to Liz:

> There are times when I really ache for you. My job is great fun, an enormous challenge and has a relentless momentum. There have been setbacks, but we have achieved a tremendous amount in a very short period since 20 December. BUT – the country is sorry for itself, dark, gloomy, cold, run-down and oppressively miserable. I really need my leave!

My family was a source of joy and strength to me and I knew this applied to many others. With half the battalion married, some three hundred families would be without their fathers for six months. Our Families Office who co-ordinated the arrangements for looking after our families were part of the Rear Party, who also maintained our buildings and equipment. Johnny Bowron later described how we set up both organisations:

> A great deal of planning, energy and resources were devoted to the Rear Party, the Families Office and the Welfare Centre and this paid dividends for us. It was an essential area that was extremely busy and had a direct effect on morale, both

that of the families and that of the troops. It gave the wives a focal point and drew them together. In our case we took a calculated risk to man Rear Party to the minimum; although they got by it was an extremely busy time and they certainly deserved their leave after the tour.

The families officer, Captain Mick Garner, and his team were co-ordinators, troubleshooters and my representatives in Paderborn. Whenever our tenuous communications allowed, Mick had a daily dialogue with the adjutant and many prospective welfare problems were nipped in the bud.

Many families went back to England for a period, particularly at Christmas, but most had school-age children and spent the majority of their time in Germany. At times mail was very slow and calls home were difficult or sometimes impossible to arrange. Mick later described the work of Rear Party in the *Silver Bugle*:

> Rear Party is actually a six-month tour in itself. Day to day administration continued. All those people arriving back from posting or going on posting from Bosnia staged through Paderborn. People were discharged and new recruits were inducted and prepared to go straight out.
>
> Sunday lunches were held twice a month, quiz nights were run, trips were organised and at times the Rear Party staff felt like a travel agent organising travel to and from the UK for families and their relatives. Throughout the tour the wives ran a coffee shop each morning which became a focal point for all those left behind in Paderborn. Families were kept in touch with the situation through a Bosnia Information Board. The wives also collected clothes for Bosnian children and at Christmas raised over DM700 carol singing for an orphanage in Banja Luka. Needless to say there were rumours and most of them were corrected through this forum. Sheets of paper were put up on notice boards for wives to write messages to their husbands. Some of these were very subtle and cryptic; others were not and were definitely risqué. They were a real boost to morale at both ends of the system.
>
> It is not a glamorous job to stay behind whilst the majority of the battalion is making modern European history, implementing the peace in a war-torn country. But somebody has to do it.

Home Leave

All of us had two weeks' mid-tour leave, usually called R&R (Rest and Recuperation). I had already seen half the battalion return from theirs. All were rested and refreshed and had renewed contacts with friends and families. Stories were already circulating about the exploits of single men on R&R, including the tale of the platoon commander whose girlfriend met him at the airport dressed in a long fur coat, boots, gloves and nothing else ...

I began my leave in the middle of the tour. After a long journey down through Bosnia to Split, we arrived worn out and dirty. The battalion had a small team at the British national logistics element there to co-ordinate our logistics and to dispatch and receive personnel travelling in out of Bosnia. Headed by Serjeant Major Noon, they had a thankless and lonely task that they executed well. The serjeant major found me a room with access to a shower, and for the first time since leaving Paderborn I slept in the next morning.

Finding that my flight back to England was delayed, I readily accepted someone's suggestion that I 'chill out'. I spent the day alternating between sleeping, standing under a shower (wonder of wonders, clean and with unlimited hot water) and reading paperbacks I had found lying on the free books shelf outside an office. J.G. Ballard's *The Comfort of Women* and Iain Banks' *Complicity* were marvellous antidotes to Bosnia, with their mixture of bizarre observation, personal tragedy, hedonism and unexpected happy endings.

Later, much later, after more delays, alarms and excursions I arrived in the early hours of the morning at an RAF base in Oxfordshire. Exhausted, I slipped into a bath. When I got up to dry myself, I noticed that I had left a thick black ring of dirt around the side – despite having had at least six long showers in the previous twenty-four hours.

I spent the two weeks with my family in Gloucestershire. How far away Bosnia seemed from this world of small villages, busy provincial towns, bypasses and out of town shopping centres. Here was an opportunity to recharge my emotional and social batteries. Central and western England at the end of a mild winter was a joy, as was renewing my family ties. I realised how ready for leave I had been.

Although I was largely able to put Bosnia to the back of my mind, on occasions I could not help seeing the landscape of southern England in the same way I had seen the landscapes of Bosnia. Visiting a supermarket I found myself calculating its suitability as a base for IFOR troops. Walking around the Gloucestershire village where I stayed, I could not help imagining it as a village on the front line like Arapuša. Whenever I drove my car along narrow single-track country lanes, I found it awfully difficult to pull onto the verges for fear that they might contain land mines. I could not stop using the mental gauges I had developed in Bosnia.

On a few occasions I tried to explain to friends or family how fragile the peace resulting from the Dayton Agreement was and how crucial to its sustainment was the military capability of IFOR. People of my parents' generation who had withstood the Second World War understood the terrible destruction around Sarajevo. But to them it was small beer compared with the destruction inflicted on London and Berlin. They also knew something of the terrible randomness of war's impact on hapless innocents. But younger people were bored with war and suffering in the Balkans.

Did they, I asked myself, have any idea how terrible ethnic cleansing really was? How would the occupants of my peaceful Gloucestershire village react to being ordered to leave by armed men, to the shooting, raping, burning, looting and casual violence so often visited upon Bosnian civilians? Did they realise how lucky they were to live in a country that had not had a civil war for more than three hundred years?

Towards the end of my leave, the IRA detonated a large bomb in the London Docklands, shattering their cease-fire. Shocked but unsurprised, I returned to Bosnia hoping that we could do better there than we had done in Northern Ireland.

While I Had Been on Leave

On the plane back I wondered what the final part of the tour would have in store for us. If everything went according to plan, we could end up with too little to do. Would I have to work hard to make sure that we did not get bored and lose our edge? Some battalions that had served in Bosnia had spent much, if not all, of their tours engaged in repetitive and undemanding routine operations.

These had been christened 'Groundhog Day' tours, after the film where the protagonist becomes trapped in an endlessly repeating time warp. During our preparation we had considered how we would tackle such a situation and had plenty of ideas up our sleeves for 'counter-boredom tactics'. I was worried. Would we end up on a 'Groundhog Day' tour? Would we need to activate our counter-boredom tactics?

Those fears were unfounded.

Waiting for me at Split Airport was a fat envelope containing a classified brief written by Chris Booth. He had been busy. Just after I had departed on leave, there had been a crisis with the VRS. The origins of this were in Sarajevo where three VRS officers had taken a wrong turning and had strayed from 'Serb Sarajevo' into ABiH-held territory. They were arrested and the senior of the two prisoners, a General Djukic, handed over to the war crimes tribunal. Relations with the Bosnian Serb authorities soured dramatically and the VRS suspended cooperation with IFOR.

It took several days before orders filtered down to the VRS soldiers on the ground to break off relations with 2 LI. Operations Group 10 and 30 Division broke off relations with us on 9 February. The next day our patrols reported that VRS soldiers were avoiding conversation with IFOR. Other work that depended on cooperation with the VRS had to be suspended. For example, in the north of our area a battalion of Hungarian engineers had begun work repairing the demolished bridge at Bos Gradiška, and needed to know where the VRS had placed mines and booby traps.

The VRS refused to supply the information and the work had to stop. IFOR worried that troops operating in VRS territory might become vulnerable to hostile action by soldiers and civilians, and security was raised. Troops were deployed to protect isolated installations and sites and reserves were put on higher readiness.

Outside VRS barracks and IFOR bases there appeared posters, handwritten in very poor English, asking IFOR not to liaise at the present time and thus make relations worse. A typical message was as follows:

We please all members of IFOR do not make relationships worser with meme-
bers of the Army of Republik Srpska and any akt of self-will and violent during
the time of duration suspensions relatins between the Army of Republik Srpska
and IFOR. Thank you.

Eventually a political deal was struck that resolved the situation, persuading
the Bosnian Serbs to resume cooperation with IFOR. In the meantime the
battlegroup had been dealing with several other problems.

Electronic Warfare

The Dayton Agreement required that all faction aircraft and helicopters
should be grounded, air defence radars be switched off from D Day and air
defence weapons be concentrated in storage sites by D+120. Romeo Troop 14
Signal Regiment were corps troops using electronic warfare (EW) equipment
to detect and identify any activation of air defence systems. Commanded by
Captain Jane Appleby, who had attended the same commanders' cadre as us
back in August, the troop was based in the Metal Factory. An excellent working relationship was quickly established between Battlegroup HQ and the
Troop HQ. They provided us with electronic warfare advice, and our patrols
were briefed to identify and report back on VRS radar and antenna arrays.
Neither 14 Signal Regiment nor the chain of command told either party to
liaise and cooperate; we just did it.

This excellent cooperation with a signals troop whose activities were normally shrouded in secrecy was in stark contrast to the problems we had with
a detachment of the divisional signal regiment. A large hill at the west of our
area had a commanding view over western Bosnia. It was an obvious location
for radio rebroadcast stations. The top of the mountain had been the site of a
large TV transmitter. NATO had attacked the site in the autumn and the mast
and half the buildings had been destroyed. Using secondary antennas the
Bosnian Serbs were continuing lower power TV transmissions and Bosnian
Serb soldiers were manning radio relay vehicles. The Serb soldiers lived in the
remaining habitable building.

Brigade security policy was quite clear – IFOR soldiers were not to share
accommodation with faction military. Our signals platoon had a rebroadcast
station on the hilltop. The soldiers manning it lived in their vehicles and
tents. But in direct contravention of the brigade orders, the detachment from
the divisional signal regiment lived in accommodation shared with the Serb
soldiers. They and some equally uncooperative Canadian signallers rejected
all security advice we offered, and any suggestion of joint administration. We
eventually had to tell the divisional signal regiment that I could not accept
responsibility for their security. Later, the signallers were surprised when a
drunk and emotional Serb pulled a grenade on them.

In the meantime, higher formation became extremely concerned about
reports of VRS radar activity. This generated a number of interesting problems.

On several occasions theatre-level EW systems detected radar emissions. Initially we were told that these transmissions had come from an air defence radar in the Kosmos Factory, an electronics maintenance facility in the centre of Banja Luka. In every case Romeo Troop detected nothing.

The battalion was involved in several operations either to ascertain whether this was the case, or to deliver formal protests. This developed into a 'bit of a saga' as Major Ian Baker described in a written report:

On 4 February we received warning of an EW inspection team. They arrived 5 February, intending that a USAF major general would inspect the Kosmos factory, where the radar would be turned on, so allowing its electronic signature to be 'fingerprinted' by IFOR's monitoring organisation. We were tasked with providing logistic support, vehicles and interpreters.

The team was not theatre aware. They were advised by me to obtain written authority from Pale to conduct their inspection and to obtain the IFOR line to take as to how far to press the issue. This was never satisfactorily achieved.

Initially the radar inspection team's visit to the Kosmos Factory on 5 February went well. The Kosmos director, his team and LOs from 1 Corps and the Air Force were extremely helpful for the preparatory visits.

Major General Short USAF arrived on 7 February, by Jolly Green Giant helicopter, which as it landed created so much downdraft that it destroyed Romeo Troop's antennas, rendering the troop non-operational. At the factory he was met by Colonel Radivojsa (director), Colonel Tomic (technical director), Colonel Cetkovich, (technical advisor) and a general (name unknown) who said, 'I am the head of the Air Force and I take my orders from General Mladić, not IFOR'. The inspection team had a confrontation with the VRS general and were refused access to the radars. Two reasons were given as to why they were refused:

(1) The inspection team had permission from Pale to visit the Kosmos Factory but not permission to turn the radars on for inspection.

(2) They stated that once their general (Djukic) is released then they will comply.

There was a heated exchange of views and General Short then left.

On 13 February, Captain Appleby was informed by Division that other EW systems had picked up radar emissions from the Kosmos Factory and that she was to go there, demand access and demand it be turned off. On my advice and on referring it to Brigade, the commander ordered that a letter be drafted and handed in at the front gate to let them know that we know the radar was on. We were not to request access and risk a refusal. Captain Appleby and I delivered the letter; however, on arrival at 1800 hrs, there appeared to be very little life around the Factory.

On 19 February Captain Appleby was again instructed by Division at 1630 hrs to try and enter the factory and to see if the radar was turned on. She was to use 'appropriate force'. What was meant by 'appropriate force' was not specified. Clearer guidance was again sought from 4 Brigade. Two Land Rovers and two Scimitars were sent. I delivered a protest to the deputy director Colonel Tomic, who was brought in from home. Colonel Tomic insisted that the equipment had not been turned on and that there had been a power failure all afternoon and that there was not enough fuel for generators. He categorically denied turning on equipment, even for basic testing purposes.

Direction on each occasion was unclear and did not seem to take account of loss of face of repeated refusals from the VRS to us. Additionally it would have been helpful to know how accurate Division's information was. On both of the most recent incidents I therefore refrained from making direct requests to access the factory.

Throughout this sequence of events, Romeo Troop had detected no evidence of any radars being used anywhere in the battlegroup area. From the outset of this saga, Chris Booth had been prepared to use force to ensure entry to the Kosmos Factory and forcibly activate or neutralise, or both, any air defence equipment there. But he considered that it should only be used as a last resort. If we did threaten to use force, we could not afford to lose face by backing down, which would significantly undermine IFOR's authority. Chris wanted to be sure that any use of force was going to have an outcome that justified the risks of a direct confrontation. He and Ian Baker asked the chain of command if the issue was sufficiently important for the battlegroup to be justified in forcibly entering the factory. After some prodding and asking of leading questions by Battlegroup HQ, Chris Booth was told that we were not to force our way into the Kosmos Factory.

Fortunately only Battlegroup HQ, a couple of LOs and Romeo Troop had been involved in the operation, thus limiting the damage that could have resulted to our own morale from all this apparent confusion of purpose. IFOR had backed down in the face of point-blank refusals to comply. This was certainly sending the wrong messages to the factions. Ian Baker christened the incident 'Mission Confusion' and the name stuck.

At the same time as Ian Baker was grappling with the Kosmos Factory, the battlegroup was dealing with VRS forces in the south of the area. The factions had all been required to declare to IFOR the locations of all their heavy weapons, tanks and artillery pieces within ten kilometres of the front line. This had not been done properly, with incomplete and inaccurate declarations being made by all three armies. The ARRC directed a surge operation to identify undisclosed heavy weapons within this area. Following ultimatums to the VRS, A and C Companies used threats of confiscation to force the VRS to withdraw undeclared tanks, artillery, heavy mortars and anti-tank guns to barracks concentration areas.

VRS cooperation with IFOR was still not good enough. So a divisional operation was launched as a 'show of force' to remind them of our considerable combat power, the battlegroup deploying the maximum number of patrols in highly visible locations. As part of this we had been allocated the entire division's force of RAF Chinook helicopters. We were already using the huge aircraft to lift the recce platoon's Scimitars as underslung loads. This astonished faction soldiers and civilians alike, all of whom freely admitted that they had never thought that 'light tanks' could be lifted by helicopter. Taking armoured vehicles or artillery by helicopter moved the weapons around the battlegroup area more quickly than by road and meant that the helicopter and its swaying cargo could be seen by a large number of people. On this occasion, the Scimitars were carried above the centre of Banja Luka, much to the general astonishment of the town's citizens.

There was friction. The RAF dropped four of the recce platoon's Scimitars at the wrong place. More worryingly, a troop of three light guns was flown in to the north of the area, ostensibly to provide artillery cover for Hungarians building a bridge at Bos Gradiška. Unfortunately, no one told the Hungarians or us that they were coming. The battlegroup only discovered the guns because a patrol saw Chinooks dropping them off – into an area we assessed as having a high threat of mines. None of the battery's observers had deployed, and the artillery troop was ignorant of our radio frequencies and locations and had no idea how they were to make contact with the Hungarians, let alone protect them.

The next day, the battlegroup was informed that the Chinook crews believed that the radars of VRS self-propelled anti-aircraft guns had illuminated them. We were given grid references but neither our records nor our patrols showed any evidence of such systems in the area of those locations. Again Romeo Troop had not detected any such activity. The battlegroup was ordered to mount an operation to provoke the radars into operation with ground forces to react. Helicopters were flown in the hope that they would also be illuminated by Serb radars and thus give us a more accurate fix. A force was deployed to holding areas with the task of seizing any radars detected. None were and a subsequent ground search proved fruitless.

Subsequently additional information trickled down Romeo Troop's chain of command. It suggested that the radar emissions that had caused all those alarms and excursions to the Kosmos Factory probably came from Hungary or Croatia! Apparently up to sixty different types of radar could have been responsible for illuminating the Chinook, although in both cases the failure of 'our' EW troop to detect any electronic emissions strongly suggested that there had never been any radar transmission from our area in the first place. These fruitless operations were not repeated.

Kulen Vakuf

Jan de Vos and Stuart Mills had been posted to new appointments. A Company's new commander was Richard Smith and Paul Kellett took over B Company. Piers Tucker handed over 127 Battery to Barry Smeaton. All three new officers were graduates of the Army Staff College and had just completed the combined arms tactics course at Warminster. I was confident that they would quickly get up to speed, though I knew that they would be glad that they were assuming command in the middle of my leave. In the event they were all well on top of their commands by the time I returned from England.

Virtually as soon as Paul Kellett assumed command, he had to detach 4 Platoon, commanded by David Livingston, to deal with a bitter territorial dispute between the Croats and Muslims in Kulen Vakuf. The town is south of Bihać, just north of the Anvil and a few kilometres away from the international border between Bosnia and Croatia. It is a small town – more likely to be regarded as a large village in England – nestling in a beautiful position in the centre of a spectacular valley, about forty kilometres' drive from the nearest IFOR location in Bosanski Petrovac. The main part of the town is situated on the south side of the river Una and is connected to the north bank by a single road bridge

Before the war the population of Kulen Vakuf was ninety per cent Muslim and ten per cent Serb; no Croats lived there. At the start of the war it fell into Serb hands, but it was 'liberated' from Serb control in the 1995 Federation offensive, though who actually liberated the town was a subject of political dispute between Croats and Muslims. The Croatian Army (HV) occupied the town and subsequently passed control over to the Bosnian Croat Army (HVO) some time after the Dayton Agreement.

A ninety-nine per cent Muslim civil population was co-existing with a company-sized HVO contingent occupying the town. Before IFOR arrived, the HVO was reported to be harassing the local population, restricting freedom of movement and damaging and looting property – all actions contrary to the peace agreement.

In February the Muslim authorities in Bihać became very anxious about this situation and threatened to resolve the problem themselves by taking armed action to forcibly evict the HVO from Kulen Vakuf. At this stage this small town was only one element of a much wider intra-Federation dispute, other flashpoints between Muslims and Croats being Mostar, Sarajevo and Bugojno. Violence in Kulen Vakuf would have probably sparked off a major crisis across the other simmering Federation flashpoints.

Intelligence was received that, after a rise in incidents in Kulen Vakuf, 5 Corps ABiH intended to send an armoured column based on their tank battalion into the town to forcibly evict the HVO. COMARRC deemed that this action would have serious ramifications for the peace process. Four Platoon was attached to A Squadron QRH, joining the squadron as it deployed into blocking positions on the road from Bihać to Kulen Vakuf, in order to prevent the ABiH gaining access to Kulen Vakuf. The ABiH commander, the aggressive General Dudakovic, drove through the blocking positions in a civilian car. He decided not to challenge the force.

Four Platoon were then tasked to move into Kulen Vakuf to provide overarching military security in the town and provide a reassuring presence for the local population. Their mission was 'to provide military security to Kulen Vakuf in order to reassure the local population and monitor the situation'.

The platoon of twenty men and four Warriors was commanded by David Livingston. It occupied a house on the north side of the river. This was not the ideal location. They were in the smaller part of the town. The larger part lay across the River Una, but the Bosnian Serbs had attempted to blow up the town's only bridge. They had demolished the roadway, but the locals had repaired the damaged span with timber. The improvised repairs were strong enough to take pedestrians, carts, cars and Land Rovers but were not strong enough to support armoured vehicles. The Warriors could not cross the bridge to establish a patrol base in the town itself and there were no other routes across the river without going through Croatia, which was politically unacceptable. The platoon therefore could only patrol the town by foot.

Communications were a big problem. A combination of ground, distance and resources prevented the platoon having radio communications with A Squadron. Instead they were given a Canadian insecure satellite telephone which proved to be unreliable – it was unable to establish a connection for at least a third of the time. When it worked, the link went straight back to the QRH Battlegroup HQ and not to A Squadron.

Undaunted, the platoon set to work. Their previous Northern Ireland experience proved invaluable. They immediately began very high-profile foot patrols into the town with a quick reaction force in the platoon base house. They set out to reassure the local civilian population, who were very pleased to see them.The patrols, consisting of four or five men, aimed to deter the HVO from harassing the local population, restricting their movement or looting property. Most of the patrols were overt – highly visible groups of soldiers wearing body armour and helmets and armed to the teeth. Others were covert, operating by night. One of these spotted HVO troops beating up a Muslim civilian. The patrol fired a flare, surprising the HVO, who fled. This deterred further beatings. The platoon's patrols had an immediate calming effect and rapidly earned the gratitude and confidence of the local population.

David also began negotiations with the faction commanders. Within twenty-four hours of arrival he had chaired a meeting between the Bosnian police and HVO officers. He began liaison with more senior commanders on both sides: the ABiH chief of police and the HVO commander from 1 Guards Brigade HVO. He convened and chaired weekly meetings between the two. These meetings allowed problems to be discussed under IFOR mediation rather than being solved by violence. He made it absolutely clear from the start that the problem in Kulen Vakuf was a federation government issue and could not be solved by local forces. The problem was indeed being discussed at the highest level: SACEUR, COMIFOR, COMARRC and the respective heads of government in the Federation were talking frequently on the subject.

A rumour evolved from these discussions that an agreement had been reached and that the HVO would hand control of the town back to the ABiH. The Muslims deployed fifty paramilitary 'special policemen' to Kulen Vakuf with orders to reoccupy the town. But the HVO had received no orders to relinquish control and stated that they had no intentions of leaving. On the evening of 9 February David learned that the situation was deteriorating and he deployed the platoon to positions around the town to be ready to deal with any eventuality. He then began frantic shuttle diplomacy between the two sides, who were now gearing up to fight each other for the town. Both sides insisted that they had clear orders and that they intended to carry them out to the last. David recounts what happened next:

Realising that the situation was becoming desperate I deployed my Warrior to the north end of the bridge, thereby blocking ABiH access to the town. The HVO meanwhile was deploying into battle positions in the town and was ready to repel the ABiH if they attempted to cross the bridge. Both sides were at this stage facing each other across fifty metres of water waiting for 'kick off'! I tried to reason with them, saying that negotiation was surely better then the inevitable bloodshed that was about to take place; however, they all seemed unfazed by the situation. One soldier explained, 'We have had four years of war, we are used to killing, we are used to seeing our friends killed – you should get out of the way.'

I had been sending constant reports to the QRH commanding officer, Lieutenant Colonel Nigel Beer, who decided to deploy by helicopter to Kulen Vakuf. By constant liaison and aggressive posturing of my troops I made it clear that IFOR would not allow fighting to take place. We were able to contain the situation until the CO arrived and, using his 'extraordinary powers' as the IFOR area commander, ordered the two opposing factions to withdraw from their fire positions and summoned their respective higher commanders to a meeting chaired by him. He laid down a series of conditions that satisfied the immediate minimum requirements of both sides and allowed them to withdraw their troops from the confrontation without losing face. A highly volatile situation was therefore defused.

The platoon continued to patrol the town after this event to ensure that all the CO's conditions subsequently endorsed by COMIFOR were adhered to.

David's account is self-effacing. He had intervened to prevent immediate conflict, negotiating between the two parties to buy time. At the climax of the incident he and four soldiers moved to the centre of the bridge to negotiate with the faction commanders. At the same time, extremely tense and trigger-happy faction soldiers and paramilitary police lined the bridge and both sides of the river, ABiH to the north and HVO to the south. The situation was very tense and David's party was in an extremely exposed position. Had one of the factions opened fire, the other side would have fired back. A misread action or a breakdown in negotiations could easily have started a gun battle, with David and his party being caught in any crossfire. This display of nerve earned him great respect. Subsequently the two sides looked to David to mediate and solve disputes.

Esla Day

While I had been away, the battalion and B Squadron had also found time to celebrate Esla Day, a tradition originating from the Peninsular War and now shared between two regiments, ourselves and the Light Dragoons. In May 1813 the Hussars Brigade had helped the 51st Foot (later the Kings Own Yorkshire Light Infantry – one of our forefather regiments) across the River Esla while advancing on Salamanca. The crossing was attempted at a ford but the swollen, fast-flowing river made it almost impassable. Soldiers survived by holding onto the stirrups and tails of the cavalry horses, and many lives were saved as result of the Hussars' assistance.

The idea to commemorate the event came some years later, when one of the two ensigns who had been saved discussed his ordeal with a visiting Hussar officer. It was agreed that the commemoration should take place on 14 February and consist of an all-ranks sporting challenge. The battalion and the Hussars (now the Light Dragoons) commemorate the occasion whenever they are in the same theatre – even so, 2 LI has not held the trophy, an oil painting of the event, since 1960!

The sports day was organised by Captain Guy Avery and Serjeant Pringle, our attached Army Physical Training Corps instructor. It is worth quoting Guy's account of the day:

> We selected football, volleyball, table tennis, darts, pool, a relay race, an obstacle course and finally a tug-of-war. The Dragoons did manage to exert some influence over the selection by suggesting the relay race should consist of cross-country skiing. We felt we had the upper hand especially as we were only competing against a squadron-size group.
>
> The weather on 14 February was very good – so good that some of the snow started to melt. This provided us with an excuse to cancel the skiing relay, as we had discovered the Dragoons had a number of Army skiers. However, we were eventually persuaded that the snow was suitable and the event went ahead as planned. The Light Dragoons comprehensively won the challenge by six events to two. The day was conducted in the intended spirit providing an enjoyable break for all those involved.

A Close Encounter

In December we had been told that dealing with the emotive issue of war crimes and war criminals was not IFOR's business. If we came across an indicated war criminal, such as General Mladić or Radovan Karadžić, we were to arrest them, but IFOR was not going to set out to hunt down wanted individuals. The example of the ill-fated US attempts in 1993 to capture the Somali warlord General Aideed was often cited as a road that IFOR travelled down only at its peril. All the factions had attempted to draw IFOR into investigating sites of atrocities allegedly committed by the other parties. We studiously resisted, telling them all this was the business of the war crimes tribunal, even though many of us found it quite a moral challenge to so do.

After arriving in Banja Luka, Brigadier Dannatt and I discussed the issue again. There was to be no attempt to deliberately hunt down war criminals, but we could not ignore one who might blunder into us. In that case he should be arrested, provided there was a high probability of success and a minimal risk of casualties to innocent bystanders. Brigadier Dannatt summarised our discussions: 'Ben, there is to be a high probability of success, and no shoot-out at the OK Corral in the middle of Banja Luka. It would be medals or court martial.' We briefed all ranks on this.

A couple of days after my leave, we were tasked to provide 'limited protection' for the Civil High Representative, Carl Bildt, and a party of Bosnian reporters who would be accompanying him to a meeting the next day in Banja Luka. The requirement had been stated to the battalion at extremely short notice, for which Brigade apologised profusely, but a British major from Carl Bildt's staff would arrive shortly and he would make the task clearer. As the main effort of the task seemed to be handling the press, Captain Steve Noble was 'volunteered' for the job.

At the evening meeting Steve Noble introduced the British cavalry officer from Bildt's staff. He had arrived in a UN Range Rover wearing civilian clothes: an immaculately tailored brown tweed suit, silk shirt, silver cufflinks, regimental tie and highly polished brown leather shoes – 'hand made, sir!' as someone incredulously observed. This outfit, together with his immaculate manners, languid air and unfailing courtesy made it appear as if he had somehow been instantaneously transported from a point to point meeting in Wiltshire to Banja Luka. His dress, so normal in a cavalry regiment's Officers' Mess, appeared incongruous in the battlegroup where everyone, including myself, was wearing dirty, dusty or oily combat clothing.

Finding it difficult not to raise my eyebrows, I ushered him into my cramped and noisy office. Over instant coffee in plastic mugs, he told us that Bildt would arrive in a French helicopter after breakfast, followed by a British Chinook helicopter containing about thirty Muslim and Croat journalists from Sarajevo. Bildt's party would use their own vehicles, which had already arrived, and the Republika Srpska authorities would provide a bus for the journalists. What was needed was for us to provide close protection of a few Land Rovers and a section of soldiers. The Srpska police would provide security for the whole time the party was in Banja Luka. Could we please allow the police into the camp and assemble the whole party so that it could travel to and from the meeting together?

Steve was confident that we could do what was required. The squad of soldiers would be assembled from Battalion HQ. The rest of the battlegroup was at full stretch and we had plenty of people who could do with a day out in Banja Luka. The operation seemed simple enough and two Land Rovers, one of which was to be armoured, were tasked.

The next morning, Steve Noble has his small force assembled next to our helicopter landing site, along with a dilapidated bus, half a dozen dusty civil police cars and couple of suspiciously clean sparkling black Mercedes saloons. Leaning against these two gleaming cars are half a dozen well-dressed men with hand-held walkie-talkie radios and a female interpreter in designer microskirt and distractingly tight lambswool sweater. Steve tells me that the men are the Republika Srpska plain-clothes security police. 'They have been checked out by Bildt's people and are legit', he reassures me. 'They seem all right to me – go and have a chat with them, they don't bite.'

I do so. They are affable and despite the presence of an interpreter, speak good English. 'Trust us, Procovnik, there will be no problems', they insist.

Bildt duly arrives in a French Puma helicopter and after a few pleasantries disappears into Banja Luka. Waiting for the Chinook, I talk to one of his aides. Who, I ask him are the journalists on the aircraft? 'I don't know', he replies, 'the prime ministers were allowed to nominate whoever they wanted'.

'What prime ministers?' I ask.

'Oh, the prime ministers of Bosnia, the Federation and Herceg-Bosna. You hadn't forgotten that they're the principal members of the Joint Interim Commission?' he explains.

I am dumbfounded. I recall that there is some kind of civil equivalent of the Joint Military Commission which is chaired by Bildt, but about which I have heard nothing more. Why has the cavalry major not told us that this was what was happening? Has he wrongly assumed that we knew what he knew? Had we failed to question him closely enough? We could be heading for a serious cock-up, with a high probability that it was caused by someone making an unjustified assumption. As these thoughts flash through my head, I start to get angry, but as my blood pressure rises, I realise that Steve Noble has to be told about the changed situation. I dash across to warn him, noticing the distinctive silhouette of a Chinook helicopter about a mile away beginning its final approach.

Steve takes up the story:

> I was told that the second helicopter did not hold press but in fact held two prime ministers, three ministers of state and various hangers-on from the Bosnian government and the Federation government.
>
> The situation had changed.
>
> The Chinook landed and thirty people got off and wandered across the landing site. An Englishman from the Bildt office pointed out the Bosnian prime minister. I went over to brief him and tell him what was going to happen. I explained that the whole party were going to get on the thirty-seater bus and drive into town escorted by the Land Rovers and soldiers as directed by Bildt's office. The prime minister told me, in no uncertain terms, that I had not thought through the security enough: two Land Rovers and six people were not enough security, it was not good enough and what was I going to do about it?
>
> I quickly explained that I could take him and three others in the armoured Land Rover. A couple of soldiers would get on the bus with everybody else. This he accepted and off we went into town. Thoughts of the French with deputy presidents and assassinations crossed my mind!

Steve is thinking of the incident at Sarajevo airport in 1992, where the Bosnian deputy prime minister travelling in a French UN armoured vehicle was assassinated during an altercation at a Bosnian Serb checkpoint outside Sarajevo airport. We had seen film of these events and I had read a detailed account of it in General Lewis Mackenzie's book. I am thinking the same thoughts as Steve takes his unusual convoy out of the Metal Factory. I suddenly realise I am holding a folded sheet of paper. With a vague recollection that it was thrust into my hand by one of Bildt's people, I unfold the list of those attending the meeting. They include not only Muratović, the Bosnian prime minister, but also the prime minister and three other ministers of the Federation Government, with the prime minister and two other ministers of Republika Srpska awaiting them in the town.

My command vehicles are already waiting to leave camp. I want to move to the site of the meeting as soon as possible. I am uneasy about the operation, which is not what we had planned. Steve and I could be so busy reacting to the changed situation that we might well not think of the bigger picture. I quickly brief Battlegroup HQ. We consider how we might generate extra forces should they be required. I leave the camp, wondering what else we should do. As the Land Rover turns onto the main road, a call from Steve comes over the radio

'Radovan Karadžić is in our area, send reinforcement as soon as possible.'

I try to call Steve, but the battlegroup command net, which has been difficult all morning, chooses this moment to stop working. I can neither talk to Steve nor reach Battlegroup HQ two hundred metres away. Since I am closer to the latter, I dash back to the operations room. They have heard Steve's message, and, yes, radio communications with the site of the meeting are very difficult, if not practically impossible. We quickly bounce some options around and I order that additional infantry, armoured Land Rovers and light armoured vehicles be sent to the site as soon as possible. I then drive as quickly as I can to the centre of Banja Luka – a frustratingly slow journey; it seems as if every horse and cart in Republika Srpska has chosen to travel on the same route as us. As I fume at this delay, the command net comes back up, although transmissions from the town centre are still of extremely poor quality.

Steve takes up the story from the successful delivery of Carl Bildt to the government buildings in the centre of Banja Luka.

Having dropped Carl Bildt and all the others off at the site meeting I remained outside and decided that the security profile should be increased immediately. Using the battalion net I requested an extra platoon of infantry, Spartan light armoured vehicles and another armoured Land Rover.

The net was intermittent and I eventually got the message through after a few attempts. Town was much busier than usual. I put the handset down with a slight sigh of relief and turned away from the Land Rover to see a corporal walking quickly towards me, pointing behind me.

'Sir, I've just seen Radovan Karadžić!' he said, and sure enough there he was. The situation had changed.

Karadžić, though President of Republika Srpska, as an indicted war criminal was not invited to the meeting. A few days earlier there had been a great deal of publicity because IFOR troops had not noticed Karadžić passing through an IFOR checkpoint. As a result the brigade commander had issued guidelines that indicted war criminals should be arrested if encountered, but only if the situation allowed.

Karadžić began to prowl around us, appearing first to our east and moving round, probing in and out like a tom cat marking its territory. I reported this on the net only to have the end of my message interrupted and cut off by my radio picking up a phone call from the telephone exchange over the road.

By now, radio communications have again failed. While Steve directs his small force of four vehicles and twelve men to do their best to look bigger than they are, he assesses his options:

Question: Do I arrest him?

Answer: looking around me, I began to realise that a great many of the extra people in town seemed to be wearing heavy jackets, walking around in twos and threes, carrying hand-held radios and what may be concealed weapons. Karadžić himself only had three people with him but were these people providing his security? If I went for him, pistols would be drawn from everywhere and, with all the civilians around, bystanders were sure to get shot. What would happen to the Federation members of the meeting as well as Carl Bildt if I took Karadžić? Would they become hostages?

Question: What if he tries to gatecrash the meeting?

Answer: Then I would have to stop him, and take the consequences.

Question: What if he tries to embarrass IFOR by staging a photo-opportunity with our troops in the background?

Answer: Nothing much I could do about that apart from keeping the IFOR profile confined to the immediate area of the meeting building.

My best bet was to do nothing immediately and hope that reinforcements turned up soon.

It was interesting to note that Bosnian Serb plain-clothes police were leaning out of the window where the meeting was happening. At one stage a plain-clothes policeman on the ground tapped a uniformed policeman on the arm, pointed to where we had just seen Karadžić and then pointed to another place. Sure enough, ten seconds later Karadžić appeared there. I began to have the feeling that things were being orchestrated around me.

Finally the reinforcements turned up and I was able to post men and vehicles on the corners, thus increasing the security profile. I was told that a Warrior platoon quick reaction force had forward deployed to the Light Dragoons base and was on immediate notice to move, a few minutes away.

We didn't see Karadžić after the reinforcements had arrived. The sight of more troops and armoured vehicles clearly had some effect.

By the time I arrive, Steve clearly has approaches to the Government buildings well blocked off with Spartans and armoured Land Rovers. He briefs me on the situation, his assessment and his plans. He clearly has the incident well in hand. I need to size up the situation for myself. I talk to the members of his small force of a dozen troops and then have time to take in the scene.

By now A Company and B Squadron are concentrated at their bases at immediate notice to move. I order A Company to move a Warrior platoon to B Squadron base, where B Squadron are to use it and all other uncommitted elements of the squadron to form a battlegroup reserve. A and Support Companies are to deploy as many armoured vehicles as they can on the route back from the government buildings to the Metal Factory. This is to deter anyone contemplating interfering with our withdrawal from the government buildings.

The meeting is being held in the large and impressive government building on the north side of Banja Luka's central square. At the entrance to the building are the besuited characters in plain clothes who had appeared earlier at the Metal Factory. Around the building are forty or fifty uniformed police in their distinctive blue camouflage overalls – not only at the entrance to the building, but on all the street corners. I notice it is an unusually balmy day as, for the first time since our final exercise in October, I begin to sweat under my body armour. The streets are very crowded with civilians, most of who appear to be enjoying the sunshine.

As soon as extra Scimitars and Spartans arrive and Steve has reconfigured his forces, I take Mr Matthews and two of the burliest soldiers from the security detail for a walk down a few of the side streets leading to the government buildings. Most of the civilians seem perfectly relaxed. What 'stands out like a dog's bollocks', as one of my imposing escorts puts it, is the presence of a large number of men wearing suspiciously thick coats or bulky jackets, all with sunglasses, carrying hand-held walkie-talkie radios or wearing radio earpieces. Many of them have large pistol-shaped bulges under their jackets and even, in a few cases, in their trouser pockets. They are making a conscious effort to avoid eye contact with us. Every street we walk down has at least one of these characters every twenty or thirty metres, with at least two on every street corner.

Mr Matthews and I cannot help grinning at each other, for these men appear to be stereotypes from a very cheap B movie. Clearly they are plain-clothes security men of some type. Are they 'genuine' plain-clothes policemen, contributing to the Banja Luka police's efforts to protect the meeting? Or are they secret police, bodyguards or even gangsters working for Karadžić? We are never to find out.

I return to Steve's cordon. The meeting closes and we make a big fuss of Prime Minister Muratović. He still insists on travelling in the back of a Land Rover. He misses the impressive sight of A Company, not only with Warriors but also reinforced by Scimitars and 432s, 'holding down' every road junction on the three-mile journey back to the Metal Factory. There are probably a dozen armoured vehicles lining every mile of the road, with turrets manned, and dismounted soldiers providing extra security and where necessary stopping traffic to allow us a smooth run back. I find the sight impressive and imagine that the Federation journalists and politicians will too.

At the Metal Factory soldiers are on alert at the perimeter of the compound and more are providing close protection for the Chinook helicopter, which already has its rotors turning. We usher the Federation party inside and breathe a collective sigh of relief as the aircraft rises suspended on a pillow of tearing gale-force winds, dips its nose and flies forward, bound for Sarajevo.

The operation is not over, for Carl Bildt is staying the night in the Hotel Bosna in the town centre. His staff ask us to provide security, a legitimate enough request but fraught with potential problems. Should Karadžić still be in Banja Luka, he could attempt to confront Bildt. If we put a guard on the hotel, we might deter Karadžić from attempting such a stunt, but alternatively he might attempt to flaunt himself to our troops in order to provoke an arrest attempt, which could in itself lead to a shoot-out in the centre of Banja Luka.

Having come within an inch of IFOR and Bildt being outmanoeuvred in the town centre, we do not wish to walk into a similar situation. We quickly consider the key factors and the courses open to us. Although a tactical problem, getting this wrong could have operational, strategic and political implications and I need to brief Brigadier Dannatt and let him know my proposed course of action before I commit troops to protect Bildt. We cannot afford to divulge our intentions to Karadžić or his henchmen, so the message must be passed over secure communications.

The problem is that we cannot talk securely with Brigade HQ. Their secure command net is not working, and the Ptarmigan 'node' in our area has gone down, denying us the secure telephone. The INMARSAT satellite telephone is unsecure and Brigade HQ does not use our KL43 secure data entry devices.

I use the artillery BATES fire control computer. Although designed to automate the passage of firing data and orders on the gunner net, the computers can pass 'free text messages' to each other. The trouble is that these take a long time to compose and are limited to a short paragraph in length. Steve Noble and I write two short messages which Barry Smeaton, the new battery commander, enters into the system. The message is passed and acknowledged. I speak to the brigade chief of staff on the insecure satellite phone, explaining that the contents of the message are an issue I want to clear with Brigade, since I have time before I commit troops.

During the afternoon Bildt is lunching with his Bosnian Serb hosts; we have until dark to decide whether to commit troops to his security and if so how to do it. Ptarmigan and the brigade command net gradually come back on line and there is considerable discussion of the advantages and disadvantages of various courses of action. It is eventually decided that Bildt should not be provided with IFOR close protection, but that 2 LI is to provide a reaction force to get him out of trouble if necessary. We will conduct mobile patrols around the Hotel Bosna throughout the night in order to deter any attempt by Karadžić or his cronies to disrupt Bildt's evening.

I order B Squadron, reinforced with a platoon, to conduct these tasks. The patrols are to be conducted by armoured Land Rovers. Their small size and comparatively low engine noise make them ideal for mobile patrols in the narrow side streets of the town centre, striking a balance between protection and discretion.

I spend some time working out clear and unambiguous orders for these patrols. If Karadžić should appear again, they must be clear that their first priority is the safety of Bildt. They might have an opportunity to arrest Karadžić, but they should only do so if there is a high probability of success and a low risk of civilian casualties.

I go to the Wood Factory to discuss the operation and these parameters with B Squadron and the platoon commander, who will be conducting the patrolling. He is Lieutenant Phil Fox, a TA officer. Until mid-afternoon his platoon was operating from a platoon house near Skender Vakuf, but they have redeployed at short notice back to Banja Luka. Phil has risen to the challenge of a completely changed situation and satisfies me that he has a good understanding of the operation.

That night I visit the small force on patrol in the centre of Banja Luka. The RSM and I take our Land Rovers around the area of the afternoon's confrontation. We park the vehicles and retrace our steps. Very few people are on the streets and all is quiet and appears normal. I return to the Metal Factory and, for the only time in the tour, sleep with my boots on – to be able to react quicker to any emergency.

The night is quiet and there are no incidents. The next morning Bildt and his party come to the Metal Factory to board a helicopter to return to Sarajevo. While waiting for the French Puma to arrive, Steve Noble and I discuss the previous day's events with Bildt and his staff. We learn that during the morning's meeting the Republika Srpska interior minister constantly left his seat to go to the window overlooking the front of the building, and also spent a long time conversing in hushed tones on a walkie-talkie. Bildt has no doubt that this man was well aware of Karadžić's appearance, and had been in communication with his henchmen. He is delighted with the way we handled the Karadžić incident and our night-time patrols around the hotel.

As soon as the French helicopter clatters away, I gather the Battlegroup HQ team to mull over the incident. I begin by congratulating Steve Noble. I have no doubt that the thwarting of the attempted intrusion by Karadžić was a decisive moment. Neither IFOR's mandate nor our rules of engagement permit the active hunting down of persons indicted for war crimes. Hard as this position is to defend against the unsympathetic questions of the media, it enhances the perceived impartiality of the force, and enables IFOR to concentrate on its main mission. A heavy-handed attempt to capture Karadžić would have run the risk of forfeiting Bosnian Serb strategic consent and thus causing incalculable damage to the mission.

In Banja Luka that day, the chances of successfully capturing Karadžić were extremely low. Steve correctly assessed the situation and, because of the difficulty with communications, acted independently. A less clear-thinking or resolute person might have taken an inappropriate course of action, leading to failure of the mission, loss of military and civilian lives and the taking of hostages. This could well have undermined the political agreement of the factions that underpinned the Dayton peace agreement, with who knows what consequences.

We initially wrong-footed ourselves, fulfilling the tasks given to us by the charmingly vague cavalry major without knowing the wider context. We should have teased out the background to the operation and then used mission analysis to derive a mission and an estimate to produce a plan, which we should have carried out as we judged necessary. We had assumed that the cavalry major was telling us everything we needed to know, and so had not planned the security operation thoroughly. So often on Mount Igman I had found fault with junior commanders for not using mission analysis. Now I have overseen an operation where Battlegroup HQ and I have fallen into the same trap. I am chastened.

We also need to rethink our policy on reserves. Although it is a well-founded military principle always to have a reserve, doctrine does not insist on it. Indeed, when forces are insufficient it is quite permissible to decide to go without one. We have done this since we left Mount Igman. As the battlegroup is so widely spread, a central reserve might take two or three hours to reach the area where it is needed. In addition, holding it at high readiness would effectively prevent it carrying out routine operations, at a time when we needed the maximum forces out on patrol. I had directed that the companies and the squadron have their own reserves of two Warriors or Scimitars at half an hour's notice to move, which Battlegroup HQ could task if necessary. This worked well for the response to the shooting at WHITE FANG and I have not re-examined the issue since we moved to Banja Luka. This I now recognise to be a mistake, for the situation has changed and our area is less far-flung than it was in January.

In the battlegroup we have a wide mix of vehicles. Warrior impresses the factions with its size, weight, and noise. Its Chobham armour makes it our best-protected vehicle. Scimitar and Spartan can reach places inaccessible to Warrior. Scimitar, Spartan and Land Rovers are useful in towns where their reduced size and noise can be more appropriate. We are already task organising at every level of command: for example, armoured infantry companies and B Squadron routinely exchange platoons and troops.

I decide to extend this principle to a new battlegroup reserve, located at the Metal Factory. It will be based on an armoured infantry platoon, using two of its Warriors, giving it capacity, protection, firepower and an imposing presence. To allow it to travel snow-covered roads, it will have a Scimitar, a Spartan and two Land Rovers, one armoured. These will also allow it to conduct operations in narrow constricted town streets, or low-profile discreet security operations. The whole force will always be on half an hour's notice to move, and can be brought to higher readiness if required. At least once a day we will stage a practice call out, to make sure it is as ready as it should be. A platoon or troop commander will lead it.

We are not to know it yet, but this little force is to prove invaluable in responding to incidents for the rest of the tour.

As we analyse the incident, we are reminded that the civil agencies do not work in the same way as we do. They have a completely different *modus operandi* to our unified, hierarchical chain of command. They will not necessarily state their requirement clearly and their communications and internal and external passage of information may be poor. We are required to cooperate with and support all kinds of agencies and it is taking patience, flexibility and very clear thinking to do so. Sometimes we have to provide co-ordination and underpinning to civil organisations operating in a way that we would regard as incredibly inefficient. If this is the price of peace implementation, we must swallow our pride and carry on.

A Terrible Accident

The next day, 28 February, I was returning from visiting Echelon at Mrkonjić Grad to Banja Luka. I had intended to visit C Company in their new base at Krupa. Suddenly Chris Booth spoke on the battalion command net:

'Hello Zero Alpha, Two Two Bravo speaking. You need to return to this location as soon as possible.'

Chris would not have sent such a message unless he had a subject he needed to discuss with me that was so confidential he could not use the brigade secure net. As we drove through the darkness to Banja Luka, I wondered if we had some really serious problem. We did.

Chris briefed me that there had been a shooting inside 4 Platoon's base in Kulen Vakuf and that Private Fox had been killed. The reports were that he had been killed with his own weapon.

I flew by helicopter to Kulen Vakuf. Arriving, we circled over the village. Another Lynx had already brought a doctor to the town; he was now leaving, accompanying Fox's body. It was a bright night and I could make out the dark sides of a huge bowl-shaped valley, the glint of a river and the lighter shapes of the buildings of the town. As the doctor's helicopter rose we began to slip into the valley. All was noise and vibration as I got out, but the aircraft clattered off, leaving me in a meadow with David Livingston and the crystal sound of running water.

Four Platoon's house was, like so many we had occupied, stripped of everything apart from floorboards, with the only furniture being the soldiers' camp beds and a few chairs. David briefed me that Fox's team were off duty in one of the rooms. The other soldiers had vaguely noticed him 'doing something with his weapon', but as they were relaxing, writing letters and listening to personal stereos they had not paid much attention until the shot went off.

The platoon were shocked and I spoke to all those I could. A terrible event had just occurred and they would feel pretty cut up about it – but the best thing to do was to build on their excellent work in Kulen Vakuf. Paul Kellett arrived. I knew that he would do everything to reassure the platoon and after a few private words with David Livingston, I flew back to Banja Luka, bitterly regretting that these were the circumstances under which I was visiting Kulen Vakuf for the first time.

Opening an Airfield

The next day we opened Banja Luka airfield. The civil airport had been closed since the imposition of the NATO no-fly zone three years earlier and the military airbase on the other side of the runway appeared similarly dormant. We wanted to fly troops and freight direct into north-west Bosnia, instead of Split, a day's travel by road to our south. The RAF liaison officer at Divisional HQ had arranged the necessary details with the civil and military airport authorities and the battlegroup was to provide the necessary security.

I decided that this should be done as a battlegroup operation. B Squadron, in whose area the airport lay, provided close protection around the perimeter of the installation. A Warrior platoon took care of security around the terminal buildings and control tower. Further out the mortar platoon were deployed in fire positions and the recce platoon patrolled underneath the flight path of the incoming RAF Hercules cargo aircraft. Tanks and Warriors were picketing critical points on the approach roads to the airport. The operation would be co-ordinated by Battlegroup Forward HQ who would include the mortar platoon and battery command posts – all operating from armoured vehicles set up in the terminal car park. Captain Jane Appleby also deployed a mobile command post for her electronic warfare troop. Division ordered an aviation squadron of missile firing Lynx helicopters to patrol around the airfield.

The forces deployed, much to the bemusement of the Bosnian Serb air force and civilian personnel lounging around the terminal building. Despite their indifference, it did no harm to show the VRS, their air force and the civil population that we could conduct a battlegroup-level operation whenever and wherever we wanted, quickly concentrating considerable force. I knew that both the VRS and the ABiH were still monitoring our communications – indeed some of their officers had told me that they did. I wanted the faction's signals intelligence people to pick up the unmistakable electronic signature of Battlegroup HQ and the mortar and artillery fire control nets.

The battlegroup's part in the security operation went without a hitch. The aviation squadron was another matter. Although we were told that they were operating 'under divisional control', they were not answering calls on any radio net. Since they had made no effort to find out about our tactical plan or to send any representative to any of our HQs, there was no way we could co-ordinate any of our operations with theirs. Had any threat to the operation actually materialised, this could have been a fatal weakness.

A helicopter brought in the brigade commander, divisional commander and Lieutenant General Pike, the deputy joint commander. A crowd of local journalists converged on the imposing figure of General Jackson while I briefed General Pike and introduced him to the soldiers. The Hercules arrived and disgorged a Spartan armoured vehicle – replacement for one of those destroyed by mines. It was hooked up underneath a Chinook helicopter and flown south to the Light Dragoons. The generals departed in the Hercules and I collapsed our security cordon and returned to the Metal Factory.

It was five days since I had returned from England and for the first time in that period there were neither battalion operations nor incidents. I walked round the Factory for an hour talking to soldiers then went back to my room. I was exhausted. The pressure of operations since I returned from leave had been intense. Private Fox's death had been a depressing shock – one I suppressed at the time, but one that now caught up with me.

But this was not the first time that I had to deal with death or serious injury amongst my subordinates or comrades. In the twenty years of my Army career I had known people who had been killed or seriously injured in training or in road traffic accidents. I had been hardened by my first Northern Ireland tour when two fellow platoon commanders were badly wounded by the IRA, one shot through the neck and the other having his legs removed below the knee in a bomb attack. Both lived and served on in the Army. My two subsequent tours had both seen deaths of soldiers, policemen and terrorists.

I can never forget the shock of hearing the incidents being described on the radio net as they happened – in one case the officer who was shot calmly and unemotionally reported the fact over the air, before he lapsed into unconsciousness. The literally sinking feeling in pit of my stomach and weakness in my legs was one that I hated every time it happened – although with experience it was easier to manage. But always within a few seconds anger would quickly start to rise quickly followed by my training clicking in and the focus would be the efforts to capture those responsible.

After the initial adrenalin surge and the all-consuming reaction born of both anger and training would come grief. I had, in my time seen tough and experienced officers with tears in their eyes; I have also had some myself. But the concept of duty, the shared ethos of both the regiment and the Army, and comradeship, were all factors that act powerfully to lift one's horizons from immediate grief – complementing it with a desire to get on with the job in hand.

My experience of incidents where casualties had resulted was that commanders at all levels tended to be buoyed up by a desire to do the best for their surviving subordinates. Commanders were, after all, trained relentlessly to lead their troops to achieve the mission and that training makes it easier for them to press on with the task in hand – even in the face of casualties.

Finally, my experience showed me that the soldiers and officers I had the privilege to command had great resilience, born of hard realistic training and long periods of shared adversity. And they all had a deep, politically incorrect and infectious sense of humour. All this would act to support my own morale.

These thoughts were in my mind as I drifted into a long, dark, dreamless sleep until the next morning.

CHAPTER THIRTEEN
'You Oughta Know'

Four Brigade were maintaining IFOR control of the Anvil, providing the only military presence between the withdrawal of the HVO at D+45 and D+90, when Republika Srpska had the right to introduce their own military forces. By now some Bosnian Serb civilians had returned to the area. Some had come in trucks and cars, but more travelled south on horse-drawn carts, loaded with families and personal possessions, the children peering out from mounds of blankets and clothing. I wondered how their parents had managed to look after them over the last six months. Many were people who had fled the Croat advance the previous September. They were lucky to be alive, and luckier still to be able to go back to their homes.

People who returned to their farms had to overcome the results of the Croats' looting, burning, arson and the abduction or slaughter of all their beasts, but they were at least able to begin scratching some kind of a living. Those who returned to the towns of Šipovo and Mrkonjić Grad were in a far more precarious position, as both towns had been extensively vandalised and looted. None of the infrastructure, services or industry was working. There was nothing to support the thousands who were moving into the towns apart from aid distributed by humanitarian relief agencies. Initially there was no overall coordination of this effort and the High Representative's organisation was conspicuous by its absence. To fill this gap and to reduce the risk of a humanitarian catastrophe, Brigade set up 'Task Force Anvil', a forum to co-ordinate the efforts of IFOR and the various relief agencies and non-governmental organisations that were operating in the Anvil.

Banja Luka was still crammed with Bosnian Serb refugees from the Krajinas and other parts of western Bosnia that remained under Federation control. We monitored the movement of civilians along the Vrbas valley road that passed C Company's base at Krupa. Brigade developed a plan to monitor and supervise the VRS move into the area of transfer. As the VRS force would have to move through Banja Luka we would provide the early warning for the rest of the brigade. The concept of operations included a strong brigade reserve comprising a tank squadron from the QRH and our A Company, with artillery forward observation officers, armoured engineers, a medical section and a psychological operations team. Their role was 'to provide a high-profile and overt presence to deter any act of non-compliance, and to be prepared to strike against any such act'.

Major Richard Smith now commanded A Company. He had come from the job of chief of staff of 24 Airmobile Brigade, spending four months of the previous year as part of UNPROFOR virtually interned in a cramped and insanitary camp at Ploce on the Croatian coast. He contrasted the frustrations and limitations of the UN with the freedom of action of IFOR. Although he took over A Company at the beginning of a more settled phase as the Dayton Agreement became more established on the ground, he and his company would soon be tested.

Alarums and Excursions

On D+88 the brigade conducts an exercise, using the battlegroup's recce squadron as the Opposing Force (OPFOR) to simulate the VRS units we expect to move into the Anvil. I take Battlegroup Forward HQ and my Warrior to Mrkonjić Grad to control our part in the operation. During the cold grey day C Squadron's patrols do their best to simulate the kind of problems that might be generated by VRS units determined to be non-cooperative or bloody-minded. As the exercise ends James Everard, the brigade chief of staff, rings me on the Ptarmigan secure telephone.

'Colonel, the exercise should end in about an hour. As soon as it ends, could you please come to Brigade HQ? We're getting reports that four or five thousand ABiH troops are refusing to withdraw from a barracks in the zone of separation in Sarajevo. There is a corps operation to assist the French in compelling compliance, using force if necessary. The British contribution to this force will be A Company 2 LI, who will be detached from the brigade reserve.'

I immediately brief Ross Gillanders and Dave Jarratt. Using Ptarmigan we call Chris Booth and Dave Wroe and have a quick brainstorming session. The battlegroup logisticians immediately go to work to produce a pack of ammunition, spare parts and medical supplies to supplement the stocks carried in the company's vehicles and begin loading the stores onto trucks.

Armed with these preparations and some questions and ideas I join in the meeting at Brigade HQ. The situation is that Tito Barracks, in the centre of Sarajevo, is now inside the Zone of Separation. Despite repeated warnings by the French, the ABiH are refusing to withdraw several thousand of their troops based there. An IFOR ultimatum that they should do so has expired, and British and American troops are to join the French division who are preparing to evict the ABiH, using force if necessary. Richard Smith will move his company to the British logistic base at Kupres, where the armoured vehicles will be mounted on low loaders and tank transporters, so as to be able to move more quickly.

All of this is immensely exciting. We know Sarajevo well and are accustomed to operating with the French. I offer the services of Battlegroup HQ and myself, but Brigadier Dannatt is reluctant to give up any more of his combat power. Disappointed but unsurprised, I concentrate on making sure that A Company wants for nothing. Since the company may have to fight, preparing it for combat will be the battlegroup's main effort over the next twenty-four hours. I give Richard Smith my Ptarmigan secure telephone to improve his ability to communicate and liaise.

Richard moves straight to Sarajevo for a reconnaissance while A Company drives to Kupres through a winding valley up to a high desolate plateau. Fresh snow has fallen over hard-packed ice. The road is narrow and twisting. Martin Bellamy, leading the company move, rates the journey as worse than the nightmare move from Mrkonjić Grad to Ćoralići two months earlier.

Meanwhile, we are still preparing for the VRS re-occupation of the Anvil. On D+90 itself two small columns of nondescript and dilapidated Bosnian Serb military vehicles move from Banja Luka, past Krupa and south into Mrkonjić Grad. By this stage the VRS are getting 'demob happy' and their chain of command is collapsing. Evidence of this is provided by the state of the VRS divisional commander and brigade commander who I find standing outside a roadside stall at ten o'clock in the morning. Both are well on the way to being drunk and do their best to get Rex Sartain and me into a similar state. There are few problems, although it becomes necessary to deny access to a couple of tanks and artillery pieces that the VRS attempt to introduce into the area without permission. As soon as the VRS brigade arrives at its destination outside Mrkonjić Grad it promptly sends most of its soldiers on two weeks' leave.

I visit A Company the next day at Kupres. Arriving by helicopter at the British logistic base I can clearly see the Warriors parked up alongside the squadron of tank transporters that will lift them, together with the additional ammunition mounted on DROPS lorries. The company is a formidable sight and is in high spirits. Not only do they take pride in having moved to Kupres so quickly, in conditions where other troops would probably have turned back, but they are also pleased to have been chosen from the whole division for this role.

In Sarajevo Richard Smith confirms that there are indeed several thousand Muslim troops refusing to leave Tito Barracks. The French HQ appears friendly, capable, well organised and deadly serious about evicting the ABiH. They are reinforced by a company of US armoured infantry equipped with Bradley, their equivalent of Warrior, and a company of Apache helicopter gunships. A company of JCOs has also flown out from the UK. As I fly away from A Company I reflect that the planned operation seems much more coherent and 'joined up' than the ill-starred Operation HORUS that had been planned by the Multinational Brigade three months earlier.

That night the ABiH begin to move out of Tito Barracks. The IFOR operation is cancelled and tank transporters bring the company back to Banja Luka, where they resume control of their area. We are disappointed that they have not had a chance to cut their teeth against the ABiH, but secretly relieved that we have not been at risk of taking any casualties.

Sustaining and Protecting the Force

The logistic elements of the battalion had quickly adapted to our NATO role. The MT platoon continued to clock up an enormous mileage delivering fuel and supplies to all our bases and outposts. The quartermasters and their small staff juggled with the necessary paperwork and records. The Ministry of Defence had directed that since Operation RESOLUTE was not a war, the full system of accounting for supplies and equipment that was used in peacetime in barracks should continue to apply in Bosnia. Our logisticians had to put in many hours manipulating the same bureaucratic procedures they had used in Paderborn, but with only a fraction of the office facilities and communications infrastructure available in Germany. Dealing with local people and businesses enlivened this grind of routine logistic staff work. Johnny Bowron later described this:

> During our training prior to deployment the G1 and G4 staffs attended the Brigade and Battlegroup Trainer and found the training both interesting and enjoyable, but thought that the incidents involving drunk and irate locals a bit over the top. How wrong we were – it would have been more realistic to double the amount of incidents and for the BBGT staff to provide more alcohol.
>
> Key to success when dealing with the locals was to converse with them in their own language initially and then revert to an interpreter. Many of the locals were very hospitable and were more than happy to agree on a deal and have a drink even at eight o'clock in the morning. It is also worth noting that many of the interpreters had in-depth local knowledge, which was extremely valuable when trying to purchase items or set up a contract. We established many contracts by asking the interpreters to find the contractors in town.

Our fleet of wheeled vehicles was posing problems. Although the fighting vehicles – the Warriors, Scimitars and FV432s – bore the brunt of our efforts to impress the factions, collection and delivery of fuel and supply was totally dependent on the trucks of the MT platoon. Our Land Rovers were being extensively used for reconnaissance and liaison, and by company commanders and myself to move quickly around our large areas. While 2 LI had brought its Warriors and Scimitars to Bosnia, the rest of the battalion's vehicles had been taken over from the Devon and Dorsets. Many of these were old and worn out, a surprisingly high proportion having been used continuously in the Balkans since 1992. Although this reduced transport and shipping bills, it meant that 2 LI had inherited a fleet of extremely worn out and tired vehicles that were on their last legs.

These were kept on the road only by dint of extremely hard work by their crews and the REME. I never ceased to wonder at the determination, adaptability, resourcefulness and sense of humour displayed by the REME craftsmen working long hours in the open air covered in oil and grease as they repaired our vehicles. But there was an increasing backlog of Land Rovers off the road and awaiting repair. The LAD had sufficient manpower to do repairs quickly, but during January, February and March the logistic system supporting us was taking an extremely long time to supply spare parts. This was exacerbated by the extraordinary variety of different types of Land Rover – all superficially similar in appearance. The battalion's fleet of forty-five Land Rovers included no fewer than fourteen different variants, all of which had different engines, brakes, tyres and spare parts.

I was told that the logistic planners in the UK had underestimated the amount of movement that the brigade would be doing and that the logistic computer system deployed to Bosnia had been unable to pass information back over the fragile and overstretched communications infrastructure. When I asked what use the logistic planners had made of the Army's considerable experience of war fighting exercises in Canada, no reply was forthcoming. The sheer geographical dispersion of British troops all over western Bosnia, the indifferent communications and the distance from the UK meant that the supply of spares would only improve slowly. Although our Land Rovers were our greatest problem, we had too many other vehicles of all types awaiting spare parts. Johnny Bowron described our efforts to keep our vehicles on the road:

> We were lucky to have company officers and SNCOs well experienced in fleet management. We attempted to husband the vehicles we had so that the REME were not swamped with minor repairs. The importance of maintenance, fault reporting and first parading became paramount and maintenance days were increasingly programmed in. All vehicles had to be properly equipped before starting on a journey, no matter how short. Snow shovels and snow chains were a necessity, not a useful extra. Chains were carried by all convoys and packets to clear routes and for self-recovery. All personnel were trained how to put on snow chains properly – if improperly fitted they were more damaging than useful.

The other way to keep vehicles on the road was to avoid damaging them in road traffic accidents. Warriors and Land Rovers had rolled off narrow icy roads and tracks and all types of vehicles had been involved in collisions with Bosnian civilian vehicles. Through some miraculous luck or divine intervention no serious casualties had resulted, although we could easily have had a dozen fatalities had the soldiers and officers concerned been less fortunate.

Many of the accidents were caused by the standard of driving of Bosnian civilians, which varied from poor to suicidal. Others were due to our drivers and commanders driving too fast on the mountainous winter roads. The average standard of British driving was far too aggressive, exacerbated by a lack of training in winter driving skills. Many of our soldiers had been taught to drive by civilian instructors and had not developed the confidence and skills they now needed. I had certainly underestimated the requirement to practise winter driving in our pre-operational preparation.

With two or three accidents a week in the battlegroup, we were making too large a contribution to the brigade average of two accidents a day. A significant proportion of the brigade's already sparse Land Rover fleet was being taken off the road as a result of accidents. This was unacceptable and unsustainable, and Brigadier Dannatt initiated a draconian crackdown on road safety. The military police mounted speed traps with radar guns and checkpoints to ensure that vehicles were fully serviced and properly equipped for winter roads. In parallel, disciplinary action was taken against drivers and vehicle commanders guilty of speeding and errors of judgement. This quickly had a salutary effect and the number of accidents was reduced by three quarters. Johnny Bowron describes how we did this:

> We had sixty-four accidents, including rolling three Warriors. Many of these were due to terrain or road conditions overcoming vehicle and/or driver capabilities. Drivers were cautioned against over-confidence: after all they had the lives of their passengers in their hands! All drivers needed to be properly trained for the vehicle they were to use in the conditions in which it was to be used, and extra training was given in theatre.
>
> We needed to get the message across that it was better to be late arriving than risk life. Better still was to plan for a much slower but safer journey. Speeding by IFOR was one of the most common complaints levelled at us by the locals. Those who sped or crashed were punished severely. We operated a two-vehicle rule. This meant that speeding was deterred and that in the event of a crash the alarm could be raised and first aid could be quickly administered. This proved crucial after the Regimental Signals Warrant Officer crashed on the way to resupply a remote rebroadcast site – if he had not been accompanied by another vehicle we could have had far more serious casualties.
>
> Careful driving helps save money and frustration but it took some time and a large number of road traffic accidents before we gave this message the priority it needed. Once we did, the message was constantly hammered home, particularly to officers: disciplining both the driver and the commander soon got the point across.

We also needed to protect ourselves against the ever-present threat of mines and unexploded ordnance. Although there had been no more British fatalities and the battlegroup had no more mine strikes, soldiers in the other NATO divisions had been killed and wounded in mine incidents, or when handling ammunition and weapons left by the factions. With each day of peace, more and more civilian casualties were caused by these impersonal dangers, especially as the winter ended and people began to use land for agriculture.

This was brought home to us by an incident at Mrkonjić Grad. One afternoon a distraught and hysterical father brought his eleven-year-old son to the front gates of Echelon's camp. The child had been badly wounded by a mine – his right arm had been sheared off below the shoulder. Lance Corporal Thompson, the Echelon medical assistant, immediately took control of this life-threatening situation, calming the father and child, stemming the blood loss and administering morphine to ease the child's pain. Thompson had not been exposed to this severe an injury before, but by remaining calm and reassuring both the child and his father he ensured that the boy survived life-threatening injuries and was stabilised for evacuation to hospital.

At Mrkonjić Grad there were two serious fires, both in the accommodation blocks of the armoured engineer squadron with whom Echelon shared the camp. The second one resulted in the death of a sapper, despite frantic attempts at rescue by both engineers and Light Infantrymen. Elsewhere, other less serious fires were caused by people trying to keep warm. Johnny Bowron describes the problem and how we tackled it.

> The soldiers became so cold in the tents that their desperation to obtain warmth became extremely dangerous. We were lucky that no one was badly injured. In each location we had a nominated NCO who constantly checked the entire location. The outposts were the most vulnerable and required the most supervision from visiting officers and the delegated NCO.

Through a combination of luck and extremely prompt action to fight the fires, we avoided any casualties.

Developing Operations

By now we had built up a picture of the social geography of our area. The effects of ethnic cleansing were easy to discern: demolished mosques and burned-out villages. Before the war the population of the Banja Luka canton had been at least five per cent Muslim. Now the homes of many Muslims had been taken over by Serb refugees and the original occupants evicted from Republika Srpska. The town's population had been reduced to perhaps one per cent Muslim.

The hills to the south of Banja Luka contained a large number of small villages, many accessible only by cart track. We could not reach all of these in our heavy Warriors, but had to use Scimitar, Land Rover, helicopter or foot. Flight Lieutenant Mark Jacklin described the way of life in these hamlets:

> Many families remain split up as sons and husbands are still away in the army. There is a distinct lack of money and the population has to rely on barter or black market dealing. Almost every household has become self-sufficient and most seem to earn their living by working on their own land, producing crops and a limited number of cattle and hens, which they sell at market. Almost all buying and selling is done in the community, or only as far as the next village. Horse and cart, bicycle and foot are the main methods of transport. Facilities are poor, with electricity connected only once or twice a week and mains water a rarity.

The balance of operations was beginning to move away from purely military operations, towards supporting civil, social and economic measures, to help promote a return to normality. This meant encouraging, educating, coaxing and, if necessary, directing the factions and the civilian population towards implementing the civil the Dayton Agreement.

We were encouraged to find that schools were reopening. Many had been used as bases by VRS troops, had lost much furniture and equipment and were in a poor state of repair. But all were well attended, with happy children and motivated teachers.

Signs of a slow return to normality were beginning to emerge. Families with all their possessions piled onto horse-drawn carts were slowly trundling long distances to return to their former homes – many of which had been devastated during the civil war. Looted and vandalised farms were being tidied up, horse and plough were tilling the land and seed was being sown by hand. In the towns local industries were trying to regenerate their plants, which had often stood idle for the past four years.

We tried to match this. We reduced our patrols by Warrior and replaced them with more foot patrols both in the towns and in the country, where they would stay out for up to three nights. We spent more time talking to local people. These operations drew heavily on the skills that we had learned in Northern Ireland.

We continued to develop operations in the city of Banja Luka, finding the urban population more literate and educated. It was important to minimise unnecessary friction with the civil community. We did our best not to be seen as an army of occupation and to remain part of the solution rather than part of the problem. To this end we refrained from close operations, such as armoured vehicle patrols in the town. We were generally successful in avoiding civil–military friction in Banja Luka.

Attitudes to IFOR varied enormously. The peasant farmers welcomed the end of the war, and all those with a chance to prosper from peace were looking forward to the economic fruits of stability. Some refugees were keen to return home, but others were happy to squat in the homes of ethnically cleansed Muslims and Croats. Many VRS officers felt that the Dayton Agreement would unravel once IFOR withdrew at the end of the year. There was no shortage of local politicians and minor officials who were keen to retain their power and privileges.

We were developing our efforts to create and sustain a climate of compliance, shaping the environment by influencing attitudes towards IFOR and the Dayton process. We did this in many ways. For example most of our battlegroup operations were transparent and open, as we had nothing to hide from the factions; little was encoded on the battlegroup insecure VHF command net and we were happy that the factions monitored the net. When serious incidents occurred, factions listening to our radio traffic would have heard the orders of our commanders.

Since we were determined to resolve any incident to our advantage those listening to our radio nets would have been left in no doubt of our intent. Conversations with ABiH and VRS officers had confirmed that this was the case. They were, they told me, clear that we had the ability to react very quickly to events. Many faction officers I spoke to considered our firepower overwhelming and had no desire to challenge our military capability.

The Message

From the outset of our IFOR operations, I had sought to explain what we were doing to the political leaders, military commanders, soldiers and civilians in our area. We knew that most able-bodied males in civilian clothes were off-duty soldiers of some kind; indeed, we had met men working on farms in villages near Kotor Varoš whom we had previously encountered in trenches near Prijedor.

We were all coming into ever-increasing contact with both civilians and the factions. We needed to make sure that a common line was taken in responding to questions about IFOR operations, the Dayton Agreement and political issues. The battlegroup produced simple *aide-mémoires* covering the practical application of Dayton and the line to take on issues that both civilians and military were likely to raise in conversation. Those were issued down to section commander level and proved invaluable.

IFOR produced a newspaper, *Herald of Peace*, explicitly designed for distribution to soldiers and civilians of all three factions. It was double-sided with the front printed in Latin script for Muslims and Croats and the back in Cyrillic for Bosnian Serb audiences. It had a lively modern appearance – particularly important when all the papers in Banja Luka were still being produced on old-fashioned manual printing presses and were printed in cheap low-quality paper. Produced by a small American team working direct to Admiral Leighton Smith, it was, we were informed, to be distributed by US Army Tactical Psychological Operations (Psyops) teams.

I changed this, not wanting the US teams to do a job that we were just as capable of doing for ourselves. The companies and B Squadron would distribute the newspapers and Ian Baker would organise distribution in Banja Luka. We were surprised but delighted that the paper was well received by the majority of Bosnian Serb soldiers and civilians. Although a small number of people would refuse the proffered paper and some would screw it up or throw it in a ditch, we found that we never had enough copies and had to put some effort into ensuring that they were evenly distributed throughout our area.

Distributing the paper became the priority for routine close operations in Banja Luka town. I commanded as many of these patrols as I could, as a good way of taking the temperature of the mood of the civilian population. We particularly targeted the town centre market, a vast array of stalls selling vegetables and all kinds of goods. My first impression was that the prices of goods seemed perfectly reasonable, if not cheaper than in Germany. My interpreter reminded me that these prices represented a fortune to people who were impoverished, unemployed, displaced, or trying to subsist on a soldier's wage of a few dollars a month. There was also an indoor meat market, similar to an Ottoman covered market in the centre of Sarajevo. On the north side of town we would visit the weekly cattle market, itself a memorable spectacle, a sprawling cross between a livestock market, an oriental bazaar, a car boot sale and a scene from a Thomas Hardy novel.

Both attracted people from throughout Banja Luka and the surrounding area – from apparently affluent town dwellers through small farmers to peasants bringing pigs for sale.

Steve Noble and any other officers or SNCOs who could be spared from Battlegroup HQ would accompany me. As well as drinking in the atmosphere I enjoyed simply talking to people. The majority were forthcoming and readily answered questions about the market, their lives, their experiences of the war and their hopes and fears for the future. I would deliberately not lay on the IFOR propaganda with a trowel, but gently attempt to engineer the conversation so that I could draw the connection between a lasting peace and the requirement for military and political compliance with the Dayton Agreement. Sometimes this tactic worked and sometimes it didn't, but it always provided a rewarding way of spending a morning or afternoon.

I never failed to elicit a reaction of surprise when I introduced myself as the 'Procovnik' in charge of the battlegroup in the Metal Factory. Sometimes I had to work hard to make the people I was talking to relax – presumably another hangover from the excessively deferential attitudes of the Titoist era. There was nothing particularly special about what I was doing: indeed I knew that our majors, young officers, SNCOs and junior ranks were doing the same. The willingness of many civilians and soldiers to talk to us was a stark contrast to the sullen hostility and frightened silences that the battalion had encountered from people living in the hard republican areas of Northern Ireland. Soldiers relished the opportunity to 'coffee house' or 'chat up' the locals. The uncomplicated open attitude of the British soldiers often disarmed suspicions and put people at their ease. This effort was most definitely the business of the whole of the battlegroup. As Steve Noble put it: 'Giving out facts is everyone's job.'

This effort to get the message across had been developed by the battlegroup from the bottom up. We had identified a need to inform and shape the perceptions of the faction civil populations and had got on and done so. We knew that there was an 'IFOR Information Campaign' and that US Psyops teams had reinforced the British division. For many the term 'psychological operations', abbreviated to Psyops, carried negative baggage, both from the impressions of the Vietnam War and from some operations that had been bungled early in the Northern Ireland conflict.

Psyops was a subject then conspicuous by its absence from Army training. I had briefly studied the subject a few years before and thought that it was an activity that had great potential. It is defined as 'activities carried out in both peace and conflict which can be directed at friendly, enemy and neutral audiences. Their purpose is to influence attitudes and behaviour, thereby enhancing the achievement of one's own political and military objectives. Psyops seek to undermine an enemy's will to fight, strengthen the support of the loyal and gain the support of the uncommitted'. This was precisely what we needed to achieve.

Brigade was joined by a 'Brigade Psychological Support Element' of US Army Psyops specialists. They came under the wing of Major Henry Joyntson, an excellent young cavalry officer attached to Brigade HQ. I had come across the US Army's Psyops capability before and believed that it could support our efforts, provided that we used them to complement rather than replace our own work. I therefore arranged for Henry to brief the battlegroup orders group on the brigade Psyops plan and the capabilities of the American teams. I directed that the battlegroup have a Psyops plan and that the companies and the squadron develop Psyops plans of their own.

The commanders got to work, initially, without too much enthusiasm, as Richard Smith of A Company describes:

> As a company commander I have to admit to scepticism when we were first briefed on the Psyops plan; I wondered if it would have any tangible effect on the ground. I was soon, however, to be convinced. Within A Company's area the towns of Čelinac and Kotor Varoš were to be key targets in the Psyops plan. Kotor Varoš was the slightly bigger town with a population of approximately ten thousand people, but both acted as feeder towns to Banja Luka. Although neither had had their infrastructure badly damaged by the civil war, both had suffered significant casualties as a result of the males having gone away to fight. Thus they were initially suspicious about the durability of the peace and needed convincing that the whole process would not degenerate into a state of violence again, especially when IFOR left.

The battlegroup and company Psyops plans revolved around gaining and spreading information. The foundation was the patrols we conducted into the towns and the surrounding countryside. They established vital links with the local community and provided the medium through which to gather feedback. Many people in the battlegroup had a natural talent for engaging local civilians and soldiers in conversation and a great deal was learned. For example Captain Mark Mortimer, the second-in-command of C Company produced some particularly useful reports:

Information Gaps
Are all Serb soldiers and officers to be arrested as war criminals?
Why did IFOR not punish the ABiH for kidnapping the two Serb officers?
How can we trust IFOR at higher political levels?
Will IFOR stay longer than twelve months if necessary?
When are IFOR leaving, where are they going?
Will IFOR collapse if the Americans leave?
Rumours
Americans will pull out in the summer.
America is training and rearming the ABiH.
IFOR are anti-Serb agents of the USA.
VRS say they have seen pictures of an ABiH tank with IFOR markings to prevent NATO air strikes.
When IFOR leaves, its equipment will be left to the ABiH and HVO.
IFOR intend to take power in Bosnia.

Mass arrests are imminent.

IFOR is going to employ truck drivers through the state and not directly, i.e. state as middleman will make a profit.

<u>Beliefs</u>

The war will restart once IFOR leaves.

The Americans are training/arming the ABiH in preparation for this.

Nine months is long enough to hold elections.

IFOR is doing a good job so far.

New political faces will be good news.

<u>Return to Normality</u>

Small family shops are reopening.

Civilian police are investigating minor crimes such as theft.

Serb civilians are becoming increasingly intolerant of the presence of the VRS in their neighbourhood.

<u>Conclusion</u>

IFOR must seriously address the Serb opinion of America. Many see IFOR as Bill Clinton's puppet. Almost all rumours, beliefs and information gaps stem from their involvement.

Low-level foot patrols talking to locals and distributing the newspaper are essential. Slowly they are building reassurance and confidence.

We must continue to encourage local leaders to brief and inform their people.

Reports like this would be passed up the chain of command allowing adjustments to be made to the Psyops plan. Liaison with the military and civilian authorities brought all this communication together. Richard Smith describes how A Company set about this:

We employed various items produced from IFOR resources. These included IFOR's own newspaper, the *Herald of Peace*, and a colouring book for children. We relearned many old lessons in this area, in that whatever you disseminate must be credible to the target audience.

Our Psyops plan also sought to generate goodwill in the local community. In mid-March, 3 Platoon vacated their base. Having carried out significant repair work, they handed it back to the village so that it could again be used as the local school. Similarly, we employed resources from the Royal Engineers, whenever the opportunity arose, to mend the dirt tracks we had damaged with the Warriors. A further example of our attempts to bridge the gap with the local community and to build their confidence in IFOR was the football games we arranged with the local sides.

The Psyops campaign gained a real momentum in a way that had not been possible under the UN, where the priority had lain in activities designed more for maintaining cordial relations with the factions on an even-handed basis rather than trying to influence them. Many of the techniques we developed were more overt and direct in their nature. There was a risk that our Psyops plan, if it was seen to be too blatant, would be rejected as the propaganda of an army of occupation. There was always the requirement for tact and subtlety.

At company level, the success of our Psyops plan depended upon the ability of the soldiers first to disseminate it to the local population, and then to provide feedback up the chain of command. Again this meant that our plan had to comprise simple and effective measures which were also credible to the soldiers who were going to have to implement them on the ground.

As a company commander the requirement to implement Psyops on the ground came as both a revelation and a real education to me. Though I had initially viewed the whole concept with a degree of caution, I was soon convinced by the tangible contribution it made towards encouraging a return to normality.

The American Psyops teams had 'Humvee' all-terrain vehicles carrying loudspeakers. As we made less and less use of armoured vehicles and more use of foot and Land Rover patrols, we began to use the services of the US teams, as much to increase the number of soft-skinned vehicles available for company operations as for their own capabilities. The Americans brought with them enormous resources including additional giveaways such as maps, mine awareness leaflets, footballs, crayons and colouring books and fluorescent armbands for children. Other IFOR units chose to rely on their liaison officers and the US Army Psyops teams as their sole means of conducting Psyops. We used the American teams and their 'freebies' as a subordinate part of co-ordinated Psyops effort that ran from myself dealing with senior faction officers, through company and platoon commanders and down to private soldiers conversing with a civilians they met on patrol.

As our effort gathered momentum, the companies continued to assess the local attitudes. We passed this information up the chain of command and also used it ourselves to refine our Psyops effort and to make any necessary adjustments to our operations. Knowing the prevailing attitudes, information gaps, questions and rumours, we could formulate 'lines to take' that our people could use to counter negative perceptions, answer questions and counter rumours with facts.

'London Calling'

We knew that however much talking we did, we could never hope to speak to all the people who lived in our area. We hoped that the messages we were spreading would be passed on, but more needed to be done. We therefore needed to identify local media and use them to explain IFOR operations to the local population. This effort was to be coordinated by Captain Steve Noble, who modestly described his role thus:

One of the problems with implementing the Dayton Agreement was the civilian information gap. While the higher echelons of the faction military understood the detail of the agreement, civilians and soldiers on the ground knew very little of the overall picture. This is when real public relations came into its own. The local population was used to the old Communist era when information was power.

The locals wanted to know what they could and couldn't do and where they could and couldn't go. To fill the gap, contacts with local radios and newspapers were developed. They were encouraged to let the locals ask questions so that we could answer them.

Steve had begun to develop this line of operation in January. Sanski Most and Klujc had a number of local radio stations – run out of a couple of rooms with low power transmitters. Steve targeted those with great success, talking on the air about what IFOR was doing and answering questions. The people running the stations showed great interest in IFOR and a hunger for information about us and the Dayton Agreement.

When we arrived in Banja Luka at the end of January the JCOs had already visited local radio stations and newspapers. Most of the radio stations were openly supportive of Pale and Karadžić. This was not the case with 'Radio Big', a privately owned independent music station. They arranged for a weekly appearance by IFOR in a talk show where the interviewer would put questions, followed by a live phone-in open to anyone with access to a telephone, all interspersed with the guest's choice of music. Initially General Jackson and Brigadier Dannatt had appeared, but once we arrived in Banja Luka I was invited to appear. Later company commanders, captains and warrant officers also took part.

The programme began with questions from one of the station's staff, but went on to questions phoned in by listeners. The live 'phone-ins' were particularly exciting, with their questions a typically Balkan mixture of the political, the emotional and the simply bizarre. Examples included:

Why are the Serbs always seen as the aggressor?
The Muslims killed my brother, so why should we ever trust them?
Why are only Serbs indicted as war criminals?
Your tanks are frightening my children.
Isn't it dangerous to carry light tanks under helicopters?
When will Manchester United come to play Banja Luka at soccer?
What do you think of our girls?
Are British troops tested for AIDS?
Have you got mad cow disease?

This programme, which had no formal name but was known to us as 'the IFOR phone-in', was run every Wednesday night. We arranged for appearances by various IFOR people involved in the Dayton process, from generals down to serjeant majors, representatives of Carl Bildt and the international police task force, to answer questions and play their own choice of music. Feedback indicated that the programmes were very successful. The locals could not believe the British were so open and relaxed – in complete contrast to the stiff, withdrawn Soviet-style image portrayed by the Bosnian Serb military. Through a bizarre sequence of events, the success of these radio programmes gained a momentum of its own.

In February I had appeared on Radio Big four times. On each occasion I had selected my choice of pop music to play between the questions and phone calls. I had tried to choose either lively, exciting music with a positive ambience (*Better Days* by Bruce Springsteen, for example) or British music that I knew to have been in UK charts in the last year or so (such as songs by Pulp, Blur and Everything But the Girl). Where possible I tried to combine the two (*Protection* by Massive Attack, *Don't Look Back in Anger* by Oasis, *One* by U2 or *Keep On Talking* by Pink Floyd). Twenty-two years earlier I had enjoyed running a small discotheque at Birmingham University. I found myself happily rediscovering the art of selecting music to fit a particular mood.

My interviews seemed well received by the station's audience, its few advertisers and its management. The interviewers, disk jockeys and engineers were intrigued that I had actually seen some of these bands perform. Time and again I found myself describing concerts I had attended. Having seen The Clash, The Jam, Elvis Costello, The Who, Richard Thompson, the Rolling Stones, The Cure, Bruce Springsteen, Ian Dury, Paul Simon, Peter Gabriel and Siouxsie and the Banshees in the flesh seemed to earn me considerable prestige. It seemed that British and American pop music was a universal language of immense popularity. One morning the station rang up the Metal Factory and asked if I would be kind enough to host a regular weekly three-hour evening slot presenting a music programme. I agreed to do a single show as a trial. If the idea turned out to have been misconceived, I could walk away.

I turned up to be given complete control of the station, including the sound engineer, who did not speak a word of English. I had already selected a play list, tapes and CDs, so Steve Noble, the interpreter and I had time to work out simple verbal and visual ways of cueing the music. We began with Springsteen, followed with (amongst others) Muddy Waters, Culture Club, Massive Attack, Ella Fitzgerald, REM, Pat Metheny, Blur, Joni Mitchell, Derek and the Dominoes, Brian Eno, Hendrix, Madonna, The Sex Pistols, Sinatra, Tori Amos, Michelle Shocked, Miles Davis, Bjork, Siouxsie and the Banshees, Billy Bragg, Ry Cooder, Oasis, Peter Gabriel, Aretha Franklin, Pulp and Iggy Pop. The evening was much more successful than I imagined it would be.

The station asked me back to present a weekly music programme in addition to the IFOR interview programme. So for the remainder of the tour Steve Noble, a selected interpreter and I would spend three hours every Tuesday evening running the radio station. I was trying to play music with genuine passion and emotion, what I called 'a higher fibre content'. I would try and sequence the music so that the first half of the show would be loud and raucous, but the second part would be more drawn out and laid back.

We approached other radio stations. Those in Banja Luka were all controlled by hard-line Karadžić supporters, but we found small independent local stations in Kotor Varoš and Laktasi. They were run on a shoestring, but they were keen to see IFOR and we arranged for people from C Squadron and A Company to broadcast regularly.

My broadcasting adventures were considered a touch unusual, both by some of the locals, some senior officers and by the Bosnian and British media.

I tried to keep a low profile, as I did not want the superficial novelty of my efforts to eclipse the good work being done by the whole of the battlegroup to spread the IFOR message. I knew that the battlegroup had reacted to my exploits with some amusement and that my broadcasts were nicknamed 'the Big Ben Show'. I was relaxed about this. I also enjoyed the experience!

More important was evidence that Banja Luka contained a significant population of intelligent young people and teenagers who seemed to have little time for the ethnic nationalism that had rent their country asunder. They saw little hope: the most popular local rock band was called 'Generation Without a Future'. If my spending three hours a week at Radio Big helped convince them that IFOR was a good thing, it was time well used.

We had received ever-increasing feedback that we were getting our messages across. Visitors to the battlegroup sometimes told us that this was in complete contrast to the approach of other IFOR national contingents, especially the US brigades, where only a small number of specialists were allowed to have any contact with civilians. The American approach seemed highly centralised, with all decisions and initiatives apparently being referred up to HQ IFOR. Our approach was as much bottom up as top down. We thought this was more flexible, adaptable and responsive.

By the end of our tour, deep operations were the battlegroup's main effort. They succeeded because they were based on a pragmatic approach and operations that had been executed by regimental officers and soldiers.

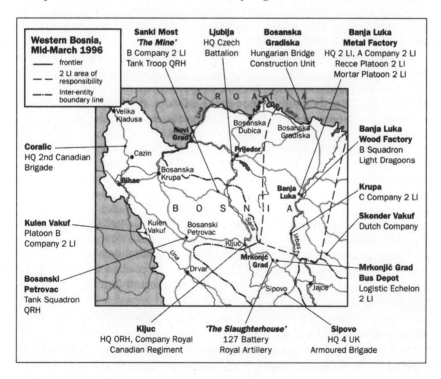

255

CHAPTER FOURTEEN
'Unfinished Sympathy'

The area that 2 LI had commanded in December and January was now the responsibility of the Canadian Multinational Brigade. The Sixth Czech Mechanised Battalion, based in Ljubija, was responsible for the area from WHITE FANG to Bos Krupa and Otaka. The other battlegroup, the QRH had everything to the south, including Sanski Most, Ključ and Kulen Vakuf. It had a British tank squadron, a Canadian mechanised infantry company and our B Company, who had remained at Sanski Most.

Although B Company was under operational command of the QRH, we were still administering and supplying them. In addition, we shared a boundary. I therefore visited them at Sanski Most every week and Paul Kellett or Peter MacFarlane came to our battlegroup orders groups so that they would know what was going on to their flank, and would not lose touch with the battalion of which they were part.

They were still responsible for the area that I had allocated them back in December, stretching from the WHITE FANG crossing point in the north, along forty kilometres of cease-fire line between Muslims and Serbs, through the hills to Ključ in the south. Although the military on both sides had reduced in strength, their area included four full brigades, two on each side.

Considerable political tension still simmered away. This was partly due to the Serb political leadership of Prijedor, which was unremittingly hard-line, and partly due to the considerable Muslim resentment at war crimes, unreleased prisoners and displaced persons who had little or no chance of returning home. Five Corps ABiH made no secret of their frustration that the war had ended before they could evict the VRS from Prijedor.

B Company retained patrol bases at WHITE FANG, BONDI BEACH and MALIBU CORNER. The company main base at Sanski Most mine remained the most austere and uncomfortable of all the battalion's bases, surviving on a minimum of resources. They detached a platoon to Kulen Vakuf and received in replacement a troop of three tanks and four Scimitars from the QRH.

Their operations were similar to those being conducted by the 2 LI battlegroup, mainly patrolling by Challengers and Warriors on both sides of the front line. They were allocated an artillery observation party from the Dutch Army, commanded by a huge Dutch officer who was his Army's champion kick-boxer. Paul made sure he took this imposing figure to any difficult meetings with the factions. The observation party had two over-snow vehicles, which provided an invaluable capability in snow-covered routes in the high hills that were beyond the ability of armoured vehicles or even Land Rovers to negotiate.

In December, the Muslim side was only partially populated, reflecting both the eviction of Muslims from the area by the Serbs at the beginning of the civil war and the subsequent haste with which the Bosnian Serb civilians had fled behind the retreating VRS in September 1995. The town of Sanski Most itself was no more than one third occupied.

In the countryside, the area was even more depopulated. Many of the villages were little damaged by fighting, but most were looted and vandalised – firstly by withdrawing Serbs and secondly by ABiH soldiers living in the villages. The result was the most appallingly chaotic mess. In a typical village, a few of the buildings might be burned out, but most would have their windows smashed. Graffiti would be scrawled all over the walls – both insults to the Muslims hastily applied by withdrawing Serbs, and the cryptic military legends applied by the ABiH. Much furniture had been stolen, used for firewood or vandalised. The streets of the villages were strewn with the discarded contents of houses that had been left by looters.

In December and January we saw a few families moving back into villages, but in February the numbers doing so visibly increased. B Company made sure that they maintained a high profile in these areas where refugees were starting to return: after all, they reasoned, the return of refugees was what the Dayton Agreement was all about.

B Company was still conducting a high level of close operations in March, when they were joined by Hugo Grenville. A former officer in the Coldstream Guards, he now had a flourishing career as an artist. The regiment had commissioned him to produce a painting to commemorate the battalion's tour in Bosnia. Hugo spent a week with the company being shown the area the battlegroup had controlled in that first month of NATO operations. He was a tall thin man with long blonde hair, eccentrically apparelled in combat trousers worn with woollen puttees and a cream skiing sweater. His enthusiasm for recording our work on canvas meant that he fitted in extremely well with B Company, particularly when he revealed that his next commission after Bosnia would be to produce a portrait of an American millionaire's young, beautiful and naked wife.

Hugo had spent the last fifteen years with little contact with the Army and, at his own admission, found both the situation in Bosnia and our operations a revelation. We had all become used to the sights of Bosnia, particularly the ethnically cleansed villages, the effects of fighting, looting and vandalism and the suffering of refugees. Hugo saw all these with fresh eyes. Later, after he had turned his sketches into a large oil painting, Hugo was to write:

> I realised that a painting that ignored the humanitarian situation would fail to present a truthful image. The mass graves, the limbs of the dead poking through

the melting snow, the domestic objects of ordinary lives scattered about the mud, the stench of rotting animals, of burned-out houses, of human degradation, the blank shocked faces of hungry refugees filled me with a sense of outrage. Only fifty years after the Nuremberg trials, western governments had tolerated 'ethnic cleansing' in Europe. The infantry had an extraordinarily challenging job and they executed it with great skill.

Hugo's painting called *Peace in Our Time* depicted B Company moving into a shattered village near the confrontation line and liaising with the local population. It showed the huge angular Warriors parked in among burned-out houses, the muddy street deep in the detritus of looting, including a cooker, a sofa and a vast amount of rubbish. Soldiers were talking to two men and a young boy, standing by their cart loaded with mattresses. The buildings were pockmarked from small arms fire and coated with graffiti, all under a darkening sky where a luminous yellow shaded quickly into the deep-frozen blue that indicated an unforgivingly cold night.

Company Operations

B Company's area of operations was bounded by the Czechs in the west, the Canadian Dragoons and Czechs in the north and the Canadians in the south. It was too easy for everyone to operate in what Paul called a vacuum mentality: everyone patrolling their own areas with little if any knowledge, other than from the QRH battlegroup's daily reverse situation reports and weekly orders group, of what was going on their flanks. The company therefore initiated a series of joint patrols with the Czechs and the Canadians. Paul Kellett describes the main reasons for this.

Firstly I wanted to find out what their capabilities and limitations were should I be tasked to undertake combat operations with them – what they could and couldn't do. Secondly, I thought it was important to show the factions that IFOR was working as a cohesive whole and that there was a unity of purpose. During several of our weekly meetings Commander 43 VRS Brigade expressed his unhappiness with the way the Czechs were operating. He said the same about me to my Czech counterpart! Thirdly, there were educational, cultural and intelligence benefits of operating with the Czechs and Canadians as we began to share information. Finally, it broke down some, though not all, operating barriers. We therefore had a menacing combat grouping on overt patrols of up to three Challengers, four Warriors, four BMPs, two BTRs and two Grizzlies as well as the odd military tourist who happened to join in. The boys thoroughly enjoyed driving and commanding BMP 2s, BTRS and Grizzlies. We escorted Commander 2 Brigade to a meeting in Prijedor with such a grouping, and I think the Serb commander thought his time was up!

There were no standard operating procedures for sub unit operations in a multinational environment. Once we had conducted joint patrolling over a couple of weeks, I, the Golf Company Royal Canadians Regiment commander and A Company, 6 Czech Battalion company commander sat down and wrote some simple procedures for patrolling in other people's areas, and how to communicate with each other. As a result I was confident that, if required, we could have responded together in an effective manner to any sudden deterioration in the situation in our area.

Platoon Operations

The centre of gravity of the company's work was its patrols. The tanks could patrol the main roads and tracks that were wide enough to allow passage to the massive vehicles, but were largely excluded from the mountainous and hilly country that made up so much of the company's area. The smaller Warriors could cover much more territory and when the roads or tracks became too difficult the infantry in the back could dismount and continue the journey on foot. This meant that the majority of the company's work to monitor the Zone of Separation and faction activities was executed by its armoured infantry platoons. Writing in the *Silver Bugle*, Lieutenant Peter Chapman described his platoon's work and its approach to the factions. He gives an accurate flavour, not just of his platoon's work, but of the work being conducted at that time by the rest of the battalion's platoons.

One of the most challenging aspects of a tour in Bosnia is working with the former warring factions. With a culture and a language so different from the British it would be easy to expect a poor working relationship, yet the practical aspect of the Dayton peace agreement demanded a close and cooperative relationship with all involved parties. For IFOR, perhaps the most significant part of the Dayton Agreement is the recurring phrase that gives it the right to 'the use of necessary force to ensure compliance'. But the simple use of force is not nearly enough. To be effective, an understanding of the modus operandi of the faction is essential, as the selective use of force can produce much better results than more heavy-handed authority. So what is there to know about the factions?

One of the strongest characteristics of the faction soldier is the importance he attaches to respect, be it respect for others or another's respect for him. The obvious focus for respect is power, and arriving at a faction HQ in two Warriors is a guaranteed way of earning instant respect. Occasionally, respect has to be taught. For instance, a Muslim military police checkpoint refused to allow a Royal Engineer's Land Rover past their wooden barrier, presumably ignorant of IFOR's right to complete freedom of movement. We parked up opposite the barrier in our Warriors with my company commander in his Land Rover in front, and the policemen quickly changed their minds. In this case the checkpoint was probably unaware that it was posing a political challenge to IFOR's rights, and the immediate threat of direct action was the best means of getting the message across.

But respect is not limited to the demonstration of hardware. As most of the Zone of Separation was inaccessible to Warrior, nearly all the joint patrolling was conducted on foot. Standard form for both ABiH and VRS soldiers is to wear minimum clothes and uniform, with little or no webbing, and an AK47 slung over their shoulders. Early on we found out that if we patrolled in helmet, body armour, webbing, day sacks and with weapons carried then we were over-equipped for the patrol, but the respect earned for keeping up professional standards was worth far more.

Small details like the cleanliness of weapons became important factors in the respect game, especially when there is so little other common ground between soldiers. A dirty weapon is more than a lapse in daily routine, it is a loss of credibility in a situation where the status of professionalism is the ultimate accolade. For the faction soldiers, many of whom have lost their homes and sometimes their families, and who have had four years of combat experience, their professional standard of soldiering is one of the few things they have left. To tell a faction commander his soldiers are unprofessional is the ultimate insult.

Closely linked to the idea of respect are the effects that fear has had on shaping attitudes. It could be argued that it was fear, fuelled by nationalistic fervour, which led to civil war in the first place. On both sides of the confrontation line near Sanski Most, however, it has been painfully obvious that while both the ABiH and VRS respect IFOR's control of the ZOS, they still have a disproportionate fear of the ZOS being violated by the other side. This has manifested itself in many ways, one of them being an early reluctance to withdraw from the confrontation line without constant reassurance that the other side was following suit.

Subsequently, there have been a number of incidents where fear has been a major factor, for instance when the Muslims admitted one day to firing into the ZOS the night before, technically a cease-fire violation. It turned out that the recruits who had been on the observation post for five days had seen two people walking along a path eight hundred metres away and in the ZOS. They were convinced that they were Serb spies, and so shot at them, although it was 2330 hours and they could not tell if the two had weapons or not! It was no use telling them that a handful of civilians lived in the area, as they were convinced that they faced an imminent attack.

Yet it would be wrong to dismiss this as an irrational fear. If the stories attached to the ever-increasing number of mass grave sites are anything to go by, Sanski Most has had more than its fair share of horror stories. It is as hard for Muslims to dismiss their deep-rooted fear of the Serbs as it is for the Serbs to dismiss their conscience-ridden fear of attempts at recrimination. But for British soldiers, who have been trained to conquer fear through positive action, it is a difficult trait to anticipate and evaluate.

In one incident two Muslim soldiers were shot in the leg, allegedly by Serb spies, at a Muslim observation post over five kilometres across the ZOS from the Serb front line. Half of the company was crashed out. As it was dark the investigation was left until the morning. It soon became clear to me that the only evidence of Serbs was the obsessive belief of the whole ABiH battalion, led by their commander, who demanded retribution by IFOR from the outset. There was not a single empty case at the firing point from the thirty rounds 'they' fired, there were two sets of footprints in the snow, but the tread was indistinguishable, and a witness had clearly seen three 'Serbs'. The two injured soldiers were in Bihać hospital, and too far away to interview.

I was then shown the contact point: a splash of bright red blood in the snow. To them it was conclusive evidence of Serb violence, to me it was an attempt at fabrication of evidence – human blood takes less than fifteen hours to congeal. Later I was shown what was the ultimate evidence – the trousers of the injured soldier complete with one (and only one) carefully ripped hole. There was not a trace of blood anywhere, even on the frayed edges of the rip!

Whatever had happened I was not being told the whole story. There was not actually any concrete evidence of any injuries in the first place, only a Muslim doctor's word for it. The only constant in the whole affair was the unshakeable belief that the Serbs were responsible, the Muslims' fear overriding any rational attempt to promote an alternative version of events.

Dealing with the local military chiefs was a complicated business. The first major hurdle was winning their confidence, as both sides fully expected us to be in secret collaboration with the other, and thus useful information was hard to come by. With time came trust, though, and after some successful joint patrolling we had developed a reasonably stable relationship with both the Serbs and the Muslims in our area. In a matter of weeks their stony-eyed stare and noncommital answers had been replaced with hearty handshakes and invitations to nightclubs (gracefully declined, of course), a progress that was good for both operations and morale.

One of the most pleasant characteristics of the factions is their hospitality. Somehow an extrasensory perception inspires HQs to put their kettle on about fifteen minutes before you arrive, even when you call in on an unplanned visit. The tradition is to do business first and offer you a coffee later. The coffee is always Turkish and always delicious. The only problem is when you're offered one small raki, which once polished off is instantly refilled. Now you've had two, and it's 'tradition' to have the Serbian three after the Holy Trinity, one of the defining features of their Orthodox religion. You can't leave without having one for the road, it would be rude to refuse; and thus at 0945 hours you escape into sunlight that seems far too bright, and the rest of the morning is lost in sleepy bonhomie. In a country where alcohol is far easier to obtain than bread, you don't want to even try and outdrink your host; he would die of liver failure before admitting defeat!

The last feature of the factions worth outlining is their pride, which surfaces as clearly as anywhere else in their attitude to sport. Perhaps it is a frustration with IFOR's influence on their lives that makes them so competitive at football, or maybe just a rare opportunity to release some aggression; whatever the reason, if we were ever to win convincingly at football I fear for a stable relationship!

Happily, we've been beaten in nearly every game we've played, the most humiliating time being a high-profile match in Prijedor. Not that we knew it was high-profile; our Serb LO told us he'd arranged for a friendly, so we picked a team from the available players in the company and turned up five minutes early. The police escort to the changing room was an early indication of our gross misjudgements, and as we entered the gym to see a packed crowd of four hundred, a professional referee, an opposition in matching strip and a TV camera crew the extent of the misjudgement became clear. Billed as a 'composite IFOR team' we took on national league players who were also soldiers, and lost the six-a-side match a convincing 11-1. It was a fascinating experience, although it was dismaying to see myself appear for the first time on Serb TV mumbling platitudes like 'it's the taking part that matters...'

Working with the warring factions has been on occasions a very frustrating business, mainly because they don't have the same background, training, standards, ideals and of course language as the majority of IFOR forces, and only rarely are there common aims. Yet it is a challenge that must be overcome, and one that is made a lot easier by maintaining a high professional standard in your own unit, and by appreciating the prominent characteristics of theirs. Handle them the wrong way, and they won't stop and warn you of the mines they've just relaid; handle them the right way, and you've got friends for life, or at least until the raki's run out.

Meanwhile in Kulen Vakuf

A few days after the death of Private Fox, 5 Platoon take over as the garrison of Kulen Vakuf. Four Platoon board a Chinook helicopter and fly to the British logistic base at Split. I join them for a short memorial service to say farewell to Fox's coffin. It is a duty that I had hoped I would never have to perform. Paul Kellett then flies to England to attend Fox's funeral and I return to Banja Luka with a heavy heart.

B Company continues to provide the platoon at Kulen Vakuf, to continue to deter the HVO from intimidating the nervous Muslim population, and the Muslim police from attempting to forcibly evict the HVO. By the end of March all three platoons of the company have taken their turn in Kulen Vakuf, reassuring a nervous population and preventing fighting between Muslim and Croat forces.

As spring approaches, I fly by helicopter to visit the town again. The RSM and I watch the landscape of western Bosnia unfold below us. It is a very cold but gloriously sunny afternoon. We fly over the huge swathe of territory bounded by Bihać in the north, Ključ and the edge of the Anvil in the south. In December and January we had concentrated on the immediate area of the front line, and had therefore ignored the vast territory over which we now fly. Much of it comprises a huge mountainous forest, but there are the familiar isolated hill and mountain villages, some completely burned out – the unmistakable indicator of ethnic cleansing.

We descend over a high plateau and are suddenly sinking over the lip of an immense bowl, edged by forests, crags and no fewer than two spectacular ruined castles straight out of medieval fable. Do they contain malevolent ghosts, I wonder. In the centre glistens the River Una, and Kulen Vakuf can be seen glowing in the afternoon sunlight its buidings of the same biscuit yellow colour as the villages of my beloved Cotswolds. As we drop towards the field where a soldier waits to marshal the helicopter, the breathtaking beauty of the location strikes me. With the awe-inspiring ring of crags, forests and castles, the sparkling shallow river and the town laid out with an intact medieval grid street plan inside a small moat, I arrive at the first Bosnian town that I genuinely consider attractive. If this were the Dordogne, it would be a major tourist site.

This is confirmed as a corporal from B Company takes me patrolling around the town. We cross the bridge. In the middle, a significant chunk of the road has been blown up; the locals have constructed a small overbridge of wooden planking sufficient for carts and small cars, but incapable of carrying armoured vehicles. The buildings in the centre of town are largely intact, albeit looted and suffering from some Bosnian Croat graffiti. On one side of the town square is the 'police station', a large building occupied by a disparate collection of Bosnian Croat paramilitaries. The RSM and I decide that 'scruffy thugs' or 'untidy macho bully boys' might be better descriptions. Lounging around in camouflage uniforms covered with menacing badges they feign disinterest in us, but with undisguised loathing they scowl threateningly at the few Bosnian Muslim civilians moving timidly through the square.

We can almost feel a solid wall of distaste from the HVO – directed both at the Muslims and ourselves. It is crystal clear that the Croat soldiers would dearly like us to leave so they could reassert their perceived right to bully the Muslim civilians out of the town. The platoon are under no illusions about the need to keep the pressure turned up in order to deter any violence, or, if fighting erupts, to react quickly enough to nip it in the bud.

Maintaining a heavy presence of foot patrols in the town is the key part of this. Indeed, my small party is now acting as one such patrol. We tour the town, talking to Muslims working on houses, making good the effects of four years of occupation by Bosnian Serbs. We discover a stream encircling the old town centre, a small moat. We linger on a bridge over the gurgling crystal clear water. The RSM and I play Pooh Sticks, and he wins.

CHAPTER 15

'Don't Look Back in Anger'

By the end of March, we knew that the transfer of territory had been successful. We could also see the faction armies begin withdrawing into barracks. As they did this, we reduced the impact of our operations, conducting fewer patrols in Warriors and more in lighter vehicles and on foot. When patrols visited villages, the locals often insisted on laying on traditional Balkan hospitality for the soldiers, who were plied with Turkish coffee, plum brandy and cakes. There was no shortage of volunteers for these duties.

We were trying to give the peace as great a chance of success as possible. IFOR had to remain part of the solution, rather than part of the problem. With the coming of spring, we could see large numbers of young men working on the farms, something they had not had the opportunity to do for the previous four years, when they would have been serving in the Army. During the civil war, spring had been a time when the armies mobilised for renewed offensives. This year it was different.

Banja Luka had become the international community's centre of gravity in western Bosnia. Although the International Police Task Force, the Organisation for Security and Cooperation in Europe and numerous aid organisations had all established offices in the town, IFOR lacked a major headquarters in Republika Srpska. The IFOR and ARRC HQs were in Sarajevo, the US Divisional HQ was in Tuzla and the French HQ was in Mostar – all in Federation territory. We could see the international relief agencies and non-governmental organisations becoming increasingly active. Many of them were making earnest attempts to promote reconciliation between the factions, but attempts to achieve any meaningful liaison between the factions were frustrated by inflexibility and intransigence.

After much negotiation, Divisional HQ secured agreement that it could occupy the Metal Factory, including an office block that had been denied to us. The size of the Divisional HQ and its communications and support meant that there would not be room for the troops and vehicles we had there.

The rearrangement of the brigade began straight away with C Company moving from their well-established base at Krupa to take over a small disused transistor factory at Previja in the western part of the Anvil. They became part of the Queen's Lancashire Regiment (QLR) battlegroup, based on the mechanised battalion that succeeded the Fusiliers. The QLR sent a mechanised company to Krupa, which came under my command. At the beginning of May we would be relived by First Battalion the Worcestershire and Sherwood Forester Regiment (1WFR). They would retain our Mrkonjić Grad base, but not the remainder of our area, which was divided between the Dutch battle-group, the mechanised company and our recce squadron operating under direct command of Divisional HQ. At the same time 1 Mechanised Brigade HQ would take over from 4 Brigade. Once all these musical chairs were over, 1 Brigade would have the WFR battlegroup with Warriors and tanks in the Anvil. The QLR battlegroup with Saxons would take over the upper Vrbas and Lašva valleys from the Dutch, resuming British responsibility for that part of central Bosnia that had originally been taken over by the Cheshires four and a half years earlier.

Until now 1 WFR had been planning to take over from us where we were. We telephoned England to find that they and 1 Mechanised Brigade HQ were both on leave, after which their advance parties were set to move straight to Bosnia. No matter, we shrugged: the plan was made and they would have to adapt when they arrived. It produced a rather complicated relief in place, with many of us handing over equipment and vehicles to the WFR but accom-modation to others; but after all the changes and uncertainties of the tour, we found this final change of plan small beer.

We began to get much more involved in civil affairs or 'G5' as it was known by NATO. There was now a civil affairs staff at Brigade HQ, headed by a British officer but largely staffed by American civil affairs specialists. The divi-sion's civil affairs staff had also opened an 'IFOR house' in the centre of Banja Luka. The idea was that civilians would be able to come to the house to seek advice, raise issues with IFOR, or get information. Many of us expected the IFOR house to be either unused, or monopolised by time-wasters. We could not have been more wrong. The house quickly proved its worth, with civilians coming to discuss subjects such as land mines, claims for damage caused by IFOR and a host of other issues.

Most of the battlegroup's people and machines were still heavily committed to patrols and other deterrent operations, but we began to identify areas where IFOR could help promote a return to civil normality. The British government's Overseas Development Administration, or ODA, had already been working in Bosnia and Division was identifying areas where the ODA could provide the money and British forces could provide the command and control and/or workforce to make things happen. We began to identify such projects. Even if we were not able to carry them out before we left Bosnia, we could pass them on to our successors.

ODA officials started visiting the divisional area. B Company was able to make good use of the visit in Sanski Most. The town was rapidly filling up with people returning home and efforts were being made to revitalise agriculture and restart industry. General Alagic, who until then had been commanding ABiH 7 Corps, suddenly became 'Mr' Alagic and took over as mayor of Sanski Most, displacing the original mayor, who we understood had actually been democratically elected before the civil war started. 'Mr' Alagic still retained the complete floor of the Hotel Sana that had been his forward command post, the small fleet of camouflage-painted Toyota Land Cruisers in ABiH colours and a posse of menacing-looking bodyguards – all the trappings of power he had enjoyed as a corps commander. Alagic had openly declared great intentions of revitalising Sanski Most and the Una-Sana canton, but presented a difficult and intransigent attitude to IFOR.

This attitude changed when Paul Kellett took an ODA official to visit Alagic. Both made it clear that there was no hope of any ODA funds being directed to Sanski Most unless Alagic gave full and unconditional support to IFOR and the other international agencies in the area. Alagic's attitude suddenly changed and he became most cooperative. B Company had no more trouble with him during the rest of the tour.

The area around Sanski Most contained a huge number of pig carcasses. The unfortunate beasts had all been shot in the previous autumn's fighting. With the spring thaw the putrefying corpses were everywhere: on roadsides, in fields, in ditches, in gardens, schools and car parks. No part of the Sanski Most area lacked its quota of rotting and stinking mounds of pink flesh. These posed a significant public health hazard to both the IFOR soldiers and the civilian population. But the civil authorities had neither the intention nor the capability to do anything about this. So B Company and a nearby British artillery battery organised Operation PORK SCRATCHING. They used their soldiers, mechanical handling equipment and diggers to find, move and dispose of, by burial or burning, as many pig corpses as they could. By the time B Company left Bosnia, they and the gunners had buried or burned more than two and a half thousand animal corpses and had run out of pig carcasses to find.

Evidence of War Crimes

B Company discovered places where a significant number of bodies had been left. The melting of snow, soil erosion and activities of wild animals were exposing more and more human remains. All of these were in Muslim territory. There was clear evidence of a mass grave near Ključ. Closer to Sanski Most, local Muslims led IFOR to a hillside cave which appeared full of decomposed bodies. Further corpses appeared to have been buried in shallow graves in the same area, scraps of clothing that had not yet rotted appearing to be of civilian origin, rather than uniforms.

These discoveries were different to the human remains we had discovered in December and January, which had been assessed to be soldiers killed in the fighting. The new finds looked much more like the bodies of civilians. Without a professional forensic and pathological examination it could not be established where and when they were killed, but it was difficult for B Company to avoid the conclusion that what they were seeing were the grisly remains of massacres of civilians. This, of course, was exactly what the local Federation authorities claimed had happened, with detailed accounts of the massacres of Muslims as dating back to 1992.

After reporting the location of the bodies up through the British chain of command to pass to the International Tribunal, there was nothing B Company could do. Guarding was not part of IFOR's mission. Even if it were, guarding the many sites would have tied up all of the company, leaving them incapable of carrying out their primary task. They therefore regularly visited the sites, aiming to deter attempts to interfere with the evidence, or at least indicate if such gross tampering had been carried out.

On one of these trips a British Independent Television News (ITN) team accompanied Lieutenant Peter Chapman and his platoon. In Bosnia to film the run up to the D+120 deadline, the team filmed a stark but moving account of two of the gravesites, with Peter Chapman showing them the pathetically sad corpses.

Multinational Operations

We worked hard to liaise with our multinational partners. To the east was the US-led Multinational Division North. The chain of command was unable to give us any information concerning their activities, apart from the fact our neighbours were the Nordic/Polish brigade, headquartered in Doboj. After some time and effort, we arranged for Ian Baker to visit their HQ.

We discovered that the northern division was focusing all its ground combat power on the immediate area of the Zone of Separation, to a depth of no more than ten kilometres on each side. We were told that the remainder of the division's territory was being 'patrolled by aviation' – in other words by helicopter overflights. The Nordic/Polish brigade's slice of the ZOS was well to the south-east of our area. With neither helicopters of their own, nor, it appeared, much call on the US helicopters based at Tuzla in the heart of Federation territory, very few helicopter patrols took place over the Nordic/Polish sector of Republika Srpska. This meant that there was little or no effective IFOR presence in the area to our east.

We, in contrast, were patrolling throughout the breadth and depth of our area, consciously seeking to ensure that no part of the territory received any more or less attention than another. This was partly to reassure all the civilian population, partly to reinforce military compliance and partly to deter infringements of the civil aspects of Dayton. In the area just across our eastern boundary there were well-substantiated allegations of Serbs intimidating Muslims and Croats, particularly in and around the town of Prnjavor. We were confident that this was not going on in our area – at least, not in such a blatant fashion or at anything approaching the same scale. We began some liaison work and visits, but despite a major effort on our part, we were never able to arrange any combined patrols or substantive liaison with the Nordic/Polish brigade.

At the south-east corner of the battlegroup area we shared our boundary with the Dutch Mechanised Battlegroup. We developed a close working relationship with the Dutch and I quickly got to know Theo Damen, the charismatic Dutch commanding officer. A Company worked with the Dutch company based in Skender Vakuf, as their platoon house at Radici was much closer to the Dutch base than to A Company's base in the Metal Factory. They quickly began an extensive program of combined patrols and cross training. The Dutch kindly allowed our soldiers to make use of their excellent hot showers and welfare telephones – facilities found in none of A Company's bases.

At the end of March, I felt that the recce platoon was becoming bored. They had patrolled all over the battlegroup area and were probably over-familiar with it. We heard that both Brigade and Theo Damen considered that there was insufficient IFOR presence in the Dutch battlegroup's area, around the towns of Gornji Vakuf, Bugojno and Donja Ljubija. I therefore offered to lend the recce platoon to the Dutch for two weeks, returning in time for the D+120 deadline.

The offer was accepted with alacrity and the platoon was duly loaded on DROPS vehicles and lifted down to Bugojno. I visited them a few days later. They had settled in well and were busy patrolling. With irony we noted that two years earlier their area had been the responsibility of an entire battalion of British UN troops, headquartered in Bugojno. Indeed, four months earlier Bugojno had contained the Fusileers' Battalion HQ and our B Squadron. Now the base was virtually empty, save for a few British signallers and military policemen.

A Mine Incident

Three days later, minding my own business in Banja Luka, I am called to the operations room. One of the recce platoon's Scimitars has run over an anti-tank mine. The vehicle is immobilised, but the crew has survived. By last light the EOD team have cleared a safe route, removing more anti-tank mines, and the crew are taken to safety. The reports of the incident show that it has occurred in the centre of an area known to be mined – indeed marked as such on the IFOR minefield maps based on those supplied by the factions. It seems that this is an incident that should not have happened. How on earth has this occurred? I send Ian Baker to Bugojno to find out.

Ian investigates the mine strike and discovers that it was wholly avoidable. Borrowing a helicopter, I fly to Bugojno the next day, passing over the site of the incident, the Scimitar sitting on its own with most of its right-hand side track and running gear blown off. The vehicle lies on a hillside track. All around are faction bunkers and trenches. How can recce platoon not have seen all these indicators of a high mine risk area?

Ian meets me at Bugojno. Together we interview the corporal commanding the patrol. He has no explanation as to how he failed to correlate the faction minefields marked on his map with his position. He admits ignoring the sight of empty faction trenches and bunkers – a sure indicator of a former front line. He claims that he had seen civilians in a logging truck driving along the same road, but all the evidence is that this was unlikely, as they would either have been blown up by mines or have come to a large barricade at the end of the track. Also, we have seen no such vehicle tracks from the air. I assess that he is either bluffing or bad at map reading.

Sending him out of the room, I talk with Ian and the RSM. The incident could have been prevented if the corporal had been paying more attention to his map, or had read the obvious danger signs. We are very lucky that he and his two crewmen are still alive.

Quickly we review all the options. I have lost confidence in his ability. I know him well, not only from this battalion but also from previous service together in another battalion. Indeed I have positively enjoyed his company, but I have no alternative but to remove him from command. He is moved from the recce platoon to another part of the battalion. He is also given a formal warning that he has three months to improve his performance or face reduction in rank.

This decision brings me no pleasure, in fact it makes me extremely angry – which I overcome in part by slamming the door of the helicopter that takes me away from Bugojno. Reflecting on the incident as I fly back to Banja Luka, I wonder if the mine strike is a symptom of complacency in us all. The weather is now much better, and in the valley bottoms conditions are positively balmy. The locals are friendlier and we see less of the faction military every day. Perhaps we are all being lulled into a false sense of security. I get out my notebook and write a short letter to all the officers in the battalion warning them about this and reminding them of the need to observe the elementary mine awareness precautions we have all been trained in.

At the next battlegroup orders group, I leave everyone in no doubt of my intent. We have already lost one soldier too many and I want to bring everyone else home in one piece. I may be getting grumpy towards the end of the tour, but I don't want any of us to lose our edge.

The International Police Task Force

At the same time as the recce platoon was supporting the Dutch and getting itself blown up, the battlegroup was helping to change the Republika Srpska police. Before the breakup of Yugoslavia, the civil police force had been neither accountable nor independent of the state. Armed police squads of all three factions took part in the civil war, including organising the suppression of minorities and the ethnic cleansing of 1992 and 1993. There was little doubt that extreme nationalists in police uniforms had played a major role in committing war crimes. Not only were there plenty of allegations that police of all sides had been linked to human rights abuses, torture, imprisonment without trial and summary executions, but there was also plenty of evidence of police corruption and abuse of power. It appeared that Karadžić and his cronies were sustained by smuggling, black marketeering and extortion. These depended on a degree of acquiescence by some of the Republika Srpska police. Hard-liners in the police could make a significant contribution to the attempts of hard-line nationalist leaders and corrupt politicians to maintain their hold on power.

It was also clear that both the civil police and the large contingents of para-military and so-called 'anti terrorist' police possessed significant firepower. Not only did all members of these units have pistols and automatic rifles, but the squads also fielded light mortars, anti-tank rocket launchers, anti-aircraft guns and even armoured cars.

To a certain extent, this was addressed in the Dayton Agreement. Although the Agreement placed no limit on the size of police forces, it restricted their armament to small arms only. It required the parties to maintain 'civilian law enforcement agencies operating in accordance with internationally recognised standards and with respect for internationally recognised human rights and fundamental freedoms'. The UN was to deploy an International Police Task Force (IPTF) to Bosnia, which was to monitor, observe and inspect this, as well as assisting with training. Such an unarmed civilian police force had been a key element of many previous UN peacekeeping and nation-building operations.

Between December and February we had seen little of the IPTF. At the beginning of March an IPTF contingent began forming up at a motel on the outskirts of Banja Luka, containing policemen from a variety of countries, most of whom were not contributing troops to IFOR. By the beginning of April the motel was full of international policemen, wearing a cosmopolitan variety of national police uniforms topped by UN berets. Ian Baker began liaison. The IPTF had established an HQ in Banja Luka, commanding a region which overlapped with that of Multinational Division Southwest. A commissioner of the Irish police commanded the region, with a Scandinavian deputy. They both seemed highly motivated and competent officers.

We were less impressed with many of the IPTF officers. It was not just that they seemed to spend most of their time in the motel, and were rarely to be seen out and about around Banja Luka. It was also that we had nagging doubts about the effectiveness of many of them. Standards seemed to vary enormously. Unlike IFOR, the IPTF had no process of 'force certification' other than a simple test of the ability to speak English. The IPTF contingent assembling in Banja Luka included a high proportion of police from Third World or recently Communist countries, some undemocratic, others notoriously corrupt. We could not see how these police could easily conform to Western standards of effectiveness, independence from political control or honesty – coming as they did from states where understanding and practice of policing was less well developed than in NATO and European Union nations. We were very disappointed to learn that no police officers from the United Kingdom would join the IPTF, as no British Government funds were available for this.

Up to this time, the factions had continued to deploy police and military checkpoints throughout the country. Some had disappeared, or been reduced in scale, but it was still impossible for civilians to move any distance on the roads without being stopped. Not only did this provide opportunities for intimidation and corruption on a massive scale, but while the factions maintained such checkpoints they would be able to prevent the free movement of civilians throughout Bosnia, including between the entities. Checkpoints also provided an excellent opportunity for dominant ethnic groups to harass minorities.

When the faction military completed their withdrawal into cantonments, they would not be allowed any military checkpoints. Recognising that a similar measure was required to constrain the entity civil police's ability to do the same, IFOR directed that from 27 March civil police static checkpoints would not be allowed.

In Banja Luka the IPTF conveyed this ruling to the Republika Srpska police. There was much 'muttering and chuntering' as Ian Baker put it. As the deadline approached the Serb police showed no sign of preparing to close the static checkpoint remaining in our area. So the Light Dragoons went with Scimitars and an engineer crane to unceremoniously remove the the shabby Portacabin of the remaining checkpoint in their area.

There was no reaction to this act of *force majeure*, an undramatic illustration of how much IFOR had achieved. In November, we had found it impossible to imagine Bosnian roads without the ever-present faction checkpoints. The complete absence of static checkpoints represented vivid proof of the transformations achieved since D Day. We had come a long way in a very short time.

Civilian movement across the cease-fire line was starting. The Federation revived a civilian bus service between Sarajevo and Bihać – the buses crossing through Republika Srpska on the road along the neck of the Anvil between Jajce and Ključ. Civilians from both sides were exploiting this meet up around Mrkonjić Grad. This was opposed by hard-line members of the Bosnian Serb police and there followed a game of cat and mouse.

The faction police were still allowed to conduct temporary vehicle checks on roads, but IFOR directed that these were not to last for more than thirty minutes, after which they had to move on to a different site. Left to themselves, the faction police would have happily stood on roads for hours on end to exercise their control. Often IFOR patrols would come across faction police who were doing this. The IFOR troops would order them to move on. They always did, but made it clear that they were unhappy about it.

The problem could have been nipped in the bud if the IPTF had been able to accompany Serb police patrols. As far as we could see, the Banja Luka IPTF was, even in April, far from fully operational. Despite the hundred-bedroom motel apparently being full of international policemen, we only witnessed occasional patrols by the IPTF.

B Company in Sanski Most made more progress with the IPTF thanks to the untiring efforts of the Task Force's commander in the town, an impressive American police officer. The Muslim civil police in Sanski Most were receptive to ideas about developing a postwar police force and the company was able to assist the IPTF in this.

In Prijedor, however little progress was made. That leadership of that police force appeared to have been taken over by hard-line Bosnian Serb nationalists and many of their truculent and un-cooperative supporters were concentrated in a heavily armed 'Anti-Terrorist Police Unit'. Indeed, the Bosnian Muslims claimed that the second-in-command of the Prijedor police, for whom these thugs in police uniform worked, had been heavily involved in the running of the Omarska prison camp, notorious for its abuse of Muslim prisoners. Paul Kellett described an incident that occurred in B Company's area that appeared to confirm this close relationship between the Prijedor Serbs and the town's IPTF contingent.

The JCOs had reported Serb police stopping traffic and people from crossing through the ZOS from north to south at a Serb police post about three kilometres north of WHITE FANG. Freedom of movement of civilians was a key issue of the Dayton Agreement and it appeared that the Serbs were violating this. The Canadian brigade therefore tasked B Company to close this Serb police post and 'dismantle' it.

I was given the freedom to use whatever force was needed to close this post. Rather than mount the operation immediately, I sought, and eventually got, permission from the Canadians to speak to the Serbs to warn them what would happen should they continue to impede freedom of movement. As this police post was in the Prijedor IPTF area, the IPTF commander, a Hungarian, was present at the talks between me and the Serbs. The Serbs stated that they would not vacate the post despite the threat of force. The Prijedor IPTF commander remonstrated with me and threatened 'administrative action at the highest level' if B Company proceeded with the action. Twenty-four hours later the company took the police post by force, and confiscated sixteen AK 47s, a number of pistols and several radios.

It was at this stage that things started to go pear-shaped. The IPTF commander demanded my presence at a meeting in Prijedor with the Serb head of police. I declined the offer and referred the IPTF commander to the Canadian Brigade HQ. The IPTF commander bypassed the Canadian brigade staff and decided to visit B Company in Sanski Most personally. After a difficult meeting at which the IPTF commander somewhat bizarrely 'sacked' me for my actions against the Serb police post, I had him escorted from B Company's location back to Prijedor by the JCOs.

The American IPTF commander for Sanski Most, who I had asked to be at the meeting, departed immediately for Banja Luka to remonstrate with the head of the IPTF delegation about the behaviour of the Hungarian police commander. This would not be the last time B Company came across this chap!

This illustrated a wider problem with the Bosnian 'civil' police and the IPTF's efforts. With the end of hostilities in 1995, a significant number of hard-liners had taken refuge within police forces of various descriptions. Although genuine professional policemen remained in the ranks of the entity police forces, there was considerable evidence of bribery and corruption. The local police forces had the capability either to disrupt or to assist a return to law and order and an enduring peace.

The IPTF had taken too long to deploy and its strength was never sufficient. It seemed to have few levers to compel compliance by civil police forces. After D+120, the faction armed forces would be under a large measure of IFOR control. Ironically, the civil police, who were permitted to use small arms, were likely to become a potentially greater threat to the implementation of the Dayton Agreement than the armed forces. The criminal justice system in Bosnia did not work to Western norms. It was difficult to see how members of the IPTF from countries where these norms did not apply could improve this.

It looked to us like the Dayton Agreement had underestimated the difficulty of establishing proper civilian police forces. The opportunity to make an early impact on the civil police of the entities had been lost and it seemed that it was going to be very difficult to change the nature and *modus operandi* of the faction civil police forces.

Preparing for Cantonment

The D+120 deadline required that all troops and weapons of the entity armed forces had to be back in barracks and cantonments. The exact location of these was subject to IFOR's approval. Troops and weapons could only leave these barracks for administration, training or any other activity with IFOR's approval.

Over a month before the deadline, IFOR had required the factions to produce their list of cantonment sites. The VRS produced a list for Banja Luka which IFOR duly approved. Although VRS Corps HQ in Banja Luka seemed to know what was going on, the IFOR-approved cantonment list did not appear to have been passed to their brigade commanders, especially those based outside Banja Luka. This may have been due to deliberate obfuscation by anti-IFOR hard-liners, but the more likely explanation was that the VRS command structure was rapidly imploding, with their divisional headquarters disbanding as Corps took direct command of the remaining brigades. Many of the more energetic and able officers were demobilising themselves – presumably to go back to civilian employment.

All this meant that the passage of information within the VRS was getting worse, causing problems in liaising with confused and unhappy brigade commanders. A Company, for example, dealt with the VRS brigade in Čelinac. Major Marković, the commander, was extremely positive and helpful, but completely in the dark about the VRS' plans. In the two weeks before D+120 Richard Smith repeatedly warned him that after the deadline passed IFOR would disarm any troops found outside barracks without permission, confiscating weapons and equipment. Yes, Marković told Richard Smith, he knew about the D+120 deadline, and yes, he could read the photocopies of the VRS' own cantonment plans that we had given him, but no, he most definitely could not withdraw troops into barracks without direct orders from Corps HQ in Banja Luka.

The brigade had some heavy howitzers, hidden in a logging site high in the wooded hills above Čelinac. Initially spotted by a helicopter patrol, the guns were unguarded, but appeared in good working order, with boxes of ammunition lying around the site. Politely but firmly A Company warned Marković that failure to move the guns to barracks would lead to them being confiscated. Marković squirmed with unhappiness at this but was unyielding, for he could not, he said, move the weapons without permission from Corps HQ. The brigade, he told Richard Smith, had only survived in the war by unyielding obedience to orders. This could not change now.

A Company could see that Marković was uncomfortable but, much as they sympathised, IFOR was not in the business of doing the factions' work for them. So the company patrolled the brigade's locations every day, checking to see if the howitzers had moved. Paul Davies, an ITN television reporter, accompanied one of the patrols. Through persistent negotiation Richard Smith persuaded Marković to agree to be filmed by ITN discussing the issue with IFOR. He, like all VRS officers, was immensely suspicious of the Western media, but eventually agreed, though reluctantly and with obvious reservations, that showing the VRS as cooperating with IFOR could help overcame the hugely negative image that the Bosnian Serbs had in the West.

Gradually problems were ironed out, but largely because we were providing a parallel chain of command by passing information to the hapless VRS commanders that should have been passed by their own chain of command.

The Republika Srpska Air Force was not showing such a high degree of compliance. When we arrived in Banja Luka liaison with the Air Force was controlled by Divisional HQ. The Air Force jealously guarded their independence from the Bosnian Serb Army and after February's electronic wild goose chase around the Kosmos Factory I was given to understand that 3 Division did not want to upset the Air Force unnecessarily. Nevertheless, the battlegroup could not avoid having to deal with them. Not only did we have the Kosmos Factory, but the Bosnian Serb's two surviving airbases were in our area, as were most of their SAM systems.

Unlike the VRS 1 Krajina Corps, whose first dealings with NATO had been with IFOR, the Bosnian Serb Air Force had been confronting NATO since the imposition of no-fly zones in 1992.The situation was effectively a slow-burning war. Bosnian Serb aircraft had been shot down and the Bosnian Serbs had fired missiles at NATO aircraft, three of which had been shot down. NATO had carried out air strikes, culminating in a sustained air offensive the previous September. Operation Deliberate Force had the Bosnian Serb air defence network as a primary target. The climax of the strikes, in which American cruise missiles attacked SAM sites around Banja Luka in the heart of their air defence network, had been profoundly shocking, especially for the Air Force, who could not stop the Tomahawk missiles from reaching their targets. Another twenty missiles could have destroyed most of Banja Luka's industrial capacity. Understandably, the majority of Bosnian Serb Air Force officers were very hostile to IFOR.

The Bosnian Serb Air Force had been required to inform IFOR of all air defence sites and anti-aircraft weapon locations. They had done this, but the declarations had been inaccurate and incomplete. Since February we had kept encountering Air Force assets in a variety of unexpected locations. An empty farm shed held a large mobile radar. The recce platoon found SA2 Guideline anti-aircraft missiles hidden along a minor forest road. Missile storage sites were identified by our patrols, who also found unauthorised radars deployed in obscure hillside locations. These were ordered back to barracks. Some of the missiles were armed and ready to fire. But there was nothing in the Dayton Agreement that specifically forbade this. We discovered another storage site where the guards told us that the missiles inside were unsafe as they were leaking propellants. Although the missile fuels included highly volatile and toxic red fuming nitric acid, an inspection by British and Czech ammunition experts confirmed that the missiles were safe enough. Patrols found stockpiles of shoulder-launched anti-aircraft missiles 'just lying around where they had apparently been dumped at the end of the fighting', as C Company put it. At all of these locations, we gave the VRS a day to move missiles or lose them. The missiles were moved.

A Visit by a Band

Before the tour I had arranged for the Band of the Light Division to visit the battalion both to entertain British troops and to help with the Psyops effort. They arrived at the beginning of April. Their trip was subsequently described by Lance Corporal Armstrong:

> We embarked on our journey to Gornji Vakuf. This was our first meeting with our driver for the tour. No one could actually determine what his name was so we took it upon ourselves to christen him 'Drivolovich', which he seemed quite pleased with. We set off in our 'Mirthmobile' to perform a marching display for the local school children. This was certainly a bizarre experience. We performed on what appeared to be a patch of waste ground surrounded by buildings which showed very obvious signs of conflict. It was certainly very well received by the locals, although they may have just been polite about the eccentricity of British musicians.

From there, the Band visited HQ ARRC at Sarajevo; they then went on to Šipovo for a weekend with Brigade HQ and the brigade troops based there and at Mrkonjić Grad, en route to five days with the battlegroup, visiting all locations, including the isolated platoon bases.

> Next morning, it was all aboard the bus bright and early for the journey up to Šipovo. As we drew near the camp, a disused gypsum factory, we encountered some of the worst devastation we had seen. That night we performed another concert in the Janj Hotel, which was very well received. The following morning, Easter Sunday, we travelled into Mrkonjić Grad to lend musical support for a

church service before performing a concert for the locals. We were a little taken aback when children came up to us autograph hunting, not the sort of reception we generally get in the UK. After much autograph signing it was all aboard the coach one more to travel to our final 'home' for the tour, the Metal Factory at Banja Luka.

Richard Smith arranged for the Band to give a concert for children and teen-agers in Kotor Varoš. A couple of hours before it was due to start, the mayor, in a highly agitated state, banned the concert from going ahead. There was nothing in IFOR's powers or rules of engagement that could compel anyone to allow a British band concert. Richard opened negotiations.

He established that the mayor had taken great umbrage at an IFOR-produced colouring book, the aim of which was to make children aware of the dangers posed to them by mines and unexploded ordnance. Half of the pictures in the book contributed to this. The other half were of apparently innocuous child-friendly images, including farms, pets and ball games. Unfortunately one of the pictures was of a knight and a medieval castle. The mayor considered that the turrets of the castle were more like the minarets of a mosque. After a couple of hours of patient negotiation, Richard calmed the mayor and secured agreement for the concert to go ahead in a local cinema.

Eventually the concert went ahead after the OC and his negotiating team laid on the diplomacy with a trowel. Following a very well received (if a little late) concert we loaded up to play a short concert in the town before performing a little light music for the duty barbecue. Next day we travelled up to 'The Mine' to spend the day with B Company rehearsing for an evening retreat. The perform-ance, although nearly obscured by the resulting cloud of dust, was very much appreciated. The following day was a national day off so we had an excellent opportunity to discover the entertainment possibilities of Banja Luka, which on the whole didn't take very long. The highlight of the day was a briefing on the situation in Bosnia, which left us a little less in the dark about things.

Our final engagement was a Sounding of Retreat for the entire battalion at the Metal Factory. This we thought would be a rather run of the mill affair, but Bosnia being what it is, nothing falls into that category. The march-on passed uneventfully, the display passed without a hitch, it was just when we came to play 'Sunset' that things started to go a little awry. Throughout the performance a steady flow of traffic had been passing behind us, but sadly one particular driver was so surprised to see a full-blown military band performing that he decided to have a good look. Unfortunately he was doing a rather rapid rate of knots at the time. When he could tear his eyes away from us to see the danger in front of him a rather lengthy squeal of tyres and brakes ensued, which must have left a quite respectable skid-mark on the road, and the resulting bang as he clearly failed, despite his heroic efforts, to stop in time caused many a wince and furtive glance over the shoulder. Fortunately there was a plentiful supply of medical staff who had been watching our performance at hand to assist.

The Factions Return to Barracks

Events around Kulen Vakuf are reaching a crisis. The HVO asks for the building occupied by their military police in Kulen Vakuf to be authorised as a cantonment. The request is turned down flat by IFOR. Division tells the HVO that they must withdraw all their troops by D+120.

As the deadline approaches, the HVO shows no sign of conforming. Keeping their military contingent in Kulen Vakuf after D+120 will be an act of deliberate military non-compliance, the first on such a scale in the division's area. This cannot be tolerated without undermining IFOR's authority and impartiality. Preparations to compel the HVO to withdraw begin.

Increasingly direct messages are delivered to both the Bosnian Croat political leadership and the HVO. General Jackson and Brigadier Dannatt leave their HVO opposite numbers in no doubt that IFOR is preparing to use whatever force is necessary to evict the HVO from the town.

The weekend before the deadline there is still stalemate between IFOR and the HVO. The Canadian brigade deploys their cavalry squadron between Kulen Vakuf and Bihać to deter or prevent 5 Corps ABiH from interfering. To the south, the Malaysian battlegroup deploy their light tanks on the routes between the rest of Bosnian Croat territory and the town. The Queens Lancashire Regiment battlegroup move our C Company from Previja to another screen position in an ethnically cleansed village high above Titov Drvar.

I met up with Paul Kellett. B Company still provides the platoon in the town. If the HVO has to be forced out, the whole of B Company will be required. Paul and I examine a range of options. These include using tactics taken directly from Northern Ireland, where the whole company would patrol the town intensively in an extremely aggressive, no-nonsense manner, so as to gain moral superiority over the HVO, essentially frightening them out. We also look at using another Northern Ireland technique, that of a mass arrest operation.

A third option we call the 'Firepower Demonstration', after an exercise regularly conducted for students and the School of Infantry on Salisbury Plain. It is an overt display of overwhelming military force. Kulen Vakuf's spectacular setting in a natural amphitheatre of uninhabited wooded and rocky hills would become the backdrop to a show of force, demonstrating both our weapons and their effects. One side of the bowl would be lined with our heavy-duty military hardware, including tanks, Warriors and AS 90 heavy guns. Lynx armed helicopters and NATO jets would fill the sky. Should this not be enough to persuade the HVO to leave, the other side of the valley would be used as a target area. The weapons would fire directly over the centre of the town, initially individually and finishing with all firing simultaneously. A narration would be provided by loudspeaker.

All of these options could produce a bloodless outcome, providing the HVO cooperated, but they all carry the risk that the HVO might open fire at any time. Whatever IFOR does, we will need to be poised to return overwhelming fire instantly on the HVO. If the HVO fire, or if all these options fail, a deliberate infantry attack with maximum supporting fire will have to be launched on the HVO. The principle will be to concentrate overwhelming force so as to minimise our casualties and maximise the chances of the HVO deciding to withdraw or surrender.

A limiting factor is the bridge across the River Una. Unless it is strengthened, or another crossing established over the river, it will be impossible to deploy armoured vehicles into Kulen Vakuf. This will reduce both the protection and firepower available to IFOR in the town. Operating with only dismounted infantry would increase the risk to our troops and the chance of IFOR casualties, the brunt of which would be borne by the infantry. Bridging the river is vital.

Time passes very slowly. Division and Brigade continued to send direct and unequivocal demands to the HVO, who show no signs of moving. Three days before the deadline Paul Kellett calls. Nigel Beer, the commanding officer of the QRH battlegroup, is to conduct a reconnaissance of Kulen Vakuf. Paul is accompanying him, together with artillery and engineer experts. By now it looks like the majority of the VRS will complete their withdrawal to cantonments in the 2 LI area and that the only enforcement action required by us will be confiscation of the artillery pieces above Čelinac. If any members of the battalion are at risk, it is B Company, who will have to plan to attack the noncompliant HVO. This looks like becoming the main effort for the division.

I offer Paul reinforcements. Firstly an additional section of the anti-tank platoon: if the Warriors cannot get across the bridge, the crews will be able to carry the MILAN firing posts and missiles into the town. Secondly the recce platoon: its lighter Scimitars may be able to get across the bridge or an improvised river crossing impassable to Warrior. Finally, I also offer the complete mortar platoon. Although the mortar bombs are much smaller than the huge shells fired by the artillery, their fuses can be set on 'delay', allowing the bombs to penetrate roofs of buildings before they explode. They can be used closer to our troops than the heavier artillery shells. This makes them extremely valuable for supporting the close-quarter infantry battle that will be necessary if the HVO fight. Paul and I also identify that we need specialist equipment to help with attacking defended buildings, such as scaling ladders, grappling hooks and sledgehammers. We also need to make explosive charges to blow holes in walls and demolish bunkers.

Active HVO resistance could cause IFOR casualties. I warn the adjutant, RSM, doctor and padre. I wonder if B Company have sufficient infantrymen to rapidly overwhelm an actively resisting HVO with minimum risk of casualties. 'The more you use, the fewer you lose' is an old military maxim that seems to apply here. The battalion is comfortable with the tactics and procedures of urban combat, having practised the art on many occasions over the last few years, including at the purpose-built facilities owned by the Allies in West Berlin and the German Infantry School in Hammelburg. Eighteen months earlier, we had used live ammunition to mount battlegroup attacks on mock-up villages on the prairie in Canada. I imagine that the QRH, an armoured regiment, is less comfortable with the idea than we are. Without wishing to deflect Nigel Beer, I hope that this will be recognised by Division, who, if the HVO show active resistance, will order a second armoured infantry company to evict the HVO, with 2 LI in charge!

I therefore let A and C Company commanders know that a second company may be needed. Battlegroup HQ is warned off to split into a Main HQ under Chris Booth, with a single company and the Light Dragoon squadron remaining in Banja Luka, and a Forward HQ, with two companies, the whole of the support company and a tailored logistic echelon, deploying to fight in Kulen Vakuf. I make no secret of these preparations. If the factions learn of them it can only reinforce their understanding of our capability and resolve. In the battlegroup, it should mean that we are all psychologically prepared to go and fight for Kulen Vakuf at short notice. I sharpen my bayonet.

By 18 April, the day of the D+120 deadline, the cantonment of forces around Banja Luka appears complete. We are surprised when A Company's patrol finds the howitzers in the woods above Čelinac gone from the hills and ensconced in a VRS barracks.

Elsewhere there is a palpable air of tension in the brigade. In the morning it appears that the HVO are as determined to remain in Kulen Vakuf as ever. An RAF Hercules transport plane delivers a pack of urban warfare equipment, including the scaling ladders and grappling hooks we had asked for. Preparations to assault continue.

In the late afternoon, I am at A Company discussing Kulen Vakuf when Battlegroup HQ comes up on the net. The HVO are pulling out of Kulen Vakuf. Like many others, I am both delighted and disappointed: delighted that there will be no casualties in any attack on the town, but disappointed that we were not called upon to execute the attack. Had we been let off the leash the HVO would have been 'terminated with extreme prejudice' as one of the A Company officers puts it.

That night Paul Davies's news report about the Čelinac Brigade was shown on a Western satellite news channel. Shortly afterwards the same report was shown on Croatian TV. The pictures were the same but the sound had been replaced by a commentary in Croatian. The original report was factual and balanced, but the Croats had changed it into a news item claiming that the VRS were poised to unleash attacks upon Croatia, skewing it into a shrill piece of blatant propaganda against the Bosnian Serbs.

A quick investigation showed that after filming their report with us the ITN team drove to Zagreb, where they used the Croatian TV studio there to edit and transmit the report to London. The Croats simply took a copy, which they subsequently doctored. Major Marković, the unfortunate commander of the VRS brigade in Čelinac, was justifiably angry. He felt his trust had been abused and that IFOR had misled him. Richard Smith went straight to Čelinac, apologised profusely and did his best to limit the damage. The incident was a salutary reminder of the deep antipathy that still existed between the ethnic groupings.

Inspections

IFOR had the right to inspect the factions' camps and barracks. This was to allow us to check weapon holdings against those declared to us. As all sides were to be inspected by IFOR it would act as a useful confidence building measure.

There was immense potential for the VRS to make difficulties while remaining within the letter of the Dayton Agreement. We therefore made it crystal clear to them that we would not tolerate the orchestrated deception, obstruction and obfuscation that had so hampered the UN weapon inspectors in Iraq. But we also set out to minimise the inconvenience of these inspections for both the VRS and ourselves. We therefore decided to give the VRS at least a day's notice of an inspection where possible. At the same time we would keep a careful watch for unauthorised movements of weapons, vehicles and equipment.

We received no guidance from the chain of command as to how to do this, nor did we need any. There was no template or standard procedure for inspecting a faction camp. Our method of operation for inspection teams was worked by 'reverse engineering' peacetime arrangements for arms control inspections that we had been liable to receive in England and Germany under the Conventional Forces in Europe Treaty. To make sure that we achieved a uniform approach, I ordered Ian Baker to set up a battlegroup inspection team headed by Tony Allport, the intelligence officer.

The inspections themselves went very well. The VRS were expecting to be inspected and had made some effort to lay out weapons and equipment so that they could easily be counted. The Air Force sites were also well laid out, but it was clear that many of them resented us being there.

After a successful inspection, I drove to a brigade conference at Šipovo. Approaching Banja Luka I was enjoying an unusually balmy afternoon, when I unexpectedly heard the sound of jet aircraft. Stopping the Land Rover, I was amazed to see NATO fighter-bombers swooping down over the town. Diving down to less than fifteen hundred feet and suddenly pulling up with a deep roar of afterburners, they appeared to be rehearsing dive-bombing attacks on the Kosmos Factory in the centre of Banja Luka.

Had this happened in January, February or March, I would have been delighted that NATO air power was visibly reinforcing our efforts. But now, with the faction armed forces corralled in barracks subject to our inspection and control regime and the battlegroup doing all it could to promote a return to normality, the last thing we needed was NATO jets putting on a loud and intimidating display of their low-level capabilities. I got straight on the brigade net to request that they stopped doing this as soon as possible. I am afraid that I swore a lot.

Another source of great annoyance was provided by IFOR troops entering Banja Luka without any legitimate reason to be there. As part our attempts to retain maximum freedom of action, extensive measures had been taken to reduce unnecessary friction with the locals. Most important of these was to avoid creating any impression that Banja Luka was a city under occupation by a foreign power.

Several times battlegroup patrols and LOs had encountered IFOR troops in the city with no legitimate reason to be there. Often they were shopping, sightseeing or socialising. This was precisely why I had banned IFOR troops from visiting the town. Although this was supported by the UK chain of command, other nations seemed neither to understand nor to enforce this. We had already found it necessary to mount a joint operation with the military police to deter unauthorised IFOR troops from swanning into Banja Luka. We called this Operation SWAN. I had thought that the extremely small number of genuine complaints from civilians in Banja Luka meant that the policy was succeeding.

Despite this we still encountered parties of IFOR troops visiting Banja Luka who did not have permission to be there and had not bothered to tell us they were in the town. The previous day, we had discovered two coachloads of soldiers from the Nordic/Polish brigade sightseeing in the town centre. The message was still not getting across. I complained to Brigade and redoubled our efforts to patrol the town.

Over the next two weeks our inspection programme continued without serious hitches, but suddenly we were overcome with official visitors. Up to now the battlegroup's distance from Gornji Vakuf and the poor weather had meant that few senior officers from outside the division came to visit us. We needed to brief these important decision makers on the realities of battlegroup operations, let them see the situation for themselves, make sure they took back a positive impression of us – and juggle with the unpredictable factors of weather, roads and unexpected operations.

Now the weather was better, the factions were in their barracks and Banja Luka Airfield was open to IFOR. In rapid succession we were visited by the British Defence Secretary Michael Portillo, a party of British politicians making up the House of Commons Defence Committee and the NATO supreme commander, an American general. Then on our last Saturday in Banja Luka Admiral Leighton Smith US Navy the IFOR Commander 'invited' himself to Banja Luka. We were to be conducting an inspection of a VRS barracks, which he would 'just happen' to drop in to see.

On the day, I waited at Banja Luka airfield, alongside four US Army Blackhawk helicopters, his 'command flight'. The Admiral arrived in a US Navy executive jet. As we strapped ourselves into the lead Blackhawk and the flight began, I briefed him about Kozara Barracks and the inspection arrangements. At the camp, as we walked round the assembled rows to anti-aircraft guns and sheds of tanks and armoured vehicles, the VRS officers showed huge surprise that such senior NATO officer should appear without warning. They were, as Ian Baker put it, 'in a bit of a flap'.

We left the VRS leadership floundering around, apparently gasping for breath as our helicopters lifted from their camp, a menacing display of the reach of American power. Yet again our speed of action had outstripped that of the factions. The Admiral and I flew to the Metal Factory. In the briefing room, we drank tea and ate cucumber sandwiches while discussing how operations could be developed in Republika Srpska. As he left, the Admiral confided in me that he wished his American troops had as much freedom of action to match operations to the threat and the environment as we did.

Arrivals and Departures

By mid-April we had all become jaded. We were too used to Bosnia. I was bored with the fact that most of the people I dealt with were wearing some kind of camouflaged fatigue uniform, albeit in a kaleidoscopic variety of different patterns – like Jackson Pollock paintings, but in limited variations of green, brown, yellow and black. Also like Jackson Pollock paintings, they were dull and monotonous in excess. I was bored with having to talk to civilians and the factions through an interpreter, having to talk slowly and simply in short soundbites, consciously avoiding the argot of British military jargon and abbreviations that so naturally peppered our speech.

Some of our equipment was wearing out. Warriors were now extremely dirty and their paint was flaked and chipped, often showing UN white or even desert yellow paint below. Of the twenty computers we had brought with us, over half had broken down – due either to the ingress of dust or dirt, or to the rough handling they received on being moved from place to place.

We were getting very tired. Although the constantly changing operational profile and unexpected events had prevented this being a 'Groundhog Day' tour, most of us were thoroughly looking forward to going home. New arrivals probably found that we were 'shot away', talking in private jargon, taking our own shortcuts and well on the way to becoming prisoners of our own particular experiences. Richard Smith and Paul Kellett had both brought a welcome fresh approach. In April three new platoon commanders joined the battalion straight from training. One of these, Lieutenant Tim O'Brien, described his experiences with C Company.

> Arriving back in Warminster suitably wet and tired after Exercise GRIM REAPER on the Platoon Commanders' Battle Course, we were informed by the Guard Commander that we would be flying to Split at 0600 hrs on 4 April 1996 – in less than thirty-six hours! A classic example of Army administration: we had been kept in the dark until the last possible moment. On release from the course, we made a quick expedition to the launderette before catching the plane to Split. Three subalterns arrived in Bosnia with wet kit hoping that they had been remembered by the battalion.
>
> The moment finally came, after sixteen months of training, to join our platoons. Second Lieutenant Epton met his platoon while they were engaged on guards and duties, allowing ample time for the company second in command, Captain Mortimer, to explain the situation: 'Snore and you'll be out of here.' Suitably chastised, 2 Lt Epton didn't even squeak.

Having arrived from a hectic course that had allowed us little chance to keep up to date with the current situation in Bosnia, the early days consisted of situation updates, meeting our platoons and being introduced to Warrior. The operations at the time were heavily influenced by the upcoming D+120, by when the former warring factions had to have withdrawn to dedicated cantonment areas. A secondary task was the increasingly important relationship with the local community.

Just as we were beginning to know the area around Krupa the company received orders to conduct a relief in place of B Company, 1 QLR in Previja. By this stage of the tour the company was so used to moving that this was accomplished with little fuss and we were under command of 1 QLR in very little time. Here the emphasis moved towards protecting groups of Serbs and Muslims attempting to visit graves and homes that they were forced to leave behind.

The benefits were great, the learning curve near vertical. There can be few better places for a platoon commander to meet his platoon than on operations. It allows him to get know his soldiers that much faster and to see them in their true light, and vice versa. On a bigger scale he receives a demonstration of how the battlegroup and its component parts work.

Throughout the second half of April we prepared to hand over Banja Luka town to the military police regiment who would control it, and Battlegroup HQ spent an ever-increasing amount of time masterminding the arrangements for the relief in place with the WFR. While all April's operations went on, the Metal Factory was being prepared for occupation by Division HQ. By the middle of the month, there were two hundred engineers building new accommodation and office units, a new helicopter pad and improved water and power supplies. Signallers were laying cables everywhere. Ptarmigan radio relay vehicles arrived and the quality of the Ptarmigan links into the camp improved dramatically. 'Strange, that', said the signals officer.

More and more shower and toilet blocks were constructed and opened. For the first three months in Banja Luka all our soldiers had was a single shower block that could not produce sufficient hot water. Even after we had got the factory showers running, the supply of hot water was always inadequate. Now there was no shortage. The Divisional HQ included a canteen and bar, with British beer, confectionery and other goodies coming up from Split every day – stark contrast to our hand-to-mouth company canteens that relied on a great deal of hard work and the purchase of local beer.

Our officers and soldiers could have been bitter and negative about the members of Division HQ being able to take for granted things that had been denied to most of the battlegroup for most of the tour. Instead they shrugged and considered it another ironic 'Bosnia bizarre', confirming their view that infantrymen could 'hack it' under much more austere conditions than the signallers and staff officers.

I felt that I should not go round the faction military commanders making farewell calls. Just as in January when we handed western Bosnia over to the Canadian brigade, we wanted the faction military to wake up one morning and find out that they had new IFOR troops to work with. Anyway I was sick of my ego being insincerely flattered. Steve Noble had arranged for me to do a 'farewell interview' on Radio Big. Igor the DJ was incredibly welcoming and polite. I handed my radio show over to a young officer of the Light Dragoons who would, I hoped, play much more modern music than I did.

A year earlier, in a time and place that seemed light years away, we had identified that, if we were to be on a dull, repetitive, undemanding 'Groundhog Day' tour we would have the opportunity to do something to alleviate some of the immense suffering all around us. In the event, the intensity of operations meant that any charitable work by the battlegroup would have had to be at the expense of our operations. So, although we saw plenty of examples of misery and suffering and many opportunities to help, I hardened my heart and ordered that no purely humanitarian or charitable projects be undertaken. It gave me no pleasure to do this – in fact I sometimes loathed myself for doing so – but the best way to reduce suffering in Bosnia was to establish a lasting peace.

Once the faction forces had successfully withdrawn to barracks, the corps commander directed that opportunities for providing assistance to civil tasks should be sought and that help was to be given where appropriate. The British division directed that its main effort would move from the military implementation of Dayton to supporting implementation of the treaty's civil aspects. The division's activity level would be adjusted to match the level of faction military compliance.

I therefore relaxed my ruling forbidding purely humanitarian activities. Sean Harris had identified an orphanage in Banja Luka and 'adopted' it. I had not been able to visit it, until my last week. Had I been repressing guilt by staying away? I did not know.

The institution was on the edge of town. It contained thirty children of various ages, half of them physically or mentally handicapped. Half a dozen support company soldiers were already there, playing with the children and helping with repairs or improvements to the buildings and the worn-out flyblown playground.

I joined in, later chatting with the hard-pressed adults running the orphanage. The able-bodied children were orphans, but families who had been either unable or unwilling to cope had abandoned most of the disabled children. The little community was living a hand-to-mouth existence, only just managing to survive on donations and support from the few international charities that operated in Republika Srpska.

The children's faces were a joy – lit up with a pleasure almost unbearable to see. They clearly loved having the good-humoured and enthusiastic soldiers to play with. The half dozen adults who ran the orphanage were all deeply careworn by the effort of looking after their charges. This microcosm of suffering and hope moved me deeply. There I saw my own small son, who by an accident of chance had been born to comfortably well off British parents, when he could so easily have been born to a refugee family.

A Protest March

The tour was ending with the IFOR mission in a state of transition. With the exception of the full lifting of mines, all the military requirements of the Dayton Agreement were achieved and IFOR had suppressed permanent checkpoints. During the Bosnian war the end of winter had been the time when the faction armies had launched the first major offensives of the year. Spring 1996 saw the faction armies' withdrawal to their NATO authorised barracks.

Freedom of movement by civilians, including displaced persons, was an important part of the civil implementation of the Dayton peace plan. Although, the closure of faction checkpoints meant that civilians theoretically enjoyed full freedom of movement throughout Bosnia, the reality was that only a very few brave individuals were crossing between the two entities, usually on trips arranged by IFOR, the NGOs or the International Red Cross. Neither the Federation nor Republika Srpska seemed willing to encourage people from the other side to cross the line.

This had been demonstrated in the middle of April when there was a serious incident at Otaka in the Czech battalion area. Back in January we had identified that the division of the town into a Muslim-held west bank and a Serb-controlled east bank connected by a battered bridge was a potential flashpoint. Before they handed over to the Czechs, A Company had played an important role in arranging meetings which allowed the Muslim and Serb civil leaders to discuss the issue.

Tension simmered and on 19 April several hundred Muslims crossed the bridge in Serb territory, after hearing rumours that empty homes on the east side, formerly occupied by Muslims, were to be used to house Serb civilians. A rival crowd of Serbs quickly appeared to contest this, and were rapidly reinforced by hard-line nationalists bussed into the town from outside.The Czech battlegroup interposed themselves between the two factions, separating them. Tensions rose, the situation rapidly worsened; Czech soldiers were threatened and responded by firing warning shots. The incident went on for over ten hours, with the Czechs firing some four hundred warning shots. There was little doubt that if they had not opened fire there would have been violence between the hostile crowds, with a high risk of IFOR troops becoming casualties.

A few days later, after the successful cantonment of forces, B Company became aware of the Muslim *Bayram* festival at the end of April and beginning of May, which involves families making visits to gravesites. The company learned that five hundred Muslims from Sanski Most wanted to travel north through WHITE FANG to visit their former homes in villages now inside Republika Srpska.

Before the war, Muslims had inhabited them. Now Serb families inhabited those houses that had not been burned out, blown up or demolished. The visit was being organised by leaders in Sanski Most – where B Company had identified much latent tension resulting from ever-increasing evidence of atrocities against Muslim civilians.

If the visit went wrong it might easily result in direct confrontation between agitated Muslims and extreme nationalist Serbs. Paul Kellett could easily imagine violence arising, and it was likely that both sides would blame anything that went wrong on IFOR. Planning for the march became B Company's main effort. Because Prijedor, from which any Bosnian Serb response would come, lay in Czech battlegroup's area, and because of the political sensitivity of the operation, it also became the QRH battlegroup and Canadian brigade's main effort. B Company however would lead the planning and conduct of the operation.

B Company would rely on the Czech battlegroup providing early warning of any reaction from Prijedor. If the situation deteriorated, extra infantry could only come from the Czechs or the Canadian company to the south. Paul drew confidence from the work that B Company had done with both nations in their multinational patrol programme, which had broken down some, though not all, operating barriers. This allowed him to quickly develop a set of multinational operating procedures for the march.

At the same time, displaced persons were attempting to visit their homes or places of origin elsewhere in the division's area. The battlegroup monitored parties of Serbs who set out from Banja Luka to visit the town of Glamoč deep in Federation territory. Six hundred set out in buses, but after discussions with the major of Glamoč, only eight cars travelled from Bosnian Serb territory to the town. A few days later five busloads of Serbs left Banja Luka to visit their former homes in Sanski Most, but decided to turn back at the edge of Bosnian Muslim territory. Both visits had been closely monitored by IFOR, including the deployment of C Company from Previja to forward positions, ready to intervene if necessary.

It was important to allow the non-governmental organisations, in particular UNHCR and IPTF, to lead in the initial negotiations between the heads of the *obstinas* – usually the mayors and their chiefs of police. It was hoped by IFOR that this would persuade the marchers that there were other, less dangerous ways of making their point than a potentially confrontational march across the IEBL.

As he planned for the *Bayram* march from Sanski Most, Paul had to work hard to liaise with the IPTF. They were structured into districts that matched Bosnian boundaries and did not correspond with IFOR brigade, battlegroup or company areas, so there was considerable scope for confusion. Paul had to deal with three different IPTF commanders from three different districts. B Company learned that the organisers had arranged for Muslim refugees living in Germany to return from Sanski Most for the march. Paul had to plan for the worst-case assumption that he would need to prevent a physical confrontation. This might require separation of the opposing forces. Key to this was, he said,

> a graded response – what I mean is, the first agencies the marchers should see are the NGOs and their own civil police. As the IFOR commander in a situation like this you need to take a back seat for as long as possible and let the NGOs get on with it.

The company did this by deploying low-profile patrols on the approaches to WHITE FANG to monitor any movement from Sanski Most. To the north the Czechs and JCOs were similarly monitoring the routes from Prijedor to WHITE FANG. Closer to the crossing point Paul had placed Warriors and tanks where they were visible, but with the crews in a relatively relaxed, non-threatening posture – for example, wearing berets instead of helmets. The tanks had their barrels lowered and pointed away from the marchers. The vehicles and troops were in a position to react very quickly, either by blocking the route, or if necessary by responding in kind to use of force or its threat by the factions.

On the day of the march, a large number of IFOR liaison officers and representatives of the various international organisations arrived at WHITE FANG. These included the Canadian brigade commander and the CO of the QRH. Paul Kellett now had to look after them and their vehicles as well as run the close operation monitoring the march.

Five buses and fifty carloads of Muslims moved north from Sanski Most, closely monitored by the company. They drove to a point just south of WHITE FANG, parked their vehicles, and then held a small demonstration and press conference with the German media. The Muslim march leaders concluded by stating that their aim had been fulfilled and the march started to disperse peacefully...or so it seemed. Paul takes up the story:

> Information was received from the JCOs that the Serbs in Prijedor had learnt of the demonstration and had commenced their own counter-march. The Czechs patrolling to the north of WHITE FANG learned that about five hundred Serbs were en route to WHITE FANG and would be arriving within thirty minutes. I requested the presence of the Hungarian IPTF commander for Prijedor to discuss the issue with him. With an angry Serb crowd now forming at WHITE FANG, I suggested that he, the Prijedor IPTF commander and a member of the Serb police take my helicopter and show the Serb policeman that the Muslims had indeed dispersed.
>
> This idea did the trick. The helicopter recce gave the Serb policeman confidence in IFOR's word and he, obviously holding a position of importance with the Serb crowd, soon ensured their peaceful dispersal. A potentially nasty incident had been avoided by an early appreciation of the situation and the talking through in the planning stages of a number of 'what ifs'. This particular episode also restored the previously strained relations between B Company and the Hungarian IPTF commander for Prijedor.

B Company breathed a sigh of relief, not only because of the peaceful outcome, but also because they could now get on with handing over Sanski Most to the WFR. Later Paul Kellett was to summarise:

> The lessons of the operation were to ensure you know the ground well and identify choke points, possible flash points, and areas for vehicles. In other words, do your intelligence preparation. Liaise early with the displaced persons

groups, NGOs, IPTF and civil police. Ensure you know who leads on what part. Understand your rules of engagement and make sure that all are briefed. Ensure you have a sound media plan – I failed to take this fully into account in my plan. Ensure that your neighbours are consulted – joint planning, which is often multinational in nature, takes time. You should also leave yourself plenty of time for rehearsals and go through mission analysis and a number of 'what if' scenarios.

This had been going on against the background of our impending relief in place. The advance party of WFR commanders and logisticians had been with us for a week. Two days before B Company's march, A Company had begun to concentrate their vehicles at Mrkonjić Grad. Their Warriors would then move to the logistic base at Lipa for 'de-bombing', the removal of their operational stocks of ammunition, while A Company of the WFR married up with their Warriors and 'bombed up'. Warriors were then transported by the same low-loaders that had delivered the WFR's armour to Split to be loaded on the ship that had brought the WFR from England. As soon as the Sanski Most march finished, B Company drove their Warriors to Lipa to begin the same process. As Warriors moved to Lipa, soldiers moved to the Metal Factory and then to Banja Luka airport to board the RAF Hercules that had delivered the WFR for flights to Paderborn.

The next day I left Banja Luka for England.

CHAPTER 16

Roads from Sarajevo

We see today in Bosnia an absence of war. IFOR, together with many civilian agencies and organisations, has made enormous progress from the savagery of last summer. But sadly, we do not have peace. Bosnia contains too much hatred, fear, and frankly a lot of stubbornness.

Admiral Leighton Smith, COMIFOR,
speaking at the Royal United Services Institute, London 19 July 1996

Departures and Arrivals

The complex dispersal of vehicles to Split port and troops to Banja Luka Airport and then all to Paderborn worked well. Once we were complete in Paderborn all of us would have a long weekend's leave.

I flew from Zagreb to England to attend the annual conference of the British infantry. The contrast with Bosnia was extreme. I had thoroughly enjoyed the tour, was never bored and had been amused by the many bizarre events. Yet I was now happy not to have to carry a weapon any more. I was sad to leave the good Bosnians that I had met, and hoped against hope that their views would prevail against the shriller counsels of the nationalists and extremists. I was equally glad to see the back of those stubborn Bosnians whom we had found obdurate, proud, cunning and manipulative and who had often treated each other with great brutality. But now I was extremely tired, events in England seemed anticlimactic and I had to force myself to concentrate. I returned to Paderborn after everyone else. That weekend, I enjoyed getting to know my family again.

In Paderborn, the battalion had always begun work on Mondays with a formal muster parade followed by fitness training. This time I ordered the whole battalion into the gymnasium, sat them on the floor and spent fifteen minutes telling the story of the tour, making sure that no significant operation or incident was left out. I knew that while company commanders and the staff of Battalion HQ had a reasonable picture of our operations, most of the junior ranks had been utterly immersed in the work of their company or platoon and knew little of what the rest of the battalion had done. I wanted to remedy this and acknowledge the achievements of every company and platoon, including the specialists in support and HQ companies.

I explained that I knew some were disappointed not to have had more chances to engage the factions in close combat. If we had done so, I had no doubt that we would have been very successful in the controlled application of overwhelming force, but our domination of the faction military had been so complete that their direct challenges had been few and far between. We should be thankful that we suffered no casualties from faction attacks and that so many people miraculously escaped being killed in traffic accidents and mine strikes. I thanked them all for everything they did.

We also had to say a last goodbye to Private Fox. A memorial service took place in Paderborn's cathedral, the *Dom*. Padre Nick Cook preached another memorable sermon.

Now there was much to be done. Paul Evanson unloaded our Warriors from the ship at Bremen, reloaded them to rail flats, offloaded them again in Paderborn and finally drove them to into our barracks. We removed the great slabs of Chobham armour so they could be used by other armoured infantry battalions and began the long task of refurbishing the vehicles to make good six months of hard wear and tear. At the same time, freight containers of equipment had to be unloaded and all our stores, weapons and radios accounted for, cleaned, checked, tested and where necessary repaired.

People had to be looked after. The battalion would be moving from Paderborn to Northern Ireland in December, some seven months hence. People were also leaving the battalion. This included some who were leaving the Army, some of whom had volunteered to extend their length of service to complete the tour, and some who were due routine postings away from the battalion. Some of the TA soldiers had so enjoyed their tour that they had volunteered for the battalion's next Northern Ireland tour, but most were returning to civilian life.

Units that had previously conducted Bosnia tours advised that it was best to spend three weeks conducting these activities before going on leave. This allowed everyone a soft landing after the stresses and concentrated experience of the tour. It also allowed time for members of the small teams that had been so close to make their farewells before they moved on.

I wanted to end the tour on a high note, by conducting a medals parade, where everyone would receive the UNPROFOR and NATO medals that they had earned. As soon as our vehicles were back, we began rehearsals, as described in *The Silver Bugle*:

Rehearsals started in earnest after the long weekend. Meanwhile Sergeant Mudd was busily preparing the seven hundred and four UNPROFOR medals, seven hundred and eleven NATO medals, thirty-one Accumulated Campaign Service medals and a single Long Service and Good Conduct medal to be presented on the day.

The Band of the Light Division joined the rehearsals on Tuesday afternoon, by which time the parade was really taking shape. The GOC, Major-General Cordy-Simpson, made his final visit to the battalion midway through the adjutant's rehearsal on the Wednesday and took the salute for the march past and double off. He then presented medals to twenty-five members of the battalion who would be part of the presentation team for the actual parade.

The colonel of the regiment, Major-General Regan, flew in from England to take the parade. Despite a wet start to the day, by 1030 hrs on Thursday 23 May 1996 the scene was set, the Union, UN, NATO and regimental flags fluttering at the far side of the square, displayed proudly on gleaming white poles. More than four hundred family members and friends, who had made a tremendous effort to be there, were now sitting waiting in anticipation.

At precisely 1100 hrs the general stepped onto the dais and was greeted with an immaculate Present Arms. After he inspected the front ranks General Regan presented medals to twenty-four members of the battalion. These had been carefully selected to represent the full spectrum of battalion members who served throughout the tour. It included personnel from all the other regiments and corps that had accompanied us to Bosnia, TA soldiers, and the youngest soldier in the battalion, Private Udale. Meanwhile, battalion officers were presenting medals to the rest of the parade. After a short speech by the colonel of the regiment, the battalion marched past and then, led by four Warriors driving past at speed with their barrels dipped in salute, doubled off to the sound of Keel Row, in true Light Infantry tradition with the commanding officer leading.

I was immensely proud to do this.

The Paderborn authorities had been very supportive while the battalion had been away. They lent us the elegant *Schloss* at Schloss Neuhauss on the edge of Paderborn as the setting for a sounding retreat by the Light Division Band. The function began with a reception in the castle's Hall of Mirrors. I had been asked to give a short speech of thanks to the *Stadt* authorities. As my German was rudimentary and of a much poorer standard than my wife's, she surprised everyone by giving the speech for me.

Parties were then held in the Junior Ranks Club, the Corporals' Mess and the Serjeants' Mess. After the reception was over, an Officers' Mess party began. This was the last time all the officers who had served together in Bosnia would be together in the same place. We danced until dawn.

Souvenirs and Reflections

That next day the battalion went on leave, all of us carrying two souvenirs. Steve Noble had come back from Bosnia a few days before the battalion to produce a magazine commemorating the tour. Filled with photographs, it contained a short descriptive history of the battalion's tour, written by Steve, Chris Booth and myself.

Steve also produced a souvenir video diary telling the story of the tour. He persuaded Forces Television, the BBC, HTV and ITN to give him copies of all their news broadcasts featuring the battalion. He arranged the reports in chronological order, interspersed with handheld video footage shot by members of the battalion. This grainy hand-held footage was set to four of the pop songs we heard on our radios during the tour. 'Search for the Hero' by M People showed our UN operations on Mount Igman. 'Don't Look Back in Anger' by Oasis accompanied clips of NATO operations. 'Country House' by Blur showed the bases and houses that we lived in. Finally 'Looking Back' by Mike and the Mechanics showed people at work, including the backroom boys and girls of HQ Company. The video was incredibly evocative. It was also very popular, as most of us had seen little of the TV news coverage of our works. Giving this video to people was an apt souvenir of their tour.

My wife had booked a house on the coast of New England for a holiday. Relaxing in a supremely quiet and isolated location, I found time to reflect on the tour.

Starting at the strategic level, by early 1995 the UN's position in Bosnia was rapidly deteriorating. General Smith recognised that the position was impossible to sustain. His leadership of UNPROFOR and the British, French and Dutch response to the summer's hostage crisis began to regain the initiative. This culminated in September, while we were conducting our second reconnaissance. The Federation offensive in western Bosnia, NATO air strikes and the Multinational Brigade's shelling of Serb positions around Sarajevo, combined with the decisive military and political engagement of the United States, created the conditions that forced all three parties, particularly the Bosnian Serbs, around the conference table.

Richard Holbrooke, the US negotiator, rapidly exploited this at the political level. He not only got the factions to negotiate, but by controlling the agenda and sustaining the initiative was able to exploit the fleeting opportunity that the fighting had created. If he had failed, UNPROFOR would have probably have been withdrawn from Bosnia. We would have played a major role in that perilous operation.

The Dayton Agreement cemented the faction's political and military consent to peace and NATO's role at the strategic level. It provided IFOR with the operational powers and 'levers' to compel military compliance, particularly the entitlement to *'use military force to ensure compliance'*, the right *'to compel the movement, 'withdrawal or relocation of forces'* and powers to protect the IFOR and implement the peace, using *'authority without interference or permission from any party, to do all that the commander judges necessary and proper, including the use of military force'*.

UNPROFOR had been hamstrung by having so many national contingents that had been structured, trained and equipped only for peacekeeping, and that soon found themselves marginalised and at increased risk. NATO was determined to avoid this problem by constructing IFOR from national contingents with a full combat capability. Compared with UNPROFOR, IFOR was operating from a position of strength with a more unified and coherent approach to operations.

Bosnia had been the UN's largest peacekeeping operation. It became NATO's first ever land operation, and the largest Western military operation since the

Gulf War. A particularly significant role was played by British troops. At the peak of Operation RESOLUTE, more than thirteen thousand UK personnel were deployed in the Balkans.

The tension and uncertainty of the initial part of Operation RESOLUTE should not be forgotten. Deployment in midwinter, the separation of the factions, the transfer of territory and the containment of the faction armed forces were all successes, but might not have been so. The military timelines of the agreement could only be achieved by IFOR reassuring both sides that they could comply without their security being threatened by non-compliance on the other side. This was particularly challenging in the first month after transfer of authority from UN to NATO, before substantial reinforcements arrived.

This was why the operations of 4 Armoured Brigade in December and January were so important. Brigadier Dannatt's assured leadership and the expert work of his headquarters not only gave us all confidence, but also created the conditions that gave the battlegroup the greatest possible chance of successfully exploiting IFOR's authority in order to achieve the tight military timelines. Central to this was the speed at which we redeployed from our UN tasks and the way we concealed our relative weakness in the first month after D-Day, using constant redeployment and demonstrating that we were capable of conducting high-intensity all arms operations.

The simplicity, clarity and practicality of the military measures in the Dayton Agreement made a major contribution to the rapid reduction of military tension. Military compliance with GFAP was high and the assertive posture and combat capability of IFOR ensured that the designated timelines were achieved. The brigade seized the initiative and maintained it, helping IFOR to achieve military dominance over the faction forces.

Our rules of engagement allowed the use of force, both for self-defence and, *in extremis*, to enforce the military provisions of GFAP. Once reinforcements were complete, IFOR possessed sufficient combat power to significantly overmatch the factions where and when it required. We called this 'escalation dominance'. By May faction military capability was controlled by IFOR, and this could be sustained for the rest of the year – provided that IFOR continued to carry out surveillance and inspections and kept control of faction training and movement.

Fighting Power

The battalion was well tested. The area over which it moved and operated was huge – the battalion area on D+1 was a hundred kilometres by seventy kilometres and contained a hundred and eight kilometres of confrontation line and a hundred and twenty thousand faction troops. For the first few months after D-Day logistic support was tenuous, intermittent and continuously overstretched. Communications were poor and sometimes non-existent and the situation was diverse and constantly changing.

Of necessity, I have spent much time discussing problems and how we solved them. But the battalion was not overwhelmed by any of these difficulties and we managed to live and move through, around, over or under all the snares, entrapments and pitfalls of Bosnia in order to carry out our missions.

Army doctrine assesses that the basis for success on operations stems from fighting power – the ability to fight. It is seen as having three components: the conceptual, the moral and the physical. These provide useful tools for analysing how we sustained our operational effectiveness in Bosnia.

The Conceptual Component

British military doctrine described the conceptual component as 'the thought process behind the ability to fight'. The battlegroup made extensive use of doctrine, both the specialist doctrine developed for what had become known as 'Wider Peacekeeping' and the tactical doctrine applicable to battlegroup war fighting operations. All this was underpinned by the philosophy of manoeuvre warfare, and the principles of British peacekeeping doctrine, namely impartiality, negotiation and transparency.

No matter how much force we had at our disposal, the factions had to see that we were even-handed. Our close, deep and rear operations were mutually reinforcing. Although we occasionally used or threatened to use force against military targets, our main targets were people's minds. We were attempting to influence attitudes – of the soldiers and their commanders and of the civilians and their political leaders.

Our philosophy of mission command aimed to promote decentralised command, freedom and speed of action and initiative. The complex nature of the task, lack of intelligence, often confused situations, poor communications and problematic passage of information were all challenges we had to solve. Doing so required a clear mission statement and full understanding of the higher commander's intent in order to be able to react quickly to changing situations or fleeting opportunities. If mission command did not exist, we would have to have invented it for Bosnia. Often the commanders' intent would be unchanged from brigade commander all the way down to the section commander.

The battalion employed mission analysis and the estimate process during all operations. As a result, we often anticipated events and identified problems before they occurred. From the outset of planning in November we had anticipated the military requirements of the Dayton timelines for both ourselves and the factions. This helped Battlegroup HQ, the company and squadron commanders and the liaison officers all understand not only the 'hows' of each action but also the 'whys'. With the exception of the difficulties posed by war crimes and war criminals, we worked out what we were going to do well in advance.

Often the battlegroup estimate largely corresponded with the conclusions being drawn from the brigade estimate. It was interesting that, in some cases, the conclusion after carrying out the full estimate was to do nothing. On other occasions, we would initiate activity without waiting for orders because our mission analysis or estimate told us to do it, only to subsequently receive instructions from the chain of command telling us to initiate that very activity. Examples of this included the restoration of freedom of movement outside Sanski Most area, the responses to the shooting incidents and the battlegroup initiating its Psyops campaign from the very outset of the NATO operation.

Some outsiders were surprised, sometimes even critical, of the battalion's method of operation. I know that one very senior British officer had commented that we exhibited *'an overdose of mission command'*. I did not agree. Mission command and the leadership of our commanders helped in overcoming the considerable friction of operations in the Bosnian winter. Without these we could have sustained only a much lower tempo of operations.

I was delighted that members of the battalion were constantly taking the initiative without waiting for orders to do so. I was very lucky to have many excellent commanders and could depend on their judgement and ability to deal with rapidly changing situations and solve unforeseen and unexpected problems. Examples included private soldiers taking charge of the scene after serious traffic accidents where all the commanders were casualties; corporals and lance corporals preventing armed and intoxicated faction soldiers and police from entering the Zone of Separation; platoon serjeants using initiative and improvisation to overcome logistic problems resulting from occupying isolated platoon bases up to three hours' drive from their company HQ; platoon commanders who happily dealt with faction battalion and brigade commanders, defusing problems where they arose without having to constantly go back to their company or squadron commanders for instructions every time the situation changed; captain liaison officers spending long periods of time working on their own, representing me with faction senior commanders; company commanders using a combination of bluff, negotiation and cunning to open crossing points across the front line between the two armies; and commanders of all ranks showing a knack for identifying the critical point and moving to it in time to decisively influence events.

In stark contrast to the faction armies, whose command structure appeared to devolve little or no authority below corps, I gave as much responsibility as possible to everyone in the battalion, limited only by the level of their training and the requirements of the mission and plan. The best ways to exploit our highly capable fighting vehicles, the tremendous firepower of our weapons and our doctrine for armoured warfare were to decentralise, delegate and, when the situation changed unexpectedly or crises occurred, back the judgement of the commander on the spot.

We often complained that the only way anything got done in the Bosnian armies was if a high-ranking commander ordered it. In 2 LI the maximum possible would get done without having to give orders – thus leaving commanders free to concentrate on the things that really mattered. We needed people, including private soldiers, who could think for themselves when the situation changed and who could assume whatever responsibility was necessary to get the job done.

We had no choice but to use mission command when conducting operations on the behalf of civil agencies, such as the Bildt organisation. Often there was neither a clear aim nor a statement of commander's intent. In these situations there was often potential for mission command to turn into 'mission confusion', and we had to conduct mission analysis on their behalf.

The battlegroup's ability to obtain intelligence from formation assets was very limited. For example, we wanted to make maximum use of helicopters for surveillance but weather and availability meant that we received only a third of the sorties we asked for. We achieved an enormous amount by patrolling, formal and informal liaison, monitoring local media and talking to the locals. This quickly produced an enormous amount of information which, when analysed by our intelligence section, helped us to build up a comprehensive picture of the faction's order of battle and attitudes.

One of the few disappointments of our NATO operations was the initial reduction in the amount of information reaching us down the chain of command concerning activities elsewhere in Bosnia. This gradually improved, but we had to rely on the BBC World Service and CNN for too long. The modern electronic news media could report events very quickly, but we should not have been depending on these and our own analysis to build up a picture of events in Bosnia and their implications for us. We needed full 'situational awareness' which NATO initially seemed slow to supply. With the proliferation of near-instant reporting by global mass media, we cannot afford to allow the chain of command to be eclipsed by radio and television news.

Even so, much of the information that flowed into our HQs was fragmentary, confused, contradictory and incomplete. The first reports of incidents were often unreliable – nothing was ever quite as bad or as good as it first seemed. There was nothing particularly new about this. Indeed gathering information and turning it into intelligence had been crucial to all our operations in Northern Ireland. But when we analysed our own mistakes and problems, we found that a common factor was that commanders had made invalid assumptions. We could take nothing for granted and at every level of command. It was essential to physically check the information on which assumptions were based.

Some operations went wrong, or were less successful than they should have been. When this happened, checking back through the sequence of events leading up to the incident usually identified a point at which a commander failed to carry out a full estimate, failed to take into account the higher commander's intent, or failed to notice that the situation had changed. Sometimes I had been guilty of this.

The tour was characterised by manoeuvre, the battalion occupying a total of twenty-five different bases. Battlegroup HQ occupied five separate locations, and one company moved its main base eleven times. This required all of us to be prepared for independent operations for substantial periods and for long moves at short notice. We were able to react very quickly to sudden changes in the situation. This flexibility was a result of well practised and efficient battle procedure, including reconnaissance, issuing of orders, and road moves over long distances.

The battalion command team was well practised. The two-month pre-tour training package at Sennelager had been excellent preparation. We were also fortunate to have conducted so much all-arms training, as we operated from the outset with engineers, artillery and helicopters, of whom many had worked with us in Germany. Once the factions were well on the way to demobilisation we were able to reduce our operational profile, but we knew that we could instantly ratchet our capability back up – as the planning to conduct combined arms assaults at Tito Barracks Sarajevo and Kulen Vakuf showed.

Although we were not politicians, all our operations had a political role and our commanders had to be sensitive not only to the political situation but also to the political results of military actions. An issue we had not anticipated was problems of a moral dimension. We also did not expect to come across quite so many occasions when the distinction between the tactical, operational and strategic levels of command would become blurred.

Physical Component

The physical component is 'the means to fight', including equipment, logistics, training and manpower.

The battlegroup was a very flexible organisation. Our approach was to integrate the strengths and weaknesses of all our arms into a 'system of systems'. The mix of Rarden cannon, MILAN missiles, machine guns, mortars, LAW 80 and small arms provided an adequate mix of firepower for all our missions. Warrior with its firepower, protection, size, weight and noise impressed the factions, while Scimitar, Spartan and Land Rovers could reach places in mountains and towns inaccessible to Warrior. Grouping tanks and an armoured recce squadron with the battalion provided a well-balanced battlegroup with an ideal mix of capabilities. It was essential to task organise equipment and vehicles at every level of command.

We took just the right number of people to Bosnia. There were usually some empty seats in the back of each of the section Warriors, but this allowed more room for supplies and all the clothing and equipment to operate continuously throughout the depth of the Bosnian winter, and still left sufficient dismounted soldiers for our tasks. The Territorial Army soldiers and officers had been a great success.

Battlegroup operations could not have been sustained without a flexible and robust logistic capability. This was particularly important in January and February when the logistic system could neither supply fuel quickly enough nor provide sufficient spare parts to sustain the complex technical ecology of our vehicle fleet. Because of the preparatory training that had made all our commanders into 'intelligent customers' of logistics and the quality and experience of our logisticians, these problems were never show-stoppers. The same was true of our equipment support capability, a chain running from vehicle crews to the stalwart REME Light Aid Detachment. Johnny Bowron identified three principles for logistics in Bosnia:

The first: planning and preparation. Without this occurring at every stage and at each level of command, units will be ineffective or slow to respond so that their response will be worthless anyway. Logistic issues cannot be left to specialists while snobs discuss tactics.

The second is the husbandry and management of personnel and equipment. Without this not only will you have no vehicles to fight from or move around in, but more importantly you will have no personnel who are able or willing to fight.

Finally the passage of information is fundamental to all activities and its absence only heralds disaster. Of course mission command was designed so communications could fail but even knowledge of the higher commander's intent relies on the passage of information. In logistic activities continuous communication is crucial.

Moral Component

The moral component of Fighting Power is 'the ability to get people to fight'. The legal use of violence directed by a legitimate government distinguishes the Army from civilian occupations. This demands the ultimate subordination of the individual to both the group and mission – being prepared to risk their life, with no ability to 'opt out'. It requires an extremely high level of cohesion at every level, built on self-sacrifice and mutual trust, fostered by teamwork, high morale and leadership.

These qualities are inextricably interlinked. The best people in the world will not bind into a cohesive military team without the influence of positive leadership. It is the single most important factor in creating the high morale that enables soldiers and officers to put the mission before self and to overcome the difficulties and frictions inherent in military operations. The battalion was outstandingly lucky in the quality of its commanders.

A key ingredient of our morale was individual, collective and special theatre training. This gave everyone such confidence in themselves, their commanders and their equipment that none of the uncertainty, setbacks or difficulties of the tour were able to dent morale. I had no doubt that had we been required to close with and destroy the faction positions in Tito Barracks Sarajevo or Kulen Vakuf, morale would have been extremely high.

Although we were in a war zone, we were not at war with the factions. Therefore, I had to minimise the chance of incurring unnecessary casualties. This meant avoiding some of the risks we would have had to accept in a war – for example, by being much more cautious about mines and road safety. I hoped that the message that I was not going to take unjustified risks with any of the battlegroup's lives had a positive effect on morale.

Morale had also been reinforced by some of the measures taken before the tour, including removing individuals who could not or would not achieve the minimum standards required, as well as soldiers with serious disciplinary problems. Combined with positive leadership at all levels, these measures resulted in very small numbers of disciplinary problems. I was delighted that the battalion had a very high level of self-discipline. This was essential to maintain trust and mutual confidence, especially in the small groups in which people were spending such long periods operating.The vast majority of the time, no one needed any prompting to get on with the job in hand and to maintain their professional standards.

When people stepped out of line, they were dealt with as quickly as possible. The company commanders and I had powers to administer summary justice and we occasionally used them. I knew that some, both within the battalion and outside it, considered our discipline harsh. I did not mind, so long as they also considered it fair, clear and unequivocal. After the tour I discovered that some had christened me 'Judge Dredd', after the cartoon vigilante who seems to spend his whole time administering summary executions. I took this as a compliment.

Operations were so far flung, diverse and widespread that there was no alternative to devolving the maximum amount of independence and authority to commanders at every level. All the commanders from major to lance corporal thrived under these challenging circumstances. They certainly enjoyed the tour, but did the soldiers? I think most of them did most of the time. The constant change prevented anyone from getting in a rut. Morale was high throughout the tour, but everyone had low points, most of these resulting from the discomfort experienced in some of the cold, austere bases before enough campaign infrastructure became available.

All the battlegroup's commanders, including me, had a duty to look after our subordinates. Generally we managed to do this pretty well. I was particularly impressed by the way young officers, serjeants and corporals both handled difficult and challenging incidents and sustained the morale of their teams throughout the uncertain and dark winter. Their leadership helped overcome the fear and stress that resulted from shooting incidents, mine strikes, traffic accidents and encounters with suffering, deprivation and the stomach-wrenching sights of human remains. The pre-Bosnia training that we had given our platoon commanders was particularly important in achieving this.

A few incidents during the tour, in particular the attempted suicide by a company storeman, emphasised the need for commanders to keep an eye on people employed in administrative posts involving long hours and often working in isolation. In the heat of intensive operations it could be easy to miss the telltale signs of loneliness or worry. These incidents were few and far between. At the end of the tour most of the experienced private soldiers seemed to have enjoyed themselves much more than they would have done on a routine Northern Ireland tour.

It was essential to do as much as possible to sustain the morale of the families who remained in Paderborn. The battalion was lucky to have an experienced and energetic families officer and team, well supported by Paderborn garrison staff. The biggest single negative morale factor was the inability of most personnel to contact friends and family by telephone. For most of the battalion deployment of welfare telephones was too little, too late.

We anticipated before the tour that preparation of soldiers and commanders for uncertainty, hardship and deprivation would be important. This was addressed in all training. It was essential that commanders made sure that soldiers had realistic expectations. We had trained hard and expected to have to live for the whole tour in austere field conditions. This helped us 'hack it' – especially during the winter months in western Bosnia, when much of the battalion had no comforts other than those carried in their vehicles. Morale remained remarkably high, despite the lack of welfare facilities, heat, light, working latrines, showers and other comforts.

The need to make the best out of austere conditions in a harsh climate demanded a far greater degree of self-reliance than was required on most exercises or in Northern Ireland. When resources were lacking, it would have been easy to do nothing; instead the majority got on with the job by applying mission command, initiative and improvisation. The tour proved that despite the most sophisticated of modern technology 'soldiering is still an outdoor sport' – a phrase apparently coined by the American troops arriving in Bosnia.

IFOR operations and the success of Dayton Agreement gave us a sense of achievement. We had done something worthwhile – relieving the terrible effects of that most miserable of wars and helping the people of Bosnia. This had a positive effect on morale. The soldiers faced constant change, considerable uncertainty and the most tenuous links with home. They persevered through a ferocious winter because of sheer toughness and a dogged determination born of hard training, comradeship and leadership. All the battalion left Bosnia as better soldiers.

The Role of Lethal Force

One of the subjects we had learned most about had been the role of lethal force. Armies of course exist to apply lethal force to their nation's enemies. The legal framework for this are the laws of Armed Conflict, as described in the various Geneva Conventions. But in Bosnia we were not *at war*, so we had to use lethal force in different ways.

Operations in Northern Ireland had been conducted under British civil law, requiring us to use lethal force only in self-defence, or to save life. On operations there we all carried the "Yellow Card" a simple *aide-mémoire* laying down the circumstances under which we could open fire. The same principles applied to the use of force for defending ourselves in Bosnia. The overriding principle in both theatres of operation was that of *minimum force;* described by our doctrine as follows:

> The measured and proportionate application of violence or coercion, sufficient only to achieve a specific objective and confined in effect to the legitimate target intended. When force is used it should be applied prudently and all positive measures taken to avoid civilian casualties and minimise collateral damage.

Simple guidance on how this was to apply was given in our Rules of Engagement. These were relatively easy to apply when we were simply dealing with faction attacks on our positions. At WHITE FANG B Company instantly responded to the machine gun attack by returning fire, within the Rules of Engagement. We followed up with a massive show of force and a forceful and uncompromising protest to the commander concerned. The reaction of the Bosnian Serbs showed that the response was effective. The same applied when A Company used cannon fire to neutralise the Bosnian Muslim bunker firing on Arapuša. But when A Company's base at Bos Krupa came under fire, the company was absolutely right not to return fire, as they could not identify from where the fire could come. In war they might have unleashed machine gun, cannon missile mortar and artillery fire on the surrounding buildings, but the need to prevent collateral damage, civilian casualties and the principle of minimum force all forbade this. We mastered the defensive use of force – in part because we had been applying similar principles in Northern Ireland.

We had to put more thought into considering the offensive use of force to persuade or coerce the factions. We knew that in September 1995, the UN and NATO had succeeded in this. The NATO air strikes and the artillery attacks of the Multinational Brigade reinforced the strategic effect of the capture of Western Bosnia by Federation forces, all three factors combining to persuade the Bosnian Serbs to give in to the UN's demands. But this had a large amount of artillery concentrated in a small area and the whole of the massive NATO air armada assembled in Italy and the Adriatic. In early 1996, the weather was bad, often precluding any air strikes, and we and our artillery were spread out over a much wider area.

Our first operation to persuade the factions to comply with the Dayton Agreement was the show of force around the front line during January 1996, whilst the factions withdrew from the Zone of Separation. Armies are at their most vulnerable when they attempt to withdraw, so we had to give the factions confidence that IFOR could provide security for them whilst they withdrew, so that their opponent could not make mischief. We therefore set out to reassure both sides. We deployed as much strengths as we could around the front line. We were achieving a coercive effect by using our combat capability to demonstrate a visible intent to use force.

The most demanding scenario would have been the actual offensive use of force to achieve our mandates or missions. We had been very lucky that the air and artillery strikes of September 1995 had succeeded. I was certain that if they had failed the UN mission would have ended and we would have been part of the NATO mission to withdraw UNPROFOR. This could well have required us to use force offensively, in order to rescue UN contingents.

In March and April we had prepared to forcibly evict non-compliant faction troops; the Bosnian Muslims in Tito Barracks Sarajevo and the Bosnian Croats from Kulen Vakuf. In these cases we opened negotiations with them, concurrent with an ostentatious movement of our forces into the contentious area, clearly showing our intent and capability to use force. In every case where we did this the factions backed down, albeit at the last minute.

This illustrates an important difference between Peace Support Operations and war. In war we set out to attack, disrupt, deceive and, if possible, destroy our enemy's command and control system. But in Peace Support Operations there is not an enemy as such and we need to get the faction's command and control systems to cooperate with us, both in physically achieving the requirements of the mandate and in influencing the attitudes of the faction military. Therefore communicating with the factions is an essential corollary to the controlled use of force.

Although we were in a war zone, we were not at war with the factions. Therefore, I had to minimise the chance of incurring unnecessary British casualties. This meant minimising some of the risks we would accept in a war – for example, by being much more cautious about mines. It also meant being prepared to use as much force as I could possibly muster against faction positions – more than time or resources might allow in war. For example, in war when attacking we would attempt to apply three times the force available to the defenders – an enemy section, for example, being attacked by one of our platoons. If in Bosnia we had been required to attack a non-compliant faction section, I might have used a whole company.

Our operations validated the British Army's overall approach to peace support operations, which emphasised a judicious and impartial use of force, balanced against the long-term requirements for peace building. All use of force, even the most offensive force should be conducted impartially with the longer-term implications in mind – use force if you have to but in the longer term you are trying to promote consent. The most appropriate approach for the conduct of Peace Support Operations will be probably based upon a combination of rewards and punishments.

So the use of force usually requires greater guidance than that offered in the Rules of Engagement. For example, an inappropriate use of too much force even if within the Rules of Engagement, may destabilise any political process, just as too weak a response can undermine the credibility of a force. Either can render the mission untenable. Whatever the circumstances, the use of force should be seen as a tool to set the conditions for the development of peace in the long term.

Decisions on the use of force and the amount of force to be deployed or employed are likely to be the most difficult that a commander will have to make. The enduring lesson is that to be effective peacemakers, you have to be combat capable war fighters. A force conducting peace enforcement needs to be able to overmatch the level of violence offered to it by the factions – 'escalation dominance'.

I worry that many who were not involved in the events of Bosnia in 95–96 are already forgetting the hard lessons that were learned. But, because of our war-fighting training and ethos, I had no doubt that had we been required to close with and destroy the non-compliant faction positions in Tito Barracks Sarajevo or Kulen Vakuf, we would have done so.

Multinational Operations

But I did wonder if some other nation's contingents in Bosnia had the warrior ethos, the combat capability and the will to see such matters through. Some of the difficulties of the UN Mission were caused by some national contingents of troops that appeared to be equipped, trained and configured only for relatively unchallenging peacekeeping tasks in a benign environment. In my view, they not only added no value to the mission, but also were quickly marginalised by the faction warlords, becoming hostages to fortune and a source of friction and drag on the mission. Had the UNPROFOR mission collapsed, getting these contingents out of Bosnia would have been extremely difficult.

During the Cold War, we had assumed that in Germany NATO would fight the Warsaw Pact in multinational army groups made up of national corps. After the Cold War, the British corps had evolved into the multinational NATO Rapid Reaction Corps. The divisions assigned to the corps were a mixture of national and multinational divisions, the latter made up of nationally homogeneous brigades. During 2 LI's NATO operations, we worked with French, Dutch, United States, New Zealand, Canadian, Czech, German, Greek, Slovak, Indonesian, Austrian, Hungarian, Romanian, Danish, Swedish, Norwegian and Malaysian troops, not to mention the Kenyans, Brazilians and Argentinians we met during our UN days. The British-led multinational division in IFOR was made up of battlegroups from five different nations. The battlegroup in which B Company served mixed UK and Canadian companies and squadrons. As the NATO operation went on, the level of multinationality descended further as both troops and platoons operated with companies and squadrons of different nations and individuals and small teams from different nations operated everywhere.

Multinationality had the enormous political benefits of demonstrating international commitment. Some capabilities which we did not have were provided by other countries. This included the US civil affairs and Psyops specialists that joined 4 Brigade, there being in Bosnia no UK civil affairs specialist and only one UK Psyops officer based at HQ IFOR. At a lower level, we had enjoyed the use of French and Dutch campaign stores and infrastructure far superior to ours during the tour. Finally, multinationality certainly helped to prevent life from becoming dull.

But the multinational nature of IFOR could reduce unity of effort. In many cases national contingents' rules of engagement were different; they had different approaches to force protection and often demanded that their national capitals be consulted if NATO wished to change the contingent's mission, tasks, or area of operations. Widely differing national operational postures sent contradictory messages to the factions.

Different contingents had different approaches to command and control. We were very comfortable with our doctrine of mission command, others contingents were less so and required more detailed and prescriptive orders than we did. This could slow down the passage of information and make command and control more difficult. Sometimes this was exploited by the factions to create obfuscation and provide excuses for foot dragging. In addition some national contingents attached less importance to some aspects of field discipline than we did. This could lead our troops working alongside them to compromise standards. The battlegroup learned to anticipate these potential problems, looking carefully at command arrangements when troops of another nation joined the battlegroup, or when our troops were put under command of another national contingent. What did we learn that might help us to overcome these problems inherent in a multinational force in the future?

The answer was not rocket science, but simply the application of some positive coalition building measures that are the tried and tested principles of successful coalition and alliance building. We have to begin by being realistic and accepting that in a military operation that is not a war of national survival, but a discretionary operation of choice, all nations will want to exert close political control over their forces and will be unwilling to risk unnecessary casualties. We have to accept that this will probably always be a problem, which arises from political, cultural and legal factors. For example British national law makes it very difficult for British troops to use lethal force to defend property, whilst other nations are less constrained.

Multinational operations put greater pressure on HQs than national operations. The sub-optimal performance of the Multinational Brigade HQ showed that attempting to improvise new HQs for each operation by assembling commanders and staff officers from the troop contributing nations is likely to result in an HQ that is extremely unlikely to be capable of achieving the required standard of effectiveness, especially in a dynamic and demanding operation. Better to base the HQ on an existing worked up HQ and use a common language and standard procedures. I favour English and NATO procedures – but foreign readers would expect me to say that!

There needs to be thorough liaison arrangements between the HQ and the different national contingents allocated to it. In IFOR both 3 Division and 4 Brigade devoted considerable effort and resources to establishing liaison links with the non-NATO contingents from the Czech Republic and Malysia. British LOs, artillery tactical groups and communications teams deployed to both contingents, and Czech and Malaysian LOs were given places at Division HQ.

We achieved a very high standard of mutual understanding upwards and downwards and sideways between all commanders and staffs. This meant that our command and control arrangements were *realistic*. There was no sense in expecting the non-NATO contingents to either apply all our NATO procedures or to be comfortable with same style of mission command orders that the British battlegroups so relished.

General Jackson and Brigadier Dannatt worked hard to achieve as much unity of command and unity of purpose as possible. They both used all their leadership skills to build mutual confidence between the national contingents. We were lucky that they succeeded so well in this. There is nothing new about commanders of a multinational force using all their leadership and interpersonal skills to create a unity of effort between their diverse national contingents – to overcome potential friction in the coalition force. There is nothing new about this, for the art was practised in coalition wars of the past – the Duke of Wellington, Slim, Eisenhower and Schawrtzkopf being notable masters of the art. These were of course highly experienced generals, operating at the highest levels of operational command. To meet the demands of operations in the twenty-first century we are going to have to establish these skills in commanders at divisional, brigade, battalion and even company level.

Afterwards

After leave the battalion reformed. Much time was spent catching up on training, administration and vehicle and equipment maintenance. People moved on, some within the battalion and some leaving it. This applied at all levels, as illustrated by the changes in the Officers' Mess described in *The Silver Bugle*:

> Ed Creswell returned to the Royal Dragoon Guards. Paul Sulyok, Will Hogg, Mark Winston-Davies and Sean Harris have all gone to a far-away place called England. Tom Welch leaves us for a wife and an old Land Rover. Kev Stainburn is off to a bigger HQ to see what software they have got! Dangerous Dave Cockburn heads back to 8 LI. Steve Liddle, on loan from the Royal Marines (and probably the nicest man in the whole world ever) goes back. He arrived single and shy, and has left us with his first girlfriend and a full black book. Mark Jacklin from the RAF Regiment returns to the Boys in Blue, and a Tuesday to Thursday working week. Peter Macfarlane on loan from the Royal Dragoon Guards has gone to Canada: apparently we spoiled him. Chris Booth has departed on promotion. In Bosnia he astounded all with his children's paintings on his office wall. Imagine our surprise when they turned out to be logistic flow charts, it's an easy mistake! Ian Baker has headed off into the confusion that is civvy street. Hearts will break all over the English-speaking world as the old uniform is finally hung up. We wish him well.

In October I handed over command of the battalion. I was sad to do so, but my two years and four months in command had come to an end. My successor was due his turn at the challenge and privilege that is battalion command. My final day began with a 'Bugle Breakfast' in the Officers' Mess, then outside to an awaiting battalion and mounting my Warrior to be pulled out of camp by the officers, warrant officers and serjeants. Half an hour later the battalion began training for Northern Ireland and I was posted to a staff job in the Ministry of Defence.

One Year After

Two anniversaries occurred shortly afterwards, that of the signing of the Dayton Agreement and five weeks later, that of the transition from UNPROFOR to IFOR. Almost all the military requirements of the Dayton Agreement had been met – an exception being the complete lifting of mines. But NATO's strategic objective of transitioning within twelve months to a non-NATO post-implementation force was not met. IFOR became the Stabilisation Force (SFOR) and remained in Bosnia.

The Dayton Agreement had many strands, with only one of the eleven annexes covering military matters. The others covered political, civil and economic issues. The treaty defined its aim as achieving a lasting peace in Bosnia. But this depended on progress in all of these mutually supporting areas. A year after Dayton it seemed to me that the lack of success reflected an initial slowness in synchronising the efforts of the international community and international agencies in supporting the implementation of each of these strands.

While the factions grudgingly complied with the letter of the civilian and political requirements of Dayton, there was no such compliance with the spirit of the agreement. There was virtually no tangible progress towards the re-establishment of a single multi-ethnic Bosnian state. For example, only a very small number of refugees had returned to their homes – especially where those lay in the territory of a different ethnic group. By the end of 1996, the entities had failed to live up to their civil and political obligations in time for NATO to withdraw at the end of the IFOR mission. Efforts to build multi-ethnic institutions and to promote reconciliation appeared largely unsuccessful.

Why was this? Was it because the Dayton Agreement failed to articulate a practical concept of how peace could be established securely in twelve months? Was it because of the lack of resources, structure and authority afforded to civil and political implementation of Dayton in 1996? Was it because the year's deadline for the withdrawal of NATO forces was a political 'fudge' to allow President Clinton to sell the initial US deployment to a reluctant Congress?

Did separation of the military and civilian structures for implementation create an unproductive division between COMIFOR and the High Representative, contributing to a vacuum at the political level that IFOR was slow to fill? Carl Bildt, the High Representative, was unable to compel compliance with civil and political requirements of Dayton. Did this lack of momentum in co-ordinating civil and political aspects of implementation make it much easier for hard-liners and intransigents in all three factions to engage in obfuscation and foot dragging?

Was the importance of the International Police Task Force in re-establishing local police forces underestimated? Was the IPTF too weak and too slow to deploy into Bosnia, and too lacking in 'levers' to compel compliance by civil police forces? Did this explain why at the end of the year insufficient progress had been made in changing the nature and *modus operandi* of the faction civil police force?

At the end of 1996 it seemed to me that the answer to all these questions was 'yes'.

It also seemed that there were unresolved questions and tensions concerning war crimes and war criminals. In setting up the International Criminal

Tribunal in former Yugoslavia, the international community had invested considerable resources and much rhetoric in an attempt to bring war criminals to justice. IFOR's assessment was that mounting deliberate attempts to capture war criminals, even if tactically successful, had the strategic risk of forfeiting Bosnian Serb consent and possibly causing incalculable damage to the mission. At the time this was probably correct. But why did the efforts of the International War Crimes Tribunal appear to be conducted in isolation from the other military and civil lines of action to return Bosnia to normality? Is there an inherent contradiction between the search for peace and reconciliation and efforts to bring war criminals to justice?

At the end of 1996, it seemed impossible to tell if Bosnia was a country with a civil war in suspended animation, to be reactivated once the international community's military commitment weakened, or if it was a country slowly emerging from madness where the two entities would agree to overcome their differences. The jury was out.

Impressions

I still find it impossible to exclude the vivid memories of the tour – a mixture of events, some important and some trivial:

The unique military *mélange* of the Multinational Brigade, the bizarre nature of our Vitez base – most of it highly fortified, but the officers living in houses 'outside the wire', with my house a good four hundred yards from the nearest UN position.

The scope and intensity of battlegroup operations in the first month after D Day, when 2 LI were the sole representatives of NATO in a vast area where the UN had been unable to operate. The effect on the factions, civilians and ourselves of our blatant displays of military capability and hardware – Warrior, Challenger tanks and AS 90 heavy guns showing that we meant business. The grinding frustration of attempting to pass messages and orders over fragile, overstretched communications systems. The surge of adrenalin in the immediate aftermath of the shooting attacks on the battlegroup. In the second half of the tour, the signs of a return to normality.

Within the battlegroup the light, easy friendships, the humour and relaxed banter, particularly amongst the members of the battlegroup orders group. The sense of common purpose so intense at particular moments – at Mrkonjić Grad Bus Depot on D Day or A Company at Kupres, waiting patiently to go to Sarajevo and evict the ABiH. The sudden concentration of the mind resulting from our preparations to attack Tito Barracks and Kulen Vakuf. A sense of absolute certainty that any attack launched by us would succeed, that the way we would use overwhelming force would be unlike anything the factions had ever experienced, resulting in the total destruction of the non-complying forces. All this seasoned with a little apprehension.

My roles during the tour: as battalion commanding officer, as battlegroup commander, as a military diplomat representing NATO to the factions and as a propagandist for the Dayton Agreement and IFOR. The exhilarating roll-er-coaster ride that is command on operations. The times when hard decisions were required, that could not be delegated, as the buck stopped with me.

Sometimes feeling frustrated that we could not use force as if we were fighting a war – especially for young soldiers and commanders trained to fight and win, consciously choosing not to use force. Defusing dangerous and difficult confrontations without force, but acting extremely firmly with the threat of force. Directly or indirectly preventing loss of life by doing so. Facing down all the confrontations and overcoming the obfuscation of the factions – apart from the half-baked operation to inspect the Kosmos factory. Returning fire, when there was no alternative but to use lethal force to counter fire directed against us.

Reducing our operational profile to help promote the return to normality and the sense of achievement arising from our projects to help the civil community. The palpable sense of evil arising from discovery of mass graves. The moral dilemmas of command, especially the issues raised by evidence of war crimes. An absurd sense of achievement from running the music show on Radio Big. Feeling guilty that I had not allowed the battlegroup to 'adopt' the Banja Luka orphanage earlier.

The battlegroup as a living social organism, whose capabilities and limitations are the sum of the characteristics of its people, further developed by training, planning, command and leadership. Soldiers enduring and doing what was asked of them – often in a very lowly capacity. The unfailing good humour of soldiers. The way the regimental system and culture worked with a unique camaraderie. The value of creating ad hoc Officers' and Serjeants' Messes and Junior Ranks Clubs as places where people could forget operations and relax amongst their peer group with a little alcohol.

Getting people to put themselves in harm's way in a planned and orchestrated fashion – an intensely human activity. The value of teamwork, not just the unification of individuals to achieve a common purpose, but also the value of a team of different people bringing their personalities to bear in solving problems and sharing ideas. The winning team in Battlegroup HQ and the excellent young commanders who were so often tested and so very rarely found wanting.

The support from so many excellent Bosnian people working for us as interpreters. Their sad, desperately sad stories about friends and family.

Interminable meetings talking in slow simple phrases through an interpreter. Drinking lukewarm, thick, mud-like Balkan coffee. The empty villages burned and demolished by ethnic cleansing – a terrible reminder of the brutal inhumanity of the civil war where neighbour had fallen on neighbour. The sheer breadth, depth and speed of the rivers of hatred that flow throughout the country. How we take for granted the fragile veneer of civilisation over our baser instincts. Could any of us actually say how we could react in a similar situation to the Bosnian civil war?

The intensity with which I and all of us missed our families, especially the opportunities to see our children growing up during the six months, making it all the more sad to see destitute families and children. The youngsters' innocence had been stolen by the war. What had they seen? How traumatised were they? Did they know that children of the other factions were just like them? How we took for granted that we would have more and better resources than the faction military and the civilians, especially our better medical cover and food supply.

The background music of the tour, the soundtrack in many of the rooms and tents of our bases: the sprawling guitars and anthems of Oasis, the minimalist hymn of aching longing, 'Missing', by Everything But The Girl, and M People's optimistic hymn of self-reassurance, 'Search for the Hero'.

The End

During those six months I lived with a singular intensity, which I have rarely achieved since. For the only time in my military career I had been relatively unshackled by the chains of paperwork and peacetime administration. I leave the final quotation to Lieutenant Pete Chapman:

> It is easy to feel cut off from the outside world, but there is great satisfaction to be had from coping with all the problems and still be making a significant contribution to the success of IFOR. As for the locals, well, they still wave at us when we thunder past, but no longer as intimidating symbols of military power, rather as a welcome contributor to peace.

What had we done? We had begun our tour strung out along the road from Vitez to Sarajevo and spent the first two months travelling that city's bloodstained roads, frustrated with delays imposed at the faction checkpoints that constrained our freedom of movement.

With the change from UN to NATO command we had left behind the predictability and frustrations of the Multinational Brigade and the journey had become a true adventure, travelling along roads closed to the UN. We had taken roads from Sarajevo, the place where the catastrophe unfurled in 1992, to Prijedor and Banja Luka, a huge area from which the UN had been almost completely absent. These places represented the heart of darkness of the Bosnian civil war and the incubator of its lethal virus of ethnic cleansing. We had travelled all over the roads of western Bosnia, where the previous autumn's losses of Bosnian Serb territory had tipped the strategic balance in favour of peace.

We had set the pace in western Bosnia. NATO's mandate meant that we could now use any road we liked, and could compel the factions to let us through their checkpoints. At the end of the tour all roads were open and all faction checkpoints had been removed.

Many roads had been narrow, dangerous and unpredictable. We had skidded on ice and met all sorts of unexpected hazards. But in travelling the roads from Sarajevo we had saved lives and acted as midwife at the birth of a fragile peace.

We had been very lucky to be there, as part of NATO's great common enterprise, and first land operation, during a crucial time in the history of the Balkans. We had helped bring the war to the end of the road it had travelled, by demonstrating the ability to use terrible violence on those who would not comply. Doing this had helped put the country on a new road, a road that offered a real opportunity for a lasting peace.

We made a difference.

What Happened To 2 LI?

Soldiers and officers continued to move in and out of the battalion. In autumn 1996 2 LI moved to Northern Ireland for a two-year operational tour. Since then it has served in England, Cyprus and Edinburgh. Operational deployments included Kosovo, Bosnia, Sierra Leone and Iraq.

On 1 February 2007 the Light Infantry merged with its sister regiment the Royal Green Jackets. They were joined by the Devon and Dorsets and Royal Gloucestershire, Berkshire and Wiltshire Regiments, to form a new regiment, the Rifles. On that day 2 LI became Third Battalion the Rifles. Formal celebrations were impossible as the battalion was deployed on operations in both Afghanistan and Iraq. A year later 2 LI's colours were laid to rest in Durham Town Hall. At the time of writing the Army plans to deploy 3 Rifles to Afghanistan.

AFTERWORD

A View from 2015

The publication of a second edition of this book to coincide with the twentieth anniversary of the events it describes seemed like an opportunity to reflect. This afterword uses the perspective of twenty years to analyse the military operations it describes in a broader and deeper context, and to identify lessons that were less obvious at the time the book was written.

Bosnia and Kosovo 1996–2003

After 2LI left Bosnia the military provisions of the Dayton Agreement continued to be successfully implemented. The entities' armed forces stayed in barracks. They greatly reduced in size and never again became threats to peace in the way they had from 1992 to 1995. The 1996 deployment of 60,000 NATO troops had created a mindset throughout Bosnia that any non-compliance would have resulted in likely destruction of the non-compliant forces.

In 1996 NATO countries agreed to the extension of NATO's military mandate into a 'Stabilisation Force' (SFOR). But the conflict continued, albeit at lower intensity and it moved from the battlefield to politics. Successful elections were held for posts in the many-layered government structures. But these allowed nationalist extremists to embed themselves in power. In Republika Srpska the malign influence of Radovan Karadžić and his supporters was an especial threat to stability. Hard-line extremists demobilised themselves from the entities' armies and moved into civil appointments, for example as mayors and police officers. Many became a malign influence, obstructing progress and making a bad situation worse. A number of these were individuals suspected of war crimes. An attempted coup by hard-line nationalists in Banja Luka was foiled by British troops. Streams of extreme propaganda were broadcast by Bosnian Serb radio stations.

As a result of these challenges, the Peace Implementation Council of France, the UK, the USA, Russia, Turkey and Germany authorised the High Representative to remove Bosnian public officials and to impose legislation. NATO also changed its attitude to war criminals. By the end of 1996 it was clear that the advantages of the existing NATO policy of abstaining from hunting for war criminals was outweighed by the disadvantages of the impunity and damaging influence being exercised by many malign actors. The UK energised an effort by key NATO states and the International Criminal Tribunal for the Former Yugoslavia to change their approach. They developed the 'sealed warrant': an indictment that would be issued to NATO, but otherwise kept secret. Intelligence was secretly collected and special forces conduct a covert arrest operation with a minimum of force, collateral damage and disruption.

The first such operation was mounted by British troops. One of the indictees was arrested without any fuss, but the other pulled a pistol on the soldiers making the arrest and was killed. He was a hard-line paramilitary who had become a senior Bosnian Serb police officer in Prijedor. The previous year, Paul Kellett had identified him as one of the key individuals in Prijedor who was actively opposing the implementation of Dayton.

Subsequent operations by British and NATO troops successfully detained other indicted war criminals from both Bosnian entities. Although a number of suspects were captured in this way, as time went on, the remaining fugitives became increasingly difficult to find.

Concurrently the situation in Kosovo deteriorated into civil war between the Kosovo Albanians and the largely Serb security forces. NATO launched an air war to force Slobodan Milošević's government to cease its brutal repression. Milošević eventually backed down and the NATO Kosovo Force (KFOR) took control of Kosovo's security. As in Bosnia, the British Army played the leading role in KFOR, with the British-led NATO Rapid Reaction Corps HQ commanding KFOR and two of the force's five brigades being British, including 4th Armoured Brigade. Security, of a sort, was re-established and British troops contributed much effort to putting the province back on its feet.

Bosnia in 2003

I returned to Bosnia in February 2003 to command NATO's Multi National Brigade Northwest. Its area of responsibility was the same as that of Multi National Division Southwest in 1996. Instead of the 20,000 NATO troops in the sector in 1996, the brigade had 3,500 troops, including three battalions from the UK, Canada and Holland. This reflected a greatly improved security situation. The three entities' armies had greatly reduced in size. There had been progress in implementing the civilian provisions of the Dayton Agreement. For example, refugees of all three ethnicities had returned to many towns and villages from which they had been evicted during the war.

I assessed that the presence of our force had utility continuing to deter the entities' armed forces from any military non-compliance. But the brigade had considerable excess capacity over and above the minimum required for this deterrence. So I sought to identify the options to widen the utility of the brigade.

We did what we could to support the energetic leadership of the new High Representative, the British politician Paddy Ashdown. He had an ambitious agenda to move Bosnia forward by improving its political organisation and culture by embedding economic and political reform and greater inter-ethnic cooperation. All of this was to make Bosnia self-sufficient economically and a credible candidate for membership of the European Union.

In Republika Srpska it was clear that there was a still a nexus of ultra-nationalists, corrupt officials and organised crime networks. There was evidence that money being illicitly generated was being used to fund the covert networks that were supporting efforts to hide Karadžić and Mladić from the attentions of NATO and the International Tribunal. The same applied in ethnically Croat areas, where the indicted Croat general Ante Gotovina still commanded considerable support. We supported operations to arrest the remaining indicted war criminals, but no arrests resulted. It seemed that that that the fugitives were by this time in 'deep cover', if they were in Bosnia at all.

We sought other ways to disrupt the networks in Republika Srpska that intelligence suggested were supporting the concealment of key individuals indicted by the war crimes tribunal. The required a variety of activity, often covert. For example, intelligence and surveillance detected a network of police corruption centred on the town of Knezevo. After months of patiently building the intelligence picture the police station was raided, hard evidence gathered and the police chief replaced.

These initiatives were complemented by an innovative operation developed by First Battalion the Highlanders. This was able to uncover vast stocks of weapons and ammunition that had been carefully hidden in Republika Srpska after the war. The battalion made ever increasing discoveries of these caches with increasing evidence that they were being actively maintained by a secret network. There was convincing evidence that this was linked to hard-line extremists, including those supporting the concealment of Mladić and Karazdic. The operation became increasingly successful over the summer. It was assessed to have put increasing pressure on the extremist elements in Republika Srpska.

The brigade also sought to support and encourage political progress. An unexpected achievement in this area was helping the Bosnian Government and police conduct the security operation for the 2003 visit of the Pope to Banja Luka. A previous visit of the Pope to Sarajevo in the previous decade had seen heavy levels of security provided by NATO troops, but this time the Bosnian Government and police would take the lead. As there were 12,000 NATO troops in the country, they would support the Bosnian security operation. The visit would take place in Banja Luka, so the brigade would lead the operation. Accordingly I found myself representing NATO on the Bosnian Government committee planning the event, as well as leading the tactical operation in Banja Luka.

We helped the Bosnian police develop their capabilities for such a large-scale security operation. They would lead the operation, but NATO would be available as a back-up should the security situation deteriorate beyond their ability to control it. To guarantee the capability to do this the brigade doubled in size. Plans were developed jointly and extensively rehearsed.

In the event most of the visit went extremely smoothly. The majority of the people attending the event were Catholic Croats, both from Herzegovina and Croatia. But there were a surprising number of Bosnian Serbs attending the large open-air Mass, as well as a minority of Muslims. Conversations with NATO troops and interviews by the Bosnian media suggested that these people wanted to see the Pope for themselves – a surprising and welcome return of the religious tolerance that had been a feature of the previous Yugoslav state.

The Mass went smoothly, but as the Pope was departing the city for Banja Luka airport, an intelligence report suggested that a Chechen assassin would make an attempt on his life. Well-developed contingency plans were put into effect; reinforcements were rapidly deployed around Banja Luka airport and its approaches and every available NATO helicopter was launched to cover the Pope's route. In the joint NATO–Bosnian police operations room the tension was palpable. When the papal aircraft successfully departed Bosnian airspace there was much applause. The success of the operation greatly boosted the confidence of the Bosnian Serb police.

2004 to 2015

The Bosnian armed forces underwent a process of integration into a single organisation under civilian political control. But efforts to integrate the entities' police forces achieved only limited success. Nevertheless, Ashdown's tenure successfully reformed and strengthened the Bosnian state sufficiently that a Stabilisation and Association Agreement with the EU was signed in 2006.

SFOR itself was replaced by a European Union Force. But after Ashdown's departure in 2006 political progress and reforms stagnated. A 2009 US-led effort to rejuvenate political reform failed. The three ethnicities remained largely culturally and politically segregated and there was insufficient support for necessary reform. Meanwhile Bosnia's neighbours made progress in overcoming the legacy of the wars of the 1990s and became increasingly integrated into Europe. Croatia became a member of NATO in 2009 and of the EU in 2013. Serbia decisively oriented itself towards the EU, becoming a candidate member in 2012.

As part of this progress, the Croat and Serb governments played an increasing role in the hunt for the major indicted war criminals. In 2005 Ante Gotovina, the former Croat military commander, was detained in Tenerife. In Serbia, Radovan Karadžić was arrested in June 2008 and Ratko Mladić was detained in May 2011. Both are now being tried for war crimes.

Twenty years after the Dayton Agreement there had been much improvement in security and some political progress. The International Crisis Group recently assessed that:

Today Bosnia is at peace, with minimal threat of relapse into armed conflict. Its standard of living has caught up with the neighbourhood; its cities, towns, roads, bridges, mosques and churches have been rebuilt or repaired. Former enemies socialise across the once-impassable line between wartime rivals without a second thought. Common institutions and services like the border police, indirect tax authority, passports, licence plates, currency, parliament and diplomatic corps are widely accepted. Others, such as the state investigative body and court, arouse rhetorical opposition but little practical resistance.

In this sense Bosnia is an example of successful conflict resolution, going from hellish wartime conditions to near-normalcy in less than a generation. The cost has been great: three years after the end of war Crisis Group estimated the annual price of international missions in Bosnia at $9 billion. Aid by 2010 may have totalled $14 billion; the U.S. share alone was over $2 billion. Sundry other costs add billions more. There are intangible costs too; for many years international officials in effect ran the country, undermining the national government.[*]

In February 2014 there were widespread popular protests against poverty, corruption and political stagnation that saw widespread rioting and burning of government buildings. Catastrophic floods in May 2014 further exposed the limited capabilities of the Bosnian state and the widespread distrust of its politicians amongst the majority of the Bosnian people.

But despite these two strategic shocks, there was little fundamental change. With the European Union's preoccupation with the Eurozone crisis and more recently with the 2015 migration crisis, it seemed unlikely that Brussels could catalyse the required changes of attitude and of Bosnia's complex constitution that would be necessary to regain the momentum of reform.

Twenty Years On: What does Bosnia tell us about War and Peace?

Much of the course of the complex military and political conflicts in Bosnia was specific that country. But it is possible to discern some lessons.

Between 1992 and 1997 force had considerable utility in Bosnia. During the war the three warring parties depended on their armies for their survival. At the same time, the UN forces' limited mandate and combat capability meant that their utility was limited. And some national contingents that lacked the military capability and national will to adequately protect themselves had zero, sometimes negative, utility.

The combined UN and NATO artillery and air strikes of September 1995 were effective in forcing all three sides to the conference table at Dayton. Just as important a role was played by the pressure exerted on the Bosnian Serbs by the Croat military offensives that evicted the VRS from large parts of

---

[*] International Crisis Group Report No. 232, 10 July 2014, 'Bosnia's Future'.

western Bosnia. This showed the Bosnian Serb leadership that military victory was now impossible and that prolonging the conflict would probably result in military defeat.

The 60,000 NATO troops that deployed through the winter of 1995–96 were very effective. This flowed from their demonstrable combat capability that overmatched the faction forces. The sheer numbers of troops based throughout the length and breadth of Bosnia meant that any actual and potential military non-compliance would be quickly detected and countered. Achieving the clear timelines for disengagement and demilitarisation specified by the Dayton Agreement created a sense of irreversible momentum. This was buttressed by the agreement's explicit authority for IFOR to use force to achieve its aims. All of these factors contributed to the rapid return of the entity forces to barracks, and the success of the subsequent inspection regime.

So in achieving the military outcomes required in 1996 by the Dayton Agreement, NATO forces had great utility, a utility that subsequently endured. The subsequent inspection regime and NATO's complete authority over the entity armed forces acted to create an irreversible momentum that over time made it increasingly unlikely that the entities could use the military instrument to restart war.

From 1997, NATO forces had continued utility, for example in countering the attempted 1997 coup by Bosnian Serb extremists in Banja Luka, and in finding and arresting war crimes suspects. These military outcomes had political effects, but increasingly politics rather than military affairs became the decisive factor in Bosnia.

But civil–military cooperation was initially sub-optimal. This was seen in the efforts made by UK forces in 1996 to integrate their actions with international reconstruction and development efforts. This had required much effort by the headquarters of 4th Armoured Brigade and 3 Division. The results were mixed at best, but the generally benign security situation meant that the decidedly sub-optimal integration of civilian efforts did not become a critical factor. NATO and the international communities' ability to mesh the utility of force with civilian efforts of similar usefulness had been tested in 1996, but the relatively benign security situation meant that they had not been found wanting. Subsequently the increasingly benign security situation served to obscure the difficulties of civil–military co-ordination that had frustrated British commanders in 1996.

However, after 9/11 the more challenging environments of Afghanistan and Iraq provided a greater test. Both the US-led coalition in Iraq and NATO in Afghanistan struggled to adequately co-ordinate military action with political activity, reconstruction and development. In 2010 the recently retired General Lord Richard Dannatt reflected on the lessons of the NATO IFOR, in the context of the Iraq and Afghan wars:

> Where military intervention is required it must be strong, robust and timely. Where a fractured state needs help, the international assistance needs to be broadly based and to cover not just the military line of operation, but governance,

the rule of law, justice, human rights, and economic support ... Perhaps of greatest importance is the requirement that strategic objectives set out by governments must be linked to tactical activity on the ground by soldiers and aid workers through a properly worked out operational-level plan – a campaign plan – drawn up by an appropriately trained and empowered theatre commander, be he ambassador or general. Strategic success is delivered by the soldiers on the ground, but is enabled by a properly thought through and resourced operational-level campaign plan. There are no shortcuts. Sadly, Iraq was to provide this point yet again.*

Re-reading this book, I was struck by other lessons that it identified: firstly, the importance of influencing attitudes, that the conflict 'was in the minds of the Bosnian people in our area'; secondly, my assessment that 'all our operations had a political role'. Operations by international forces in Iraq and Afghanistan also saw an ever-greater interaction between military operations, political factors and efforts by all parties to influence attitudes of populations and adversaries. Often characterised by British officers as 'national building under fire' or 'armed politics', counter-insurgency operations in both countries were essentially contests for the minds of people: the populations, the insurgents and militias, and their military and political leadership. There was nothing new about this; indeed, it had long been a central feature of insurgency and counter-insurgency warfare. The evidence of Iraq and Afghanistan suggests it will probably apply to much conflict in the future.

From Bosnia to Basra: The Dangers of Overconfidence

My last job in the Army was to write the British Army's final analysis of its role in the stabilisation of Iraq. This was a much more demanding operation that Bosnia. The Army was faced with far greater challenges than it had expected. There were periods of intense fighting. Most soldiers, officers and units performed well, often outstandingly so. But the British campaign in Basra came close to failure. Overall, the British in Iraq were not as effective as they could have been. Britain's military reputation and confidence was damaged. These sentiments were widely felt across the Army.

I assessed that the reasons for this were complex. The failure to prevent instability and to find weapons of mass destruction, and the rising toll of casualties rapidly eroded public support in the UK. Following the fall of Saddam Hussein, both the British and US governments struggled to achieve the necessary match between ends, ways and means necessary for tactical success to have the desired operational effects that would achieve progress towards both coalition and national strategic objectives. These were complex

---

* *Leading from the Front: The Autobiography* by Richard Dannatt, Bantam Press, 2010, p. 173.

failures, with many contributing factors and multiple examples of sub-optimal decision-making in Washington DC, London, CENTCOM, Baghdad and Basra.

After regime change, British commanders in Basra sensed a profound lack of civil–military co-ordination in London, a palpable lack of top-down leadership and a government approach to southern Iraq that was under-resourced and inadequately led and co-ordinated. These factors made achieving an adequate British inter-agency civil–military effort difficult. Some modest improvements were seen in the last year of the war but these were too late to reverse many of the effects of earlier failures.

Underlying all this was a sense that the US and UK military and political leadership had expected that stabilisation operations in Iraq would most likely resemble operations in Bosnia and Kosovo in the previous decade. For example, my researches showed that in 2004–05 many British commanders considered the situation in southern Iraq to have more in common with peace support operations than anything else.

In retrospect, it can be seen that the British Army that entered Iraq in 2003 had a quarter of a century of successes from Northern Ireland, Zimbabwe, the Falkland Islands, Operation DESERT STORM, Bosnia, Kosovo, East Timor, Sierra Leone and the 2002 formation and leadership of the International Security Assistance Force in Kabul. All these operations were supported by Parliament, public and the media. There were remarkably few casualties. Many aspects of these operations were demanding, but in all these conflicts the opposition was of lower average quality than British, US and NATO forces, were mostly unwilling to stand and fight, and were overmatched by the arms and joint war fighting capabilities of the UK and its allies.

When I look back at the operations in Bosnia described in this book, I am struck that the challenges and demands they made on the British troops seemed at the time to be exceptional. The British Army had not faced similar demands before. But NATO and its British contingent's military superiority meant that there was relatively little actual combat. Indeed, the only two fire-fights involving IFOR in north-west Bosnia are those described in this book. There was a similar lack of close combat in the British sector in Kosovo. And the British operation in Sierra Leone saw only two periods of intense fighting involving British forces.

All these brief battles were successful. But I believe that this success may have resulted in a degree of overconfidence, an expectation that future opponents would be as easily countered by British forces. Looking back on the period between Easter 1996 and the beginning of efforts to stabilise Iraq in April 2003, I have a sense that the British Army and the UK Ministry of Defence were probably a bit too pleased with themselves.

So when British troops in Iraq found themselves fighting against enemies who rejected Western values and were prepared to stand, fight and die, the shock was profound. British troops quickly reacted, falling back on proven combined arms war fighting tactics, but the unexpected intensity of the fighting, combined with the unpopularity of the war, served a serious strategic shock to the British government, its Ministry of Defence and the Army. All were too slow to adapt.

I am not seeking to denigrate or belittle the achievements of the 2LI Battlegroup, or of the other British and NATO troops that deployed over that fierce winter of 1995–96, across front lines that had seen close-up evidence, intense fighting, terrible war crimes and ethnic cleansing. Nor do I forget the great strategic and tactical uncertainty, and the considerable difficulties of communications and logistics, together with the novelty of what we were attempting. But I now assess that our very success in those difficult and dangerous operations, in part, contributed to overconfidence that gave rise to some of the many difficulties that the British faced in Iraq.

The lesson for armed forces is that they should measure themselves against competent enemies who are willing to stand and fight. And that operational success is always relative and historic. Armed forces must always guard against becoming victims of their own success.

Further Reading

Different Perspectives on This Book

Twelve years after the events described in this book, many other complementary accounts are available. Two books give very different perspectives on 2 LI's operations and others give useful accounts of events in Bosnia from 1991 to 2006. Alternative views on 2 LI's operations can be found in:

Winter Warriors by Les Howard (Book Guild 2006). A lance corporal in the TA who was outraged by the Bosnian war, Howard volunteered to join 2LI for the tour. He served in the Signal Platoon. I would strongly recommend this unvarnished account of the tour, from a perspective at the other end of the telescope from mine. It is also one of the few books on recent British operations written by a soldier, as opposed to an officer, academic or journalist.

Leading from the Front: the Autobiography by General Lord Richard Dannatt (Bantam Press, 2010). This military autobiography contains a chapter describing Dannatt's command of 4th Armoured Brigade in Bosnia during the period covered by this book.

Soldier by General Sir Mike Jackson (Bantam 2007). This is an autobiography covering Jackson's whole military career. The chapter on Bosnia provides an illuminating account of the events of 1995 and the role of IFOR from the point of view of 2 LI's divisional commander.

The Bosnian War

Many books have been published about the disintegration of Yugoslavia and the war in Bosnia. Most were by journalists. I have not read all of them. Readers interested in learning more about the background to the events described in this book my find the following books, which I have read, useful. I list them in approximate chronological order of the events they illuminate.

The Fall of Yugoslavia by Misha Glenny (Penguin 1996). An account of the disintegration of Yugoslavia.

The Death of Yugoslavia (BBC Worldwide). A BBC TV documentary series providing a good overview of events from 1991 to 1996.

From Cold War to Hot Peace by Anthony Parsons (Michael Joseph 1995). A history of UN interventions from 1947 to 1995. Although only covering the UN operation in Bosnia until the beginning of the Dayton negotiations in 1995 this book is an invaluable summary of the full spectrum of UN military operations. Written by a British ambassador to the UN it concentrates on the political and diplomatic spheres, but Parson's military analysis is always admirably clear and perceptive.

Peacekeeper by General Lewis MacKenzie (Douglas and McIntyre 1993). A first hand account by the Canadian General who was the first commander of UNPROFOR in Bosnia. It provides a good account of the initial UN involvement in 1992, particularly around Sarajevo.

In Harm's Way by Martin Bell (Hamish Hamilton 1995). A British journalist describes the war in Bosnia and how he reported it. It covers events from 1992 until summer 1996. Very strong on atmosphere and one of the best books ever written by any war correspondent.

Broken Lives by Colonel Bob Stewart (Harper Collins, 1993). Stewart's account of his command of the First Battalion the Cheshire Regiment, the first British battalion in Bosnia, is a highly personal narrative. Stewart gives clear picture of the successes and failures of British operations with a limited UN mandate, where the three warring factions held the initiative.

Bosnia Warriors by Major Vaughn Kent-Payne (Robert Hale, London 1999). Kent-Payne's book is an account of the author's dangerous and bizarre adventures as an armoured infantry company commander in 1993,. The book gives a particularly good picture of the way British troops dealt with the obdurate and truculent faction armies whilst the Bosnian civil war was raging

My War Gone By, I Miss It So by Anthony Loyd (Doubleday 1999). Loyd, a former Army officer, hitchhiked to Bosnia in 1993 and after living in Sarajevo became a reporter. It combines stark and shockingly vivid descriptions of the fighting and suffering with a traumatic journey of self-discovery. Loyd's descriptions of the war and his own inner turmoil make the book a British equivalent to Michael Herr's similarly personal account of the Vietnam War *Despatches*. The book includes vivid and exciting descriptions of the fighting around Bihać and 5 Corps ABiH's offensive in autumn 1995 that captured Sanski Most. The account finishes as the Dayton negotiations begin and does not discuss NATO's work. Excellent though it is, the book is of a radically different nature to this one.

Fighting For Peace by General Sir Michael Rose (Harvill Press, London 1998). Rose's book discusses his command of the UN Protection Force in 1994 and the many challenges he faced.

The Utility of Force by Rupert Smith (Allen Lane 2005). Perhaps the best book on strategy and the operational art in the modern age written by a practicioner, Smith shows how difficult it is for force to achieve the poltical effects that governments seek. Central to his arguments are events in Bosnia in 1995, during his time as the commander of UNPROFOR. Chapter 9 *Bosnia: Using Force Amongst the People* is highly recommended. Deliberately designed to read on its own, it is the best free-standing military account of the ending of the war.

Srebrenica: Record of a War Crime by Jan Honig and Norbet Both (Penguin 1996). An account of the fall of the Bosnian Muslim enclave of Srebrenica to Bosnian Serb forces, and of the subsequent massacres. It shows the practical impossibility of implementing the UN 'safe areas'.

Deliver Us From Evil by William Shawcross (Bloomsbury Publishing 2001). A very perception journalists account of UN peacekeeping in the 1990s. Chapter 6 *Bosnian Endgame* is a useful account of the end of the war.

Operation Deliberate Force by Tim Ripley (Lancaster University 1999). Ripley's book describes the NATO air strikes of August/September 1995. It is a good account of the background to the overlapping military and political crises that climaxed in the strikes and the concurrent fighting between the Bosnian factions. It finishes with the US negotiated cease-fire of autumn 1995.

To End a War by Richard Holbrooke (Random House 1998). A political account of US policy towards Bosnia. The central matter of the book is the negotiations to achieve the Dayton Peace Agreement.

What Happened Next In Bosnia?

I have been unable to find any single account of events in Bosnia from the signing of Dayton until the present day. Useful snapshots can be found in:

Peace Journey by Carl Bildt (Weidenfeld 1998). An account of Bildt's role as the first High Representative in Bosnia. Concentrating on the political level, it shows how on D Day Bildt had to build his civilian implementation team from scratch, with a fraction of the resources available to NATO. The book's account of the meeting in Banja Luka in February 1996 that was almost interrupted by Radovan Karadžić is very different from that in Chapter 12 of this book.

Waging Modern War by General Wesley Clark (Public Affairs 2001). Clark was SACEUR, NATO and the US' top military commander in Europe from 1997 to

2000. Much of this book describes the Kosovo crisis, but Chapter 4 *"Wearing Two Hats"* describes NATO's military confrontations with Bosnian Serb hard-liners in 1997. An earlier chapter *To Dayton and Back* complements Holbrooke's book by describing the drafting of the military annex to Dayton in 1995. <u>*Swords and Ploughshares* by Paddy Ashdown</u> (Weidenfeld and Nicholson 2007). As a UK politician Ashdown had immersed himself in the Bosnian war from its outset. From 2002 to 2006 he served as the High Representative in Bosnia, responsible for co-ordinating the civil implementation of Dayton. This book uses numerous examples from Bosnia to illuminate its discussion of rebuilding states after conflict. It also has a lengthy annex that begins with an authoritative analysis of what the international community had achieved in Bosnia from 1996 to 2002. The annex and subsequent postscript then shows how Ashdown used military political and civilian instruments to take the country forward.

Index